CW01497564

Ferranti: A History

MANCHESTER
1824
Manchester University Press

Ferranti: A History

Volume 3
Management, mergers and fraud 1987–1993

John Wilson

Manchester University Press
Manchester and New York

distributed in the United States exclusively
by Palgrave Macmillan

The right of John Wilson to be identified as the author of this work has been asserted by him in accordance with the Copyright, Designs and Patents Act 1988.

Published by Manchester University Press
Oxford Road, Manchester M13 9NR, UK
and Room 400, 175 Fifth Avenue, New York, NY 10010, USA
www.manchesteruniversitypress.co.uk

Distributed in the United States exclusively by
Palgrave Macmillan, 175 Fifth Avenue, New York,
NY 10010, USA

Distributed in Canada exclusively by
UBC Press, University of British Columbia, 2029 West Mall,
Vancouver, BC, Canada V6T 1Z2

British Library Cataloguing-in-Publication Data
A catalogue record for this book is available from the British Library

Library of Congress Cataloging-in-Publication Data applied for

ISBN   978 0 7190 8839 1   hardback

First published 2013

Typeset
by Action Publishing Technology Ltd, Gloucester
Printed in Great Britain
by TJ International Ltd, Padstow

Contents

Illustrations

Figures

Tables

To Anna. With my love and thanks. Outstanding!

Preface

WITH THE PUBLICATION of this third volume in the Ferranti series comes the end of almost a lifetime of research and writing. Having first visited the Ferranti Archives in March 1978, it would have been impossible to predict that the project would last almost thirty-five years. Few business historians could have been given such support in charting the rise (and fall) of a major company.

Inevitably, I have accumulated a plethora of debts in completing the commission. As I noted in the Preface to Volume 1, first and foremost, one must start by noting that there would have been no project (and no company!) without the Ferranti family. In particular, without the support of Sebastian de Ferranti the research would never have progressed from a dry doctorate into a full-blown corporate history without the encouragement and funding provided by this remarkable man. Although he has always criticised my writing for its academic nature, I would like to thank him for his support; not only does he have a true sense of history, but he is also willing to back his instincts. Just as Sebastian's grandfather pleaded for more men like Matthew Boulton to support technological innovation, I would like to state that with more men like Sebastian de Ferranti British business history would be in a position to match American efforts. Similarly, his brother Basil was a great help when consulted on any aspect of the company's history.

The respective Ferranti archivists – Charles Somers, Bob Campbell and Cliff Wimpenny – have also assisted me enormously. While none have been professional archivists, as I note in the Bibliography each in his distinctive way has contributed to the collection of an impressive array of documents and artefacts. In addition, their assistants, respectively, Edith Walsh, Doreen Scott and Chris Pennington, were equally important in supplying everything I wanted. I will always cherish the memories of those trips to the archives, because I was always made so welcome.

Apart from the archivists, a legion of Ferranti employees either agreed to be interviewed or wrote copious notes on my stumbling efforts. While it would be invidious to describe the help of all of these kind people, a special mention must be given to the late Tom Lunt, the former Staff Manager, whose easy charm and affinity with academic life provided an ideal introduction to the complexities of a firm with which he had been associated for over fifty years. In addition, two of the trustees of the Dr Ferranti Centenary Memorial Fund, Tom Grime and Albert Dodd, have been unstinting in the amount of advice they provided on the first two volumes. I would also like to thank several senior people who provided information and guidance, including: Sir Derek Alun-Jones, Eugene Anderson, Ian Ball, Mark Billings, Phil Burton, Bruce Calveley, Graham Clarke, Alan Cooper, Edgar Ernstbrunner, Lester George, Roy Handley, Alan Heron, Tony Hopgood, Norman Jones, David Knowles, Sir Donald McCallum, Charles Scott, Alan Keable Smith and Dr Alan Shepherd. Tony Mason at Manchester University Press has also provided great support in seeing this project to fruition.

This preface would not be complete without thanking the many librarians and professional archivists who have assisted me over the years, especially in Preston and Manchester. Jan Hargreaves has been a special source of assistance over many years.

John Wilson, Preston 2012

Abbreviations

BNL	Banca Nazionale del Lavoro
CE	Capital Employed
CIA	Central Intelligence Agency
COMED	Combined Map and Electronic Display
DTI	Department of Trade and Industry
EFA	European Fighter Aircraft (*Tornado*)
EGM	Extraordinary General Meeting
ERM	Exchange Rate Mechanisms
ESA	European Space Agency
ESL	SC Electronic Systems Ltd
FA	Ferranti Archive (at Manchester Museum of Science and Industry)
FBM	Ferranti board minutes
FBPG	Ferranti-Bendix Power Generation Ltd
FCO	Foreign & Commonwealth Office
FCSL	Ferranti Computer Systems Ltd
FDSL	Ferranti Defence Systems Ltd
FEL	Ferranti Electronics Ltd
FICC	Ferranti Industrial Controls Corporation
FIDL	Ferranti International Dynamics Ltd
FIEL	Ferranti Industrial Electronics Ltd
FIL	Ferranti Instrumentation Ltd
FN	*Ferranti News*
FSSA	Ferranti Shareholders Support Association
FTSS	Ferranti-Thomson Sonar Ltd
GEC	General Electric Co.
ICAEW	Institute of Chartered Accountants of England and Wales
ISC	International Signals & Control Inc
LGB	laser-guided bombs
LICOS	Liquid Cargo Operations Simulator
MoD	Ministry of Defence

MEP	Member of the European Parliament
MESS	Micro-electronics Support Scheme
NATO	North Atlantic Treaty Organisation
NC	Numerical Control
NEB	National Enterprise Board
OPEC	Organisation of Petroleum Exporting Countries
PEWS	Platoon Early Warning System
PGM	precision guided munition
PMM	Peat Marwick Mitchell
RICO	Racketeering-Influenced Corrupt Organisations Act
SEC	Securities & Exchange Commission
SFO	Serious Fraud Office
SZF	Sebastian Ziani de Ferranti
TAI	Technology Associates International
TMD	Tactical Munitions Dispenser
TQM	Total Quality Management
UAE	United Arab Emirates
UN	United Nations
WMD	weapons of mass destruction

1

Ferranti by the mid-1980s

BY THE MID-1980S, having effected a widely acclaimed recovery from the
liquidity problems of the previous decade, Ferranti had become a significant member of the British corporate community. One might even go as far
as to say that Ferranti was a microcosm of that heady decade dominated by
privatisation, increasing dominance of the financial services sector and
intense merger activity, alongside the introduction of new telecommunications technologies that were to have a profound impact on society over the
following generation. Although the firm had passed through similarly
exciting phases in its long history – witness the 1903 crisis, not to mention
contributing to two world wars[1] – for many the pride in achieving the status
accorded Ferranti by the 1980s exceeded any other episode. Of course, it is
vital to stress that these achievements were based on the legacy inherited
from the founding de Ferranti family, specifically an engineering-led strategy
combined with a highly devolved organisational ethos that encouraged
experimentation and entrepreneurship. It was this style of management that
had spawned a host of successful products listed in Appendix H of Volume 2,
the bulk of which had been capable of generating sound profitability well
into the 1980s. On the other hand, most Ferranti personnel would also
attribute a lot of the successes achieved during the late 1970s and early 1980s
to the management team assembled by Derek Alun-Jones, the managing
director brought in by Sir Don Ryder after the firm was controlled and mostly
owned by the state from 1975. Similarly, the government was also pleased
with this team, because having invested £8.5 million in the firm, it received
over £55 million from the institutional shareholders that bought up Ferranti
shares on divestment in 1980.[2]

While the difference of opinion over who was most responsible for the
firm's rapid recovery reflected internal debates over the manner of the firm's
progress at that time, there is little doubt that Alun-Jones wanted to move the
firm even further along his chosen trajectory. This chapter will consequently
assess both sides of the debate, providing a detailed overview of both the
status Ferranti had achieved by the mid-1980s and the context in which it

operated. We shall start by identifying the key characteristics of both the family and Alun-Jones regimes, reiterating some of what we discussed in Volume 2, yet ensuring that the key characters who dominated the story during the 1980s are at centre-stage. In particular, it will be important to assess the firm's corporate governance structure, because in analysing the decisions leading up to the 1987 merger with ISC one can only fully understand these by ascertaining how the various levers of power (internal and external) operated. It will then be necessary to discuss the environment in which Ferranti was competing by the mid-1980s, highlighting especially the dramatic changes in its principal market (UK defence), growing pressures from shareholders concerning the firm's profitability, and some severe problems in certain civil markets that demanded significant reallocations of resources. While it would be a gross exaggeration to say that by the mid-1980s Ferranti was struggling, in the light of decisions made in 1987 it is essential to assess the range of influences that resulted in a decision that sparked a chain of events and culminated in the firm's demise. Many lessons can be learned from this exercise, an issue to which we shall return in the concluding chapters.

1.1 Ferranti traditions and key people

One of the recurring themes of Volume 2 of this history was the extent to which by the 1980s Ferranti had become a different type of firm. After all, given the changes in the highest echelons of management, and especially once the Conservative government had curtailed the activities of the National Enterprise Board (NEB) and disposed of its shareholdings in a variety of British firms, Ferranti had starkly differing ownership and managerial characteristics. These changes are recorded in Table 1.1 (replicated from Volume 2), highlighting how the replacement of the de Ferranti brothers as executive directors with Derek Alun-Jones, alongside the dispersal of the firm's equity to largely institutional shareholders, converted Ferranti from being a family firm into a more conventional expression of managerial capitalism. Taking this comparative exercise further, the third row in Table 1.1 highlights how Derek Alun-Jones refined the organisational structure, introducing an executive committee, meticulous financial planning and tighter controls over cashflow. Of course, Sebastian de Ferranti had clashed with Alun-Jones over these changes, arguing that they were merely ways of marginalising the former owners' influence over strategy. This relationship deteriorated to such an extent that by 1982 Sebastian had resigned from the board, resulting in his brother Basil taking over as non-executive chairman, a move Sebastian regarded as treachery.[3] Indeed, the de Ferranti brothers never quite resolved this disagreement over motives, even though Basil publicly stated that he had not planned the change.

Table 1.1 A comparison of Ferranti in 1974 and 1987

Categories	1974	1987
Ownership structure	56% of equity held by two de Ferranti brothers; only 15% held outside family	Dispersed across large number of institutional shareholders
Board composition	de Ferranti family as executive chairman and managing director, as well as deputy chairman, divisional managers and one bank representative	Non-executive chairman (de Ferranti), managing director, finance director, divisional managing directors, non-executive directors
Organisational structure	Loose divisional structure, with control over operating departments exercised by chairman through informal meetings with senior managers	Executive committee created to monitor tight accounting controls, and one- and three-year planning exercises; divisions converted into closed companies
Product range	Power Transformers; Meters; Instrumentation; Electronic Components; Avionics Devices; Airborne Radar and Navigational Systems; Displays; Digital Computer Systems (defence and civil); Connectors; Lasers; Navigational Equipment; Graphics Systems; Simulation Equipment	Avionics Devices; Airborne Radar and Navigational Systems; Displays; Digital Computer Systems (defence and civil); Connectors; Lasers; Navigational Equipment; Graphics Systems; Simulation Equipment; Tele-communications and Office Equipment
Core technologies	Electricity Distribution, Instrumentation and Metering; Electronics (including components and computer systems); Avionics; Lasers; Gyro-stabilisation	Electronics (including components and military and civil computer systems); Avionics; Lasers; Gyro-stabilisation; Telecommunications Systems
Geographical spread	Mostly UK, with Canadian subsidiary and holdings in firms in Italy, Germany and Australia	Mostly UK, but with subsidiaries and joint ventures in the USA, Brazil and Western Europe
Gearing	215%	20%
Return on capital employed; stock exchange reputation	0.1%; only preference shares traded on the London Stock Exchange; equity regarded as highly risky	21.5%; equity traded extensively on the London Stock Exchange at healthy premiums; regarded as a 'buy' stock
Workforce	16,079	21,683

It was unfortunate that Sebastian and Basil were never able to agree about the circumstances surrounding the former's resignation from Ferranti, not simply because it was a family dispute, but also because, as we shall see later, it was imperative that significant shareholders[4] needed to work together when assessing the ISC merger proposals in 1987. While as non-executive chairman Basil de Ferranti was highly respected both at Ferranti and across the business community, it is clear that he had little influence over corporate strategy throughout the 1980s. It was also during this period that as a Member of the European Parliament (MEP) from 1979, representing the Hampshire West constituency,[5] Basil became a Vice President of the European Parliament, committing a considerable amount of his time to political affairs. This would have suited Derek Alun-Jones very well, leaving him free to determine corporate strategy without de Ferranti family interference. Of course, Basil never neglected Ferranti affairs, even when from 1987 his health deteriorated badly as a result of being diagnosed with cancer. Similarly, Sebastian closely observed developments at Ferranti, albeit from 1983 as a non-executive director of General Electric Co. (GEC). Continuing his close relationship with Arnold Weinstock,[6] he felt that he had a responsibility to act as an external commentator on the strategies pursued by the board.

Having a member of the de Ferranti family at the head of the firm, of course, also raises the issue of continuity, because while one can point to the key changes in the first three rows of Table 1.1, it is equally important to reflect on the extent to which Ferranti sustained the highly informal character that had been its hallmark since its very beginning.[7] This freebooting environment has been encompassed in the widely used phrase, the 'Ferranti Spirit', reflecting the sense of community that was felt by most who worked for the firm. While it is impossible to detect the culture from what we have presented in Table 1.1, the many thousands of former Ferranti employees would empathise with this view. Indeed, a consistent feature of the interviews conducted for this history, as well as the many messages received from former employees, is the feeling that in stark contrast to many other British electronics corporations, it was fun to work at Ferranti.

Regardless of this 'fun' element, however, one should nevertheless emphasise the nature of the organisational culture that prevailed by the early 1980s. On the one hand, the financial planning exercises brought a new managerial discipline, especially at divisional management level, while Charles Scott as finance director was responsible for tightening control over liquidity. At the same time, it is crucially important to stress that organisationally Ferranti in the 1980s operated in much the same devolved manner as in previous generations, with the divisional 'barons' wielding considerable influence over both their own destiny and at board level. Throughout the

1970s and 1980s, Ferranti continued to operate as a highly devolved business, in spite of the introduction of an executive committee, planning and stronger accounting systems. The divisional 'barons' – Donald McCallum; Peter Dorey; Albert Dodd; and Dr Alan Shepherd – were so well-versed in Ferranti traditions that it was impossible for Derek Alun-Jones to overcome the inherent centrifugal tendencies across Ferranti. It was also these 'barons' who implemented the engineering-led strategy that had been the hallmark of the family regime, pursuing a style of management that encouraged initiative and enterprise.[8] Indeed, it has often been noted that Derek Alun-Jones was never able to rein in the two most powerful 'barons',[9] Donald McCallum and Peter Dorey, given that their pivotal contributions to Ferranti profitability and turnover ensured their independence from central control. This organisational characteristic must always be borne in mind when assessing the events of the 1980s, given that while Alun-Jones was pursuing certain objectives for the business as a whole, at times it was difficult to persuade the major divisions (computer systems and Scotland) to follow this line rigidly. This highlights the weakness of Alun-Jones' managerial style, in that while he often used harsh words to describe divisional strategies, rarely was this converted into decisive action on product range or capacity.

One of the most dangerous manifestations of the tendency of the 'barons' to pursue their own strategies was the accumulation of factory capacity. As the finance director, Charles Scott, frequently complained, the divisions seemed intent on buying and equipping new factories, adding a considerable burden to their overheads. 'Keeping busy what were often excessively substantial and old factories' was, according to Scott, a deflection of divisional finances that could have been avoided through the more effective use of existing capacity.[10] This challenge had been especially apparent at the Avenue Works, where the NEB's involvement ensured that management time was devoted to utilising a facility which was no longer viable.[11] Similarly, though, Moston, Gem Mill and some of the computer and Scottish factories proved to be major financial millstones impeding divisional performance. One especially wonders about the wisdom of buying the factory adjoining the Wythenshawe site, while some of the Oldham facilities required such extensive modernisation that valuable resources were soaked up in this process. Furthermore, because of the continued failure to streamline intra-group activities (especially in the computer systems field) the problem was compounded by the purchase of further capacity as short-term solutions to production problems.

This highlights one of the major organisational shortcomings of the new regime, because one might argue that managers embarked on projects with the aim of filling factories as a means of justifying a place in the corporate pecking order, a strategy that poses important questions about the commercial viability of their businesses. It is vital to stress, though, that Derek Alun-Jones was content to nurture the autonomous organisational culture that had been such a prominent feature of Ferranti under family management. The managing director was also heavily influenced by John Pickin, the company technical director who believed in the 'Small is Beautiful' philosophy that purportedly allowed innovative individuals to flourish. The 'barons' were consequently given a tremendous amount of freedom to develop their own strategies, especially in the Scottish and computer systems divisions. While this could well have resulted in excessive replication of capacity, not to mention the continuing failure to foster intra-group collaboration that would have saved considerable amounts of money otherwise spent on this additional space, the board encouraged autonomy as a decisive feature of the 1980s organisational culture.[12]

Another feature of this philosophy was the Ferranti tradition that each division should have its own site, or more often sites, compounding the problems associated with filling old factories with business. A major exception to this rule was the emergence of a centralised industrial relations function, headed up to the mid-1980s by Albert Dodd. As we saw in Volume 2, Dodd had been given the responsibility by Derek Alun-Jones for harmonising industrial relations across the Ferranti group, developing a much more collegial style that helped to overcome the era's acute challenges in this area.[13] Overall, though, divisional autonomy severely hindered the much-needed rationalisation of capacity and limited the extent to which engineers from different departments might co-operate in the development of new products. Of course, in sustaining the Ferranti commitment to engineering innovation and excellence, this autonomous structure was regarded as an essential basis by both the 'barons' and the board. On the other hand, not only did it cause extensive replication of both projects and capacity, it also reinforced the tendency to adopt ideas which would fill up newly acquired factories, creating pressures on divisional managers at a time when synergistic benefits could have been achieved.

At the corporate level, this worrying tendency amongst the divisional 'barons' was by the mid-1980s beginning to have an impact on the balance sheet. As Donald McCallum noted at the 1987 Chief Executive's Conference, the firm's gearing (borrowing to equity ratio) had recently started to rise precipitously, after having fallen progressively from the late 1970s levels of 45%. Indeed, by 1986–87 Ferranti gearing had exceeded 20% for the first time in six years, providing clear warning signs for senior management of the need for careful management of resources.[14] It was consequently imperative, argued McCallum, that each division should take immediate action on stock control, especially in view of what we shall see later was the MoD's changed attitude towards the way in which this could be accommodated into profit calculations, not to mention the stark reduction in progress payments on defence contracts. This action would also have to be accompanied by improved purchasing procedures, combined with an increased emphasis on quality, tapping into the growing fascination in British business with the Japanese techniques of total quality management.

In reviewing these financial imperatives, it is worth questioning the role played by both the executive committee and the three-year plans introduced by Derek Alun-Jones from the outset of his tenure as managing director. As we noted in Chapter 2, although Alun-Jones disputes the claims of Goold and Campbell that after 1975 the Ferranti planning mechanism was more concerned with financial than long-term strategic aims,[15] above all this technique was concerned with imposing some financial disciplines on the divisional 'barons'. Indeed, the whole purpose of insisting on forward projections from each division was based on the need to maintain financial consistency across the group as a whole, while at the same time ensuring that the divisions kept to agreed budgets. It is clear, however, that especially when it came to the performances of the three smaller divisions (Ferranti Engineering, Ferranti Electronics and Ferranti Instrumentation) they were rarely capable of meeting their agreed targets.[16] Furthermore, Ferranti Computer Systems was only able to meet its mid-1980s targets by manipulating the way in which stocks were included in the profit figures for its Wythenshawe division.[17] Again, one must be wary of condemning the Ferranti planning exercises as complete failures, given the enormous efforts that went into compiling and monitoring the data generated at divisional levels. On the other hand, there is little evidence to suggest that planning had been a great success, especially in controlling what happened within the divisions.

In coming to this conclusion, one returns to a recurring theme, namely, that while Derek Alun-Jones had succeeded in introducing various changes to the way Ferranti operated as a group, these had barely made a dent in the shields raised by divisional managers to protect their local interests. One might even go as far to say that the 'barons' had successfully resisted the incursions from Bridge House or Millbank Tower, with the Scottish division and Ferranti Computer Systems especially operating almost as independent businesses. Of course, the divisions would defend this position by arguing that in giving the operating departments such latitude to develop their own products and markets, this underpinned the undoubted successes of that era. After all, Ferranti had flourished on the basis of a highly devolved organisational culture that encouraged intrapreneurship, resulting in progressive diversification into the latest electronics technologies.[18] In addition, the 'American Strategy' and other overseas ventures added considerably to the burden of co-ordinating and funding an expanding group. At the same time, this proliferation of products and departments was by the mid-1980s beginning to impose heavy costs on a group that would appear to have reached a financial plateau. Even though the Ferranti share price continued to rise up to 1988, one might argue that this position was only achieved by buying the loyalty of shareholders through generous dividend payments (see Table 1.1). Charles Scott also warned that the three-year plan produced in 1987 contained excessively ambitious targets, especially for the various civil ventures established over the previous decade.[19]

In spite of this apparent weakness, one ought to stress that by the mid-1980s Derek Alun-Jones had laid out five principal strategic objectives for the group as a whole:

- 25% return on capital employed;
- 15% pa real growth in turnover and profit;
- better balance of commercial and defence businesses;
- to expand overseas, in particular the USA and possibly the Pacific Basin;
- remain independent and financially strong with gearing less than 40–45%.

While one might debate whether these were sufficiently ambitious aims for a firm competing in one of the boom sectors of the 1980s, it was clear by the time of the Ferranti Chief Executive's Conference, held in January 1987 at the Selsdon Park Hotel in Surrey, that Ferranti would struggle to meet especially the first three. As we shall also see in the next section, achieving the balance between civil and military businesses was by the mid-1980s dropped, in favour of boosting the latter. Donald McCallum noted in concluding his review of the previous ten years' performance: 'The question which has to be considered is whether we have the ability and the will to continue to expand … and to meet the challenge of the financial objectives which have been laid down for the company by the Chief Executive.'[20] Ultimately, though, while financial management and effective merger strategies would dictate the degree of success Ferranti would achieve in these respects, it would be innovation that would ensure effective growth, placing the emphasis on something not even mentioned in Alun-Jones' five-point plan.

The engineering-led strategy, of course, had been at the heart of the de Ferranti family approach to business since the 1880s, acting as the benchmark against which much was *really* done right across the firm well into the 1980s. It was this engineering-led strategy which facilitated the constant metamorphosis of the firm's product range, as we can see from Table 1.1.[21] While the core technologies (electronic systems, avionics, lasers, and gyro-stabilisation) played significant roles from the 1950s through to the 1990s, the older activities associated with electricity distribution, metering and instrumentation had disappeared, with telecommunications systems emerging during the 1980s. As far as the latter was concerned, senior management committed considerable financial and engineering resources to this expanding sector, indicating how they were always on the look-out for opportunities that could be exploited by the application of Ferranti talent and capital. Nevertheless, it is striking that Alun-Jones failed to mention innovation when outlining the firm's five key objectives, sending a message to the engineering-oriented divisional managers that few could ignore.

It is already apparent that the issue of continuity at Ferranti is clouded in uncertainty: a lot depends when making this judgement on which particular criteria one chooses to stress. However, in one respect there is absolutely no dispute at all, namely, financial performance. When one assesses the quantitative criteria included in Table 1.1,[22] it is above all apparent that by the 1980s Ferranti was enjoying an era of unprecedented profitability. The gearing data is perhaps the most impressive, indicating how the ratio between debt and equity was much more favourable by the 1980s as a result of the firm's consistent ability to generate better returns and reduce its borrowing. Similarly, as Figure 1.1 reveals, the return on capital employed recorded by the 1980s was much more impressive than in the 1970s. Even though after the 1984 peak this particular measure fell off worryingly, a point to which we shall return later, the firm's reputation in the City was much enhanced. A final point to be made about the data in Table 1.1 is that even though the labour-intensive transformer and meter divisions had been either closed or sold, Ferranti employed more people in 1987 than at any other point in its history.[23] There is, indeed, a plethora of data to demonstrate that by the mid-1980s Ferranti was a much stronger commercial operation than in the early 1970s.

Having made this point, however, one must also highlight how the financial strength exhibited by Ferranti was both an advantage and a

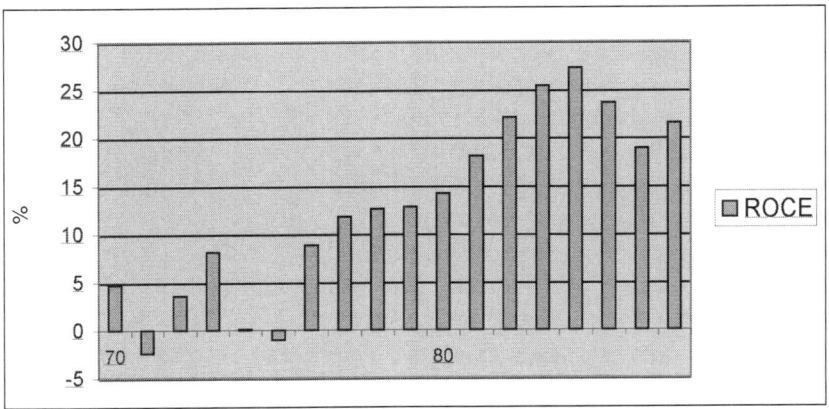

Figure 1.1 Return on capital employed (ROCE) at Ferranti, 1970-87

potential weakness. The injection of fresh capital in 1975 by the Labour
government, as well as the various financial innovations introduced by the
NEB-appointed finance director, Maurice Elderfield,[24] created a much more
solid foundation for the firm's recovery. In 1981, Ferranti also made a
£21million rights issue, bringing more equity capital into the company and
providing the resources for an ambitious growth strategy (see Appendix A).
On the other hand, thereafter Ferranti was much more vulnerable to the
demands of City investors, placing different pressures on the board when
considering both dividend and investment strategies. Of course, this
approach was by the 1970s common in much of British business, because
with the changes in company ownership since the 1950s, firms had become
increasingly vulnerable to the implicit threat of a take-over bid, unless by
paying out good dividends and boosting share values they could pay for
shareholder loyalty.[25] While investors have a right to expect an adequate
return on their investment, especially when they fund a firm's recovery, this
can prove extremely damaging when the balance of management decision-
making swings in favour of sustaining shareholder loyalty at all costs, forcing
up dividend payments especially and draining the very lifeblood from a firm.
This represented the classic challenge associated with a divorce between
control and ownership, a challenge that Derek Alun-Jones and his board
wrestled with for many years.

A key influence in this respect was Robin Broadley, of Barings Bank, who
advised the Ferranti board throughout this period as a non-executive
director. In particular, Broadley was able to guide the board on City
sentiment, stating in a report to the board that 'the basic strategy should be to
increase the high level of support and confidence which the company enjoys
among its shareholders, to sustain the company's perceived potential for
growth in earnings, and to develop and expand the company's business'.[26] It is
consequently no surprise that, as Table 1.2 indicates, Ferranti dividend
payments increased significantly over this period. Indeed, when compared
with the era of family management, dividends as a proportion of net profits
were four times the rate by the 1980s (see Appendix A). While it is also
apparent from Table 1.2 that the sound state of the company's finances
provided the funds for this distribution policy, one cannot avoid the conclusion that, like much of British business, the firm was at least partially
subjugated to the short-term considerations of City financial institutions.
Overall, though, the board was capable of achieving a balance between
serving City requirements and developing the business. Derek Alun-Jones
and Charles Scott especially reject the notion that Ferranti struggled to
achieve this balance, pointing to the manner in which by the 1980s the
company could afford the investment funds which allowed some divisions to
initiate a host of new ventures.[27] This is a justifiable position to take, espe-

cially when the early 1980s are contrasted with the early 1970s. On the other hand, it is apparent that as a proportion of net profits dividend payments rose even more significantly after 1983 (see Table 1.2), indicating how City pressures intensified. Moreover, as we shall see in the next chapters, as a result of these pressures, and especially rumours of a take-over bid, the board started to consider other strategies that might strengthen the business and sustain the growth track that had been initiated in the late 1970s.

Apart from noting Robin Broadley's role, it is also important to note the changing composition of the main board, because by 1987, while the divisions accounted for five of the directors, Derek Alun-Jones had been careful to bring in other people who could provide a breadth of experience and advice on many aspects of corporate strategy, in addition to the two non-executive directors appointed by the NEB in 1975, Gavin Boyd and Wilfred Broad.[28] In 1986, they were joined by Sir John Hoskyns, who apart from sitting on the board of several leading companies, had been a member of the Prime Minister's policy unit during the early 1980s, as well as director general of the Institute of Directors. While there has been much debate about the role of non-executive directors, resulting in a substantial increase in their duties,[29] at Ferranti they were always used as sounding boards for company policy, adding a useful dimension to the decision-making process. At the same time,

Table 1.2 Profits, dividends and retained earnings at Ferranti, 1976–87

Year to March	Profit (loss) pre-taxation (£ M)	Capital employed (£ M)	Return on capital employed (%)	Net[a] profits/ (losses) (£ M)	Dividend payments[b] (£ M)	Dividends as a proportion of net profits (%)
1976	4.1	46.7	8.8	3.6	0.1	2.8
1977	6.1	51.8	11.8	4.8	0.5	10.4
1978	9.1	72.3	12.6	5.8	0.6	10.3
1979	9.9	77.1	12.8	7.8	1.3	16.7
1980	11.2	78.8	14.2	4.7	1.6	34.0
1981	18.1	99.8	18.1	14.9	2.9	19.5
1982	23.8	107.7	22.1	19.4	3.7	19.1
1983	31.5	123.9	25.4	29.8	4.8	16.1
1984	38.8	141.9	27.3	22.3	5.7	25.6
1985	46.0	195.1	23.6	30.1	6.8	22.3
1986	41.1	217.0	18.9	28.0	7.5	26.8
1987	50.2	233.5	21.5	31.5	8.5	27.0

Notes: Key: [a] Net profits are defined in the balance sheet as the funds attributable to the ordinary shareholders, having deducted taxation, minority interests and extraordinary charges from the figures given in column 2.

[b] This sum includes both preference and ordinary share dividends, but it is important to emphasise that the former never cost the company more than £100,000 per annum.

Source: Ferranti Annual Reports, 1976–93.

and in spite of what we noted earlier about the degree to which the 'barons' were allowed to dictate their own strategy, especially in the larger avionics and computer systems divisions, it is also clear that over the course of the 1980s Alun-Jones was able to determine the way in which corporate strategy was devised. This will become even more apparent when we assess the reasons behind the firm's major acquisition in 1987, because Alun-Jones' wishes clearly prevailed over those of other directors. Furthermore, as the equity had been distributed across a large number of institutional shareholders, with no one organisation ever owning more than 5%, little concerted external pressure was ever exerted on Alun-Jones. Indeed, the 1980s strategy of paying generous dividends ensured shareholder loyalty, with AGMs and EGMs passing by without much debate over the direction taken by Alun-Jones and his team.

Having noted Alun-Jones' desire to involve some prominent members of the British business community in board discussions, above all it is apparent that most of the 1980s board changes reflected the traditional tendency within Ferranti to convert divisional managers into directors. The exception to this rule was Charles Scott, who in 1981 was elevated from his position as company financial controller to the post of finance director. Scott had only joined the company in 1979, as deputy financial controller, having previously been with Price Waterhouse since 1962. To the managing director, Scott's promotion was vital, because as he had yet to be imbued with the Ferranti culture, he would be capable of providing a source of objective advice at a time when most of the executive committee was composed of long-standing company men. As finance director after 1981, not only did Scott act as a close advisor to the managing director, he also made some detailed improvements to the manner in which data was presented to senior management. These contributions account for his promotion in 1986 to the post of deputy managing director, with specific responsibility for finance and administration.

Another board appointment in 1981 was Dr Shepherd of Ferranti Electronics, giving him an opportunity to represent this division's interests at the highest level of management. By 1986, though, he had given up his duties at Gem Mill to become deputy managing director of Ferranti, with specific responsibility for operations. Similarly, after the substantial organisational changes to the Scottish division in 1985, Donald McCallum became a non-executive director with prime responsibility for advising on general developments in the firm. On the other hand, not only was Phil Atterton (managing director of Ferranti Defence Systems) made a director, McCallum continued to push for his old division, giving the Scottish activities a powerful position on the board. Peter Dorey of Ferranti Computer Systems also continued to sit on the board, while on Lester George's retirement in April 1987, Albert Dodd of Ferranti Instrumentation replaced his predecessor. In fact, with Basil de Ferranti as non-executive chairman, this created a board composed of five divisional representatives and five other directors. While the City remained impressed by Derek Alun-Jones's achievement in ensuring that outside advice would always be heard, there is little doubt that as the most substantial contributors to company funds, Ferranti Defence Systems and Ferranti Computer Systems very much held the whip hand when it came to crucial decisions. This demonstrates how, in spite of the board changes, the divisional interests remained paramount throughout the 1980s, a conclusion which helps to explain the direction of the firm's acquisition strategy at that crucial time.

Overlaid on the divisional stories, of course, are the corporate activities of the small team that Derek Alun-Jones assembled at Millbank Tower. There is considerable disagreement over the impact of Millbank Tower executives like Derek Alun-Jones and John Pickin (the technical director), because while there were no doubt many sound ideas on corporate finance and organisation emanating from these quarters, and some divisions profited substantially from central support, it is unclear whether this involvement was on balance beneficial. In the first place, not simply would their actions have been seen as excessive interference in divisional strategy formulation, we have also seen how some of the schemes proved to be calamitous failures.[30] Paradoxically, in retrospect there was clearly also insufficient integration of divisional activity, leading to a failure to exploit economies of scale and scope in developing a competitive product range. Furthermore, while 'Creating wealth from technology' was a slogan Derek Alun-Jones proudly used to represent his philosophy, problems arose when the balance in this philosophy swung too far in favour of wealth creation, putting at risk the technological viability of projects which just might never come to fruition. This fuelled a constant internal debate over balance and credibility in the strategies devised by the Millbank Tower team, even if overall the firm's finances improved significantly from the mid-1970s.

Another point to make is that for personal reasons John Pickin ceased to be concerned with defence technologies. Of course, this disadvantage could well have been used to the firm's benefit, in focusing Pickin's activities on essential diversifications into civil technologies and markets. On the other hand, many in the defence-oriented divisions were left without any input from the centre, placing an even heavier burden on them in negotiations with the MoD or foreign governments.

A final point to discuss in relation to the state of Ferranti by the 1980s is the explanation for the firm's improved performance. On the one hand, as Sebastian de Ferranti would argue,[31] the most profitable businesses of the 1980s – avionics and computer systems – were those established under family management, while some of the ventures created after 1975 – telecoms; some of the US subsidiaries – were commercial disasters. Crucially, the acquisition strategy pursued from the late 1970s proved to be catastrophic, both for individual divisions and, ultimately, for the company as a whole, in contrast to the organic growth strategy pursued by the family. Conversely, it was under Derek Alun-Jones that Ferranti took the hard decisions to deal decisively with the ailing power division at Chadderton[32] and meter and instruments businesses in Hollinwood and Moston,[33] respectively, allowing the profitable divisions to reinvest their own profits in expanding businesses, rather than bail out loss-makers. Moreover, the introduction of financial planning techniques and Charles Scott's improvements to the accounting system ensured that management had a much better understanding of both divisional performance and liquidity. Many members of the senior management team of that era have also attested to the diligence with which the executive committee oversaw divisional and corporate performance, providing much tighter control of the expanding business. While it is difficult to contradict the claims made about the post-1975 acquisition policy, and especially the 'USA Strategy' introduced by the board as a means of securing business in the world's largest market for those technologies in which Ferranti excelled,[34] one should also add that many of those accusations have since been made with the benefit of hindsight, undermining their credibility.

In many ways, then, the period 1975–87 can consequently be characterised as an elusive combination of continuity and change; coming to a decisive conclusion on this issue defies rational thinking. One can conclude, however, that after 1975 a devolved style of management and an engineering-led strategy linked up with decisive decision-making on loss-makers and aggressive market-building policies aimed at strengthening core competencies. Of course, one might add that the new regime was given an enormous initial fillip through the provision of taxpayers' funds, combined with the lucky coincidence that for once in its generally unprofitable existence Ferranti-Packard generated substantial surpluses that arrived just in time for Derek Alun-Jones to announce his first set of results.[35] On the other hand, especially once the NEB had divested itself of its Ferranti shares in 1980 and two years later the government-imposed moratorium on trading in these stocks expired,[36] the board had to operate like any other firm that was owned by hundreds of financial institutions. It was also the reputation achieved by Derek Alun-Jones and his board that persuaded those financial institutions to retain their holdings, rather than sell them for a short-term profit, such was the level of trust that Ferranti equity had earned by that time. As we shall see later, however, this relationship with City financial institutions was a source of both strength and weakness, providing management with greater resources and more intense pressures, creating a conundrum the reconciliation of which would determine the firm's future.

1.2 The mid-1980s business environment and Ferranti response

Before expanding further on this conundrum, it is first of all necessary to provide the context in which the company operated. Of particular importance in the 1980s was a robust economic recovery from the dire problems of the 1970s and early 1980s. Although unemployment remained a major socio-economic feature of this era, having risen to just over 11% of the active workforce between 1982 and 1986, falling steadily to 6% by 1991,[37] living standards improved considerably, in spite of stubbornly high rates of inflation. Indeed, the 1980s has often been characterised as an affluent decade, perhaps best characterised by the boom in financial services, and especially the City of London. This boom was fuelled by a 'Free Market' Conservative government headed by Margaret Thatcher that was committed to macro-economic policies aimed at reducing the economy's dependence on manufacturing, not to mention its desire to close the coal industry after the highly damaging 1984–85 miners' strike. Indeed, this government eschewed the advantages of intervening to preserve industrial employment, preferring instead to boost service sector activities that appeared to offer more consistency. At the same time, by liberalising the restrictive post-war financial regulatory system and instigating what has passed into history as the 'Big Bang' of 1985, the British financial system experienced a boom decade that was characterised by intense merger activity, substantial investment in City of London headquarter premises, and the internationalisation of financial investment activities. The City also benefited significantly from the wave of privatisations that the Conservative government enacted, passing the ownership of formerly nationalised utility and manufacturing operations into the hands of the financial institutions that eagerly bought up the shares.

Of course, the late 1980s boom precipitated a major collapse in the early 1990s, when both interest rates and inflation increased to alarmingly high levels. The principal reasons behind these changes were the lax monetary policies of the late 1980s, while joining the European Exchange Rate Mechanism (ERM) in September 1990 proved to be catastrophic. By the time the UK had withdrawn from the ERM in July 1991, interest rates had surged to 15%, precipitating a major recession that severely limited the availability of capital and resulted in major governmental cutbacks. Even though in 1990 Margaret Thatcher had been replaced as Prime Minister by John Major, it was clear that similar economic policies were going to be pursued as long as the Conservatives were in power. Above all, and in stark contrast to the 1970s, there would be little chance of governmental support for ailing firms, highlighting how the macro-economic and political environments had changed markedly in such a short space of time.[38]

Another important dimension of the policies pursued by successive

Conservative governments during the 1980s and 1990s was the reduction in spending on defence. Indeed, a moratorium on defence spending was imposed in 1979–80 as soon as the Conservative government came to power, as part of its drive to fulfil its electoral promises to cut public expenditure as a means of reducing taxation. This was followed in 1981 by the publication of *The United Kingdom Defence Programme: The Way Forward* by John Nott, Minister of Defence. This document stated boldly that: 'Defence spending on the scale we have decided is a heavy burden on the British people.'[39] Ironically, this moratorium could also have precipitated the Falkland Islands conflict, in that the reduced British presence in the South Atlantic encouraged Argentina's military rulers to reclaim what they regarded as home territory. The British Prime Minister, Margaret Thatcher, proved more than willing to engage Argentina over the Falkland Islands issue in 1982, committing the country to both a war in the South Atlantic and enormous expenditure on defending this small territory. This significantly undermined the Treasury's moratorium on defence spending, because over the period 1978–79 to 1984–85 it rose from almost £22 billion (at 1991 prices) to £25.7 billion.[40]

Thereafter, however, successive defence ministers were placed under enormous pressure by the Treasury to trim spending, leading to dire predictions for those heavily committed to this market.[41] It is also vital to note that in 1985 the Ministry of Defence, by then headed by Michael Heseltine, was preparing a new approach to tendering and contract management. These moves resulted in, firstly, a planned decline in British defence spending over the course of the next seven years, reaching £22 billion in 1992–93, or 14% less in real terms than in 1984–85. Secondly, and arguably more importantly, Heseltine and his team devised radical changes to procurement policies and contract conditions in 1985, leading to the imposition of competitive tendering and a dramatic reduction in the old system of providing progress payments for contracted work. Dubious claims were made by Heseltine that the policies would 'galvanise British industry' and improve competitiveness. In reality: this was simply political rhetoric that attempted to hide the real reason why the Conservative government introduced these new rules: namely, as part of its assault on the general levels of government expenditure and a desire to roll back the influence of the state on economic activity.

Not surprisingly, after these policies were announced considerable concern was expressed by both Ferranti and its external commentators about the prospects for what had been its principal contributor to turnover and profits for over forty years. Of course, the most threatening aspect of Heseltine's innovations was the implication that American and European corporations would from the mid-1980s be able to compete for British defence contracts on an equal basis with indigenous suppliers, thereby significantly reducing the potential profitability of this market. A clear illustration of how this would work in practice was provided by the Ferranti naval systems business,[42] in that a French contractor was found for contracts that would in the past have normally been placed in the UK. While export markets like the Middle East remained buoyant, and Ferranti divisions were making strenuous efforts to break into the USA and Latin America, it was business from the Ministry of Defence on which the firm principally relied. These pressures would also intensify after 1989, when the Cold War was officially brought to an end and the global defence business received yet another shock, an issue we shall assess further in Chapter 8. Crucially, though, as far as British defence suppliers were concerned this trend had already started four years earlier, precipitating a detailed reassessment of corporate priorities at firms like Ferranti.

It is consequently clear that by the mid-1980s serious reservations were being expressed by an influential number of internal and external commentators about defence market prospects. The blaring warning signs for Ferranti, of course, were the events at its naval computer business in Bracknell,[43] because the loss of its premier position as the Royal Navy's preferred supplier of automated systems ought to have forced the board to reassess its preference for focusing an ever greater share of corporate resources on defence. In short, the Ferranti aura was slipping; having recovered in the 1970s from the *Bloodhound*-induced problems of the 1960s,[44] by the mid-1980s the Ferranti reputation was no longer held in such high regard. It should also be stressed that the Bracknell problems were a symptom of another emerging weakness, namely, the firm's deteriorating relationship with the MoD. Although it is vital to note that this did not affect the Scottish operation, given the deeply embedded relationships McCallum and his senior managerial and engineering teams had enjoyed for many decades, other parts of Ferranti lacked this rapport. Crucially, Derek Alun-Jones did not enjoy a good relationship with the senior civil servants in the Procurement Branch of the MoD, mainly because he failed to talk frequently with the key people and develop an empathetic approach. The Heseltine reforms further exacerbated this lack of empathy, while the defence-oriented parts of Ferranti failed to break away from the old cost-plus mentality that had been such an important characteristic of this market for so long. As Table 1.3 also reveals, Ferranti was considerably smaller than its major British defence market rivals, while sales growth looked pedestrian when compared to Racal, Plessey and Lucas. These factors worried the Ferranti board immensely, principally because it was increasingly unlikely that the MoD would use the firm as a prime contractor for major systems. Although there was still good business to be secured in subcontracting, dependence on other firms carried other dangers, while at the same time making Ferranti increasingly vulnerable to a take-over in those merger-mad years and exacerbating the board's fears about future independence.

Table 1.3 Balance between defence and civil (output %)

		MoD	Military exports	Civil
FCSL	1974–77	41	23	36
	1985–86	53	10	37
FDSL	1974–77	63	28	10
	1985–86	47	48	5
FEL	1974–77	14	0	67
	1985–86	16	3	81
FIEL	1974–77	14	0	67
	1985–86	5	0	95
FIL	1974–77	59	3	38
	1985–86	62	11	27
Totals	1974–77	35	14	51
	1985–86	42	20	38

Note: FCSL (Ferranti Computer Systems Ltd); FDSL (Ferranti Defence Systems Ltd); FEL (Ferranti Electronics Ltd); FIEL (Ferranti Industrial Electronics Ltd); FIL (Ferranti Instrumentation Ltd).

Given these challenges in what was the firm's principal market, it is important to assess how the board chose to effect a better balance between civil and defence activities across the Ferranti product portfolio.[45] With regard to the latter, in the 1960s and 1970s senior management had made some bold moves to reduce the dependence on defence markets, and divisions pursued an ambitious diversification strategy based on the application of internally generated technologies to civil applications. By far the most significant manifestation of this strategy was the design and production of the *Argus* process control computer, a system that was derived from the launch control post of the *Bloodhound* guided missile originating from the Wythenshawe division.[46] Similarly, during the 1980s the Cheadle Heath division of Ferranti Computer Systems diversified its product base into civil markets, applying the core technologies employed in military simulation systems to develop new products. An excellent example was the liquid cargo operations simulator (LICOS), produced in 1983 for the College of Nautical Studies, at Warsash, in association with the chemical engineering department at Edinburgh University and partially funded by the DTI.[47] Although Warsash accounted for most of LICOS's sales, when in the mid-1990s Cheadle Heath was sold off an American corporation, Ship Analytics, acquired this off-shoot and developed a highly successful business using the core design.

Under Donald McCallum's management, the Scottish division also made considerable efforts to convert its military technologies to civil markets. In this context, developing Europe's most advanced numerical control systems as a result of reassessing the way it manufactured wave guides for its military radar, AI23, was perhaps the most outstanding example.[48] In the 1970s and 1980s, Donald McCallum persisted with this attempt to diversify the Scottish division's product range, encouraging engineers to apply their world-renowned expertise in gyro-stabilisation and laser technologies to a range of markets.[49]

Of course, the most daring civil venture of the 1980s was Ferranti Instrumentation's foray into telecommunications (hereafter, telecoms), moving the firm into a market that has expanded enormously since then.[50] We shall return to the telecoms venture in Chapter 7, but it is vital to stress that civil markets were never totally neglected by Ferranti management. Indeed, the petrol-pump and Dundee components businesses demonstrated that at times Ferranti succeeded in certain civil markets, adapting core competencies to sectors that proved extremely remunerative. On the other hand, it is apparent that by the mid-1980s the Ferranti board was concentrating an even greater share of its resources on defence markets, both at home and abroad. In many ways, of course, this move was entirely reasonable, not least because Ferranti had for many years struggled to generate much profit from its civil businesses. While Ferranti civil products were generally regarded as extremely well-engineered, frequently competitors were able to undercut them on either price or service levels. Jonathan Aylen has also produced fresh evidence to demonstrate that while Ferranti enjoyed an initial competitive advantage in process control computers, the failure to improve key aspects of the *Argus* range – sensors, software and instrumentation – meant that even its established customers such as ICI were turning to US suppliers when considering new investments in this area.[51] As we also saw in Volume 2, the *Argus* business range was cross-subsidised by the military simulator and sonar businesses based at Cheadle Heath.[52] Another issue was the marketing of Ferranti products, a weakness that in 1987 the board attempted to tackle by acquiring an American firm that was allegedly superior in this respect, a move analysed in detail in the next chapters.

Apart from these problems in the civil market, the Ferranti board was also convinced that the global defence market would provide a much more conducive environment for the firm's core competencies. Again, given the consistent record of success in designing, developing and manufacturing defence products, from shell fuzes through to guided weapons, avionics and naval computer systems, this was an entirely rational strategy that appeared to offer much more secure routes to increased profitability. Above all, it was apparent to senior management that maintaining the status quo was a recipe for disaster in sectors like electronics, computer systems and avionics, leading the board in 1986 to ask Lester George to instigate a major review of the firm's position. Working closely with a team from Barings Bank,[53] George focused on three considerations: firstly, the balance of the business between military and civil; secondly, acquisition strategy; and, thirdly, which new technologies should the firm exploit. This reveals how corporate strategy at Ferranti was both proactive and positive, rather than being responsive and passive, indicating once again that the 'Ferranti Spirit' was very much alive and flourishing in the 1980s. This approach also percolated down into divisional management hierarchies, because a succession of conferences and workshops were held throughout the 1970s and 1980s in order to involve as many people as possible in the firm's development.

The impact of George's report, of course, was ultimately subsumed in the build-up to the acquisition in 1987 of ISC, a move that decisively reflected in the starkest terms the board's preference for defence markets. Although throughout the 1980s frequent allusions were made in the annual reports to an intended policy of creating a better balance between civil and defence businesses, even in 1986–87 almost 83% of the operating profit and nearly 62% of turnover was derived from the latter. Table 1.3 also provides the divisional breakdown of civil and defence output, confirming once again how FSCL, FDSL and FIL relied significantly on the latter, while overall by the mid-1980s the former accounted for just 38% of output, compared to 51% in the mid-1970s. Crucially, this made the group extremely vulnerable to the dramatic late 1980s changes in MoD activity, raising a key issue when assessing the long-term viability of the Ferranti strategies pursued from the late 1970s. Of course, it was entirely rational that Ferranti should have exploited its internationally renowned expertise in defence technologies. As Alun-Jones noted, 'it is no good being the 42nd manufacturer of something. We look for things where we have something special to contribute', namely, defence equipment.[54] On the other hand, much more effective preparations for the market changes could have been enacted earlier, rather than built into a situation which the firm found difficult to control.

Of course, the Ferranti board was well aware of these evolving circumstances, devoting a considerable part of its 1987 Chief Executive's Conference to analysing current and future market prospects. Given the highly dispersed nature of Ferranti equity ownership by the 1980s, it was also apparent that these concerns about UK defence market prospects fed directly into the price of its shares traded on the London Stock Exchange. Although immediately after the Falkland Islands conflict with Argentina defence stocks had experienced a significant boom, by the mid-1980s there were widespread concerns within the City over the long-term trends in defence electronics.[55] This was why by September 1987 the Ferranti 10 pence ordinary share was trading at 137 pence, compared to an equivalent of 162 pence in July 1982.[56] Although Figure 1.1 has already revealed that the firm's return on capital employed was far superior in the 1980s, especially when compared to the 1970s, Figure 1.2

indicates that the earnings per share recorded by Ferranti over the period 1981–87 did not surge ahead as rapidly as the board would have liked.

The key issue here, of course, is the extent to which in these circumstances Ferranti could remain independent or fall victim to a predatorial take-over, at a time when British merger activity was booming.[57] In the early 1980s, as we saw earlier in this chapter, Barings Bank had strongly advised the board to pay as much out in dividends as possible, in order to ensure shareholder loyalty and limit the potential for a take-over.[58] While this inevitably diverted a higher proportion of profits to dividends than the de Ferranti family had ever allowed,[59] this was inevitable given the dominance of financial interests over British business by that time. Regardless of these concerns, one should still stress that between the release of Ferranti shares by the NEB in 1980 and 1987 City institutions generally regarded them as a 'buy'. This consistent record reflected extremely well on the management style and structure introduced by Derek Alun-Jones in the immediate aftermath of the Nicholson Report.[60] Indeed, while Nicholson had concluded in 1975 that 'This is a good business, but it must be properly run, and while [at chief executive level] it has been well led, it has been badly managed',[61] had he written a similar review in 1987 he would undoubtedly have changed the last part of that judgement. This was why the firm's marketing slogan 'Creating wealth from technology' was widely appreciated, given that the divisions continued to pursue the engineering-led strategy inculcated into management by the de Ferranti family, while under Derek Alun-Jones much more careful monitoring of performance criteria was effected through the executive committee as a means of ensuring that the devolved system did not descend into chaos. It was this combination of styles that mostly lay behind the commercial successes of the period.

Having stressed the value of organisational innovations such as the executive committee, planning and tighter accounting controls, one must not

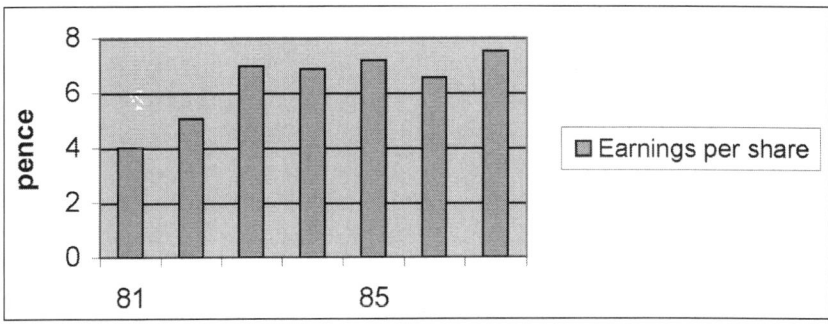

Figure 1.2 Earnings per share at Ferranti, 1981–87

be misled into believing that the central management regime was averse to taking risks on new projects and technologies. Of course, throughout its history Ferranti had continually responded to fresh engineering opportunities by diverting funds and personnel into development projects, frequently producing radical innovations that acted as the basis for new commercial departments. We have also noted in this chapter how after the mid-1970s crisis the divisional managers continued to encourage their engineering staffs either to keep abreast of the latest developments or push the boundaries of knowledge even further forward. At the same time, the Ferranti technical director John Pickin was continually searching for opportunities that might complement divisional competencies. Furthermore, as Pickin worked for the most part in Millbank Tower, he was in direct contact with the managing director, advising him regularly on the results of his investigations. In other words, at both divisional and central levels an entrepreneurial element continued to be a prominent feature of management activities, providing direct input into discussions at executive, board and divisional levels throughout this period.

1.3 Conclusions

One might argue that the early 1980s especially was a 'Golden Age' for Ferranti, with the return on capital employed rising to unprecedented heights (see Figure 1.1 and Appendix B) and the company name becoming a byword for both continued engineering excellence and solid dividend performance. Certainly, Derek Alun-Jones had worked hard to gain the City's confidence in, and backing for, the company's expansion plans, ensuring a regular supply of funds at reasonable rates. Of course, there are significant caveats that one must add to this positive conclusion, not least that as the firm after 1980 was wholly owned by professional investors who were only interested in the return on their capital, a new discipline was being imposed on management. Crucially, this contrasted sharply with the way in which the de Ferranti family was able to keep control and ownership together, limiting the potential for outside interference in decision-making. After 1980, however, because all at Ferranti were keen to secure continued independence, it was essential that adequate dividends were paid to shareholders as a means of buying their loyalty. Moreover, at regular intervals the firm was obliged to open itself to external scrutiny, with institutional fund managers poring over every aspect of the business in order to verify any claims made by the board concerning corporate viability. This was all part of the much more transparent relationship all firms were expected to have with their City owners, even if in some notorious cases management was less than scrupulous in their financial dealings. At Ferranti, however, guided consistently by Barings Bank, the board took the view that it was essential to maintain healthy relations with the City, devoting considerable time to liaising with fund managers and ensuring that future supplies of capital would be forthcoming.

Although many in senior management would regard this as an excessively pessimistic note on which to conclude a review of the firm's most consistently profitable period in its history, several warning signs were blaring in the board's ears. In particular, the defence market changes, failures in several of the civil and American ventures, and the threats imposed by what seemed to many to be an imminent bid from a rival electronics firm, all added up to a worrying scenario for Ferranti. Indeed, it was exactly these pressures that persuaded the board to enter into a major acquisition in 1987, a decision that effectively precipitated the collapse of Ferranti just six years later. This story will be the subject of the remaining chapters, presenting a plethora of detail on the acquired firm, as well as a thorough analysis of the build-up to the creation of Ferranti International plc. Above all, though, the Ferranti board was responding to the principal threats just outlined, emphasising how in many ways the firm was beginning to lose control of its own destiny. Of course, one might argue that this was the case in the vast majority of firms where there had been a divorce between control and ownership, indicating in stark form the inherent dangers associated with managerial capitalism. But this was only part of the story for Ferranti, given what was happening internally and externally, and especially at a time when its main market was undergoing radical change. This highlights again the weight of the challenge facing senior management, posing fundamental questions concerning the orientation of its main divisions and the prospects for its weaker activities. It was the response to these challenges that would determine the extent to which Ferranti would continue to flourish.

Crucially, one should stress that while Ferranti succeeded in remaining independent, the board was exercised by constant rumours that either a rival electronics firm or a conglomerate seeking further diversification would bid for the equity. As Derek Alun-Jones reported at one board meeting, 'Ferranti has been widely seen as a bid stock'.[62] This climate of fear was also at least partially responsible for persuading the board to embark on an even bigger acquisition, given its relatively small scale (see Table 1.4). Again, as far as we know, not a single formal bid ever materialised, but the implicit threat to Ferranti independence persuaded the board to build ever-higher defences against predators. Indeed, the 1986–87 debates about corporate strategy were at least partly stimulated by the need to obviate these threats, bringing Barings Bank fully into the analysis of future aims and objectives. Similarly, Derek Alun-Jones was keen to encourage the divisional managers to build ever-stronger links in the USA, given the central importance of this market to

Table 1.4 The ten largest British defence companies, 1985–86

	[1985–6]		
	Turnover (£ M)	ROCE (%)	Annual sales growth 1984–86 (%)
British Aerospace	2,647.7	6.5	7
Rolls-Royce	1,601	(17.2)	10
Hawker Siddeley	1,592	12.3	5
Racal	1,266.3	22	25
Marconi	1,195	41	15
Plessey	1,146.9	56.3	23
Lucas	886.5	(60.9)	28
Vickers	611.2	6.6	(3)
Ferranti	595.2	23.4	15
Land Rover	521	(13.9)	0

Source: Financial Weekly, 24 Dec 1987

the firm's core competencies in electronics, computer systems and avionics. As a consequence, an extensive acquisition programme was enacted by three of the divisions, Computer Systems, Electronics and the Scottish operations, adding yet another significant dimension to the business. As we noted earlier (see Table 1.4), because Ferranti was much smaller than some of the major British defence contractors, an acquisition programme would go some way to making up the yawning gap.

Ultimately, of course, the key decision was the acquisition in 1987 of International Signals & Control Inc (ISC), of Lancaster, Pennsylvania, because this represented both a major foray into the US defence sector, as well as another mechanism by which Ferranti might defend itself from predatorial behaviour. It is consequently at this point that one must finish the introductory chapter and move on to analyse ISC in much greater detail. We leave Ferranti in a position of unprecedented financial strength, with investors eagerly buying and retaining its shares as a result of the strategic and structural decisions made by a team that was based on both a consistent organisational ethos and dynamic entrepreneurial instincts. Indeed, what some referred to as 'the Oxford and Cambridge of British electronics'[63] was in the mid-1980s riding high on the contemporary sentiment that British business was booming, with the City of London especially recording record levels of activity and investment growing impressively, both at home and abroad. Like many such 'bubbles', however, the promise proved illusory, not least for a firm that had sought to exploit every aspect of the boom by spreading its wings ambitiously and aggressively into American business.

Notes

1 These incidents have been extensively covered in Vol. 1 of this history: J.F. Wilson (2000), *Ferranti. A History*. Vol. 1. *Building a Family Business, 1882–1975*, Carnegie Publishing. See especially pp. 135–42, 282–6.

2 This story is told in greater detail in Ch. 9 of Vol. 2: of this history: J.F. Wilson (2007), *Ferranti. A History*. Vol. 2. *From Family Firm to Multinational, 1975–1987*, Crucible Books.

3 These events are related in greater detail in Vol. 2, pp. 58–66.

4 Although both had sold significant tranches, Sebastian and Basil combined (including the various family trusts) still held 8% of the Ferranti equity in 1987.

5 In 1984, this changed to Hampshire Central, a constituency he represented until his death in 1988.

6 Sebastian and Arnold had been close friends since the 1950s, when both came to prominence as leading figures in the British electrical industry. As we saw in Vol. 2 (pp.35–44), Weinstock had also played a major role in the 1974–75 negotiations between Ferranti and the government, advising the de Ferranti brothers on strategy and financial matters.

7 This issue has been discussed at length in Vol. 1, pp. 533–6 and Vol. 2, pp.14–24.

8 See Chs 1 and 9 of Vol. 2 for more detail on this atmosphere.

9 This point was made to the author during many of the interviews conducted with senior Ferranti employees.

10 Interview with Charles Scott.

11 See Ch. 3 of Vol. 2.

12 For insights into this feature of the organisation, see Vol. 2, pp. 14–24.

13 Vol. 2, pp. 316–27.

14 D. McCallum, 'Ten year performance and our position in 1987', Ferranti Archive (FA).

15 Interview with Derek Alun-Jones. See M. Goold, and A. Campbell (1987), *Strategies and Styles. The Role of the Centre in Managing Diversified Corporations*, Blackwell pp. 137–8.

16 See Chs 3–5 in Vol. 2.

17 See Ch. 6 in Vol. 2.

18 See Ch. 1 in Vol. 2.

19 C. Scott, 'The 1987–90 three year plan and its message', 1987 Chief Executive's Conference, 1987, FA.

20 McCallum, 'Ten year performance and our position in 1987'.

21 See also Appendix H, Vol. 2.

22 See also Appendix A, this vol.

23 In fact, Ferranti employed more people (21,791) in 1986, indicating how as a result of some rationalisation in computer systems a peak had already been reached.

24 See Vol. 2, pp. 336–49, for a review of these innovations.

25 See John F. Wilson (1995), *British Business History, 1720–1994*, Manchester University Press, pp 201–8.

26 FBM 10835, 24 Sept 1980.

27 Interviews with Derek Alun-Jones and Charles Scott.
28 Broad had retired by 1985, while Boyd continued as a director into the 1990s.
29 See J. Charkham (1995), *Keeping Good Company. A Study of Corporate Governance in Five Countries*, Oxford University Press.
30 See Vol. 2, pp. 14–24, for details on these failures.
31 Interviews with Sebastian Ziani de Ferranti (SZF).
32 See Ch. 3 in Vol. 2.
33 See Chs 3 and 4 in Vol. 2.
34 See Ch. 9 in Vol. 2.
35 D. Alun-Jones (1982) 'My business experience at Burmah Oil and Ferranti' paper presented to the Business History Unit, LSE. See Vol. 2, pp. 345–7.
36 See Vol. 2, pp. 344–56, for an analysis of these issues.
37 P. Chapman (1994), 'Overview: the UK labour market', in T. Buxton, P. Chapman and P. Temple (eds), *Britain's Economic Performance*, Routledge, p.279.
38 G. Owen (1999), *From Empire to Europe. The Decline and Revival of British Industry since the Second World War*, HarperCollins, pp. 455–7.
39 Quoted in M. Seagrim (1992), 'The effect of defence spending upon the UK economy', *Royal Bank of Scotland Review*, No. 173, March.
40 J. Lovering, (1995), 'Opportunity or crisis? The remaking of the British arms industry', in R. Turner (ed.), *The British Economy in Transition*, Routledge, p. 100.
41 D. Greenwood (1984), 'Managing the defence programme and budget', *The Three Banks Review*, No. 142, June, 34–50.
42 See Ch. 6 in Vol. 2.
43 Described in detail in Ch. 6 of Vol. 2.
44 See Ch. 10 of Vol. 1, for a study of the *Bloodhound* story.
45 See Appendix H in Vol. 2 for an overview of the firm's product range in 1987.
46 See Ch. 10 in Vol. I.
47 I am indebted to Edgar Ernstbrunner for details of LICOS's development.
48 See Ch. 8 in Vol. 1.
49 See Ch. 7 in Vol. 2.
50 See Ch. 10 of Vol. 2.
51 Private correspondence with author, 6 Feb 2008. See also J. Aylen (2012), 'Bloodhound on my Trail: Building the Ferranti Argus Process Control Computer', *International Journal for the History of Engineering and Technology*, Vol. 82, No. 1, 1–36.
52 See Ch. 6 in Vol. 2.
53 The board debated this report on several occasions, including FBM 8 May 1986 and 29 May 1986.
54 Quoted in Owen, *Empire to Europe*, pp. 22–3.
55 *Financial Times*, 27 Sept 1987.
56 The Ferranti share price in July 1982 was 810 pence, but given that in 1985 each 50 pence nominal share was converted into five 10 pence shares it is essential to divide the 1982 figure by five.
57 See John F. Wilson and Andrew Thomson (2006), *The Making of Modern Management. British Management in Historical Perspective*, Oxford University Press.

58 See Ch. 9 in Vol. 2.
59 See pp. 353–5 in Vol. 2.
60 See pp. 354–6 in Vol. 2 for coverage of this Report.
61 Nicholson Report to the NatWest Bank, 1974, FA.
62 FBM 10883, 23 Dec 1980.
63 This is a term used frequently in the 1960s and 1970s when civil servants referred to the firm. See Vol. 2, p. 1.

2

The rise of ISC

WHEN ON 21 September 1987 the Ferranti board formally announced the merger with International Signals & Control plc (hereafter, ISC), few contemporary commentators were publicly willing to make anything other than positive comments about the prospects for this amalgamation. Although coincidentally – some would say, prophetically – shareholders approved the merger on what has passed into financial history as 'Black Monday', on 19 October 1987, when share prices collapsed precipitously across the industrialised world, it is difficult to detect any public predictions that the merger would not work. Indeed, as we shall see in the next chapter, it was seen as a good move for both companies, given the apparent complementarities. On the other hand, key figures in both business and political circles privately regarded ISC as highly dubious, highlighting the need to investigate a corporation that few could claim to know very well. The analysis of this debate will be divided into two main sections: firstly, we shall examine ISC's progress since its creation in 1971, outlining what to many seemed to be extremely impressive progress; secondly, it is also necessary to disclose the firm's covert activities, given their crucial role in underpinning its expansion, especially in the 1980s. Janus-faced, ISC managed to fool the financial establishment that it was a credible operation with a sound balance sheet; in reality, much of its alleged progress was based on either illegal or fictitious contracts that were negotiated or contrived by its founder, James Guerin. At the same time, it is vital to stress that Guerin's covert activities were conducted with the permission of both the US and UK governments of the 1970s and 1980s. While in the 1990s both countries refused to acknowledge any responsibility for the links Guerin built with South Africa, Iraq, Pakistan and China, all countries that were at that time on the United Nations embargo list, there is little doubt that successive American Presidents and British Prime Ministers were aware of his covert work in disseminating conventional weapons technology and equipment. In spite of various UK governmental inquiries in the 1990s, little of this has still to come to light, making it even more remarkable that Guerin was able to use ISC as a front for his arms dealing that operated under a protective cloak provided by high-level officials and their political bosses.

2.1 Foundations and growth

Born on a New Jersey farm in the 1930s 'Great Depression' and educated at Roxbury High School, in Succasunna, New Jersey, James Guerin was initially interested in agriculture, taking a degree in this subject at Rutgers University, New Jersey. After serving in the US Navy during the Korean War, he was retrained as an electronics officer while on destroyer duty, persuading him to take up this subject when he returned to civilian life. He first of all took an undergraduate degree in electrical engineering, again at Rutgers, gaining a *magna cum lauda* distinction, while a Masters degree had been acquired at the University of Arizona by 1959. This change of direction was no doubt brought on by the attraction of joining the booming American defence industry, in which enormous opportunities were emerging as the USA geared up for the Cold War. After graduating from Arizona, he joined Lockheed Missile & Space, one of the leading US defence corporations at the heart of building the Cold War armaments that dominated the era. As well as working on the *Polaris* missile programme, he would eventually rise to the position of programme manager in a part of the enormous *Poseidon* project. Managing a 280–strong engineering department based in Sunnyvale, California, at Lockheed he gained invaluable experience of working in the rapidly expanding US defence industry, building a network that in future would prove invaluable. It was experience he put to good use in securing the post of general manager of Hamilton Technology Inc, a subsidiary of the Hamilton Watch Co, of Lancaster, Pennsylvania, which had diversified into the defence business in 1968. In August 1969, he and his wife Helen consequently moved the family of five children (Tom, James, Beverly, Shirley and Nancy) to Lancaster, close to some of the most religious communities in the USA. Apart from his devotion to building up Hamilton's new electronics division, it is also apparent that he became a dedicated member of the Church of God, in Landisville, a Christian fundamentalist congregation that believed in the Bible as the unassailable word of God. It was in this capacity that 'he culti-vated the "guy-next-door" image in Lancaster as a personable, sober, God-fearing family man',[1] contributing significantly to various religious and arts activities in order to position himself as a pillar of that community.

   Hamilton Watch was one of Lancaster's leading firms, employing over 3,000 people, with sales of $89 million, mostly from its long-established watch-making business. By the late 1960s, with growing competition from Far Eastern and European watch-makers, Hamilton recruited Donald G. Cooper from IBM to lead the diversification into the much more lucrative

defence business, a strategy that would see them establish military electronics
and fuze assembly operations in and around Lancaster. To manage the
military electronics business, Cooper head-hunted Jim Guerin from
Lockheed, reminiscing that: 'He appeared to have a solid combination of an
entrepreneurial spirit, a desire to make the organization grow, a strong
technical background, and a knowledge of how businesses operate.'[2] This
glowing reference demonstrates at the outset the considerable ability Guerin
possessed to persuade people of his innate ability and trustworthiness. It is an
asset that he was to use extensively over the following twenty years in building
both his own business and laying the foundations of a personal fortune. At
Hamilton Technology, he also started to fashion the core elements of his
business philosophy, an approach built on rapid growth and extensive internationalisation. It was this business philosophy that was offered as the
foundations on which Hamilton might diversify out of its troubled watch-
making activities and become a major international defence supplier,
adopting ruthless tactics that would speed the processes of adaptation and
expansion.

Unfortunately for both Guerin and Hamilton, however, the strategy was
fatally holed by what Guerin tried to do with the first product they chose, the
AN/PRC-77 portable radio, to be supplied to the US Army. The prime
contractor for this radio was RCA, but given certain capacity problems at
their Camden plant they were looking to subcontract some production.
When he heard about this opportunity, Guerin tendered at the extremely low
price of $7.5 million for 16,000 radios, in the hope that this loss-leader would
provide an entrée into defence markets. It was later calculated that Hamilton
was losing at least $200 per radio, while the substantial investment in a refur-
bished factory further sapped the ailing corporation's resources. Undaunted
by these problems, Guerin talked to colleagues about opening a division of
the business in South East Asia and buying a corporate jet to transport executives between the proposed far-flung parts of the Hamilton empire. He also
used his charismatic style of leadership to inspire staff, working long hours as
an example to others who questioned the commercial base on which the
strategy was built. This reveals how Guerin had already started to elaborate
features of the corporate vision and managerial style that would later become
key features of his own business, inspiring others to buy into this vision for
the future.

While Guerin's leadership certainly proved instrumental in building up
Hamilton Technology in its first two years of trading, the vision was dashed
by harsh commercial realities. By 1970, Hamilton was reporting losses of
$41.1 million, the bulk of which was attributed to the declining watch-
making business. In spite of Guerin's strong advocacy of the potential in his
military electronics business, in such circumstances Hamilton just could not

afford to continue to subsidise the loss-leading strategy he had enacted with the military radio, which by then had accumulated losses of $6.7 million on a $75 million contract. When it became apparent that the board was about to sell off the military businesses, Guerin then stepped in with a management buy-out offer that would have provided him with a base on which to implement his emerging corporate vision. This offer was rejected, mainly on the grounds that the board had received a better price for the military radio contract from LTV Electrosystems Inc, of Huntingdon, Indiana, making Guerin and his team redundant.

Although it would be difficult to place all of the blame for the failure of Hamilton Technology on Guerin's shoulders,[3] it is apparent that he was already formulating a highly ambitious corporate vision based on lucrative defence contracts, internationalisation and the use of corporate jets. Using what was widely acknowledged as a charismatic personality, combined with a very strong work ethic and highly religious orientation, Guerin aspired to running a multinational defence electronics firm that would fund his personal interests. It was a vision that he would eventually implement at his own corporation, because unbowed by the Hamilton experiences, and recognising in Lancaster a sound base for his ambitions, in 1971 Guerin borrowed $150,000 from a local bank, Meridian, recruited four of his colleagues from Hamilton Technology, and established a small operation ambitiously named International Signals & Controls (ISC), using the basement of his Landisville home as their initial premises. One of the former Hamilton employees who joined Guerin in 1971 was Carl Dreyer, who served ISC until his sacking by Ferranti International in November 1989. Just like Guerin, Dreyer had a Masters in electrical engineering and worked in the US defence industry for some years, specifically United Aircraft Corporation and Honeywell. At ISC, he became director of product assurance, working intimately with Guerin on a host of arms contracts that were to have major implications.

With his Pentagon and electronics industry contacts built up over the previous two decades, Guerin secured contracts to manufacture sub-assemblies for the *Shrike* and *Sparrow* guided missiles, moving production into a small facility on the outskirts of Lancaster. Although the highly ambitious name chosen to implement Guerin's vision offered a portent of things to come for this business, to most observers ISC was in the 1970s a struggling venture that latched on to virtually any product that might turn a profit. His long-term aim was to create a business capable of acting as a major turnkey systems supplier in a variety of fields, including missile propulsion systems, advanced weapon systems and communications and information integration. This reflects his considerable optimism and entrepreneurial skills, not to mention an ability to negotiate lucrative contracts from the military establishment. As one journalist later noted: 'He filled the company's ranks with former military and intelligence officers, and filled their heads with visions of "a billion dollar technology empire" in the rich farmland outside Lancaster.'[4] One of these early recruits was Stuart Pindell, a Cornell University graduate and former US Navy combat pilot who had flown many missions over Vietnam.[5] After leaving the Navy, Pindell had joined Hamilton Watch Co's new electronics subsidiary, where he met Jim Guerin and started to discuss their mutual interests in the international arms trade. Although when Hamilton closed this subsidiary Pindell first moved on to Novox Inc, a Vermont corporation, by 1974 he had been recruited by Guerin to become president and general manager of ISC's international division. Over the following twelve years, such was Pindell's alleged success that he claimed to have brought $850 million worth of contracts into ISC, an issue we shall examine at some length over the next three chapters.

Of course, Pindell had moved from a relatively large business to what was still a very small player in the US defence industry. Nevertheless, he shared Guerin's desire to build ISC into a highly successful business, working tirelessly on its international contracts. Crucially, though, one should stress that Guerin was the inspiration behind this vision, later explaining in another remarkably predictive statement that 'I begged, borrowed or stole as much money as I could get together', when building the business in the early 1970s.[6] Little did people realise how close to the truth was this typical piece of hyperbole from a man who appeared to pursue a ruthless approach to business expansion. It was also an approach that over the 1970s would appear to have worked, because by 1980 ISC had expanded into a business with a turnover of £36.5 million. As early as 1973, a separate division, ISC International Technologies Group, had been formed to cater for overseas orders, the parent company having won business for testing equipment, control devices and electronic components. A year later, the firm had diversified into ordnance and communications equipment, building up a major international order-book that underpinned its initial growth. Although as we shall see in the next section Guerin was operating a highly lucrative covert business for the CIA and various overseas partners through ISC International Technologies, these contracts did not come to light until the late 1980s, demonstrating how the other ventures were used as little more than a cover for activities that would later to be investigated by US legal authorities.

Apart from the *Shrike* and *Sparrow* sub-assembly work, the most visible aspect of ISC's 1970s business was a range of civil products that smacked of opportunism, even desperation. By far the most successful of these was *Pestolite*, a device that used a fluorescent light-bulb to lure flying insects either into a tray of water or on to a sticky paper cylinder, the rights to which were acquired in 1974 by Guerin from a New York entrepreneur, Henry Lorin.[7] Although there were rumours that the industrial version of this product was prone to bursting into flames if it was not regularly maintained, between 1974 and 1981 ISC sold up to 500,000 per year of the domestic variant, mostly by mail order at around $20 each. While it is impossible to calculate the profitability of this business, given that ISC's financial records for this period have been shredded, it is fair to claim that *Pestolite* would have sustained the public image of ISC as a viable business, keeping the Lancaster factories busy at a time when Guerin was struggling to break into other markets. For example, ventures into making vacuum cleaners and golf clubs proved to be calamitous commercial failures, while a move into producing two-way radios inserted in firemen's helmets generated extensive hate-mail from those fire departments unfortunate enough to purchase ISC's design.[8]

It is difficult to exaggerate the importance of *Pestolite* to ISC's first decade in business, because whether or not it generated a reasonable profit from the impressive growth in sales, this helped Guerin cover up the income derived from his covert activities (to be described in the next section, where we shall also stress how the South African conglomerate Barlow Rand also bailed Guerin out during a difficult period in the mid-1970s). One should also note that covert trading was being used to extend Guerin's Lancaster presence, because by the early 1980s he had either acquired or created a string of other businesses, including: Four Seasons, a sports and restaurant complex; a small savings bank called Parent Federal Savings Bank; a travel agency; Micro-Precision Tool & Manufacturing Inc, a small high-technology machine tool firm; and Sierratronics, a Sacramento, California, electronics sub-assembly operation, with forty employees. All of these activities were eventually absorbed into a new holding company formed in 1982, Parent Industries, a move that his London merchant bank, Robert Fleming & Co, advised as part of the flotation of ISC in the UK. The choice of the word 'Parent' is interest-ing, because this was another dimension of his Christian beliefs: as his parents had given him his Christian principles, he wanted to further this tradition to employees in his adopted county of Lancaster.

The London flotation will be described later, given its central importance to this history, but it is vital to stress at this stage how as a result of receiving clear guidance from his London merchant bank, Robert Fleming & Co, Guerin was keen to split his defence and civil activities. However, *Pestolite* and the other civil ventures were not placed within Parent Industries alongside Guerin's Lancaster ventures; instead, he decided to sell them to another vehicle he had formed in 1978 with his brother-in-law, Carl E. Jacobson, and James B. Christian, United Chem-Con Corporation, with financial support from the local Meridian Bank. Chem-Con, as we shall refer to it, was created in order to tap into potentially profitable opportunities afforded by the Pentagon's programme to allocate defence contracts to firms owned and run by ethnic minorities. This had led Guerin to recruit one of the leading Black

American entrepreneurs of his era, James B. Christian, who in 1985 was awarded the title of 'Black Entrepreneur of the Year' by President Reagan. Although as we shall see over the next three chapters this particular story ended up in Christian's imprisonment for corruption,[9] Chen-Con was yet another vehicle employed by Guerin to cover up his arms trading activities. For example, few were aware that in selling *Pestolite* and the firemen's helmets to United Chem-Con for $2.5 million he was saddling the firm with what by then were major loss-makers. Christian remembers trying to persuade Guerin not to force him to buy these businesses, to be paid for in twenty instalments of $156,625 (including interest of $632,500), but his entreaties proved fruitless and ISC delivered what the Chem-Con's chief executive described as 'a truckload of useless components to Chem-Con's parking lot … and much of it sat there, in a trailer, largely untouched for years'.[10] Moreover, while this sale took place in 1982, according to the accounts published by ISC in advance of its London flotation, claims were made that what Guerin chose to call his 'special products division' had been unloaded in 1980. When the US bankers for both corporations, Meridian Bank, discovered this inconsistency and asked Chem-Con why this had not featured in its accounts, Guerin embarked on a campaign of disinformation and bluster that attempted to claim the sale had never happened. As by then the London flotation of ISC had succeeded and Guerin was in possession of a substantial amount of British investors' money, he decided to reclaim the special products division for Parent Industries, unsaddling Chem-Con of its $2.5 million debt.

This highly unusual incident can only be regarded as yet further evidence of Guerin's willingness to manipulate both his own colleagues and the auditors and Meridian Bank officials who asked questions about his business affairs. It is also clear that throughout the 1980s *Pestolite* was used by Guerin to support United Chem-Con's balance sheet, even if the sale of this civil business had never occurred. These ruses will be described later, when the extent of Chem-Con's nefarious activities, as well as Guerin's involvement, will be assessed. Again, one should note that in spite of Meridian Bank's 1982 concerns over the alleged sale of the special products division, the nature and pervasiveness of Guerin's financial manipulations did not come to light until 1989–90, by which time other decisions had been taken which would dramatically affect Ferranti and British investors. Nevertheless, it is clear that Guerin was willing to shuffle assets between his corporations, using them in varied ways, firstly, to borrow heavily from banks, and secondly, to persuade investors to put large amounts of money into ISC, thereby making him extremely wealthy.

Needless to say, had Sir Derek Alun-Jones and the Ferranti board known about Guerin's dealings with Christian, Jacobson and other Lancaster businessmen, the 1987 merger would never have gone ahead. Instead, to all intents and purposes they were negotiating with a man who had not only built up an extensive reputation as a successful entrepreneur, but also established himself as a highly regarded philanthropist. Indeed, ever since moving to Lancaster he had pursued a vigorous mission to ingratiate himself with the Lancaster community. Apart from being a major figure in the Church of God, Landisville, where he sang in the choir at least twice a week, he also accepted the post of Director of the Lancaster Chamber of Commerce and Industry, sat on the Fulton Opera House committee, and acted as a trustee of the Pennsylvania School of the Arts. By the 1980s, he was widely regarded as perhaps the leading business figure in Lancaster, frequently either supporting personally a series of charitable causes or chairing fund-raising committees aimed at helping local activities. In 1986, the Urban League of Lancaster County voted him 'Man of the Year', reflecting his new-found status. As one contemporary described him:

> Guerin is a man oriented towards action. Associates describe him as very bright, competitive, energetic and optimistic. When things go wrong, he is not one to listen to excuses. He wants to hear solutions .. While, on the one hand, he is described as compassionate and sensitive, Guerin also prods people to do their best.[11]

One is left with the abiding impression of a highly personable, plausible and hard-working individual who had Lancaster's best interests at heart in everything he did. The tall, bespectacled and quiet-spoken Guerin was consequently able to persuade a lot of people that he had much to offer. Although some speak of his ability to look straight through a person, even when in supposedly deep conversation, most felt that he came across as a highly genuine, sincere workaholic who was committed to invigorating Lancaster. Even after all the revelations, there are still people in Lancaster who are eternally grateful for his charitable work, not least in the religious and educational circles on which he lavished large amounts of money in the 1970s and 1980s.[12]

A further reflection of Guerin's philanthropic activities was the creation in 1982 of a charity known as Parent Foundation, linked directly to his holding company, Parent Industries. Administered almost single-handedly by Landisville Sunday School teacher and executive director of the United Way,[13] Susan Eckert, this operation dispersed substantial amounts of money to a wide range of institutions and individuals. By the 1980s, Eckert was personally responsible for distributing $200,000 per year, mostly to individuals who were either never able to afford Medicare or failed means tests imposed by local government. In addition, Guerin was extremely generous to his own church, the Church of God, which received $75,000 annually from Parent

Foundation, while other Lancaster charities received sums ranging from $20,000 to $40,000. This was also matched by similarly impressive donations to the Pennsylvania School of Art and Design and the Lancaster Symphony. The *Lancaster New Era* calculated that between 1982 and 1989 Guerin contributed at least $10 million to local charities and cultural activities, as well as funding an orphanage in the Philippines.[14] It was all an essential part of the image that Guerin was building for himself, as the industrious, Christian entrepreneur who was willing to distribute his wealth to less privileged people in his community. How could anybody doubt the veracity of his statements?

2.2 Building the ISC empire

By the early 1980s, this image was also being disseminated much more widely than Lancaster, given Guerin's increasing recognition that if he was going to sustain both aspects of his business, it was going to be necessary to find a way to hide the covert activities. As a first step in implementing this plan, in 1979 he formed ESI London, principally as a means of exploiting British and NATO military markets, while $10 million worth of equity in ISC was also sold on the Luxembourg Stock Exchange. To run the British operation, Guerin recruited a member of the British establishment, Sir David Checketts KCVO, who following a distinguished career in the Royal Air Force had been Equerry to both the Duke of Edinburgh (1961–66) and Prince of Wales (1966–70). Throughout the 1970s, Checketts was Private Secretary and Treasurer to the Prince of Wales, having been assigned to support Charles while he was still at Gordonstoun School. This confirms his position as an extremely well-connected person who was capable of linking a new company to the British establishment. At the same time, though, one should stress that Guerin was always in charge of ISC strategy, whether at the central or subsidiary levels, reducing people such as Checketts to very much a subordinate, non-executive role. As one can see from Figure 2.1, by 1986 Checketts had also been moved to ISC International Technologies, as a result of some important changes to the group's location and identity. Crucially, though, while Checketts earned a high salary as an ISC director, and would later hold options and shares in Ferranti International plc worth £750,000,[15] he was never responsible for any of the key strategic decisions that took this subsidiary into illegal territory – his role was almost solely as a source of contacts within Whitehall and British business.

The British subsidiary of ISC would appear to have proved to be a great success, building up what to many outside observers seemed to be an excellent business in Africa and the Middle East. This success was used in August 1980 to persuade investors on the London Stock Exchange to invest

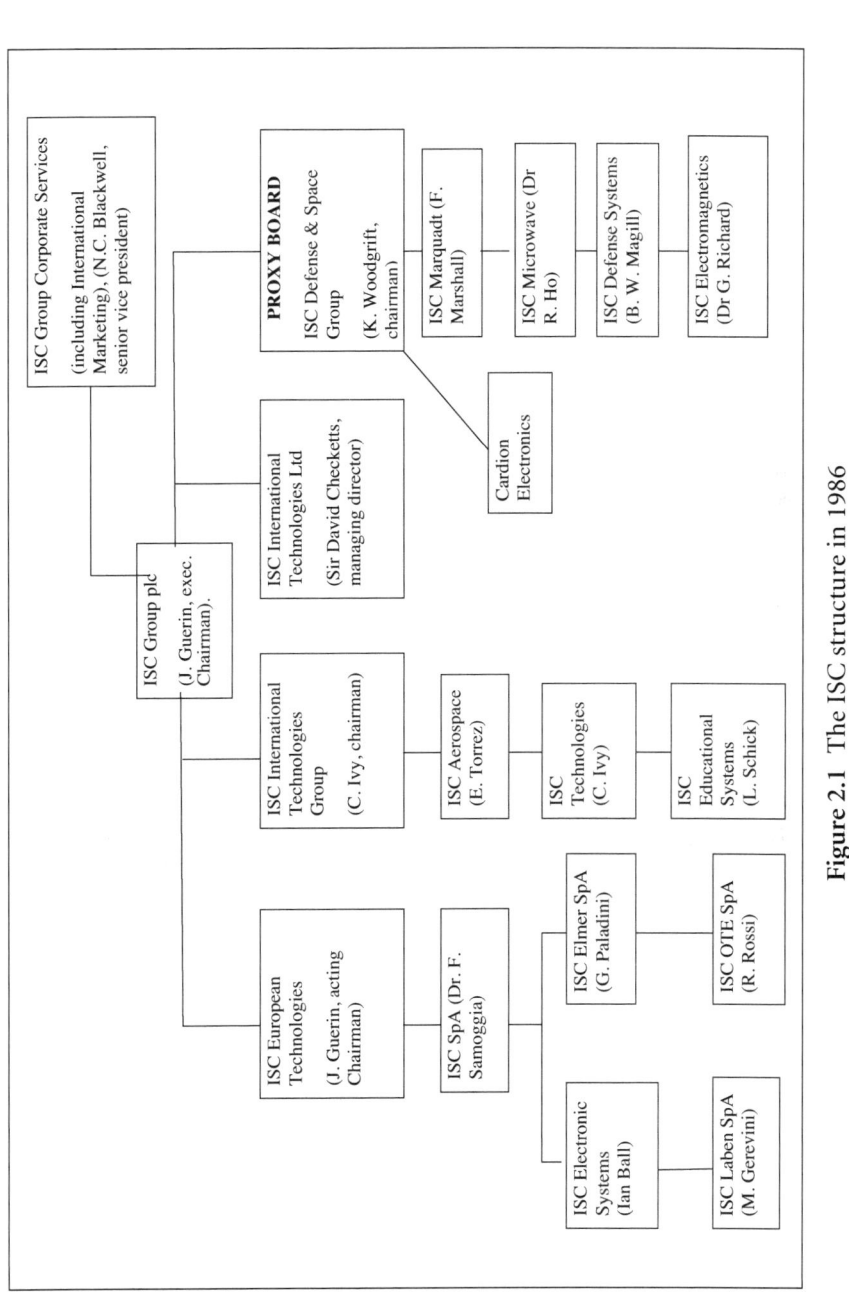

Figure 2.1 The ISC structure in 1986

£4.2 million in the business. By September 1982, the entire ISC Group had also been incorporated in England and Wales, as a prelude to acquiring all of its US operations and obtaining a listing in London. The latter was achieved in October 1982, when a share issue managed by Robert Fleming & Co Ltd raised £21.8 million for the now-British firm, by which time ISC's turnover had grown to just over £50 million. When one considers why ISC should incorporate in England, however, clues start to emerge about a more sinister aspect of Guerin's activities. In a report on ISC prepared by the research division of Robert Fleming & Co, one of the City of London's most prestigious and long-established merchant banks,[16] it was stated that:

> The main reason why London was chosen in preference to New York for ISC's flotation was that ESI London already had an enthusiastic following in the London financial community. A further reason was that [American] SEC [Securities & Exchange Commission] regulations might have required disclosure of information about the Group's major overseas clients which would have been inconsistent with ISC's confidentiality agreements with those clients.[17]

Of course, while one cannot predict whether ISC would have been able to raise its funds in New York, it is obvious that the second sentence contains the real reason why Guerin chose London and English company law as the safer base for his activities. Floating in New York would have obliged him to abide by the SEC's much more stringent regulations on corporate disclosure, a point on which we shall expand in some detail in the next section.

Another crucial point to make about the 1982 flotation is that while ostensibly converting ISC into a British company, with the support of the prominent merchant bank Robert Fleming and influential investors such as Guardian Royal Exchange,[18] in effect it was still controlled from Lancaster. Guerin himself held 16.6% of ISC equity (21.2 million shares) after the flotation, giving him a tight grip on the board of directors (who together held 2.5 million shares), while as executive chairman and president of the company he kept an extremely tight grip on all aspects of corporate strategy and structure.[19] At the same time, just as he had done when establishing his business in Lancaster, Pennsylvania, Guerin launched an ambitious public relations exercise aimed at giving ISC some credibility in the UK business scene. Hiring Sir David Checketts had been a part of this strategy, in providing links with the British establishment, while every year ISC hired substantial chalets at key events such as the Wimbledon Lawn Tennis Tournament and Farnborough Air Show. Not only were guests treated to lavish hospitality at these events, but Guerin would also spend a lot of time talking to each person, using his charismatic personality to impress on all and sundry that he was a highly credible businessman and entrepreneur who could be trusted. It was a campaign that clearly worked, given both the enormous success of the 1982 flotation and the apparent expansion of the business over the following five years.

When one looks more closely at ISC (see Figure 2.1), it is vital to stress that beneath the ISC Group plc holding company there were three main subsidiaries, the Defence & Space Group, International Technologies and European Technologies, each of which had their own subsidiaries operating either in the USA, the UK or in Italy. The key to understanding this chart, however, is that the Proxy Board running ISC Defense & Space Group, located in Lancaster, effectively ran the whole company, given that within those companies ISC maintained its principal US and export contracts. By the mid-1980s, ISC had also opened a 'Government Liaison Office' in Washington, from where top-secret discussions were conducted into the licensing of international sales and technology transfers. The ISC description of this office's activities also mentioned that: 'Our attention to the law and to detail assures that objectives are achieved with propriety.'[20] One can only marvel at the duplicity in this statement, but it is one that helped Guerin assure all observers he was operating legally and with the sanction of various US government agencies.

While in the next section we shall outline the nature of this group's businesses, it is vital to remember that the conversion of ISC into a British firm was an attempt to prevent either the authorities or investors discovering what Guerin and his closest business colleagues were actually doing. While a 1986 Flemings report on ISC claimed that the company had 'a decentralised management structure, aimed at giving maximum entrepreneurial freedom to the individual companies within the group',[21] it failed to note the existence of the Proxy Board and the central role it played in determining the flow of resources across the subsidiaries. Crucially, to fulfil a statutory requirement to maintain the group's security clearance with the US Defense Department, three of the Directors on the Proxy Board (General Guthrie, Admiral Inman and Barry Shillitoe, a former Assistant Secretary of Defense) held the voting proxy on the group's shares. The role of this Proxy Board, and specifically Admiral Inman, a former National Security Advisor, will become apparent over the next chapters, but it is obvious that in maintaining close links with ISC's key source of custom, namely, the US security services, it continued to play a major role in fashioning a range of strategies well after the merger with Ferranti.

Another distinctive feature of ISC was its extensive use of front companies to deal with various contracts. As the PMM audit report on ISC noted in 1982:

> The reason for the growth of ISC over the past five years is almost wholly attributable to the international division. Much secrecy

surrounds this business and, in many instances, the identity of both
suppliers and customers are concealed by intermediate companies.
Often in the past business came to ISC primarily because of the desire
of the US Government and certain US public corporations not to be
seen dealing with some politically sensitive foreign governments particularly in products with military uses.[22]

While this is an issue to which we shall return in Chapters 3 and 4, when
assessing the nature of the fraud perpetrated by Guerin and his immediate
associates, it is nevertheless clear that many within the City of London were
aware of the methods adopted by ISC to hide much of its activity from prying
eyes. By the 1980s, though, ISC had clearly changed significantly since its
inception in 1971, adding many different activities through both organic
development and mergers. The latter strategy proved especially popular after
ISC's flotation in London, starting with the acquisition of Marquadt in July
1983, SI EL (an Italian electronics group) in December 1984, Eletro-Magnetic
Processes (EMP, a Californian telemetry business) in April 1986, and Cardion
Electronics (a New York radar firm) in August 1986. As a result, having been
mostly based in Lancaster, Pennsylvania, where 90% of its workforce was
located in 1981, by 1986 these premises employed only 30% of ISC's
employees.[23]

By far the most prestigious of ISC's acquisitions was Marquadt, given that
this firm provided ISC with an entrée into the American space industry.
Although it was later alleged that Guerin paid a $350,000 bribe to encourage
the Marquadt management to agree to the merger,[24] diversifying into this
sector significantly enhanced ISC's prestige, especially as the firm was being
linked to Ronald Reagan's highly controversial 'Star Wars' nuclear defence
system. Established in 1944 to develop airbreathing propulsion systems (or,
ramjets), Marquadt's facilities in Van Nuys, California, were amongst the
most advanced in the world. By the 1980s, as well as ramjets, it had also diversified into liquid-fuelled rocket systems, the first of which had helped the US
Lunar orbiter to circumnavigate the moon in 1966, laying the foundations for
a long-term business with NASA. By 1986, 800 of these rocket engines had
been sold to NASA and a range of international satellite programmes
(including EUROSTAR, INTELSAT VI 83, MILSTAR, and the Ford Aerospace
collaboration with the Japanese satellite programme). Lucrative contracts for
the Space Shuttle had also been acquired, providing the subsidiary with a
promising future.

Apart from propulsion systems, in the early 1970s Marquadt also diversified into ordnance. Its first major contract was *Rockeye*, a 500 lb air-launched,
free-fall, cluster bomb containing 247 armour-piercing bomblets. This was
later replaced by the Tactical Munitions Dispenser (TMD), a 1,000 lb free-

fall, cluster dispenser weapon which had first been developed by Honeywell, but subcontracted to Marquadt in 1986, with the prospect of up to $1 billion worth of contracts. Alongside the prestigious propulsion systems businesses, this ensured that Marquadt would generate a good return on the $43.5 million paid by ISC for this business. Furthermore, the ordnance activities significantly complemented the original work in this market conducted by ISC since the early 1970s from its Lancaster base. Given the greater significance of Marquadt's work, however, when these businesses were merged into ISC Defense and Space Group (see Figure 2.1) in 1985, the former chief executive of Marquadt, Ken Woodgrift, was made executive chairman and the headquarters was moved to Santa Monica, California.

Linked closely to the markets exploited by Marquadt was ISC Aerospace. Although part of the ISC International Technologies Group (see Figure 2.1), this subsidiary was another branch of the expanding ISC defence activities. As a systems house, ISC Aerospace was specifically interested in designing, developing and producing tactical guided missiles, giving it a position of central importance to Guerin's aspirations to be a major international arms trader. It was specifically created as a vehicle for Clyde Ivy's missile work, something we shall assess in greater detail later, because its principal facility was in Westlake, California, where ISC had invested in advanced research and development facilities. More importantly, ISC Aerospace worked closely with potential customers on the design and production of these guided missiles, maintaining the high levels of confidentiality that became the hallmark of the group's activities throughout the 1970s and 1980s.

The central significance of the ISC Defense and Space Group to ISC's total activities is also reflected in two further acquisitions, EMP and Cardion Electronics. Formed in 1972, EMP had developed a niche position in the market for telemetry systems, as well as diversifying into radar training equipment and electronic news gathering. Its acquisition in 1986 for $13.5 million indicated how this part of the ISC Group was developing a significant presence in the market for microwave systems, because (see Figure 2.1) in 1986 they joined with an established expert in this field, Dr Raymond Ho, to form ISC Microwave and ISC Datacom. Of even greater significance was the purchase in 1986 of Cardion Electronics, formerly part of the General Signals

Table 2.1 Geographical analysis of ISC International Technologies' sales ($ m)

Year to 31 March	1982	1983	1984	1985	1986
Middle East and Africa	49.2	83.8	101.2	136.8	213.5
Europe	1.5	2.5	7.0	15.8	91.9
Other	11.4	5.6	28.8	29.0	12.1

Corporation and a major supplier of naval radar systems and displays. Although in 1985 Cardion had made a loss of $8.1 million, on a turnover of $37 million, explaining why General Signal was willing to offload this business, much of the deficit was attributable to excessive development expenditure on a series of radar projects. ISC Defense & Space was nevertheless confident that integrating this firm into its group would produce the required results, not least in adding a new branch to its military business that by the mid-1980s was burgeoning. Moreover, with ISC's marketing expertise, centrally co-ordinated by N.C. Blackwell (see Figure 2.1), it was anticipated that sales would expand significantly after the acquisition.

In the 1980s, ISC was clearly willing to spend significantly in building its defence businesses, another example of which was the acquisition of SI EL in March 1985, for $36.5 million, giving it an entrée into both Italian and NATO markets. This Italian firm was the result of a series of mergers, starting in 1966 when the Edison and Montecatini groups combined to form Montedison. Although primarily a chemicals company, Montedison built an electronics division, Montedel, that through its subsidiaries (Elmer, Gregorini, OTE and Laben) established a prominent position in the Italian defence sector. Montedel was eventually sold to the Italian conglomerate, Bastogi IRBS, but as a result of some financial difficulties this group was broken up, leading to the formation in 1982 of SI EL to consolidate the electronics businesses. After ISC acquired this business in 1985, Giorgio Geddes was appointed chairman and Dr Franco Samoggia was made chief executive, having played a major role in assisting the parent company to enter the Italian market. By that time, SI EL had sales of approximately $73 million, but with profits of just $2 million it was apparent that the business struggled to develop commercially viable products. Working from a small head office in Florence,[25] though, Geddes and Samoggia were keen to develop ambitious plans to double turnover in the following three years and significantly improve profitability, principally by securing both domestic and overseas contracts across its four subsidiaries.

By far the largest component of SI EL was Elmer, a manufacturer of military communications equipment that could be traced back to 1961. By the 1980s, not only was Elmer supplying this equipment to the Italian variant of the *Tornado* military aircraft, it had also exported to twenty-eight countries, principally those linked by NATO. Working with American and British companies, it had jointly developed highly advanced communications equipment for use in NATO projects, including the Manassas Programme which was run jointly with Magnavox (a subsidiary of the US firm Philips), producing nuclear-hardened HF receiver-transmitters used by the US Army in Europe. Coming under the ISC umbrella resulted in much greater investment in capacity to boost production from $30 million in 1984 to an estimated $70 million by 1988, reflecting the confidence its new owners had in the core technology developed by Elmer engineers.

Another significant subsidiary within the SI EL family was Laben, an instrumentation firm that sold extensively to both the nuclear industry and the European Space Agency (ESA). By the 1980s, with specific regard to its work with the ESA Laben had developed an extensive experience in areas such as satellite links, systems integration and ground instrumentation, providing a solid position as one of Europe's leading firms in this sector. Similarly, in the European nuclear industry its range of instrumentation had brought Laben into contact with many of the world's leading firms in this sector, giving its management and engineers strong links with the most advanced technology. Indeed, while Laben was only a relatively small operation, with sales in 1984 of $1 million, its well-established positions in the expanding nuclear and space industries offered rich promise.

The third significant element of SI EL was OTE, a firm that had been established in Florence as long ago as 1954, principally to design and manufacture multi-channel trans-receivers for the Italian Air Force. Over the 1950s and 1960s, apart from developing its radio business, diversification into telemetry and tracking devices was pursued, leading to contracts from the ESA. After merging into the Montedel group, however, it was decided that in order to avoid overlap with Elmer and Laben, OTE should focus on civil communications equipment. This resulted in the development of products for the police, air traffic control and mobile radio, building up sales to approximately $5 million by 1984.

Clearly, acquiring SI EL had not only given ISC access to sound communications, nuclear and space technology, but also helped the American executives develop stronger links with NATO, ESA and other customers across Europe. It is important to stress, though, that the subsidiaries were not major businesses in their own right, while Ian Ball described ES IL as a group of 'likeable enthusiasts, full of plans for tomorrow!'.[26] Indeed, while one might optimistically claim that Guerin had identified and seized an opportunity to expand from his well-established British base into broader European networks and markets, it remains a mystery why ISC should embark on this acquisition. Ian Ball's views on the entire ISC group were also by 1987 based on inside information, because after his unfortunate experiences with Peter Dorey over the profit projections of the Wythenshawe division of Ferranti Computer Systems,[27] he had left Ferranti and joined ISC as managing director of ISC Electronic Systems Ltd. As Figure 2.1 reveals, this subsidiary was a component of the newly created European Technologies Group which Jim Guerin ran as acting chairman. At the same time, Sir David Checketts (see Figure 2.1) had been given responsibility for a new venture, ISC International Technologies Ltd, what was in effect the public relations arm of the British-based subsidiary of ISC. This reiterates the view expressed earlier, that Checketts was employed by Guerin principally for his impeccable establishment connections, because he rarely played much of a role in the operational aspects of any of the British or European subsidiaries.[28]

Another part of the ISC group that Checketts managed was a subsidiary established in Nigeria, ISC Electronic Systems Ltd.[29] This operation was set up as a joint venture with the State Security Services, known locally as The Secret Service, in the hope that access to substantial government contracts could be acquired. To this effect, a retired Nigerian General, G. Wahishi, was hired by ISC, while Checketts recruited as managing director a former RAF Squadron Leader, Roy Handley, who since retirement from active service had been involved in various Middle East ventures. In spite of considerable pump-priming investments from Checketts' branch of ISC, however, during its two-year existence the Nigerian subsidiary failed to secure a single major contract, apart from providing some security equipment for the Presidential Palace in Abuja. Little is known about why Guerin encouraged Checketts to pursue this venture, but it again illustrates the preferred modus operandi of ISC, in working directly with high-level government sources to secure big public sector contracts.

Ball's recruitment into ISC at the beginning of 1987, on the other hand, marked a decisive upturn in the profile of ISC Electronic Systems Ltd (hereafter, ESL). Based in Hanworth, near London, the subsidiary had been formed early in 1986, after ISC had acquired two small defence-related businesses and Dr Simon Wilder had been recruited from STC as managing director. The two businesses were, firstly, a producer of electrical windings for radar equipment and torpedoes (purchased from the receiver for £110,000), as well as a management systems business (acquired from Power Engineering Associates for £32,000) that ran projects for the MoD, including work on the *Trident* nuclear submarine. By the time Ball arrived at Hanworth in January 1987, however, it was apparent that ESL was losing substantial amounts of money,[30] having failed to expand the newly acquired businesses. Indeed, Ball felt that ESL was saddled with a top-heavy management at Hanworth, not to mention two loss-making businesses that would always struggle to generate any profits. Consequently, several of the senior executives were released, on extremely beneficial terms, while Ball recruited a former Ferranti man, Ken Goodwin, to help him restructure ESL's finances. In spite of ESL's losses, Guerin also provided the funds for Ball to continue to build ESL, principally by buying other small defence-related businesses that would complement the global ISC portfolio. This resulted in the purchase of CSR Ltd, a small computer software firm based in Ilkley, Yorkshire, and Solartron Simulators, a subsidiary of Schlumberger based in Farnborough.

We will need to return to Ian Ball's work within ISC at a later point,[31] given the insights he gained into the various missile contracts allegedly secured by Guerin and his team. Crucially, one should remember that ESL's principal base at Hanworth also housed the missile production facility operated by ISC Technologies, a subsidiary of ISC International Technologies (see Figure 2.1), run by one of Guerin's closest confidants, Clyde Ivy. Interestingly, access to this subsidiary's facilities at Hanworth was limited to a select group of senior employees, on the orders of Jim Guerin himself. One should also note that, reflecting the central importance of ISC International Technologies (hereafter referred to as ISC International), according to the Fleming's report it consistently accounted for 60% of ISC group turnover and up to 75% of pre-tax profits.[32] While ISC Defense and Space co-ordinated strategy across the conglomerate, ISC International was the alleged mainstay of the group, placing considerable importance on what went on within its various subsidiaries. Interestingly, though, the Fleming's report went on to note that '[ISC] International does not disclose its customer list, out of respect for certain clients' requirements for confidentiality'. Nevertheless, it went on to provide the information in Table 2.1, indicating that the bulk of its business was done in the Middle East and Africa (and in reality, by far the preponderance in the former rather than the latter). What credence one can give to this data we shall examine later, but again it is indicative of the level of revelation that Guerin preferred, especially when it came to ISC International's activities.

While ISC was willing to reveal the geographical destination of ISC International's sales, however, it was extremely vague when identifying both the specific customers and the actual product sold to them. Indeed, after noting that 'a small number of customers have accounted for a large proportion of its sales', the Fleming's report talked only about 'Customer A' and 'Customer B', and specifically how on average they accounted for over 75% of the subsidiary's sales. While the report also went on to note that 'it is not appropriate to discuss its products and services in the normal fashion',[33] we shall see in the next section that there were very good reasons why ISC preferred to keep this information from official eyes. One of the contracts was what would come to be known as the PGM air-to-ground missile (precision guided munition, also known as a *Paveway* bomb), 1,500 of which were to be funnelled from ISC companies in the United Kingdom through the United Arab Emirates and on to Iraq. Although none of these ever reached Iraq, it will be vital to assess this contract in the next section as a key element of Guerin's worldwide covert military operations. Apart from this covert missiles business, ISC International was also heavily involved in either the production of ordnance and electronic systems or transferring this technology to various countries, building on what ISC had been developing since its inauguration in 1971. At the core of this activity was *Rockeye*, an air-launched, anti-armour weapon, as well as security systems and communications equipment, demonstrating that ISC's existence was heavily dependent upon ISC Defense and Space Group run by Guerin's Proxy Board in Lancaster, Pennsylvania.

Again, it will be vital to reassess this network of contracts and subsidiaries in the next section, where more information will be provided on the covert nature of this activity. At this stage, though, one can note that as a result of ISC's externally driven growth in the 1980s, it had clearly expanded significantly from the humble base established by Guerin in 1971. As we noted earlier, only 30% of its workforce was by 1986 based in Lancaster, while a further 24.3% were located on the West Coast of the USA, and 41.5% worked in Italy. At the same time, publicly ISC was still predominantly based on its core businesses of ordnance, communication systems and electronic equipment, although the acquisition of Marquadt and some of the Italian subsidiaries had created new opportunities in propulsion systems and instrumentation. Of course, this ignores the substantial guided missile business that we shall examine in the next section, but publicly very little was made of this activity, for various reasons. Through his network of companies, in the UK, the USA and Italy, Guerin encouraged co-ordination of product development, for example in ordnance and electronic systems, providing some synergistic benefits to emerge in these areas. In general, though, this was extremely limited, with Ian Ball noting that within the Hanworth facility occupied by ISC Electronic Systems, ISC International Technologies (run by Sir David Checketts) and ISC International (run by Clyde Ivy), they rarely met together to discuss business.

In spite of these reservations, however, it is apparent from Figure 2.2 that ISC was expanding impressively over the period 1978–87, from a turnover of £21.8 million (£27.5 million at 1980 prices) in 1978 to £393 million (£258.1 million), with the period of greatest growth coming after 1983 when the acquisitions were made. Even more impressively, the trading profit had increased from just £1.3 million in 1978 to £45.5 million by 1987 (see Figure 3.1 for more profit data), persuading investors on the London Stock Exchange to stump up another £70.5 million in response to ISC's 1986 rights issue. These funds were used, firstly, to repay the loans raised to buy Marquadt and the Italian subsidiaries, and secondly, to buy Cardion Electronics for cash. To some insiders, though, it was difficult to identify the exact source of ISC's financial strength. As Ian Ball noted:

> With hindsight I realise I was becoming very disillusioned: it was fairly obvious that no ISC business competence existed in the UK, so the Company's profits must have been generated elsewhere ... there did not appear to be the infrastructure in any of the subsidiaries capable of

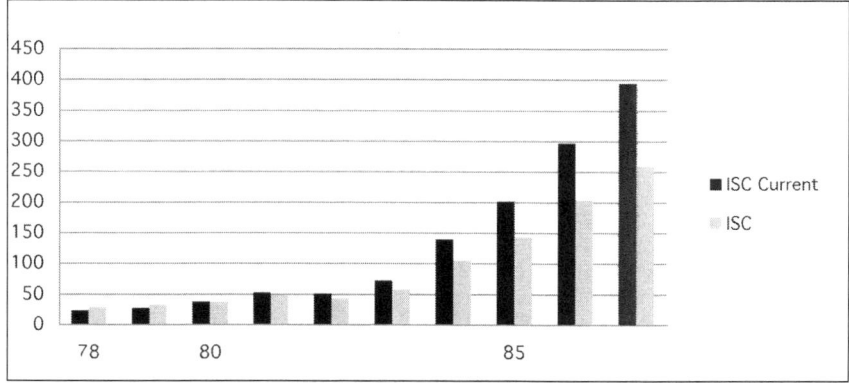

Figure 2.2 ISC turnover in constant (1980 prices) and current prices, 1978–87

generating the profit expansion which must have occurred. Jim Guerin was supremely confident, and much of this confidence rubbed off on others, but the actual business, the contracts, just didn't seem to be there. Marquadt were always going to sign big contracts, Cardion were in a recovery situation, Data Comm and EMP were start-ups, Defense Systems in Lancaster were in the build-to-print market (highly competitive and therefore low margin), and the Italian Group were likeable enthusiasts, full of plans for tomorrow![34]

Although Ball admitted that hindsight helped him to form these views, he notes that they were a genuine reflection of the way he felt in 1986–87, when working for ISC at Hanworth.[35] Moreover, given that ISC's 1986–87 profits failed to match the Stock Exchange's expectations, the share price had fallen by almost 20% in the summer of 1987, indicating that others were beginning to express some concerns about the financial basis of the firm's growth.

In trying to unravel Ball's speculative comments, one is significantly hampered by ISC's traditional reluctance to reveal any performance data on its constituent parts: the annual accounts were always presented in consolidated form. As these accounts were tightly controlled by Guerin, it was impossible for Ball, or indeed anybody else, to discover any more information than was publicly available in the published accounts. This again highlights the nature of ISC's business operations, in that just as with the Proxy Board that ran ISC Defense and Space (see Figure 2.1), only Guerin and his closest associates knew exactly what was happening across the group. Consequently, such questions as 'Where do the profits come from?' would always remain unanswered as long as this regime was in place, leaving Ball and similarly curious people in a state of ignorance that would persist up to the autumn of

1989. Another matter of growing concern was how ISC extracted profits from contracts, an issue that needs to be assessed in much greater detail as we open up the reality that Guerin and his associates mostly withheld from the world outside his Proxy Board.

2.3 ISC's covert activities

Having outlined the public face of Guerin's efforts to build ISC into a major electronics outfit, it is now necessary to scratch beneath the surface and reveal the covert activities that mostly explain why his corporation was able, firstly, to survive a shaky start, and, secondly, grow significantly in the 1980s and generate purportedly impressive profits. As far as the latter was concerned, of course, not only were commentators concerned about how ISC extracted profits from contracts, but it also became apparent that Ian Ball's reservations about the lack of substance behind ISC's British activities were well-founded. The story takes us from Lancaster, Pennsylvania, to secret service offices in Washington, and on to South Africa, the Middle East, Pakistan, China, Chile and back to the UK, involving some of the world's most prominent politicians of that era, as well as individuals with whom few of these people would admit to having a relationship. One can only be amazed at the intricate web that connected Guerin to a source of business which underpinned his aspirations and Janus-like provided the money which he spent liberally on not only jet aircraft and an international lifestyle, but also churches, the arts and other local charities. It is also vital to reveal that very few people knew the full story behind these duplicities, because Guerin was both architect of and principal actor in the scenario, hiding his business affairs from all but a close circle of associates.

ISC and South Africa

Whether out of desperation or pure serendipity, it was in 1974 that James Guerin first came into contact with a new source of business, bringing him into contact with some highly influential US government operatives and politicians who were pursuing policies, official and covert, that provided enormous commercial opportunities. As we noted in the last section, ISC had struggled to develop a viable product base in its first three years of trading, hopping from missile sub-assemblies to bug-zappers and radios. All this was to change when in 1974 he established Gamma Systems Associates, ostensibly a technology-transfer operation, but in reality what in the intelligence community is known as a 'cut-out' company. This term refers to an innocuous corporate entity that mostly performs wholly legitimate business, but on occasion acts as a contractor for the United States Central Intelligence

Agency (CIA), albeit on the condition that official recognition is never granted. The key agent in the Guerin–CIA relationship was Admiral Bobby Ray Inman, one of the leading influences in American intelligence who was at that time extremely concerned about shipping movements in the South Atlantic. Based in a small building at Kennedy Airport, New York, and surviving until 1987, the principal purpose of Gamma Systems was to export highly sophisticated, and politically sensitive, missile technology, ordnance and other electronic equipment, none of which would ever have export licences. When one considers that the beneficiary of the first phase of Gamma System's activities was going to be the apartheid regime in South Africa, it is patently obvious that Guerin was willing to involve ISC in trade that was always going to be secret and illegal.[36]

While it is impossible to say who initiated these links between ISC, the CIA and South Africa, it is first of all necessary to remember that because at that time its regime was built on apartheid, it was illegal to trade with the country, and especially to sell military-related equipment to a government that was pilloried by every other democratic nation. As the South African regime feared for its survival, it was investing significantly in armaments, initiating in 1971 a programme to develop nuclear weapons. While to a significant extent supported by Israel, it was apparent that the nuclear weapons programme required the assistance of Western nations, technologically and strategically, given that this sector was tightly regulated. Another factor of some significance was the US's growing concern about the control effected by Russian submarines in what was known as the Cape Route, a highly strategic link connecting the Atlantic and Indian Oceans. Specifically, Admiral Inman (at that time Head of US Naval Intelligence) was increasingly concerned about the concentration of Russian nuclear weapon submarines in the South Atlantic, arguing that this represented the single most important threat to the USA, not least because it was impossible to track the fleet accurately.

Having identified this threat to US security, Admiral Inman set about securing permission to resolve the problem, firstly by successfully asking permission from President Richard Nixon to open up negotiations with South Africa,[37] then providing the requisite equipment. Approved by the US government in 1976, and in total worth $200 million, this resulted in the construction of advanced radar stations in Cape Province, South Africa, to monitor an extensive network of underwater sonar devices planted in the South Atlantic. In addition, electronic surveillance and countermeasure systems were constructed on the northern borders of South Africa, to monitor possible insurgent activity. Crucially as far as our story is concerned, ISC played a leading role in facilitating the transfer of this equipment to South Africa, using Gamma Systems to ship freight provided by ESI Manufacturing subsidiary from Kennedy Airport using commercial aircraft, yet without the requisite export licences. One should also note that the South African conglomerate Barlow Rand was used as the local agent, establishing links between the two firms that lasted many years.

Gamma Systems used a freight-forwarding operation, Public Brokers International, to do this job, resulting in its owner, Gerald Schuler, later being prosecuted for illegal arms trading.[38] Inman apparently chose Guerin partly because ISC at that time was a very low-profile operation based in a small Pennsylvania city, while Guerin's experience on the *Poseidon* programme (when he worked for Lockheed in the 1960s) provided appropriate skills in prosecuting large-scale defence contracts. Although ISC only manufactured a small proportion of the equipment supplied, given that it was too sophisticated for its limited Lancaster activities, Guerin reaped a rich financial reward from this business as the sole owner of Gamma Systems. As no accounts survive for this period,[39] naturally it is impossible to say just how much Guerin earned from his South African business, but it certainly made him a wealthy man, judging from his private expenditure on Lancaster cultural and religious activities. Ferranti International later claimed that in 1983 $1.2 million was placed in a Channel Islands bank account by a South African contact, money the board tried to recoup through the courts.[40] Moreover, the *Intelligencer Journal* has claimed that Barlow Rand leant $2 million to ISC in 1974, in order to pump-prime the illegal trade, money which was later written off as a bad debt. The report also goes on to note that in 1974 some of this money was used to purchase Pro Line Golf Corporation, in order to supply Barlow Rand with golf clubs, demonstrating how Guerin covered up his covert activities with what were ostensibly legal trading ventures.[41] In effect, Inman's gift elevated Guerin from being a small-time electronics manufacturer into a significant player in the international arms trade.

To substantiate this claim further, one need only examine the multiplier effects of the South African deals. Given its political isolation, not to mention the implied and explicit threats to its independence emanating from other African countries, most notably Angola, the South African government was minded to extract a hard bargain from Admiral Inman in return for co-operation over the radar stations. This bargain took the form of an agreement to supply nuclear weapons technology to South Africa, including appropriate delivery systems, giving the regime a major advantage over other African countries. Recent research by Sasha Polakow-Suransky has revealed that this support was provided via Israel, which gave the apartheid regime a considerable amount of technical expertise during the 1970s,[42] making South Africa the only African nation with a nuclear capability and limiting the willingness of its neighbours to invade the country and end the apartheid regime. The USA consequently became a major bulwark of apartheid, albeit in the interests of monitoring what Inman had identified as its greatest military threat in the South Atlantic. Such were the delicacies of international politics that successive American Presidents provided Inman with total backing. Even when the Democrat Jimmy Carter was elected President in 1977 and all American military links with South Africa were officially curtailed, he accepted the need to maintain the surveillance programme, providing Inman with implicit authority to continue supplying nuclear and missile technologies to the ostracised regime.

By 1979, it is also apparent that this covert support for South Africa extended to the UK, because the election of a Conservative government in that year, headed by Margaret Thatcher, heralded a softening of British attitudes towards the apartheid regime. Although Thatcher realised that it was impossible to circumvent the United Nations restrictions on trading with South Africa that had been in existence since 1964, she convened a meeting of British and South African ministers and businessmen in Schloss Freudenberg, on the shores of Lake Geneva in Switzerland, to discuss how sanctions could be obviated.[43] By the time that Ronald Reagan had replaced Jimmy Carter as US President in 1981, an Anglo-American alliance over this issue was also emerging, allowing South Africa not only to continue its nuclear weapons programme, but also to import most of the commodities it required, including food and oil. While as we saw earlier it was the laxity of English company law that persuaded Guerin to transfer the registration of ISC from the USA to the UK in 1982, the Conservative government was not going to object to its covert operations in South Africa.

Although South Africa had been building a nuclear weapon capability jointly with Israel since the early 1970s, the development programme was attenuated by a shortage of both core technologies and components. These problems were mostly overcome by Jim Guerin, because throughout the 1970s he transferred the expertise and equipment that allowed the apartheid regime to develop and build a long-range ballistic missile capable of delivering a nuclear warhead. First tested in 1979, this missile was built by Kentron, the specialist missile development branch of the formidable state-owned South African armaments firm, Armscor, for whom Guerin became a consultant in 1977. This missile programme was managed by Clyde Ivy, a highly regarded expert in this field who from 1977 would play a major role in ISC's activities. Up to the mid-1970s, Ivy had been working for the industrial conglomerate Teledyne, of Huntsville, which had legitimately been working in South Africa on civil projects, under licence from the US government. Having been approached by Armscor to establish a missile development and production operation, Ivy was instructed to contact Guerin and offer his services to ISC. Ivy was then moved to South Africa and established Kentron, initiating a relationship with Guerin that proved central to ISC's expansion. As we have already seen, by the 1980s Ivy had become head of ISC

International Technologies Group, based in the UK, at their principal facility in Hanworth, where Ivy master-minded the PGM project. Although Ivy actually became an ISC employee in 1977, however, it is clear that until the mid-1980s he spent most of his time in South Africa helping Kentron develop the nuclear missile that was so central to that country's defence strategy. Although Israel had been helping South Africa since 1971 to develop, test, and produce long range missiles and rockets, based on its own *Jericho II* missile, clearly the Armscor-Gamma Systems-ISC link proved crucial to the success of this programme. In September 1979, an American satellite detected a distinctive double flash off the southern coast of Africa which, using the satellite data, offered strong evidence that it had been caused by a low-yield (up to 3 kilotons) nuclear explosion.

It is now clear that during the 1980s the ISC subsidiary ESI Manufacturing provided through Gamma Associates more than $30 million-worth of military-related equipment for South Africa, including telemetry tracking antennae to collect data from missiles in flight, gyroscopes for guidance systems, and photo-imaging film readers, all of which were crucial to the further development of missile systems. Furthermore, again using ESI Manufacturing as the vehicle, Clyde Ivy assisted two of South Africa's most notorious arms importers, William Metelerkamp (head of Kentron's procurement department) and Colonel Hendrix Botha (of the South Africa Defence Ministry), to support Kentron's continued efforts to develop guided missiles.[44] In 1984, Metelerkamp and Botha were arrested by the UK authorities for organising an illegal arms trading operation, a year after they had visited Ivy in Lancaster, when they secured a supply of essential electronic components, to be provided by ESI Manufacturing. It is consequently a cause of some concern that after being vetted by the British intelligence services, Ivy was in 1987 cleared to be a director of a major British defence supplier, given what would have been the extensive knowledge of his links with South Africa. Although Metelerkamp and Botha were allowed to return to South Africa in 1984, reflecting the Conservative government's attitude towards that country, ISC continued to work with them over the next five years, as part of the extensive covert trade Guerin had built since the early 1970s.

South Africa consequently achieved its strategic aim of becoming the only African nuclear power principally because of the covert support provided by US and British governments, using ISC and Gamma Systems as their well-remunerated vehicles to obviate international law. Another vehicle created by Guerin to facilitate this trade was ISC Educational Systems, which ostensibly existed to supply South African black communities with personal computers and educational aids, but in practice supported Armscor's missile and weapons development programmes. This also involved another firm, LearnTech Pty, jointly owned by ISC and Barlow Rand, leading one federal source to note that: 'To say ISC was owned 100 per cent by Barlow Rand might be somewhat of an overstatement. But to say they were a US arm of Barlow Rand would be right on target, so to speak'.[45] Guerin instructed key staff to set up the accounts through which ISC was able to shuffle millions of dollars in payments for the illegal trade. A 1995 BBC Radio programme entitled 'Special Assignment' claimed that since 1974 ISC had annually sold approximately $16 million worth of night-sights, missiles and cluster bombs to the apartheid regime in South Africa, providing Guerin with a sound financial base for his corporate and personal activities. Given the involvement, and approval, of the world's leading politicians, however, is it any wonder that Guerin rejected any notion that he was acting illegally? Such was his confidence that by 1986 he was even attempting to market one of Armscor's products, the *Striker* munitions-delivery system that closely resembled ISC's *Rockeye*. ESI also carried over $9 million worth of orders destined for South Africa as late as September 1988, demonstrating that Guerin sustained this link in spite of the 1987 merger with Ferranti. One should also stress that little credibility can ever be attached to Guerin's defence that he was merely providing the CIA with information on South African military activity,[46] because he was not only working directly and covertly for the intelligence agency, but ISC was also building up a substantial and highly profitable business that he was reluctant to give up, even after Ferranti had acquired his business.

As we shall see in Chapter 4, it was only once Ian Ball had started to play a more prominent role in ISC's activities that this trade with South Africa was eventually terminated. Ball sought advice from senior civil servants at the Foreign & Commonwealth Office, who noted that as South Africa remained on the United Nations embargo list, it would be illegal to sell Armscor products. Marketing *Striker*, nevertheless, demonstrates both the extent to which ISC was linked with Armscor and Guerin's growing confidence that he could circumvent international law. Chapter 4 will also outline a wide range of covert contracts that Guerin's ISC fulfilled for Armscor and its many subsidiaries, demonstrating that up to the merger with Ferranti and beyond the illegal arms trading continued apace. Indeed, ISC was a key vehicle in South Africa's defence exporting activities without which the apartheid regime would have struggled to keep up with its increasingly well-armed neighbours.

ISC and Iraq

Although the covert ISC story would be sufficiently sensational if it only involved South Africa, as we shall go on to see it was merely the starting-point from which ISC built an extensive international arms trade that would take in

Iraq, Chile, Pakistan and China. Starting with Iraq, one might express some surprise at the discovery that a country with which the USA has fought two wars since the 1990s, and recently over the alleged existence of so-called weapons of mass destruction (WMD), benefited from American and British technology and finance to build these capabilities. Once again, though, just as in the case of the need to monitor Russian submarines in the South Atlantic, this was all bound up in geo-political strategic concerns, specifically those arising from the Iran–Iraq war of 1981–89. Before discussing this conflict, however, it is also important to note that relations between Iran and the USA had deteriorated badly after the revolution of 1979 that had seen the overthrow of the Shah, to be replaced by Ayatollah Khomeini and a deeply religious Islamic government intent on rejecting Western ideas and influence. This rejection was especially manifested in the November 1979 invasion of the US Embassy in the capital, Tehran, by revolutionary Islamic students, who in taking sixty-six hostages humiliated the American government by withstanding all efforts to repatriate its citizens. Futile military attempts to free the hostages exacerbated the situation, and even though some of the hostages had been freed by the end of November, it was January 1981 before the siege ended, precipitating an antipathy that has persisted up to the present.

Recognising the dangers associated with isolating their country from the rest of the Middle East, which was mostly allied to the USA, the Islamic clerics were keen to secure financial independence. One of the most effective ways of achieving this strategic aim was to seize various oil deposits that existed in the disputed territory of Khouzestan which its neighbour, Iraq, had been exploiting for some years. At the same time, the ruler of Iraq, Saddam Hussein, who was a Sunni-Muslim and had in turn come to power as a result of a 1968 coup, saw in the Iranian revolution an opportunity to extend his empire. As the American government was anxious to recoup some credibility after the Tehran hostage fiasco, Saddam Hussein was encouraged to order his troops to invade Iran in September 1980, starting a bloody and devastating war. It is estimated that this war cost half-a-million civilian and military lives, given that it lasted until August 1988 and compares in many ways – the use of trench warfare, bayonet charges and chemical weapons (by Iraq) – with the First World War. Whatever the accuracy of this comparison, for the less scrupulous, not to mention Machiavellian politicians, this created an enormous market for military equipment, resulting in a series of machinations that would shock many. As Iraq spent approximately $43 billion on armaments between 1981 and 1987, this was an opportunity some just could not resist.

For the major Western powers it was clearly vital to pay close attention to the swinging balance of power between these two oil-rich countries that were located close to the USSR. Not surprisingly, given the USA's poor relationship with Iran since the Islamic Revolution, successive Presidents (the Democrat Jimmy Carter up to 1981, followed by the Republican Ronald Reagan) 'tilted' towards Iraq by reopening diplomatic channels and lifting restrictions on the export of what has passed into the vocabulary as dual-use technology (namely, machine tools that could be used to make either civilian or military products).[47] Apart from the covert transfer of third-party designs for military hardware and operational battlefield intelligence from US satellites, this also involved the creation of 'front companies' with secret ownership, the use of middlemen, and secretive shipping arrangements that contravened all aspects of United Nations embargoes and general international law. Much of the US activity was funded through an Atlanta subsidiary of Italy's largest bank, the State-owned Banca Nazionale del Lavoro (BNL), which channelled $5 billion to Iraq during the 1980s, using US government-backed loans as security.[48] Other countries involved in this trade included the UK, France, the USSR, Singapore, Italy and Chile. At the same time, such are the complexities associated with international politics, the USA,[49] USSR, Portugal, Spain and Yugoslavia also supplied arms to Iran, while the Communist regime of North Korea was another source of equipment that was mostly manufactured in various Eastern European countries.

As we shall see again in succeeding chapters,[50] while this was not reported extensively at the time, ISC Technologies was one of the beneficiaries of BNL's largesse, receiving letters of credit for military exports to Iraq.[51] We shall examine these exports over the course of the next chapters, but this information demonstrates that ISC was involved in the illegal trade. At the same time, one must also stress that the most prominent British involvement in the Iran–Iraq war was through the engineering firm Matrix Churchill.[52] While space limitations prevent a detailed examination of how this Coventry-based company came to play such a prominent role in providing Iraq with dual-purpose technology,[53] specifically some of the world's most advanced machine tools capable of producing armaments and nuclear-related equipment, the case illustrates some of the issues that will recur later in our analysis of ISC's activities. Matrix Churchill had only been created in 1987, after the head of Iraqi military procurement, Safa al Habobi, funded a merger of TMG Engineering and TI Machine Tools, as a means of ensuring a reliable supply of advanced equipment for the Iraqi war machine. At the same time, as the British directors of Matrix Churchill were supplying the Ministry of Intelligence with extensive information about Iraq, no official barriers were put up to limit the firm's extensive exports. However, even though the Minister for Trade, Alan Clark, was prepared to state in the House of Commons that all exports to Iraq were covered by appropriate licences, three Matrix Churchill executives were in 1990 arrested for illegal arms trading with that country. This prosecution preceded the First Gulf War, popularly known as *Desert Storm*, when following Iraq's invasion of Kuwait in 1991, a US-led Western Alliance had forcefully ejected Saddam Hussein's forces from that oil-rich country. Although the Western Allies refused to follow through on their military success and oust Saddam Hussein, extensive United Nations investigations into Iraq's ability to produce weapons of mass destruction revealed the extent of its purchase of foreign-made equipment. Nevertheless, the Matrix Churchill trial, which did not happen until 1992, collapsed amidst acute government embarrassment, when Alan Clark (by then no longer a government minister) admitted that in his 1980s Commons statements he had been 'economical with the *actualité*',[54] uncovering the duplicity of official attempts to assist Iraq. Much to the chagrin of the intelligence establishment, Clark admitted that the government had given a 'nod and a wink' to Matrix Churchill executives to export dual-use equipment to Iraq. The resulting inquiry, headed by Sir Richard Scott, laid bare the extent of both officially sanctioned British dual-technology exports to Iraq and the lengths officials and politicians went to in keeping this information secret.[55] The extensive use of 'public interest immunity certificates' had initially allowed politicians and senior civil servants to hide behind arcane parliamentary privileges, putting four Matrix Churchill executives through two extremely difficult years, when all they had done was follow UK government directions.

Much to the amazement of some, and the considerable relief of others, the Scott Report is notable for failing to discuss any of the activities perpetrated by ISC Technologies during the 1980s, even though it was well known by that time that BNL had funded its military exports to Iraq. This omission was not perpetrated for a lack of evidence, because it was reported in 1994 that the Scott Inquiry investigated whether the MoD had sanctioned ISC's *Hakim* PGM contracts.[56] While ostensibly supplied to the UAE, there was widespread suspicion that both versions of *Hakim* were ultimately destined for Saddam Hussein's Iraqi army.[57] Nothing could ever be proved on this front, however, explaining why the Scott Report ignored ISC. At the same time, apart from significantly destabilising the Conservative government, by now headed by the beleaguered John Major, the Scott Report brought to light a range of covert Middle Eastern activities that had been sponsored, maybe even initiated, by both British and American governments that shocked most citizens on both sides of the Atlantic. Major would go on to win the decisive House of Commons vote on the Scott Report, by 320 votes to 319, but this was mostly made possible by a refusal to allow anybody other than two Labour politicians sight of the Report until just three hours before the debate, thereby severely limiting the availability of appropriate information.

Members of the British and American armed forces that fought in the First Gulf War (or, *Desert Storm*) were amazed to discover that their adversaries were using equipment that had been manufactured using technologically advanced machine tools supplied by their own countries. This trade originated in the early 1980s, when the Reagan administration decided that in order to prevent either Iran or Iraq dominating the oil-rich Middle East region, a policy of 'active neutrality' was devised. Apart from demonstrating their ability to stretch the English language, it was also clear that politicians and officials at the highest levels were willing to embark on work that clearly contravened international law. Vice President George Bush was responsible for this policy, working closely with the Director of the CIA, William Casey, and the USA's special envoy to the Middle East, Donald Rumsfeld,[58] to supply equipment and intelligence to both countries. Although Iraq would appear to have been the principal beneficiary of this policy,[59] given that in 1982 it appeared to be losing the war with Iran, the latter also benefitted from the USA's 'active neutrality'. In this section, we shall focus on the extensive network of contacts and financial channels that supported Iraq's expanding military machine, demonstrating that while the USA co-ordinated the multi-lateral supply chain, this involved almost every country in Western Europe, China, the Soviet Union and some Latin American countries. Iraq became the world's largest buyer of arms during the period 1980–88, spending $43 billion on weapons, offering the leading nations and traders an opportunity that was not resisted.

When one comes to consider the role of ISC in this enormous trade, its complicity extended to much more than machine tools, because it is now clear that the Lancaster firm was also responsible for supplying the specifications for some particularly nasty weapons to Iraq, presumably with financial support from BNL. Although one must stress that ISC would not have appeared to have shipped any weapons to Iraq directly, Jim Guerin was responsible for both passing the technical specifications of his firm's principal munitions product, *Rockeye*, to a South African firm, as well as directly exporting key components of this product to South Africa, which he knew would be transferred to Iraq.[60] The South African customer for the latter, which was a 'proximity fuze', enabling artillery rounds to explode above enemy troops and thereby killing more people, was Fuchs Electronics Pty, Ltd, the electronics subsidiary of Barlow Rand, the country's largest industrial and mining conglomerate that worked closely with Armscor.[61] Given that sand deadens the blast effect of high-explosive bombs, *Rockeye's* ability to explode just above the ground and distribute its armour-piercing and anti-personnel bomblets proved highly advantageous in Middle East conditions.[62] Some 300,000 of these 'proximity fuses' were supplied by ISC to Fuchs, worth $4.4 million, all of which were sold on to Iraq and used in the Gulf War of 1991 against US and Allied troops. Crucially for South Africa, in acting as an intermediary in this covert trade, it was able to acquire invaluable oil supplies from Iraq in return for the fuzes, demonstrating how ISC was directly bolstering the apartheid regime by ensuring that it was supplied with a commodity that would otherwise have been difficult to buy. The factory (known as Sahad 38, located close to Baghdad) where *Rockeye* was manufactured, was one of the first targets of US laser-guided weapons during *Desert Storm*, indicating the strategic importance of this facility to Iraqi defences.

Another link in this circuitous trade was the Chilean firm Industrias Cardoen, run by Carlos Cardoen, one of South America's most notorious arms traders who sold approximately $200 million worth of cluster bombs to Iraq.[63] As an engineering PhD (University of Utah), Cardoen had established his defence equipment business in order to service the requirements of one of his main sponsors, the military regime headed by Augusto Pinochet in his home country. From this base, Cardoen ran an international arms firm that would supply weapons and equipment to any country that had the money. In order to exploit these links and cover up their direct involvement, the American intelligence services approached Cardoen in 1981 with an offer to provide him with the technical specifications for ISC's *Rockeye*, on condition that he supplied Saddam Hussein with the end product. The Iraqi forces had identified a need for this kind of cluster bomb, because in countering the infantry charges typical of their war with Iran, this technology was especially devastating. With a killing range of several hundred yards, these bombs could cut off a charge before it had really started, giving Saddam's army a distinct advantage over its rivals. It has been estimated that Cardoen supplied 700,000 cluster bombs to Iraq, worth approximately $200 million, during the 1980s, profits from which he invested in an extensive property portfolio in Florida, run by an investment company called Swissco. In addition, Cardoen shipped explosive zirconium pellets supplied by another US firm, Teledyne Inc, directly to the Iraqi military for fitting to cluster bombs. Following the First Gulf War (*Desert Storm*), when just as in the UK politicians were obliged to investigate how Iraq had become such a powerful military force, and in this case use *Rockeye* against the American-led coalition, Swissco's assets (worth $30 million) were seized by the authorities and a writ was issued for Cardoen's arrest.

Although cluster bombs are a particularly nasty form of weapon, another more sinister aspect of Guerin's links with South Africa and Iraq involved the transfer of nuclear weapon technology. It is now known that in 1983, as a result of a request made by William Casey, Director of the CIA, James Guerin personally delivered the technical specifications to Israel for the electronic fuse that triggers the fuel-air bomb which was a crucial component in a nuclear bomb.[64] This was regarded as an acceptable action, given the USA's close strategic links with Israel, even though once again this was done covertly in order not to upset their other allies in the Middle East. We have also mentioned earlier that ISC worked directly with Armscor's subsidiary, Kentron, to develop a guided missile capable of delivering a nuclear weapon, establishing the relationship between James Guerin and Clyde Ivy that became so crucial to later activities. What most alarmed commentators in the 1980s, however, was that Armscor was transferring this technology to Iraq, including equipment which could be used to develop a missile capable of carrying nuclear warheads, photo-imaging equipment for determining the performance of missile tests, and gyroscopes used in inertial navigation systems. In addition, it is also now clear that between 1984 and 1988 Stuart Pindell of ISC set up a project to supply the United Arab Emirates (UAE) with a strategic air-launched missile known as a 'precision guided Munition' (PGM, also known as a *Paveway* bomb), to be fitted to their fleet of French-made *Mirage 2000* jets. The contract was for 1,500 PGMs, later renamed *Hakim* (Arabic for 'The Wise One'), a laser-guided missile that weighed 1,000 kg and had a range of 40 km carrying a small nuclear warhead, to be supplied by ISC's British operation at Hanworth and ISC Aerospace in California. *Jane's Defence Weekly* later questioned why the UAE had not purchased the American-made *Maverick* surface-to-air missile, given that this was regarded as highly reliable and proven in battle.[65] At that time, however, as a very strong Jewish lobby had persuaded the US regime not to sell to potential enemies of Israel, a British-registered firm such as ISC could obviate this kind of obstruction, giving Pindell an opportunity to push the PGM sale.[66] Whatever one thinks of the use of *Hakim* – 'The Wise One' – as the name for the PGM missile, it certainly provided Guerin and ISC with the opportunity to launch a myriad range of fraudulent derivations of this contract, persuading many investors and business counterparts that the firm had become a major player in the international arms trade.

Initially, considerable confusion reigned over exactly when the first *Hakim* contract was signed, Guerin having originally claimed that this occurred in 1986. However, as we shall see in Chapters 4 and 5,[67] following the meticulous investigations by Ian Ball and Alan Cooper (the Ferranti International company secretary), it is now apparent that since the early 1980s Stu Pindell, ISC's senior overseas marketing director, had been pressing the Head of the United Arab Emirates (UAE) Air Force, Major Khalid, to buy ISC-designed laser-guided bombs (LGBs). One should stress that nobody within ISC had started work on an LGB design, reflecting the audacity and hype to which ISC executives frequently resorted, but Pindell persisted with his efforts in the hope that Clyde Ivy's South African connections would fill the technological gap.[68] Nevertheless, ISC included a 1984 missile contract in its accounts for that year, as part of Guerin's attempts to convince investors and other commentators that his firm was continuing to expand impressively and diversify into even more sophisticated product areas. In fact, however, in spite of aggressive lobbying by Pindell, including presentations to a member of the ruling family, Sheikh Mohammed, it was May 1986 before the UAE agreed to pay $138 million for what by that time were designated *Hakim* missiles. This proved to be highly lucrative work for Pindell, because it has been estimated that he earned a $6 million commission on this contract alone, a point which helps to explain why he pushed the UAE so hard to sign.[69]

For various reasons which we shall track over the course of the next chapters, delivery of these missiles was delayed until 1991, at which point *Desert Storm* ensured that they would remain in a United Arab Emirates warehouse. Crucially, though, UAE provided a down-payment of $8.6 million when signing the 1986 *Hakim* contract, funds that were mysteriously applied to ISC's 1985–86 balance sheet under the heading of 'Missile R&D', even though they had only been paid in May 1986. In an even more sinister turn, it is also now clear that having secured the signatures of Sheikh Mohammed for the *Hakim* contract, another version of this document was produced in Lancaster that would be presented to ISC's auditors, with five pages added that gave a false impression of the financial benefits to be derived from this business. Only in the latter months of 1989, however, did any of this come to light, providing Guerin and his closest associates with the time to fool both Ferranti executives and the auditing team that ISC was built on solid financial foundations.

To demonstrate further the secretive nature of the PGM contract, it is interesting to note the contents of a memo sent by Jim Guerin to Clyde Ivy and other senior ISC executives.[70] In this document, Guerin continually refers to the UAE as 'a unique ASSET', indicating that by this time he had adopted the vocabulary used by his CIA supporters. The word 'asset' is often employed in the intelligence community to denote either a specific relationship or source of information, a point confirmed by Guerin's memo, which stated that: 'This ASSET, which is essentially a relationship of trust with a complex client, must be treated with great care and in a manner to maximize its return.' Guerin went on to warn his colleagues that it was essential to understand the 'customs, mores, and culture of the client . . . to ensure preservation of the ASSET'. To liaise with the UAE, a 'function' was established within ISC Aerospace, with specific responsibility for all negotiations on technical specifications, delivery and future upgrades, and reporting directly to Guerin. This 'function' was actually Clyde Ivy, using the experience he had acquired in working with the South African missile programme to ensure the total confidentiality required by UAE, further illustrating the highly covert nature of ISC's PGM work.

Alongside Saddam Hussein's desire to build a chemical weapons capacity, his regime's work on nuclear weapons carried the biggest threat to stability in the Middle East, making it all the more surprising that the CIA would sponsor the technology transfers via Gamma Systems and Armscor. Ultimately, though, it was the West's fears over weapons of mass destruction which precipitated the second war with Iraq, when in 2001 coalition forces used this threat as a pretext to invade the country. As we all know full well now, Saddam had terminated his nuclear and chemical weapons programmes in the 1990s, largely because the source of essential technology and compo- nents had (not surprisingly) dried up after the First Gulf War. The roots of the problem, however, can be traced back to the 1980s, when American and British governments and firms conspired to provide Iraq with access to this technology, on grounds that today seem highly specious.[71]

ISC in China and Pakistan

By the mid-1980s, James Guerin had built up an extensive international arms dealership, consisting of forty-eight front companies, as well as the open businesses charted in Figure 2.1. As a further dimension of his dealings, Guerin was operating at least sixty-one bank accounts in countries such as Switzerland, the Cayman Islands and Bahamas, and Panama, namely, those which were rarely concerned about the means by which any money deposited had been earned. As we shall also see in Chapter 4, Guerin used all of these accounts as a means of persuading more honest business colleagues that ISC was actually generating money, as well as keeping his covertly earned wealth from the prying eyes of tax and customs officials. With highly lucrative cluster bomb, missile and technology transfer contracts that accumulated significant profits, this kind of clandestine banking became an absolute necessity for Guerin. Moreover, his collaborators in the CIA and National Security Agency did not want him to reveal the nature of his business activi- ties, a point that helps to substantiate further the claims made earlier in this chapter, that ISC was registered in England specifically for this purpose. When one comes to consider Guerin's activities outside South Africa, Chile and Iraq, it is also increasingly evident that the last thing he wanted was official scrutiny of his international trading. Such an investigation would reveal that having gained a taste of the wealth and excitement associated with international weapons trading, Guerin extended his vista from Africa and the Middle East into other countries that were on the United Nations 'blacklist'.

This claim is further substantiated by ISC's evolving relationship with the China North Industries Corporation, normally referred to as Norinco. Established in 1980, Norinco resembled South Africa's Armscor, in that not only was it responsible for manufacturing a wide range of engineering equipment, from trucks, cars and motorcycles to military firearms and more sophisticated weaponry, but also selling arms to any terrorist or criminal operation with the funds. While initially dependent on Soviet technology for many of its designs, during the 1980s Norinco was used by the US intelligence services to supply American-made military equipment to Iran. As we noted earlier, President Reagan's regime had developed the view that victory by either side in the Iran–Iraq war would destabilise the Middle East, and thereby affect the supply of Persian Gulf oil to the West. This so-called 'active neutrality' resulted in supplies of military equipment to both countries. However, while South Africa and Chile acted as intermediaries for Iraq, in the case of Iran the American intelligence services developed a relationship with Norinco, the common thread being James Guerin and his network of front companies.

It is not known exactly when Guerin started working with Norinco, but it is more than likely to have been just after Iraq seized the initiative over Iran in 1982, when the American 'active neutrality' position became operative. Initially, the relationship revolved around the supply of munitions to China, the bulk of which were immediately sold on to Iran's military. As we shall see in Chapter 4, however, Clyde Ivy especially extended this link with Norinco by initiating discussions about missile contracts. Although one cannot say whether these were also destined for Iran, it is now clear that the development of an Iranian nuclear missile capability was based on Chinese technology.[72] In the short term, Ivy and Guerin attempted to persuade Norinco that ISC's PGM technology would significantly enhance China's defence capabilities. Allegedly, this campaign was also successful, leading to Guerin's claims in 1986 that he had acquired the *Alpha* contract, worth $138 million. In order to cover up the Chinese link, once again the UAE connection was used as the official source of this business, with Chilean and South African subcontractors involved in supplying a range of sub-assemblies, all of which would eventually end up in Norinco's warehouses. Again, this contract will be analysed in much more detail over the course of the next two chapters, demonstrating that while ISC claimed to have received $116 million in progress payments on *Alpha*, the substance behind the project was difficult to find. Just to illustrate one source of confusion, while ISC was buying rocket motors from Norinco to be fitted to the *Hakim* missiles, the former was also allegedly supplying the same equipment to the latter for *Alpha*. Even though it is now clear that the *Alpha* contracts were fictitious, in the consolidated accounts of ISC it was claimed that profits of $89.7 million were derived from the Norinco link, with $52.8 million appearing in 1985–86 alone, artificially boosting its share price at a time when Ferranti executives were considering a merger.

At the same time that Guerin and Ivy were building the mirage that ISC had secured significant contracts from Norinco to manufacture and supply variants of the PGM design, similar moves were afoot with regard to Pakistan. Yet another country on the United Nations embargo list, Pakistan had been ruled by a military regime since General Muhammad Zia-ul-Haq (widely known as General Zia) had overthrown the democratic government of Prime Minister Zulfikar Ali Bhutto in July 1977. General Zia was responsible for imposing Islamic rule over the country, brutally suppressing civil liberties by introducing draconian martial law that severely marginalised all opposition to his government. At the same time, he rejuvenated the Pakistani economy through a policy of denationalising industries and reducing the level of regulation on private enterprise, using increased tax revenues to boost the indigenous nuclear and conventional defence programmes, in order to defend against possible invasion by India. Crucially as far as the USA was concerned in the 1980s, as Pakistan neighboured Afghanistan, which in turn was engaged in a major military struggle with the Soviet Union, it was very much in American interests to support General Zia. Moreover, as General Zia was ideologically opposed to communism, he was keen to assist the Mujahadeen resistance movement in Afghanistan. This combination of strategic and ideological aims conspired to persuade President Reagan to provide over £1 billion in aid to Pakistan and Afghanistan. The key agent in prosecuting this policy was Reagan's US Secretary of State, General Alexander Haig, who struck up a close relationship with General Zia.[73] Paradoxically, of course, this aid also bolstered what would in the 1990s become the Taliban and Al-Qaeda terrorist movements, because the Mujahadeen of the 1980s were later converted into these Jihadist outfits once the Soviets left Afghanistan in 1988. Of course, it would have been beyond the abilities of American politicians and intelligence experts to have predicted that on the basis of their 1980s actions there would have been either the atrocities of 9/11 (when the Twin Towers of the World Trade Center were destroyed by Al-Qaeda terrorists) or the Second Gulf War (that lasted much longer than the First). Nevertheless, in arming the Mujahadeen and bolstering the military dictatorship of General Zia in Pakistan, the Americans were guilty of creating movements that would eventually be impossible to control.

While the most significant features of the US aid package to Pakistan were the provision of *Stinger* missiles and *F-16* strike fighters, early in 1987 ISC Technologies was able to secure two contracts worth a total of £42 million to supply *Rockeye* cluster bombs from the Lancaster plant. Guerin had effectively exploited the strong links between the US and Pakistani governments in order to secure these cluster bomb contracts, paying General Alexander Haig $600,000 for services rendered in facilitating this business. At the same time, Guerin used this contract as a front to claim that he had also been given a much larger order worth over $500 million to supply guided missiles to Pakistan, ostensibly through a firm called KP Industries Pty. As we shall see later, it is now known that while Guerin claims that the KP contract was signed in November 1986, KP Industries Pty was not registered until March 1987 and the existence of several of the Panamanian-registered subcontracting firms was, to say the least, uncertain. Guerin would later claim that the missile contract had been negotiated personally with General Zia. Indeed, a top-level Pakistani mission to Lancaster and Washington occurred in June 1988, including Major General Masood, the Head of Pakistani military procurement. It is also known that General Haig was present at meetings between ISC executives and General Masood,[74] substantiating Guerin's claim that a major contract existed. Nevertheless, Guerin had his senior staff concoct a raft of paperwork to cover up the real situation, that Guerin had already created a false trail to boost the value of his firm.[75]

The fraudulent nature of this contract will be fully revealed over the course of the next three chapters, highlighting the way Guerin was able to combine elements of reality (the cluster bomb contracts) with sheer fantasy. It is possible, however, that his biggest problem was an event that is still shrouded in mystery, because just as the Soviet troops were departing Afghanistan in August 1988, one should also note that General Zia died in an air crash, when his American-built *Hercules C-130b*, code-named 'Pak One', dropped out of the skies near Bahawalpur, in the Punjab.[76] As neither the 'black box' flight recorder was ever publicly examined, nor were any autopsies conducted on the twenty-five people killed in that crash,[77] the exact causes of this crash continue to puzzle even the most astute observers. A range of likely candidates has inevitably been compiled, including: Soviet spies instructed by the Kremlin to dispose of the man responsible for arming their Afghan enemies; disaffected Pakistani groups linked to either the Bhutto family or other generals who aspired to power; Indian militia directed by Delhi to undermine Pakistani efforts to assist the Sikhs in their campaign to create a separate state; and even the CIA. The latter might seem surprising, given that amongst the dead were the American Ambassador to Pakistan, Arnold Raphel, and General Herbert Wassom, the head of the US Military aid mission to Pakistan. On the other hand, by 1988 there was growing concern in Washington that General Zia was beginning to develop Islamic policies that did not synchronise with American interests, while it has also come to light that Raphel and Wassom had never intended to accompany the Pakistani dictator on his flight back to Islamabad. One should also add that all American investigations into the crash were summarily ceased one day after the crash, more than likely on the grounds that these could well reveal facts that would inflame one of the other sectional interests that prevailed in that highly sensitive region. It now seems likely that the aircraft fell from the sky because poisonous gases had somehow been released into the cockpit, thereby killing the crew and preventing either the transmission of a *Mayday* distress signal or one of the passengers taking the controls. As the official Pakistani inquiry concluded, 'the most probable cause of the crash was a criminal act of sabotage perpetrated in the aircraft'.[78]

Speculation concerning the perpetrators of what would appear to have been this terrorist act will continue, especially as General Zia's death precipitated developments in that region which still today have serious repercussions for the West, given the consequent emergence of the Taliban and Al-Qaeda. Of central concern to this chapter is the heavy American presence in Pakistan, with the deaths of Ambassador Raphel and General Wassom in that *Hercules* demonstrating in graphic form the extent to which the two countries' military and strategic interests were intertwined. James Guerin was also well positioned to exploit this connection, because by 1987 he was claiming the existence of a missile contract, code-named KP, that would allegedly generate up to $300 million-worth of business for ISC. The KP name – the initials of the Khyber Pass – derived from the alleged partner with which ISC was linked, KP Industries (Pvt) Ltd, which in turn was supposedly acting as an agency of the Pakistani government. Ian Ball would later write that the documentation left in the Hanworth offices of ISC Technologies 'should have caused any reasonably diligent auditing body to ask more searching questions, at least as early as 1985',[79] indicating that just as with the *Alpha* missile contract, the substance was lacking. Crucially, as we have just noticed, KP Industries was not even officially registered until March 1987,[80] even though by 1987 ISC was claiming profits on the KP contracts of $25.2 million, with much more to come. These phantom profits will be further examined in the next two chapters, bringing to light the lengths to which Guerin went in boosting ISC's image on the London Stock Exchange. Whether the KP contracts would have materialised had General Zia not been murdered is a matter of considerable conjecture, because while Guerin was later to use the assassination as cover for his activities, many doubt whether KP Industries was anything more than a component in an extensive and cunningly conceived fraud.

2.4 Conclusions

Everything that has been revealed in the last section contrasts sharply with what was said about James Guerin in earlier sections of this chapter: having played the role of a god-fearing, charitable entrepreneur in Lancaster, Penn., at exactly the same time he was selling electronic equipment, munitions and guided missiles to some of the most unacceptable regimes embargoed by the United Nations. Indeed, Guerin was covertly involved in almost all of the major scandals of that era, not only in arming Iraq and Iran, supporting the apartheid regime in South Africa, and bolstering the military dictatorships of Pakistan and China, but also reaping massive financial rewards that were at least partially used to bolster his image of the classic Christian philanthropist. By pursuing this Janus-faced approach, he was able to build ISC into a significant electronics company that ostensibly resembled a major success story, if one believed the data provided in successive annual reports. We shall leave until the next chapters the assessment of how difficult it was to peel back the veneer of credibility from the real story that underpinned ISC's growth, because it is first of all necessary to understand why Ferranti entered into a merger with this firm. Above all, it is apparent from what we have seen in this chapter that James Guerin had built a flourishing business with a well-connected leadership capable of sustaining this trajectory. A trap had effectively been set for a company to step in and buy ISC.

Notes

1 *Financial Times*, 5 Feb 1990.
2 This section is based on an extensive report in *Lancaster New Era*, 29 March 1990.
3 *Intelligencer Journal*, 9 Nov 1999.
4 *Philadelphia Inquirer*, 13 Sept 1991.
5 *Lancaster New Era*, 17 March 1992.
6 Reported in *Independent on Sunday*, 16 June 1991.
7 Lorin was later prosecuted for share price manipulations on Wall Street. This section is based on the *Lancaster New Era*, 15 Jan 1990.
8 *Lancaster New Era*, 15 Jan 1990.
9 See later, pp. 88–9, for a full description of Chem-Con's demise.
10 *Lancaster New Era*, 15 Jan 1990.
11 *Lancaster New Era*, 28 December 1984.
12 'Phantom empire', *Independent on Sunday*, 16 June 1991. See later, pp. 85–8, for further contemporary views on Guerin and his contributions to Lancaster.
13 The United Way was a Lancaster charitable foundation that worked closely with Guerin in administering support to the disadvantaged of that county.
14 *Lancaster New Era*, 18 Aug 1989.
15 *The People*, 20 May 1991. Checketts' salary was £72,000 per annum by 1988.
16 Flemings was established in 1873. It was sold to Chase Manhattan Bank in 2000 for £4.5 billion.
17 Flemings Research, 'International Signal & Control Group plc', 9/86, p. 10 [hereafter, Flemings Research].
18 Guardian Royal Exchange held 9.91% of ISC equity.
19 ISC Offer for Sale by Tender, published by Robert Fleming & Co Ltd, Aug 1982.
20 ISC publicity document, *An Insight into ISC*, published by ISC.
21 Flemings Research, p. 10
22 Quoted in M.S. Chance (1996), 'The investigation of the audits of the International Signal and Control Group PLC', Joint Disciplinary Scheme of the ICAEW, June, p. 8, Institute of Chartered Accountants for England and Wales.
23 Flemings Research, p. 9. 1,153 worked on the East Coast of the USA, 953 on the West Coast, 1,626 in Italy, and 188 elsewhere (including the UK).
24 *Intelligencer Journal*, 28 Feb 1997.
25 Dr Samoggia had been running his own firm, PRO-EL Technologie, from

Florence. This firm had been created in 1984, jointly with ISC, to provide venture capital for ambitious new Italian electronics firms.

26 Ian Ball Report to the FBI, 8 Jan 1990.

27 See J.F. Wilson (2007), *Ferranti. A History*. Vol. 2. *From Family Firm to Multinational, 1975–1987*, Crucible Books, pp. 233–6.

28 According to Ball, Checketts spent most of his time working for charity.

29 I am indebted to Roy Handley for this information.

30 Accurate data is difficult to acquire, due to ISC's refusal to report subsidiary finances, but Ball has estimated that on a turnover of £3 million, ESL was losing £2 million.

31 See pp. 142–3.

32 Fleming's Report, pp. 7–11.

33 Fleming's Report, p. 11.

34 Ball report for the FBI, 1990.

35 Interview with Ian Ball.

36 Evidence of this activity was brought out in Guerin's 1991 trial.

37 Nixon's successor, Gerald Ford, also sanctioned Inman's activities.

38 *Intelligencer Journal*, 16 Nov 1992.

39 Even if the ISC accounts survived, it is not clear whether these South African contracts would have featured, given US corporate regulations on the revelation of contracts.

40 *Lancaster New Era*, 25 Aug 2000.

41 *Intelligencer Journal*, 19 Jan 1990.

42 Sasha Polakow-Suransky, *The Unspoken Alliance*, reported in the *Guardian*, 24 May 2010.

43 *Sunday Business*, 28 July 1996.

44 This section is based on a report in the *Independent on Sunday*, 11 Feb 1990.

45 Reported in *Intelligencer Journal*, 13 Jan 1991.

46 *Lancaster New Era*, 29 May 1991.

47 For more detail, see Alan Friedman (1993), *The Spider's Web. The Secret History of How the White House Illegally Armed Iraq*, Alan Friedman Books.

48 The local Atlanta BNL manager, Christopher Drogoul, later gave evidence that the US, UK and Italian governments were fully aware of his work for Iraq. See http://www.pinknoiz.com/covert/drogoul.html, accessed 3 Aug 2011. He was prosecuted in 1992, but eventually released two years later after admitting all offences.

49 This came to light in 1986, during the so-called 'Iran-Contra Affair'. President Reagan was obliged to admit publicly that his regime had traded weapons for hostages held by Hezbollah guerrillas in the Lebanon, in the course of which Colonel Oliver North had diverted funds to support Nicaraguan terrorists.

50 See below, pp. 151–2.

51 *Independent*, 18 Sept 1989.

52 One should also stress that Astra Holdings PLC was heavily involved in supplying ammunition and weapons to Iraq, allegedly working closely with the British intelligence services. See G.R. James, *In the Public Interest*, Little Brown, 1995. In addition, a so-called 'super-gun' was being developed by Dr Gerald Bull, the

technical head of a Belgian company, Space Research Corporation, which had subcontracted the manufacture of the barrel to Sheffield Forgemasters. Bull was assassinated in 1990.

53 For a detailed analysis, see D. Miller (1996), *Export or Die. Britain's Defence Trade with Iran and Iraq*, Cassell.

54 For deep insights into the various machinations, see Alan Clark (1993, 2002), Vol. 1: *Diaries. In Power 1983–1992*; Vol. 3 *Diaries. The Last Diaries 1993–1999*, Weidenfeld & Nicolson.

55 See Scott Report (1996), *Report of the Inquiry into the Export of Defence and Dual-Use Goods to Iraq and Related Prosecutions*, House of Commons Papers 115, 1996.

56 *Observer*, 2 Oct 1994.

57 Ibid.

58 Rumsfeld was later to play a leading role in the Presidency of George W. Bush, 2001–09, as Secretary of Defense (2001–06), when the USA invaded Iraq.

59 For more detail on the extent and nature of these supplies, including helicopters, missiles, and other armaments, see 'How we supplied Iraq' on www/wf.org /iraq-west.htm, accessed 12 Aug 2011.

60 *Scotsman*, 23 Jan 1991.

61 J. Cock and L. Nathan (1989), *War and Society. The Militarisation of South Africa*, David Philip.

62 *Scotsman*, 23 Jan 1991.

63 US Department of Justice bulletin, 20 Jan 2000.

64 Court records.

65 *Jane's Defence Weekly*, 20 Jan 1990.

66 *Oberver*, 21 Jan 1990.

67 See below, pp. 142–5, for further clarification.

68 This information is derived from 'Ball FBI Report'.

69 Ibid.

70 This document was given to me by Ian Ball.

71 The Scott Report made similar points in a series of highly damaging conclusions.

72 In 2003, Norinco was sanctioned by the USA to supply missile technology to Iran.

73 Haig had also been a former White House Chief of Staff and Commander of NATO forces in Europe.

74 *Observer*, 21 Jan 1990.

75 *Financial Times*, 16 Jan 1990.

76 He had been persuaded to go there to witness a field trial of the latest American *Abrams* battle tank.

77 Apart from General Zia, several other senior military personnel died in the plane crash, including his closest advisor, General Akhtar Abdur Rehman, General Mian Muhammad Afzaal, Major General Mohammad Sharif Nasir, Major General Abdus Sami, Major General Muhammad Hussain Awan, Brigadier Najib Ahmed, Brigadier Moin Ud Din Khawaja, Brigadier Siddique Salik, Brigadier Muhammad Latif, Brigadier Abdul Majid, Colonel Safdar Mohammad, Squadron Leader Rahat Mujeeb Saddique, Captain Zahid, Naib Subedar Mohammad Shafiq and Jan Muhammad.

78 For more detail on this event, see E.J. Epstein (1989), 'Who killed Zia?', *Vanity Fair*, Sept 1989.
79 Ball, FBI Report, 1990.
80 FBM 3, 25 May 1988.

3

A step too far? Merger with ISC

OVER THE COURSE of the last two chapters, attempts have been made to provide a balanced view of the relative positions of Ferranti and ISC by the mid-1980s. The dual analysis will be sustained in this chapter, especially in trying to explain why the two companies entered into a merger in September 1987, outlining how the relationship between Ferranti and ISC evolved slowly over the course of that decade, culminating in extensive rounds of detailed investigations by both executive teams and a plethora of professional advisors selected from amongst the best the City of London had to offer. Given what happened to Ferranti as a consequence of this merger, inevitably one must question the nature of these investigations and the practices adopted by City professionals, because they patently missed several pertinent facts. Similarly, it is important to look more widely at the range of advice Ferranti especially was receiving, from Sebastian de Ferranti, counterparts in prestigious firms such as GEC, and the Ministry of Defence (MoD), and how this was absorbed into the decision-making process in 1986–87. While we are at no stage claiming that Ferranti executives were guilty of perpetrating a fraud on their share-holders, serious questions must be asked about the quality of information accumulated and the way it was utilised. One dimension to all this was the prevailing attitudes towards corporate governance, in that the board, and in particular Derek Alun-Jones as chief executive, would appear to have taken decisions without the need to take into consideration the interests of other stakeholders. At the same time, it is necessary to assess the environment in which the board came to its conclusions, because there is no doubt that external pressures were persuading Ferranti executives that a merger with ISC was almost obligatory. Ultimately, it could well have been these external factors that forced their hand, in spite of the reservations expressed by internal and external sources, demonstrating in graphic form the most damaging implications arising from the particular form of financial capitalism that had emerged in the UK and USA by the 1980s.

There has been considerable debate since the 1980s concerning the benefits associated with merger and acquisition strategies, most of which has demon-

strated that while since the late 1960s British business had indulged extensively in this form of external expansion, few firms had managed to achieve
substantial (if any) synergistic benefits from the strategy.[1] The main obstacles
to success have been a combination of inadequate defensive thinking behind
moves to buy companies and the adoption of ineffective management struc-
tures that have proved wholly incapable of exercising the appropriate levels of
control over newly acquired operations. This demonstrates that both the
motivation behind the Ferranti-ISC merger was by no means exceptional,
while the consequent organisational arrangement merely typified the shortcomings of other combinations, further reflecting the weak corporate
governance pressures exerted on Derek Alun-Jones and his fellow-directors.
Compounding these issues, however, were the fraudulent and cleverly hidden
contracts featuring in ISC's accounts, not to mention the extensive covert
arms trading perpetrated by Guerin and a small clique of his senior staff, all
of which ensured that the merger would never work. While the unravelling of
the ISC fraud will be the principal subject of the next chapter, it is here
essential to explain why the two companies came together and the organisational structure that was put in place once the merger had been formalised,
illustrating how Guerin was able to hide his criminal actions for a significant
period of time.

Linked with this issue is another debate that has raged for decades, namely,
the need for regulation of City activities. As we shall see over the course of the
next two chapters, it was clearly possible for unscrupulous people to conduct
their operations without fear of intrusive investigations, given the lax nature
of financial regulation. Indeed, while changes to the way the Stock Exchange
was run resulted in some radical innovations, the City was mostly allowed to
regulate itself, relying on trust as the basis of commercial relationships.
Inevitably though, cases such as BCCI, Barings Bank, Polly Peck and the
Maxwell/Mirror Group demonstrated that trust can be exploited by individuals who worked to different rules. Of course, the UK was not unique in
having a monopoly of financial scandal, but the way in which the City was
regulated left much to be desired in protecting investors from the actions of
ruthless individuals who cared little for the interests of other stakeholders.

3.1 Ferranti merger strategy and the USA

Under family management, of course, Ferranti had rarely indulged in
external growth through mergers and acquisitions, preferring instead organic
development arising from engineering innovation and astute market
selection. Indeed, up to the 1970s Ferranti was probably better known for
divesting loss-making activities, such as television and radio, mainframe
computers, and numerical control equipment,[2] graphically illustrating the

inherent dangers of remaining a self-financed operation. After the 1975 financial crisis, however, it is apparent that the board headed by Derek Alun-Jones was much more interested in external growth. The aggressive merger strategy was first clearly laid out by the Ferranti board during a meeting in September 1980. It was at that meeting, which focused almost solely on corporate strategy, that non-executive director Robin Broadley (representing Barings Bank, the firm's merchant banker) 'suggested that the basic strategy should be to increase the high level of support and confidence which the Company enjoys among its shareholders, to sustain the Company's perceived potential for growth in earnings, and to develop and expand the Company's business'.[3] As we noted in both Volume 2 and Chapter 1 earlier, this resulted in a significant increase in dividend payments, largely as a means of encouraging shareholder loyalty at a time when the government was preparing to sell its equity.[4] Crucially, though, in assessing how the firm could operationalise Broadley's advice, prime consideration was given to a 'major acquisition', if possible in the USA, demonstrating that from that time Ferranti was continually searching for such an opportunity. In a later board debate about long-term corporate strategy, Alun-Jones came out with the prescient comment that 'if a major acquisition went wrong, it could have a significant impact on the Group',[5] inadvertently predicting what would happen later in the decade. Overall, though, as the chairman noted in the annual report and accounts for 1986–87: 'Growth through acquisition will continue to play its part in our development.'

Of course, an acquisition strategy had first been introduced as a means of attempting to secure a more stable commercial base for Ferranti Engineering Ltd, where between 1975 and 1980, using funds provided by the NEB, Bruce Calveley closed down the power transformer business and replaced it with a range of activities – container handling equipment; agricultural equipment; and fabrications – purchased from other firms.[6] As if to substantiate Alun-Jones' fears, this strategy proved to be a dismal failure, with Ferranti Engineering having closed down by 1985 and the substantial Chadderton factory sold off (to a newspaper publisher).

Although the Ferranti Engineering adventure had been a bold move to save many hundreds of jobs in that depressed area of East Lancashire, its failure would not appear to have disabused the board of the efficacy of merger strategy. Indeed, from the late 1970s all divisional managers were encouraged to pursue a dual strategy based upon, firstly, extensive product innovation, and secondly, backed up wherever possible by acquisitions of complementary companies that would secure greater market share, especially in the USA. Of course, the first aspect of this dual strategy sustained the 'Ferranti Spirit' about which we have heard a great deal in this history. In this sense, managers were not doing anything different to not only that which had motivated them to join Ferranti in the first place, but also made working for this firm so exciting over the previous decades. The second dimension, however, was a new skill that had to be acquired speedily, providing legal, commercial and organisational challenges that few had experienced. Bearing in mind the point made earlier, that British merger activity rarely resulted in significant synergistic benefits to the predator, it is apparent that this strategy was fraught with dangers, issues that can only be compounded when experience of such activity was so limited across Ferranti. Nevertheless, as Derek Alun-Jones noted during an interview for *Ferranti News*, managers were obligated to buy into substantial and growing markets where Ferranti expertise could be harnessed to boost market share, a philosophy that was to have dramatic consequences for the firm over the following fifteen years.[7]

Even if most of the 1980s acquisitions were small-scale, and often associated with specific product ranges, the logic behind this strategy was entirely rational: firstly, by pursuing an aggressive stance, it was easier to defend the firm against other predators; and secondly, as the emphasis was placed on extending the firm's links with the largest high technology market in the world, the USA, Ferranti could expect to open up significant commercial opportunities for those divisions that possessed a competitive advantage. As far as the latter was concerned, given the quality of the products developed by the Scottish, computer, instrumentation and electronic components divisions, the USA was seen as the obvious market, stimulating respective management teams to conduct extensive investigations into prospective acquisitions. The divisional teams were also often supported by the work done by John Pickin, the Ferranti technical director who worked mostly in the Millbank offices in London, from where he continually investigated the possibilities of securing strategic alliances that would keep the firm independent. This *modus operandi* sustained the Ferranti acquisitions strategy throughout the 1970s and 1980s, combining divisional expertise with the opportunistic work of John Pickin and a very small team operating out of Millbank Tower.

Although UK acquisitions by Ferranti divisions were by no means negligible in number at that time, the principal emphasis was consistently placed on the USA as the focus for external growth. To facilitate this activity, in 1980 Ferranti High Technology Inc was created as a vehicle allowing Ferranti plc to acquire shares in American companies, while separately certain divisions built substantial bridgeheads in the USA.[8] Of course, apart from the Canadian subsidiary which had been formed as early as 1912,[9] Ferranti had been present in the USA since 1926, when Ferranti Electric Inc was created in New York as the base for the firm's North American activities. However, as R.H. Davies discovered in the 1950s and 1960s when he ran Ferranti Electric, persuading either American government officials or private companies and consumers to buy British equipment proved to be a frustrating experience, given the inherent protectionism of that country. It was especially apparent that in sensitive markets associated with either advanced technology or defence equipment, American firms would always be preferred to foreign suppliers, even when the latter were able to produce superior designs.[10] Above all, it was apparent that if Ferranti wanted to secure a share of the world's largest defence and electronics markets, it would have to build local bases in the USA as a means of overcoming the bias against non-American products. Davies' role was consequently focused on providing information to Ferranti divisions about American technological developments, rather than orders for the UK divisions.

Apart from Ferranti Electric's activities, the only significant US successes for the parent company had been the licence Bendix had acquired to use Ferranti numerical control (NC) technology. Although this relationship proved short-lived, by the time Bendix had been acquired in 1963 by the Sheffield Corporation, the licence had brought in almost £200,000 worth of orders, compensating to some extent for the sluggish rate of growth in domestic NC sales.[11] The Scottish division was also successful in selling its combined map and electronic display (COMED) system to the USAF, but again it was only after Bendix was involved as a partner in the contract that the American government placed a substantial order. This contract encouraged the head of the Scottish division, Donald McCallum, to establish in 1982 Ferranti Electro-Optics Inc, based in Huntington Beach, California, to provide sales and maintenance services in North America. By that time, the Scottish division also had two other American subsidiaries, Ferranti ORE Inc, at Falmouth, Massachusetts, and Ferranti Indiana Inc, at Spencerville, Indiana, indicating how even in civil markets McCallum's team was attempting to develop a strong presence.[12]

The desire to push key divisions much more extensively into the American civil, space and defence markets was an entirely rational strategy for Ferranti, particularly in view of the significant changes affecting UK defence markets from the early 1980s.[13] In June 1983, an entire edition of *Ferranti News* was devoted to a 'Special USA Report', in which the existing American ventures and future expansion plans were extensively described. The lead article also quoted Derek Alun-Jones expressing his hopes for a future which would see many parts of the business build strong alliances in the USA. Given the ever-present take-over threats and domestic market changes experienced by Ferranti, again one can see the sense in this strategy. While inevitably hindsight inevitably clouds any judgement of the ensuing acquisitions, and clearly some proved to be distinctly less than successful,[14] the board was taking decisive action for all the right reasons. It is also fair to note that the history of British forays into the US business world was littered with calamitous investments.[15] On the other hand, while it is notoriously difficult to target a lucrative acquisition in another country, it was clearly essential that the strategy should be implemented effectively through careful planning and rigorous rationalisation of the acquired assets. This placed a tremendous premium on the ability of John Pickin and his acquisitions team to identify potential synergies, while it was left to the local management to integrate the subsidiary into core Ferranti activities.

Ferranti subsidiaries in the USA (and dates of ownership)

Interdesign Inc (Silicon Valley, California) – 1977–93
Electro-Optics Inc (Huntington Beach, California) – 1982–93
Curtis Technology Inc (San Diego, California) – 1981–87
Spectrum Ceramics Inc (San Diego, California) – 1981–87
Ferranti Indiana Inc (Indiana) – 1982–93
Venus Scientific Inc (Long Island, N Y) – 1981–87
Ferranti ORE Inc (Falmouth, Mass) – 1982–93
Ferranti Electric Inc (New York) – 1926–93

By 1983, Ferranti had eight subsidiaries operating in the USA, including Ferranti Electric Inc, the sales agency formed as long ago as 1926 and various operations acquired since Alun-Jones had joined the firm.[16] The formation in 1982 of Ferranti High Technology Inc was central to the development of this strategy. While only a small operation, this corporation's brief was to investigate possible American partners for the UK divisions. It was largely run by John Pickin, the technical director, who worked mainly from the Ferranti office in Millbank Tower, London. It is vital to emphasise that the UK divisions always took charge of any operation that was acquired. Frequently, though, it would be John Pickin who either initiated discussions or encouraged departments to make contact, indicating how the American strategy was implemented in practice. By 1983, a total of $50 million had been invested in American operations, apart from which a substantial commitment of managerial resources had been made. This indicates the extent to which Derek Alun-Jones was committed to the 'American Strategy'. At the same time, it is not clear whether these significant investments really made much difference to either divisional or group performance, given the depth of the problems experienced in converting the plan into commercial successes. Of course, making such a judgement over a short time period could be described as harsh, but Ferranti shareholders were never interested in the long term, pressurising the board into extending this chosen course of action.

While one can point to some successful dimensions to this 'US Strategy', most notably the defence-related businesses initiated by the Scottish division, one must conclude that spending in excess of $50 million on American acquisitions did not generate the kind of rewards anticipated by the Ferranti board. The most obvious cases where reality failed to resemble anything like the projections were: Venus Scientific, the New York-based manufacturer of miniature high-voltage power supply packs, mostly for use in military aircraft;[17] Interdesign Inc, the electronic components operation in California;[18] and what has passed into Ferranti folklore as 'The Texas Ranger', namely, Ferranti International Controls Inc. The Venus Scientific case is especially interesting, because while under Bruce Calveley's management this subsidiary fulfilled the principal aim behind the acquisition, namely, enhancing the Ferranti name in the eyes of the American military establishment, this was achieved at a high price. Although substantial orders were placed by leading American defence contractors like Westinghouse and Raytheon for its power packs, to be fitted in twelve separate American military aircraft, such was the heavy commitment to engineering development that profitability proved elusive.[19]

Judging from what we have seen elsewhere in this history, the Venus Scientific saga would appear to have typified the nature of Ferranti forays into the USA: while the rationale behind the acquisition would appear to have been sound and the product range offered significant possibilities, rarely did the ensuing operation contribute to group or divisional profits. However, while Venus Scientific and Interdesign Inc proved to be commercial failures, their losses paled into insignificance when compared to the calamitous 1984 acquisition by Ferranti Computer Systems Ltd of TRW Controls Corporation, of Houston, Texas. At the time, spending $10.7 million on a venture that had an order book worth over $60 million would appear to have been a clever piece of business by the Wythenshawe division of Ferranti Computer Systems. Renamed Ferranti International Controls Inc, its intended development of an advanced energy management system, marketed as the *Ranger*, promised even richer rewards. This was also regarded as vital for the further development of the division's civil order book, in that the heavy dependence upon defence contracts at the Cheadle Heath and Bracknell divisions of Ferranti Computer Systems was creating an imbalance that needed to be corrected. However, Ferranti International Controls also demonstrated another weakness in the way that Ferranti pursued its acquisition programme, in that the original owner of the firm, Roger Grooms, was left in charge of the business, having persuaded Ferranti executives that he was capable of converting the potential of *Ranger* into commercial success. Sadly, though, mostly as a result of poor project management and over-ambitious planning, the subsidiary was to become a significant financial liability for Ferranti. Indeed, a failure to inject fresh managerial talent into the venture prevented the discovery of the problems that would eventually result in massive write-offs arising from flaws in the design of the *Ranger* system, doing considerable damage to the Ferranti reputation amongst civil customers, not to mention write-offs amounting by 1992 to $110 million.[20] As we shall see later with regard to the ISC merger, leaving the original management in charge of acquired companies was to prove deeply troublesome, even if it reflected the long-held Ferranti belief in devolved responsibility.

Again, it is possible that in studying these acquisitions over such a short time period we are imposing excessive standards on their performance. On the other hand, as Ferranti management was charged with the task of maximising the returns on its investors' capital, it was essential that any American purchases should add successfully to the group's commercial profile. One cannot ignore the conclusion, however, that Ferranti International Controls provides an object lesson in the acute dangers associated with venturing abroad, warning British businesses in general that disaster awaits the over-ambitious, especially when existing owners are allowed to continue to run acquired businesses. Clearly, in normal circumstances one might have expected the Ferranti management to have learned from its experiences, preventing the acquisition of similar financial troubles. Unfortunately, though, it was 1989 before the board realised the implications of committing the firm to *Ranger*, two years after the firm had embarked on another acquisition which makes even the Houston losses look relatively paltry. One must nevertheless add that apart from reputation and status, and with the glorious exception of the Scottish division's success with COMED and some other small avionics contracts,[21] it is difficult to discern any obvious commercial benefit arising from the American acquisitions. Again, it is important to stress the value of hindsight in drawing this conclusion, the Ferranti board never having had access to a crystal ball. On the other hand, there were clearly fundamental problems with the American strategy, and especially with the manner in which it was implemented. Indeed, management and organisation would appear to have been the key weakness in this respect, because in keeping with the highly devolved culture that Ferranti had traditionally maintained, the American subsidiaries were never fully integrated into the UK divisions. Of course, they were subject to supervision by the executive committee, having been instructed to produce regular financial reports by Charles Scott, the finance director. Members of the executive committee also made regular trips to the USA, in order to look personally at the operations and question executives, while in 1985 the main Ferranti board actually met in San Francisco when touring the various facilities. At the same time, rarely were the American ventures remunerative enough to warrant the kind of investments made in the 1980s, while organisationally they lacked rigorous supervision.

3.2 Ferranti and ISC: the courting stage

Having come to this damning conclusion on the firm's American activities, it is now necessary to consider how over the course of the 1980s Ferranti was persuaded to contemplate a merger with ISC. Of course, in view of the Stock Exchange's regulations on insider trading, only a select group of senior management and financial advisors was ever involved in the build-up to the Ferranti-ISC merger. In 1980, though, the initial contact came at divisional level, when John Pickin, Ferranti technical director, introduced an ISC product to Mike Richards, marketing director of Ferranti Instrumentation Ltd, based in Moston. As we saw in Volume 2, Ferranti Instrumentation was at that time desperate to rebuild an ailing product portfolio, leading its managing director, Lester George, to investigate a series of possibilities.[22] The ISC product was a military detector device known as PEWS (platoon early warning system), but it soon became apparent that George's engineering team would not be able to convert the design into a commercially viable product. Even though the head of the Cheadle Heath division, Ian Ball, was brought in to the discussions with ISC, such was the scepticism expressed by his engineering team that the collaborative venture was dropped.

Regardless of this false start, Jim Guerin continued to maintain contact with Ferranti, eventually asking the Ferranti board to lend $1.4 million to ISC, for fifteen months at a rate of 1% per month, in exchange for a mutual trading agreement on missile technology.[23] Although some might have regarded this as a highly risky move by a firm that was still state-owned, it proved to be an extremely astute bit of business, because not only was the loan repaid in full in April 1982 with an exchange rate profit of £206,000, but also when the American company was floated on the London Stock Exchange in August 1982 Ferranti took up the option to acquire 100,000 ISC shares at £3.50 per share. After a further reorganisation of the ISC share capital in September 1982, which converted the holding into 600,000 shares, the Ferranti investment was worth £930,000.[24] When these shares were sold in December 1982, their value had increased to £1.2 million,[25] adding significantly to the profit made on the original loan. This cemented a link between the two companies that was to persist throughout the 1980s, with infrequent contact between the respective engineering teams on various missile-related issues, especially on the Ferranti side from Ian Ball's Cheadle Heath division.[26] Nothing of substance came of these contacts, however, until in the summer of 1986 John Pickin was again lobbying Derek Alun-Jones in favour of a more formal merger that would exploit the potential economies of scale and scope in areas like missile technology, munitions, computerised control techniques and electronic systems.

While certain divisions were beginning to develop a close relationship with

ISC, by the mid-1980s Derek Alun-Jones and John Pickin were also conduct-ing negotiations with Guerin which would ultimately lead to the merger announcement of September 1987. As we have already noted, John Pickin especially was convinced that a more direct link with ISC would offer substantial opportunities to exploit economies of scale and scope in a wide range of product areas. Furthermore, as an extension of the 'American strategy' outlined earlier, Derek Alun-Jones could see tremendous logic in a merger. By the mid-1980s, however, other factors had started to influence attitudes at Ferranti, creating a much greater sense of urgency which could well have blinded the board to some of the dangers associated with this merger. In the first place, as we saw in Chapter 1, after major changes were introduced in 1985 to the way in which UK defence contracts were allocated and funded, ISC's extensive links in American and Middle East defence markets offered certain possibilities which might benefit the Scottish and computer divisions as they struggled to come to terms with new domestic pressures. Secondly, by 1986 rumours abounded in the City that Plessey was about to bid for control of Ferranti, ironically as a means of protecting itself against a predatorial bid from GEC. This explicit threat to the company's independence convinced Derek Alun-Jones especially that a defensive alliance would strengthen his hand in any ensuing take-over battle. Robin Broadley of Barings Bank also noted in a lengthy board discussion of corporate strategy towards the end of 1985 that Ferranti should consider more significant acquisitions, because to date most purchases had been rela-tively small-scale and would never have pre-empted a take-over bid.[27] This was contradicted at a later board meeting, in May 1986, by Sir John Hoskyns, who 'pointed out [highly prophetically] it would be wrong to make a large acquisition just to avoid a takeover as the acquisition could prove disas-trous'.[28] Overall, though, Alun-Jones was more prone to listen to Broadley's advice, given that they had been working effectively together since the mid-1970s and trusted each other implicitly. At the same time, Hoskyns' advice resonated with something Alun-Jones had himself said at a previous board meeting,[29] acting as a warning-sign in what was about to transpire.

In view of the conflicting hindsight views which cloud the debate over the Ferranti-ISC merger, it is essential to address the reasons why Derek Alun-Jones and the board led the company into what proved to be a disastrous deal. Of particular importance in all the negotiations was the enormous trust placed in James Guerin by his future partners. As we saw in Chapter 2, Guerin was a key figure in the Lancaster community where he lived, contributing extensively to local charities, singing in his church choir, and employing a growing number of highly skilled engineers and administrators in both Lancaster and other American cities. Whenever Ferranti executives visited him in Lancaster, not only were they flown from Philadelphia Airport in one of Guerin's own aircraft, they were normally treated to presentations that emphasised his status as a god-fearing, patriotic philanthropist. Moreover, while serious questions were asked about ISC's product base, few would fail to be impressed with both the rate at which the firm had expanded, as well as the range of its customers, from the US government to Middle Eastern countries. They would also read statements from Guerin in ISC literature that claimed: 'Responsible commitments will be made and kept. This comprises the primary performance rating tool at all levels of management. We are persons of our word.'[30] How could anybody find fault in such an organisation? Who could predict that they were merely hollow words that reflected the most duplicitous type of corporate communication?

The apparent logic behind a merger with ISC consequently strengthened as the decade progressed, and especially in 1986 when Ferranti shareholders were being courted by Plessey management. It was during this period of uncertainty that not only did Derek Alun-Jones and John Pickin meet privately with Jim Guerin, the Ferranti finance director, Charles Scott, was also instructed by Alun-Jones to conduct a detailed audit of ISC. To assist him in this task, Scott recruited Alan Bardsley, the finance director in Ferranti Instrumentation who had been responsible for negotiating several of its major acquisitions (for example, Ferranti GTE).[31] Scott and Bardsley produced a highly authoritative report that provided the Ferranti board with a detailed grasp of both the benefits and (especially, financial) risks associated with linking up with ISC. While they were well aware of what by then had become a commonplace within both Ferranti and ISC, namely, the combination of ISC's international marketing expertise and ability to secure turnkey contracts with the renowned engineering excellence at Ferranti, their objective analysis made all aware that serious issues remained over such issues as the nature of the American firm's business practices, its customer base, and the valuation placed on it by the London Stock Exchange.

In trying to synthesise the Scott-Bardsley report,[32] it is clear that a plethora of evidence was presented that would dissuade a predator from entering into a merger with ISC. Crucially, it was stressed that because of ISC's rapid growth since its flotation in 1982, as well as a successful 1986 rights issue worth £73 million, the London Stock Exchange valued the firm at £452 million (with a share price of 265p). Even though Ferranti turnover (£596 million) was almost twice that of ISC's (£296 million), this meant that the latter was worth £4 million more than the former (with a share price of 104p), a situation which even Jim Guerin regarded as unacceptable. It was actually a matter of record that since the defence sector boom associated with the 1982 Falklands War, Ferranti shares had generally underperformed the market, while the combination of the MoD's 1985–86 review of contract conditions and concern about the electronic components division exacerbated City fears that they would not rise much, at least in the short term.[33]

Another problem that the Scott-Bardsley report highlighted was what they referred to as an 'extremely thin' top tier of senior managers, with just five individuals (Jim Guerin; Joe Zilligen; Stuart Pindell; Clyde Ivy; Clive Woodgrift) singled out as key decision-makers. This contrasted sharply with 'the breadth and depth in the Ferranti Group', with its corporate and divisional structure featuring a plethora of executive talent. This also raised the curious organisational feature to which we alluded in the last chapter, namely, the proxy board that ran ISC Defense & Space Group, in order to secure US Department of Defense security clearance. As Scott and Bardsley concluded on this issue, 'we should be cautious about this structure', because it was unlikely that ISC would abandon the proxy board and risk losing its security clearance, thereby detracting significantly from the attraction of buying the firm.

When it came to assessing possible product and technological synergies, Scott and Bardsley were on more positive ground. Indeed, given ISC's position in markets such as munitions, defence systems, and electronic equipment, there was every possibility that the two companies would be able to exchange technological expertise. Of course, Guerin accepted that ISC was more of an 'innovative technical follower', rather than an engineering pioneer, but it would be possible to achieve technological synergies by combining the firms. Of much greater significance, though, were the international markets in which ISC operated, specifically the Middle East, Far East, Africa and Chile, regions in which Ferranti had rarely competed. The PGM contract was held up as the arch example of this ability to secure significant turnkey contracts which were proving extremely lucrative, judging from the data provided by Guerin's accountants. While concerns were expressed at the extent to which ISC subcontracted the production of key components to international suppliers, especially in countries such as South Africa, it was emphasised that opportunities existed for Ferranti divisions to secure some of this business at what were regarded as excellent prices. Indeed, a range of opportunities existed for several Ferranti divisions to acquire development and production contracts from ISC, including laser designators, sighting systems, fuzes, and microwave systems.

Having stressed these synergistic benefits, however, it is once again vital to stress that the emphasis of the Scott-Bardsley report was extremely cautious. Above all, they argued that a 60:40 merger (in favour of Ferranti) was much more preferable than the current City valuations which put them on a level footing. Whatever the quoted prices, it was also argued that as soon as the merger was announced, this would 'put a price on their heads', possibly stimulating counter-bids from well-known predators such as Plessey, GEC, BAe and even Siemens. This was why they insisted on 'the utmost secrecy' when discussing their report, otherwise one of these firms could well develop an alternative approach, while the MoD would also need to be assured that a merger would not create difficulties. On the other hand, the combination of ISC's businesses in the USA and Italy (jointly worth £250 million per annum) with the apparently lucrative Middle East contracts (one of which was worth £250 million) were highly attractive features of the proposed deal. Although serious concerns were expressed about the PGM contract, failure on which 'could have a profound effect on [ISC] profit and on the company's market credibility', they had received such assurances from Guerin, Ivy and the engineering team that it seemed to be a risk worth taking. Scott and Bardsley were also worried about ISC's South African links, given that country's dubious status, leading them to stress the need to talk directly with both British and American government agencies if the merger proceeded.

When the Ferranti board came to consider this report, it was clear to all of the executives that a merger with ISC was too great a risk, not least because the City valuations did not give Ferranti shareholders a good deal. Of course, nobody knew of the covert activities that had underpinned ISC's growth since the late 1970s (see Figure 3.1), even though deep suspicions surrounded the reliance on two customers and ISC's tendency to extract large profits from these contracts at an early stage in the production cycle. Indeed, the scant information emanating from ISC and its City advisors, Robert Fleming & Co, was a cause of great concern, leading Scott and Bardsley to advise Derek Alun-Jones and the board to move very cautiously towards any merger talks. At the same time, as the report concluded: 'A UK-based joint venture between Ferranti and ISC might be one way to prolong an involvement [in PGM] and retain a strong relationship with ISC for the future.' With the Scottish defence division in particular looking likely to secure missile production subcontracts,[34] this was indeed the way forward chosen by the board, offering up the opportunity that merger talks could be revived if City share prices moved in a direction that was much more favourable to Ferranti shareholders.

As Figure 3.1 reveals, over the course of the 1980s ISC had grown considerably: while in 1978 Ferranti turnover was 7.2 times the scale of ISC, by 1986 it was just 1.7 times larger. Of much greater concern to Charles Scott, however, was the data featuring in Figure 3.2, because this underpinned the impressive improvements in ISC's share value. Indeed, judged by the published accounts the gross profits of Ferranti and ISC were almost reaching parity by the mid-1980s, accentuating Scott's fears that in any merger discussion this would create unwanted imbalances. When this factor was added to the other revelation that ISC took a higher proportion of a contract's profit, rather than commit some of the funds to a contingency against future problems, this made Scott extremely nervous about the nature of their accounting policies. This was also a point made in a report from Lazard Brothers which was commissioned by Sebastian de Ferranti, the merchant bank noting that 'ISC should accept more conservative accounting policies on longer-term contracts'.[35] For example, on the PGM air-to-ground missile contract ISC had released up to $20 million more in profit than would have been the case under Ferranti methods. On a similar basis, the missile technology transfer contract with Pakistan, code-named KP, had provided over two-thirds of ISC's first quarter profits in 1986–87, fuelling further increases in the ISC share price.

It was revelations of this nature that persuaded the Ferranti board not to proceed with detailed merger talks in August 1986. This was a cause of some disappointment to Guerin, because he was extremely interested in a merger with Ferranti, no doubt because this would provide him with even greater

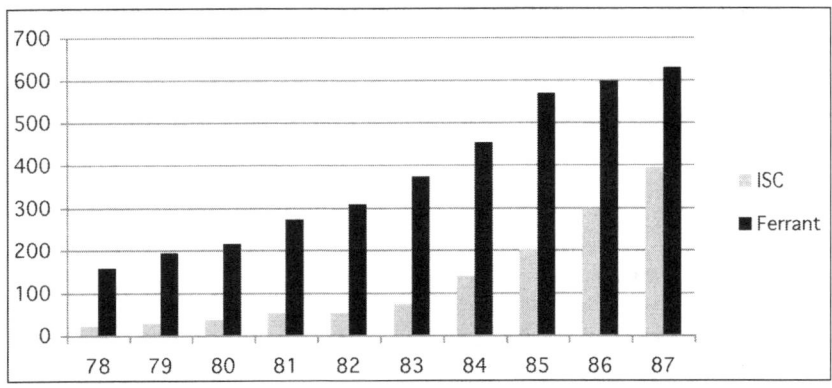

Figure 3.1 Turnover at Ferranti and ISC, 1978–87 (£ m)

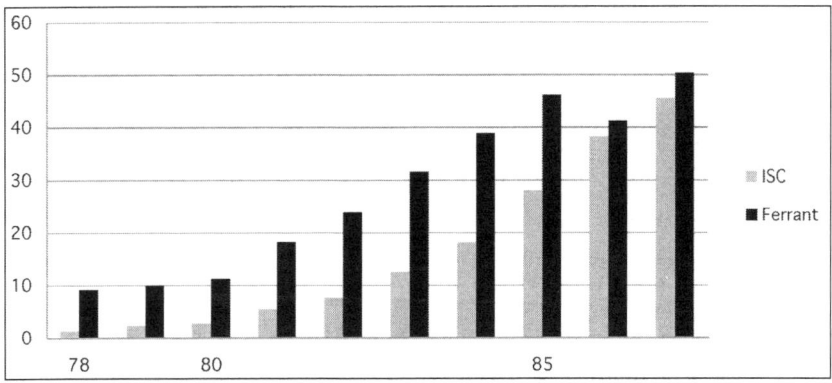

Figure 3.2 Gross profits at Ferranti and ISC, 1978–87 (£ m)

financial security if he was able to sell his business to an established British operation. According to Ian Ball, who by early 1987 had joined ISC and started working at the Hanworth facility, Guerin continually mentioned a possible merger with Ferranti, given that he was frequently talking to Derek Alun-Jones about a series of issues. One outcome of these talks was the award to Ferranti Defence Systems of an £18 million contract to produce the seeker equipment for ISC's PGM system, providing clear evidence of the potential benefits of a fully fledged merger. During the summer months of 1987, there were also discussions between Ian Ball, Derek Alun-Jones and Jim Guerin about Ferranti performing the full assembly of PGM, talks which clearly precipitated more serious analysis of the issues that had stopped the process in 1986.

It was at this juncture that something rather odd happened within Ferranti, in that following the rejection of a merger with ISC in September 1986, thereafter the minutes use 'IBIS' as the code-name whenever the American firm is mentioned. It is not clear why the board decided to adopt this clandestine approach, given that the minutes were confidential and never distributed to stockbrokers who might use the information to manipulate share prices. Perhaps it reflected Guerin's tendency to use the vocabulary of the intelligence community,[36] but whatever the case from September 1986 ISC was only referred to as IBIS.[37]

While the prospect of taking on more of the PGM work would have provided a major attraction to Ferranti executives, of even greater concern were the renewed entreaties from Plessey that rumbled around City institutions.[38] It was also apparent from various share price movements that by July 1987 the respective capitalisations of Ferranti and ISC had moved to what was regarded as an acceptable 60:40 split, persuading Alun-Jones and Scott that the time was ripe for a move. Although as Figure 3.2 illustrates ISC's gross profit for 1986–87 was higher than in 1985–86, throughout 1987 Guerin had led the City to expect profits of approximately £65 million, in spite of reported delays on some overseas contracts. This immediately raises the possibility that Guerin was manipulating the ISC share price, so that in relation to the Ferranti valuation the two companies were moving towards the 60:40 ratio advised in the Scott-Bardsley report of August 1986. As the Lazard Brothers report noted: 'It is unclear why [ISC] management allowed the market to have significantly higher profit expectations'. Guerin's explanation at ISC's 1987 AGM was his decision to introduce a 'more conservative approach' towards accounting for the enormous missile contracts he had secured, following critical comments made by his auditors, Peat Marwick Mitchell, about previous policies.[39] Whatever the case, the Ferranti board was sufficiently satisfied that conditions were much more favourable to a merger, especially as the Ferranti share price had risen from a low of 103 pence in

November 1986 to reach 126 pence by August 1987, while the ISC share price plunged by almost 25%. These movements prompted Charles Scott to solicit a full report from Guerin's auditors, Peat Marwick Mitchell (hereafter, PMM). This report would prove crucial to the ongoing merger discussions, given that as another independent source concluded, while there were certain politically sensitive features of ISC's operations, especially in South Africa and the Middle East, there is no evidence of any 'creative accounting' which might have warned off the Ferranti board.[40] The path consequently seemed much clearer, leading to detailed evaluations at board level and an agreement on the terms for a merger.

We shall return to the PMM audit of ISC, given the central importance of this document. At the same time, it is also vital to stress that Ferranti conducted its own evaluation of ISC, just as Scott and Bardsley had done in 1986. In July 1987, a small investigating team was asked to assess whether anything had changed since the previous summer. This team was once again composed of Charles Scott and Alan Bardsley, but in addition the deputy managing director (operations), Alan Shepherd, and the former head of the Ferranti operations in Scotland, Sir Donald McCallum, were asked to join the original investigators. McCallum had actually gone on record at a previous board meeting in support of a merger with ISC, a position based on his fear that the MoD and its European partners in developing the next generation of military aircraft were expressing concerns about the ability of Ferranti to participate in what would be an enormous project. If the Scottish avionics division was not involved in this project, Phil Atterton (MD of Ferranti Defence Systems) and McCallum feared for its future, leading him to suggest in the spring of 1987 that Ferranti should reopen merger talks with ISC, principally as a means of building the scale that would reassure the MoD.[41] With hindsight, of course, McCallum deeply regrets offering this view, but such were the pressures under which Ferranti was operating by that time. In addition, of course, City rumours abounded about an imminent take-over bid for Ferranti, adding considerably to the board's sense of urgency.

Just as in August 1986, the Ferranti internal evaluation of ISC was extremely thorough, involving a series of meetings with executives in both the UK and USA. Indeed, the whole Ferranti team flew to Lancaster, Penn., in order to assess for themselves what was happening at ISC's headquarters and interview Jim Guerin as intently as possible. Guerin treated the Ferranti executives to the usual courtesies, including flights in his personal jet from Philadelphia Airport to Lancaster, tours of the city and ISC premises, and in-depth discussions about any issues they wished to raise. It was a full-frontal charm-offensive, confirming the views of other Ferranti people that Guerin was a likeable person with a big commitment to his local community. Much to the credit of the Ferranti team, however, while acknowledging the credibil-

ity and status of Jim Guerin, the report produced in September 1987 highlighted several problems which clearly caused the board to think more deeply
about the merger. In the first place, they reiterated the Scott-Bardsley reservations about the extent to which ISC extracted profits from large contracts
such as PGM. More worryingly from a technical point of view were the
concerns expressed by Sir Donald McCallum that Clyde Ivy's team had yet to
tackle the challenges associated with assembling PGM. Were these challenges
to attenuate delivery, this could severely compromise the overall profitability
of the contract, even though ISC had already extracted over £20 million in
profit from PGM. Of even greater concern was Guerin's refusal to allow the
Ferranti team to inspect the Hanworth facility, where allegedly some of the
PGM development was taking place. As we have noted earlier,[42] not even Ian
Ball, who by then was an ISC employee, was allowed into that part of the
factory allocated to PGM work. Finally with regard to PGM, the extent to
which ISC relied on subcontractors alarmed some Ferranti executives, given
the high degree of self-dependence that had always characterised Ferranti
activities. As we have noted in the previous chapter, ISC was merely an
assembler of products developed elsewhere, creating severe quality challenges
in co-ordinating this army of subcontractors, not to mention the political
sensitivities involved in working with firms in Chile and South Africa.

While Ferranti engineers and senior managers might have been confident
that they would be able to deal with any technical issues arising from these
aspects of the missile contract, the investigating team was concerned at the
shroud thrown over PGM by ISC. Another key issue was the political sensitivity of ISC's overseas markets. In particular, as some of the missile
technology was derived from Clyde Ivy's former contacts in South Africa (still
very much on the United Nations embargo list), Ferranti executives were
extremely nervous of entering territory which was alien to them. Guerin
assured all who inquired about these contacts that the contracts were 'cleared
by Washington', while the auditors, PMM, were shown a letter from the MoD
'which, though it does not give carte blanche, does address this project'.[43]
When all of these concerns were added to those linked with the KP contract,
for the supply of missile technology to Pakistan (another country on the UN
embargo list), as well as the links ISC had built with the likes of China, Iraq,
Chile and Greece, it is clear that Ferranti was becoming involved in markets
that had rarely passed across its radar screens. All Guerin would ever say
when confronted with these concerns was either 'Washington is fully aware'
or the contracts were cleared at the highest government levels. With
hindsight, of course, we know that these assurances were patently exagger-
ated, given the alacrity with which American government agencies withdrew
their support for Guerin at his trial in 1992. This raises the key issue of trust,
because in spite of the report's comment that 'the very nature of ISC's market

area political risks exist on a scale unusual in Ferranti markets', and that 'ISC could be left on a limb' if the political interests moved in adverse ways, the Ferranti board must have accepted Guerin's assurances. Of course, Guerin added the alluring prospect that the profitability of this work was commensurate with the risks taken, a factor that would have offered a strong financial incentive to minimise the political dangers. Nevertheless, the Ferranti internal report laid out in cold detail that these risks extended to work in the UAE, Pakistan, China, Iraq, Turkey, Israel, South Africa, Chile and Greece, all countries that could have – and in some cases did – sparked grave international repercussions.

As if to exacerbate all of these concerns, the Ferranti team was also given a presentation on another major contract, code-named *Express*, which was an anti-tank missile based on technology developed in South Africa, to be supplied to China. While it was worth up to $150 million, representing a significant opportunity, it transpired that the contract with China had not yet been signed, even though ISC had allegedly spent $350,000 on development. As the team concluded: 'This project is a prospective risk and is illustrative of the continuing international complexity of ISC's type of business ... political risks exist on a scale unusual in Ferranti's markets.' They acknowledged that as long as the contracts came to fruition at the prices reported by Guerin and his senior management team, then acquiring ISC would prove to be a superb piece of business. ISC's international contacts and marketing strengths, combined with its ability to secure turnkey contracts, were also seen as significant incentives to go ahead with the merger, complementing the engineering competencies and established market position achieved by Ferranti. It was consequently a matter of the board's judgement on the balance between these potential, but by no means assured, advantages and the risks highlighted by several of ISC's overseas contracts, providing the directors with the kind of challenge that they had never before faced. In addition, of course, there was Jim Guerin, the apparently trusted entrepreneurial philanthropist who had built an industrial empire from virtually nothing, surrounded by City advisors that were willing to vouch for his business probity.

The internal Ferranti report, of course, was not the only document circulating at the time which expressed some concerns about the nature of ISC's overseas business. As a major shareholder and former executive chairman of Ferranti, Sebastian de Ferranti had commissioned a report on ISC by Lazard Brothers, another distinguished City institution, which struck right at the heart of the organisational issue that would arise if a merger occurred. While a British company listed on the London Stock Exchange, as we noted in the last chapter, the bulk of the ISC business was controlled by a proxy board in the USA. This structure had been designed to serve the dual purpose of, firstly, avoiding US corporate regulations that insisted on extensive revelation of financial information, but, secondly, projecting the image through the proxy board of being an American firm that can bid for defence contracts. As the Lazards report noted, however, not only would this limit any synergy benefits from the proposed merger, because access to sensitive US military technology would be severely limited, but also the Ferranti board would not be able to interfere in the proxy board's activities.

Moving on from this central organisational issue, Lazard Brothers went on to highlight a series of other issues that Sebastian argued ought to have prevented further consideration of a merger. These ranged from the by now familiar refrains concerning both the heavy reliance on a small number of overseas customers and that Ferranti accounting policies were much more conservative than those used by ISC. Lazards also noted that the latter was a highly cash-absorptive business, having either extended its borrowings or issued fresh share capital in every year since 1982. As ISC still reported in American dollars, currency-driven volatility could creep into the financial planning exercises, thereby creating future difficulties that would affect the combined group. In addition, grave concerns were expressed about the polit-ically sensitive nature of ISC's principal customers, concluding with a report from another sound City institution, Prudential-Bache: 'We regard the [ISC] stock as more akin to a high-risk venture capital play moving between rounds of post-launch financing than as a stable company in conventional trading circumstances.' Sebastian used this report to denounce publicly the merger strategy, an argument that was further strengthened when he discovered from conversations with the GEC chief executive, Sir Arnold Weinstock, that Guerin's approaches had been rejected by Britain's major defence and high-technology company.[44] Nevertheless, it is important to note that while the Lazards report on ISC contained some critical elements, the merchant bank revealed that most brokers' analysts were very much in favour of the merger, offering only an equivocal opinion on which direction the de Ferranti trusts should vote. As a later commentator stressed when Sebastian was trying to use the Lazards report as a weapon to beat the Ferranti International board into mass resignations, he would be better advised not to reopen 'old wounds', given his role in bringing the company to the brink of collapse in 1974.[45]

Apart from the weighty evidence offered by Sir Arnold Weinstock, Sebastian de Ferranti and Lazard Brothers, and although not directly related to the Ferranti-ISC merger talks, another warning to shareholders, executives and employees of the dangers associated with colluding with Jim Guerin was being paraded in a Philadelphia court from the summer of 1987. As we saw in the last chapter, Guerin had been highly supportive of the creation and early development of United Chem-Con Corporation, headed by one of the leading examples of Black American entrepreneurship in the form of James B. Christian. Guerin had not only invested in Chem-Con, his brother-in-law,

Carl E. Jacobson, had also been given a senior management position at the defence electronics firm. By 1987, however, both Christian and Jacobson had been indicted by the Justice Department for defrauding the government of $16 million and bribing US Navy purchasing officials.[46] This not only initiated a two-year investigation into Chem-Con's activities, but also precipitated Jacobson's flight to Chile in a failed attempt to avoid prosecution. It later transpired that Guerin's associate Carlos Cardoen had orchestrated Jacobson's move to Chile, demonstrating the lengths to which ISC's chief executive was keen to limit the adverse publicity associated with this scandal. Although it was only in June 1989 that Christian revealed the full extent of Guerin's involvement, when after being sentenced to six years in jail he made an impassioned speech to the court in which he directly implicated his former supporter in the illegal activities, it was apparent to some in the US tax agency by the summer of 1987 that the ISC's chief executive was culpable. Indeed, Christian stated that Guerin masterminded the ploy to defraud the government of $16 million from its special scheme to support minority-operated businesses.[47] It was yet further evidence that linking up with Guerin and ISC could well be too much of a risk,[48] even if this only became public knowledge two years after the merger.

Delving further into the evolution of United Chem-Con, and linking with the material provided in Chapter 2,[49] it is apparent that Jim Guerin had formed this business in 1978 as a front for his illegal trading, using the Black American entrepreneur James B. Christian as cover for this work. By placing his brother-in-law, Carl Jacobson, in a senior management position, Guerin also ensured that Christian would follow all instructions passed on from ISC. We saw in Chapter 2, for example, that Christian had been obliged to take over ISC's dubious *Pestolite* business, just at the time that ISC was being floated on the London Stock Exchange in 1982, while in the same year Chem-Con executives were paying out bribes to the Director of the US Navy's Office of Small and Disadvantaged Business Utilization, Richard D. Ramirez, to the tune of $120,000, for various contracts to supply $135 million worth of sea shed cargo containers.[50] Chem-Con was also aided in its lobbying for business by Raymond S. Wittig, who was minority counsel to the House Small Business Committee of the US Senate, remuneration for which took the form of both significant financial payments and various gifts and holidays. Wittig was consequently one of the twelve people prosecuted in the Chem-Con scandal, all of whom received sentences of varying degrees of severity.

Another dimension of Chem-Con's trading activities that deserves attention was the way in which a fake contract to supply Pakistan with up to $8 million worth of intercom equipment was used in the early 1980s to create the misleading impression that the firm was in a healthy financial state.[51] The remarkable similarities with what Guerin perpetrated with the KP contract are instantly recognisable, although it is important to stress that Christian only revealed the intercom fraud after he had been prosecuted for bribing US Navy officials. Indeed, no physical evidence exists to support Christian's claims against Guerin. On the other hand, the accusations were made at a time when Guerin's reputation was deteriorating rapidly, creating the widely held impression that much of his empire-building had been based on fraud and illusion. Although Christian's sentence was not reduced in return for the substantial amount of evidence he produced on Guerin's earlier activities, it undoubtedly prompted the Philadelphia Grand Jury investigations which resulted in his later prosecution and jailing. Crucially, as Christian was to argue in court during his sentencing: 'Even though there was a minority person in charge [of United Chem-Con] on paper, a minority person was not calling the shots.'[52] This highlighted graphically to many people that Guerin's activities deserved much closer attention, sparking investigations that would eventually lead to revelations that amazed many people. Although he claimed that the closure of United Chem-Con in May 1987 cost him $8 million, representing the amount he had allegedly invested in the firm since 1978, few were willing to voice any sympathy for a man whose reputation was sinking fast, not least the owners of Merdian Bank, which lost $3 million on the bankruptcy.[53]

Having noted these developments, it is nevertheless important to stress that while the Ferranti board was presented with evidence of ISC's high-risk nature, both from its own assessments and those of objective outsiders, the real situation only became apparent well after the merger. One should also note that the Lazards report completed for Sebastian de Ferranti was never presented to the board, while the former chairman failed to attend the EGM that approved the merger.[54] In any case, the Lazards report would have been dismissed as self-serving, given that it was conducted on behalf of Sebastian de Ferranti and the family trusts that still owned a considerable number of Ferranti shares, while it did actually report that ISC was regarded by many brokers as a 'buy' stock. On the other hand, the internal report by Scott, McCallum, Shepherd and Bardsley contained enough powerful evidence that must have placed serious questions about any merger proposal. A City of London electronics analyst at Shepherds, Peter Minton, would also later comment that:

> Allowing for the libel laws, I came as close to saying Guerin was fraudu-lent as makes no odds. The company had no substance, most of its alleged operations were placed off limits by a US Pentagon-nominated proxy board and it was so dubious that it could not get a US stock exchange listing. The real question is, where did the non-shareholder money that kept it afloat for so long come from?[55]

Of course, these were hindsight views that did not register in internal Ferranti debates, even if Minton was a highly respected source of comment. Once again, though, the issue of trust must be considered, because while it is clear that each Ferranti director was fully apprised of ISC's accounts and business, any reservations expressed privately and publicly, whether at the time or in hindsight, were apparently soothed by the claims of Guerin and his team that all was totally above board and financially sound. Indeed, throughout July and August Guerin and his senior management team travelled frequently to London to talk directly with Ferranti board members, discussions that clearly laid the foundations of a productive working relationship.

To assist them further in coming to a decision, the Ferranti board also instigated objective investigations of ISC's accounts by trusted advisors. However, in this context it is fascinating to note that the board took the highly unusual decision to solicit an audit from ISC's own auditors, PMM. Charged with the task of rigorously analysing ISC's finances, there is no evidence that PMM staff failed in this respect. Clearly, though, it is difficult to see how they could remain totally objective in assessing their client's activities and making recommendations to a potential purchaser. Whether or not the board should have listened to the warnings expressed by Sebastian de Ferranti, they ought to have commissioned an independent report on which objective conclusions could be based.

The role of the objective assessor comes under the City convention known as 'due diligence'. Although not enshrined in company law, it had been accepted practice since the first surge in take-over bid activity during the 1930s, imitating American practices that had been introduced during the 1930s in response to the highly speculative investment boom that had sparked the 1929 Wall Street Crash. 'Due diligence' was based on the notion that predators were obliged to undertake a full and frank analysis of a target-company's accounts and business. This practice would normally involve a team of auditors crawling all over a firm, in order to be able to report back to the predator that what they were acquiring was fundamentally sound. One should also stress that PMM was a long-established auditing operation that was used by many leading British and international firms, having become a major component of City activities, employing highly talented and experienced professional accountants that could normally be trusted to perform their duties to the highest possible standards. Judging from the investigation of PMM's audit of ISC, performed by Michael Chance on behalf of the Institute of Chartered Accountants of England and Wales (ICAEW), it complied with all current standards.

To place all of this into a wider context, one should remember that the mid-1980s was a period of considerable change within the City of London. Frequently referred to as 'Big Bang', these changes amounted to a radical overhaul of practices that had been employed since the early nineteenth century.[56] Running in parallel was a merger wave of considerable proportions, with the average annual expenditure by British companies on acquisitions running at £15.6 billion (at 1987 prices) between 1985 and 1987, while in the following two years this rose to an incredible £24.3 billion.[57] This 'merger mania' not only exacerbated the tensions felt within Ferranti, but also led to improved codification of the auditing process, when in 1985 the Auditing Practices Committee of the ICAEW issued a document entitled 'Fraud and other irregularities'. While this provided welcome clarification of the processes to be followed, crucially one must stress that these guidelines placed the primary responsibility for the prevention and detection of errors firmly in the hands of management, rather than the professional auditor. The auditor's responsibility was 'limited to designing and evaluating his work with a view to detecting those errors or irregularities which might impair the truth and fairness of the view given by the financial statements'.[58] Of course, one might question why management should be given more responsibility for detecting fraud than the professional auditor, but in any judgement of the utility of PMM's report on ISC it is vital to remember the contemporary conventions that ruled such activities.

Having made this important point, there is a peculiar feature of the PMM audit that does need to be mentioned: namely, that a substantial part of the audit work on the ISC subsidiary which held what came to be seen as fraudulent contracts was performed by PMM's American associate company, based in New York. While this might be seen as logical, given the geographical dispersion of ISC's activities, Chance noted that this was contrary to the Auditing Guidelines, given that ISC was an English company and its activities ought to have been fully audited according to the conventions in that country. On the other hand, one should stress that the London branch of PMM conducted the bulk of the audit on ISC, with a team headed by Alan Comber and Robert Ferguson, highly experienced engagement officers at PMM whom Chance said 'approached their audit tasks conscientiously, appreciating the risks associated with the business of the ISC group and its dealings with front companies, and had sought to devise audit plans and tests to satisfy themselves that the value of contracts in the accounts on which they were reporting was appropriate'.[59] Of course, as the PMM auditors noted, the use of front companies was by no means an indication that ISC was committing any offence, especially given the nature of the defence business. One should also stress that PMM made every attempt to acquire the kind of information that would verify the credibility of those contracts conducted mostly through these front companies, even though it was acknowledged that they were dependent on the quality of the information provided by ISC. Indeed, as Chance concluded, 'all the overt indications were that [the KP] contracts were being performed'. Intensive investigations by a US Grand Jury from 1988 also revealed 'a blizzard of paperwork' that had been drawn up by Guerin aides, especially Robert L. Shireman, Lawrence L. Resch and Wayne Radcliffe. As the programme manager for KP, Resch was responsible for showing PMM auditors a bonded warehouse in Belgium which allegedly contained sealed containers of missile components and equipment. Although it is now known that the containers were empty, PMM staff chose not to request that Resch substantiate his claims.[60] Similarly, it might seem odd that PMM made no efforts to investigate the existence of the front companies involved in what turned out to be fraudulent contracts, especially as KP Industries had not even been incorporated at the time the KP contract had allegedly been awarded.[61]

As we shall see later in Chapter 4, one of the strongest cases against PMM was their failure to investigate the front companies and KP Industries, when Ferranti International sued the auditor for providing inaccurate advice on the merger. In the case of KP, however, it is important to remember that PMM auditors met with a senior figure in the Pakistani military establishment and received assurances that it would be honoured. Although it later transpired that Guerin had paid this person $250,000 to say such things, this bribe only came to light in 1992 at Guerin's trial. Furthermore, not only did Comber and Ferguson meet all of the ISC board of directors and questioned them on the missile contracts, in August 1987 the PMM auditors met the Ferranti internal team that investigated ISC just prior to the merger and heard no evidence to place this work under a cloud. During the course of the work of the multi-agency team that investigated Guerin from September 1989, it also came to light that during its 1987 audit of ISC the PMM auditors had been highly critical of the corporation's internal controls, insisting on radical changes as part of a general overhaul of the accounting system.[62] Indeed, PMM would appear to have investigated every possible means of checking these contracts, conducting the audit as rigorously as possible, with extensive checks conducted on the flow of both subcontracted parts and payments; little did they know that false documentation was being presented to them, while the bribed Pakistani official proved to be highly convincing. One might reply by stating that PMM evidently missed something, given the extent of the fraud. On the other hand, referring to the contemporary notion of auditors' duties at that time, as Chance noted in his report: 'It is not the duty of an auditor to obtain every possible piece of audit evidence.' Indeed, according to the 1985 Audit Guidelines, it was the responsibility of the acquiring company's management to detect errors, leading Chance to conclude that:

There is no scope for the suggestion that PMM were faced with clear evidence of dishonesty and failed to pursue it because, for example, they had allowed themselves to become too close to their client's senior management and were unwilling to confront them. The reality is that PMM were among those comprehensively deceived by a fraud which was designed and executed with extraordinary care and skill.[63]

Of course, this ignores the potential problem highlighted earlier, that the New York branch of PMM conducted the audit of the American subsidiaries, contravening the 1985 Guidelines. One might also wonder why so much trust was apparently placed on the words of a Pakistani military official who had been chosen by ISC for the PMM auditors to interview, while the failure to investigate the front companies more rigorously would appear to have resulted in the absence of crucial material, not least the timing of KP Industries' incorporation. Moreover, a more detailed investigation of the engineering and production facilities at the disposal of ISC could well have raised similar concerns to those expressed by Ian Ball when he first joined the firm at the beginning of 1987, as well as those of Sir Donald McCallum. On balance, though, given the nature of the auditor's role in the mid-1980s, with the ultimate responsibility placed on an acquirer's management to detect fraud, it is difficult to blame PMM for what was to come out over the course of the period 1987–89. Although one would expect 'due diligence' to be conducted objectively and honestly, this is also dependent on the nature of the terms agreed by client and audit firms. In this respect, one should remember that not only was the Ferranti board granted access to the PMM audit report, allowing them the opportunity to scrutinise the overseas contracts, but also Grant Thornton, the auditors to Ferranti, would have worked closely with Comber and Ferguson while the merger was going through in September–October 1987, providing yet further evidence that Guerin had spun such a tangled web of intrigue that some of the best accounting professionals in the City of London were unable to detect the problems.

3.3 The merger

The last section has demonstrably illustrated that far from being conducted on a wing-and-a-prayer, the Ferranti-ISC merger was thoroughly assessed by a series of both internal and external teams, none of whom could find any fraudulent contracts. Admittedly, common issues were raised by them all, not least the sensitive nature of ISC's links with South Africa, China and Pakistan, a reliance on a small number of customers in these potentially difficult regions of the world, the heavy reliance on subcontractors for key components, and accounting conventions that lacked any commonality with the conservative practices used by Ferranti. In addition, some were sceptical of

ISC's engineering base, while the proxy board was regarded as an obstacle to total assimilation of the American activities into Ferranti divisions, thereby undermining any attempts to achieve the anticipated synergistic benefits. Whether these issues amount to a case against the merger is a matter of judgement, but one must conclude that the unanimous decision of the Ferranti board of directors to embark on the merger was based on a full and frank assessment of the *known* facts. The Ferranti board consequently accepted the accuracy and efficacy of the information provided by PMM, especially once Grant Thornton had surveyed their paperwork in September 1987 and verified it as credible. Any misgivings about ISC activities in what were described as covert policy areas (South Africa, China, Chile and Iraq) were disregarded as an element of risk in the deal, even if in hindsight it is clear that the board should have been much more cautious. On this point, Sir George Younger, Secretary of State at the Ministry of Defence, informed Sir Donald McCallum that he had personally warned Sir Derek Alun-Jones that ISC was not a company he would trust.[64] At exactly the same time, MoD officials in the Procurement Executive offered anecdotal evidence that should have set warning lights flashing in the MD's mind.[65] On this point, though, it is worth noting that Alun-Jones had not developed a very good working relationship with the Head of Procurement at the MoD, Peter Levene, limiting the degree of intimacy between customer and supplier, especially when considering matters of a covert nature. Similarly, one should stress that neither Younger nor MoD officials were willing to provide categoric evidence that ISC was doing anything illegal, substantiating Alun-Jones' later statements that nobody ever persuaded him that he was doing anything other than taking a credible commercial risk.[66]

Although Alun-Jones chose to keep this information to himself, there was considerable debate within senior management about the firm's acquisitions strategy. Indeed, at the Ferranti chief executive's conference in 1987, Charles Scott gave a presentation on the subject, stressing how to date the company had been extremely timid. This caution was demonstrated by the limited prices paid for new operations, TRW Controls Inc being the largest acquisition at $10 million. Furthermore, as we noted earlier, Scott reminded his audience that little financial benefit had been derived from these acquisitions, raising question marks over the way they had been conducted. Whether or not Scott was preparing the senior management for what was about to happen, he concluded that 'acquisitions have to play a part in the growth of our business and that the part must be larger and more successful than it has been in the past'.[67] This reveals how Alun-Jones frequently used Scott to reinforce his own messages, especially in persuading the board that a particular strategy was credible. Indeed, while as we noted in Chapter 1 the divisional 'barons' were given considerable latitude in the way that they ran their fiefdoms, it is above all apparent that when it came to corporate strategy Derek Alun-Jones held the reins decisively. This also highlights the weak nature of corporate governance pressures on the chief executive, because not only did the board acquiesce in his decisions, but also the widely dispersed ownership of Ferranti equity ensured that he was never challenged at AGMs or EGMs on any strategy. Although Sebastian de Ferranti constantly agitated against Alun-Jones, few took this opposition seriously when major issues were being discussed, emphasising how the board and shareholders were willing to place their total faith in the chief executive.

While all of these factors were being endlessly discussed by executives, accountants and other advisors, in explaining why the Ferranti-ISC merger went ahead there is one factor above all that overrode all reservations and caveats, namely, the trust placed in Jim Guerin by all those with whom he came into contact. Apart from his growing reputation as an entrepreneur who had built an industrial empire from virtually nothing, many were willing to attest to both his patriotism and outstanding philanthropic activities in Lancaster, Pennsylvania, where he spent several hundred thousand dollars supporting religious, educational and cultural institutions of importance to that community, not to mention the boost he gave to local African-American entrepreneurs. Who would mistrust such a person? Why would you not believe him when he assured all and sundry that the sensitive overseas contracts and supply chains were all approved by US government agencies? How could one deny the efficacy of his business practices? Although some asked these questions in 1987, and even fewer offered negative answers, unless they were benefitting from excessive hindsight, the Ferranti board was willing to accept that subject to satisfactory auditing by established firms such as PMM and Grant Thornton, the merger ought to proceed. Moreover, an august institution of the calibre of Baring Brothers was willing to promote the merger, continuing its support of Ferranti that had been so important over the previous decade.[68]

While Ferranti and ISC executives, as well as an army of advisors, had been discussing the merger for several weeks during the summer of 1987, it was 21 September before an official announcement was made revealing the proposed move. The Ferranti board had met six days earlier to discuss what was reported in the minutes as a merger with what they continued to refer to as 'IBIS',[69] sustaining the secretive nature of the process. This resulted in a unanimous vote in favour of the merger,[70] leading to further meetings between Alun-Jones and Guerin to finalise the details of the share-swap, and culminating in another Ferranti board meeting at Barings' headquarters in Bishopsgate, City of London, when finally the pseudonym IBIS was dropped and specific reference to ISC was made. Although only attended by Alun-Jones, Scott and Shepherd – it was a Sunday – this meeting approved the merger announcement which would be made the following day on the London Stock Exchange. By that time, the 60:40 split in favour of Ferranti had been agreed, converted into an offer of nine 10 pence Ferranti Ordinary Shares for every five 10 cent ISC shares. This made each ISC share worth 232p, valuing the entire operation at £411 million.[71] In view of the 1989 revelations to be discussed in the next chapters, we now know that this valuation proved to be nonsensical, but one should stress that *in public at least* no adverse comments were forthcoming from contemporary observers.

Indeed, newspaper comments were entirely positive, the *Financial Times* leading the way with a report noting: 'Stockbrokers were unanimous yesterday in praising the industrial logic of the merger of Ferranti and International Signals & Control.'[72] Other newspapers made the usual allusions to the marital nature of such events, the *Oldham Evening Chronicle* describing 'An exciting marriage' and accusing Ferranti of 'cradle-snatching', given the relative ages of the two companies.[73] There were also comments such as: 'Such marriages are made in heaven'[74] and a 'Love Match'.[75] Sir Derek Alun-Jones sustained them, saying that 'if you take a girl out for long enough, you nearly always end up marrying her',[76] giving a heavy hint that the 'courting' had been going on for some years. Overall, the *Daily Record*'s positive comment – 'Sky's the limit in space deal'[77] – was typical of the general consensus that this represented a sound move by both companies, even if some felt that it would prompt more decisive action from other predators.[78] The key to *Investors Chronicle* was that in acting defensively against recent share price movements, Ferranti and ISC were making it increasingly difficult for a predator to step in and make a bid.[79] This is ironically described in City circles as taking a 'poison pill', in that it prevented a take-over bid. Little did City commentators know about the full implications of this vernacular term, given the way it eventually killed off Ferranti. Nevertheless, *Corporate Money* was willing to go as far as to say that 'Ferranti is preparing to swallow a foolproof "poison pill"'.[80] As we shall argue later, pre-empting a merger was perhaps most powerful force working on Alun-Jones's mind at that time, given the threatening noises from the likes of STC, Plessey and other defence giants. Crucially, though, the largest holder of Ferranti shares, Guardian Royal Exchange, with 5.6% of the equity, was reportedly very pleased with the merger,[81] confirming the efficacy of the board's actions and further substantiating the claim that corporate governance pressures on the board were extremely weak.

Once the announcement had been made, it was vital for Ferranti and ISC shareholders to receive all of the official documentation that laid out the timetable for the merger. Produced by Baring Brothers, this material ('Listing Particulars' and 'Proposed Merger') was posted out on 2 October, giving shareholders until the 23rd to return their Form of Acceptance. Not surprisingly, shareholders were informed in letters from the two boards that unanimous votes in favour of the merger had been passed by both, on the grounds that not only was it consistent with their mutual aims of becoming major international players in defence and civil electronics, but also brought together a complementary range of engineering and management skills that would help them achieve those aims. Comprehensive consolidated balance sheets were also provided for both companies, tracking performance over the previous five years. Interestingly, though, no reference to the characteristics analysed earlier in this chapter was made, leaving shareholders ignorant of ISC's dependence on a limited number of politically sensitive overseas markets, its links with South Africa, and the existence of the proxy board. Instead, apart from tracking the kind of information represented in Figures 3.1 and 3.2, it was explained that the combination would have over 26,000 employees in the UK, USA and ten other countries, while the order book stood at £1.5 billion and profit growth was assured. The new board of directors would be composed of six ISC executives (Guerin; Blackwell; Fox; Heywood; Ivy; Zilligen) and ten from Ferranti (Alun-Jones; Atterton; Boyd; Broadley; Dodd; Dorey; de Ferranti; Hoskyns; Scott; Shepherd). Crucially, Sir Derek Alun-Jones would become executive chairman, while Guerin would be made deputy chairman (as well as executive chairman of the ISC proxy board). This reflected a decisive change from the pre-merger Ferranti organisation, because Basil de Ferranti was relegated from his position as chairman to non-executive director. While Basil was surprised about this, one should also stress that it was not handled particularly well by Sir Derek, because Basil was only informed of this change by his chief executive when going up in the lift to the 24 September board meeting.[82] In order to accommodate Guerin in the new system, apparently Basil had to be sacrificed, ending over fifty years of there being a de Ferranti at the head of the firm. It was later agreed that Basil would become president of the new group, but this was merely a token gesture and he was effectively excluded from future board meetings.

As if to reassure Ferranti shareholders, another feature of the merger documentation worthy of note was a clause on page 23 of the 'Proposed Merger' booklet that reported how Guerin had agreed not to sell any of the new Ferranti shares acquired as a result of the merger until the new company had announced its 1988–89 results. As Guerin held 18,225,236 ISC shares at the time of the merger,[83] converted into 31.8 million Ferranti International shares (or, 4.26% of the new firm's equity), had he sold a large tranche of his holding in the new company, this could have been to the detriment of the share price. One might add that since the 1986 ISC rights issue, Guerin had sold over 8.2 million shares in his company, earning him £24.5 million. He was consequently willing to agree to a moratorium on future sales from his personal portfolio, especially as he would be in line for a substantial return in the summer of 1989 from the steady rise in the value of the new firm's equity. Indeed, as a result of the merger announcement the Ferranti share price jumped from 117p to 129p, reflecting the City's confidence in this combination and assuring Ferranti shareholders that they ought to vote in favour.

Coincidentally, and some might even say prophetically, Ferranti shareholders approved the merger just four days after 'Black Monday', when on 19 October 1987 stock markets around the world crashed precipitously. Although it is likely that the crash occurred because of what is known as 'programme trading',[84] rather than any fundamental problem in the world economy, the FTSE 100 index on the London Stock Exchange fell by 26.4% and the Wall St index by 22.7%, following massive share price declines in Hong Kong (46%) and Australia (41%). Nevertheless, Ferranti went ahead with its planned extraordinary general meeting (EGM) on 19 October, called to approve the acquisition of ISC, while on 23 October it was announced that the offer went unconditional, given that votes representing 74.3% of ISC equity had accepted the Ferranti offer. At this stage, it was essential to consult the Office of Fair Trading on whether the merger would be referred to the Monopolies and Mergers Commission, a discussion on which the Ferranti board was pleased to report a negative answer. The Ferranti board also agreed to extend the deadline for acceptances to 13 November, by which time 78.3% of the equity had been placed behind the offer, allowing them to declare the merger unconditional. Baring Brothers was duly deputed to announce this formally to the Stock Exchange on 16 November, by which time acceptances had crept up to 84%, making it much easier for the ensuing technicalities to flow smoothly. Indeed, when Ferranti International Signal plc was registered in January 1988, prospects appeared to be extremely bright for a group with an issued capital of £74.6 million (see Appendix A) and borrowing facilities of £250 million. The first board meeting of the new group had already taken place, on 3 December 1986, at which extremely optimistic projections were tabled by Guerin on behalf of ISC and Sir Derek Alun-Jones for Ferranti, allowing the directors to wallow in what to them seemed like a superb piece of business. As the next chapter outlines, however, all of this 'patting each other's backs' was merely the prelude to a period of acute crisis within Ferranti International, a crisis that ultimately precipitated the disappearance of a company that in 1987 appeared to have such great prospects.

3.4 Conclusions

In view of the conflicting hindsight views which cloud the debate over the Ferranti-ISC merger, it is essential to address the reasons why Derek Alun-Jones and the board led the company into what proved to be a disastrous deal.

It is first of all vital to quote the Ferranti MD's own words on the merger decision:

> ISC was a UK quoted company introduced to the Stock Exchange by Flemings. Its shareholders were very much the same large institutions that owned Ferranti. It was audited by PMM, the largest accountants. It was investigated by Barings, Grant Thornton and by our management in considerable depth. Maybe when crime is involved – we can claim to be as much the victims of others as ourselves.[85]

Even though this ignores the warning-signs given off by the MoD procurement executive and other informed observers, not to mention the Scottish division's desire to acquire missile business from ISC and build a bigger business that would guarantee the EFA radar contracts, this balanced point deserves to be remembered when assessing the credibility of the Ferranti board's decision. Crucially, by acquiring ISC Ferranti was buying into the US military-industrial complex, colloquially referred to as the 'Beltway Bandits' (namely, the hordes of defence suppliers and agents that operated within driving distance from the Pentagon in Washington that grew significantly in both size and influence during the Reagan era).[86] Even though entering this military-industrial complex carried a high price, in the form of the ISC Proxy Board and limited communication between the two companies, this was the logical fulfilment of Alun-Jones' 'US Strategy' formulated in the early 1980s. One should also note that by September 1987 the board was dominated by Derek Alun-Jones, because the two men who had in the past been least pliable, Peter Dorey and Donald McCallum, were no longer as influential as they had been. Tragically, by that time Peter Dorey's health was deteriorating badly, while Donald McCallum was obliged to retire as a director, having reached sixty-five. McCallum actually offered to continue as a director, but Alun-Jones was reluctant to allow this, given that the Scottish divisions were already well represented on the board, leading to the departure of a man who had sagely guided FDSL through an era of rapid and profitable growth.

When considering the wide range of reasons why the merger went through, however, of particular importance in all the negotiations was the enormous trust placed in James Guerin by his future partners. Guerin was actually a person of importance in the Lancaster religious community; while it is well known that some American evangelists certainly cannot be trusted with other people's money, clearly the Ferranti board was willing to accept his answers on issues like the ISC accounts or his links with the CIA. As several have since noted, he was a credible and persuasive man who exuded charm. In particular, John Pickin was convinced that Ferranti would benefit enormously from a merger with this man's company. One should remember that while for personal reasons in 1983 Pickin had been obliged to resign from his post as technical and planning director, he continued to act as a consultant to the firm. This gave him a highly influential role at Millbank Tower, where because of his training and background, Derek Alun-Jones placed considerable faith in Pickin's technical expertise. One should also remember the rumours that Plessey was about to bid for Ferranti, largely in order to forestall a GEC bid, pressuring Derek Alun-Jones and the board into developing a defensive strategy which would maintain the company's independence. Furthermore, in spite of the reservations expressed by Donald McCallum about the engineering competencies at ISC's US factories, Ferranti Defence Systems in Scotland was beginning to accept the case for a stronger link with ISC, not only in view of the entrée this would provide into the American and Italian defence industries, but also because a merger would maintain its dominant position within Ferranti.

While there are those who rather unfairly heap considerable blame on Derek Alun-Jones and the whole Ferranti board for agreeing to the merger, it is clear that in coming to this momentous decision they had rationally appraised all the available information and considered the various pressures mounting on the company. In performing these tasks, they been assured by the reports from PMM, all of which were ratified by their own auditors, Grant Thornton, as well as receiving encouragement from such august institutions as Barings and Flemings. In this context, though, it is especially important to remember that the 1985 Audit Guidelines laid the principal responsibility for detecting fraud or other irregularities firmly on the shoulders of the acquiring firm's management. While the professional auditors were expected to conduct a thorough examination, ultimately senior management at Ferranti were to blame for the failure to detect Guerin's antics, a fact that undermines any accusations levelled at PMM or Grant Thornton. Of course, the board double-checked their information as far as possible, for example, by consulting Ian Ball, who had joined ISC at the end of 1986. Although Ball would never have revealed any confidential information, he was willing to verify the general view that Guerin was a highly entrepreneurial leader who carried the support of his employees at all levels. Similarly, question marks hang over the advice MoD officials gave Sir Derek Alun-Jones, because although it is clear that George Younger (Secretary of State for Defence) had expressed his deep reservations about ISC, and senior figures in the procurement executive informed the Ferranti managing director of various activities that *at the very least* should have lit an amber light, no concrete proof was ever presented to the Ferranti board.

Above all, irrespective of these warnings, it was the efficacy of the advice and data presented in the various audit reports and private discussions that persuaded all Ferranti directors to favour the merger when the issue was finally brought to a vote in September 1987. In spite of its reputation for advanced engineering and ambitious innovation, Ferranti was not known for taking silly risks; strategic decisions were only ever taken after a full, rational appraisal of the available information by both the executive committee and the full board. Above all, the key issue was the trust placed in Guerin as a potential partner, a trust which Guerin exploited to the full throughout the negotiations and overrode any question marks that the MoD might have put in Alun-Jones' mind. If the Ferranti board was culpable, and in spite of the 1985 Audit Guidelines, it was only in the sense that it failed to see through the veil of integrity with which Guerin cloaked all his activities, the key weapon in the hands of all successful fraudsters. As Sir Derek later stated: '[Guerin] was full of energy and life and I must say that my directors felt that one of the assets of the merger would be this wonderful man coming in.'[87] This indicates the extent to which the board was taken in by the God-fearing Reaganite who openly boasted of his international arms links. One might add that the dual external pressures associated with UK defence market changes and a threatened take-over bid from Plessey might have put undue pressure on the board, forcing them into such a quick decision that they had little time to assess Guerin's true personality. On the other hand, both at divisional and corporate levels, senior Ferranti managers had known him since 1980 and none had voiced any fears about fraudulent activities. In retrospect, of course, it is easy to see how warning signals relating to ISC's trading should have been recognised, although there again neither the MoD nor any American authorities were willing to provide categoric proof of any illegal activity. The board would have had to possess the proverbial crystal ball in order to predict the enormous problems which were to beset Ferranti as a result of the merger, an asset which is beyond all but the luckiest of firms.

Having come to this balanced conclusion, it is vital to stress that Ferranti had agreed to the merger for six main reasons: firstly, acquiring ISC would give the firm an enhanced presence in American, Italian and Middle East markets at a time of considerable uncertainty in the UK defence sector; secondly, the two companies would appear to have had highly compatible product ranges, especially in defence markets; thirdly, as a turnkey systems supplier ISC could help Ferranti make the decisive move from being a subcontractor to a major player in high technology sectors; fourthly, the Italian subsidiary (valued at approximately £70 million) could always be capitalised if its potential remained unfulfilled; fifthly, the board would appear to have been entirely taken in by the American evangelist who ran ISC; and finally, it would be increasingly difficult for firms like GEC or Plessey to acquire Ferranti if it was so much larger and more dispersed. In terms of relative importance, clearly the latter two would appear to have played the most significant role in persuading the board to go ahead with the deal at that point in time, providing the opportunity for Jim Guerin to shelter the more dubious aspects of his business within the confines of an estab-lished member of the British defence industry, as well as making him even wealthier. Moreover, the Ferranti board had accepted Guerin's arguments that it was vital for the proxy board to continue to run the American side of ISC's activities, providing yet further protection for the carefully constructed fraud that within a few years would bring the newly created group to its knees. While this decision gelled with the devolved organisational culture that had been a prominent feature of Ferranti for many decades, as we shall now go on to discuss, it merely compounded the problems associated with managing Guerin and acquiring accurate information on his network of companies.

Moreover, this unusual organisational feature of the new firm was but one of a series of warning signs that might have persuaded the Ferranti board to resist Guerin's entreaties, because in addition to the proxy board, one might point to a series of issues of similar gravity. Firstly, ISC's refusal to reveal the identities of customers that accounted for a substantial proportion of sales and profits was an extremely worrying feature of its accounts, giving even those with a propensity for high-risk investments some cause for concern. When this is added to ISC's accounting conventions, which allowed Guerin to extract high levels of profit from contracts well before they had been completed, an image had already been created of a firm that differed in fundamental respects from the risk-averse Ferranti. Many were especially curious about ISC's profit shortfall in 1987, given that Guerin had led brokers to believe that they would be at least $8 million higher, resulting in a signifi-cant fall in the ISC share price to levels that persuaded Ferranti and its advisors that were more conducive to a merger. Thirdly, the extensive reliance on subcontractors revealed the relatively weak technological base of ISC, not to mention the associated problems of ensuring quality standards were main-tained. Moreover, the fourth issue was ISC's intimate connections with South African firms, most of which were linked to the state-owned defence conglomerate Armscor, as well as similarly sensitive work with operations in Chile, Pakistan and China. Fifthly, Sir Derek Alun-Jones had been personally advised by the Secretary of State for Defence, Sir George Younger, as well as officials in the MoD procurement executive, that these overseas contacts could well cause problems in the future, while Sebastian de Ferranti told everybody who would listen that the chief executive of GEC, Sir Arnold Weinstock, had refused even to meet Guerin, let alone discuss a merger. In addition, the testimony of Chem-Con's James B. Christian revealed other dimensions of Geurin's activities, even if this could be rejected as the words of a bitter man about to go to jail. While these factors represent a powerful case against the merger, however, the Ferranti board regarded those in the previous paragraph as far more convincing, leading to a unanimous vote in favour of the move. The next chapter will reveal how Guerin's tissue of lies and obfuscation was rent asunder by a combination of time and astute investigative work by key Ferranti executives such as Alan Cooper, Ian Ball and Charles Scott. Whether or not the board should have seen through Guerin in 1986–87 is a matter of personal judgement, even if hindsight and vested interests frequently distort the thought process.

Notes

1 For further material on the late twentieth-century business scene, see Wilson, *British Business History*, pp. 234–6.
2 See J.F. Wilson (2000), *Ferranti. A History*. Vol. 1. *Building a Family Business, 1882–1975*, Carnegie Publishing, pp. 514–22.
3 FBM 10835, 24 Sept 1980.
4 J.F. Wilson (2007), *Ferranti. A History*. Vol. 2. *From Family Firm to Multinatonal, 1975–1987*, Crucible Books, pp. 352–3.
5 FBM 9, 26 March 1985.
6 See Vol. 2, pp. 94–106.
7 *Ferranti News*, June 1982.
8 Vol. 2, Chs 5–7.
9 Vol. 1, pp. 169–71.
10 See Vol. 1, pp. 301–3 and 337, for instances of these problems.
11 See Vol. 1, pp. 337, 480 and 572.
12 For further details on these activities, see Vol. 2, pp. 356–65.
13 See Ch. 1, as well as Lovering, `Opportunity or crisis?', pp. 97–102.
14 See examples of difficult American acquisitions in Vol. 2, Chs 5, 6 and 7, especially Interdesign Inc and Ferranti International Controls Inc.
15 G. Jones (2005), *Multinationals and Global Capitalism*, Oxford University Press.
16 See FN, June 1983, for a fuller description of their activities. Vol. 2, p. 360 also provides a map identifying their location and further detail.
17 See Vol. 2, pp. 359–63.
18 See Vol. 2, pp. 175–9.
19 Data on turnover and profitability have been difficult to find, but the annual reports produced by Ferranti plc always refer to Venus Scientific as a loss-maker.
20 See Vol. 2, pp. 223–4, for more detail on this story.
21 See Vol. 2, pp. 276–7, for the COMED success story.
22 Vol. 2, pp. 109–18.
23 FBM 10883, 23 Dec 1980.
24 FBM 16, 22 Sept 1982.
25 FBM 10, 15 Dec 1982.
26 Interview with Ian Ball.
27 FBM 13, 27 Nov 1985.
28 FBM 14, 19 May 1986.
29 See earlier, p. 72.
30 ISC publicity material published in 1986–87.

31 See Vol. 2, pp. 117, 119–20 and 133–7.
32 The following section is based on 'A report on International Signal & Control Group plc', hereafter known as the Scott-Bardsley report.
33 *Financial Times*, 22 Sept 1987.
34 FBM, 15 Sept 1986.
35 Lazard Brothers report on ISC, provided to author by SZF.
36 See above, pp. 15–24.
37 FBM 18, 24 Sept 1986.
38 *Sunday Times*, 24 Sept 1989.
39 *The Times*, 18 May 1990.
40 Chance Report, 1996.
41 Interview with Sir Donald McCallum and FBM 14, 29 April 1987.
42 See above, pp. 60–1
43 This section is derived from the investigating team's report.
44 Interview with SZF.
45 Andrew Alexander in *Daily Mail*, 19 Jan 1990.
46 Jacobson later pleaded guilty of paying $255,000 in bribes between 1982 and 1985 to the Director of the US Navy's Office of Small & Disadvantaged Businesses. *Intelligencer Journal*, 10 June 1989.
47 *Intelligencer Journal*, 9 Nov 1989.
48 In total, twelve people were successfully prosecuted for their involvement in Chem-Con's illegal activities.
49 See above, pp. 85–8, for further information on Chem-Con.
50 Ramirez was also paid $80,000 by another minority-owned firm, Wedtech, to award $54 million worth of contracts to supply pontoons. *Lancaster New Era*, 5 June 1990.
51 *Lancaster New Era*, 12 June 1990.
52 *Lancaster New Era*, 13 Oct 1989.
53 *Lancaster New Era*, 8 Aug 1989.
54 There is an apocryphal story that Sebastian had asked Lazards to send a representative to the EGM, but after a lengthy liquid lunch this person failed to make the meeting.
55 *Business Age*, July 1992.
56 Wilson, *British Business History*, pp. 235–6.
57 The previous peak year had been £13.4 billion in 1973, although the average for the early 1970s was just £9.1 billion (at 1987 prices). Wilson, *British Business History*, p.225.
58 Chance Report, p. 5.
59 Chance Report, p. 8.
60 *Lancaster New Era*, 7 Nov 1991.
61 See Ch. 2, pp. , for a summary of the KP contract.
62 *Lancaster New Era*, 17 May 1990. These revelations were made during William Clark's case claiming $2.75 million compensation from Guerin and ISC, arising from his resignation as the corporation's legal counsel. See later, pp. 134–8, for details of this case.
63 Chance Report, p. 14.

64 Evidence provided by Sir Donald McCallum.
65 Letter to the author from David Knowles, 19 May 2008.
66 Interviews with Sir Derek Alun-Jones.
67 C. Scott, 'Acquisitions strategy', Ferranti Chief Executive's Conference, 1987.
68 See Vol. 2, pp. 352–3, for evidence of Baring Brothers involvement in Ferranti.
69 FBM 2, 15 Sept 1987.
70 Sir John Hoskyns was the only director not present at that meeting, but Alun-Jones reported that he had consulted this non-executive director and gained his approval of the merger.
71 Some newspapers valued the acquisition at £540 million, but £411 million remains the accepted figure.
72 *Financial Times*, 22 Sept 1987.
73 *Oldham Evening Chronicle*, 24 Sept 1987.
74 *The Times*, 22 Sept 1987.
75 *Today*, 22 Sept 1987.
76 *Daily Mail*, 25 Sept 1987.
77 *Daily Record*, 22 Sept 1987.
78 *Corporate Money*, 24 Sept 1987.
79 *Investors Chronicle*, 25 Sept 1987,
80 *Corporate Money*, 24 Sept 1987.
81 *Daily Telegraph*, 22 Sept 1987.
82 Interview with Sir Donald McCallum.
83 ISC had issued 171 million shares by September 1987, giving Guerin almost 11% of the equity.
84 This occurred when computers that are programmed to respond automatically to price changes in related securities, a process that could result in rapid reductions in share prices.
85 Letter to author, 9 June 1997.
86 Alex Brummer in *Guardian*, 20 Sept 1989.
87 *The Times*, 27 Jan 1990.

4

From honeymoon to divorce

W ITH THE FERRANTI-ISC merger greeted by the business world as an astute response to a combination of market-cum-technological pressures and take-over threats, from November 1987 the two boards were then obliged to discuss in minute detail a wide range of issues. In the first place, it was crucial to decide on both the management structure and key appointments, assimilating the best talent into a hierarchy that would work effectively. Secondly, and very much linked to the first point, senior management was charged with the challenge of securing sufficient synergy across the combined firms, not least in terms of harmonising the marketing and technological complementarities that had been trumpeted in the build-up to the merger. Whether or not ISC possessed the kind of international marketing skills claimed by Guerin and his team will become a theme of this chapter, given that it increasingly became apparent that this revolved around a series of deals of a highly specious nature. Thirdly, the new board needed to convince its City followers that the synergy could be converted into improved financial performance, even if again it was soon obvious that ISC brought little of value to the table in terms of technological expertise and profitable business. Indeed, just as the Scott-Bardsley report had warned in 1986, apart from Guerin's inner team ISC was not exactly blessed with the depth of managerial and engineering talent that Ferranti had developed,[1] illustrating yet again the superficial nature of the business that Guerin had fashioned. At the same time, as Guerin was allowed to retain the Proxy Board that had managed the covert and US defence contracts that underpinned ISC's recent expansion, Ferranti was never going to be able to extract full value from its acquisition. Of course, there were sound reasons why the Ferranti board permitted this arrangement, even if in retrospect it is now possible to say that it prevented an earlier discovery of the fraud perpetrated by Guerin. Above all, though, returning to a key theme of the last chapter, the Ferranti board had placed their trust in Guerin and his Proxy Board, in the expectation that the combined firms would generate the kind of benefits anticipated from the summer of 1987.

This chapter will analyse these issues in some detail, explaining how fundamental problems emerged in the way that Guerin not only continued to act in a mysterious manner over certain contracts, but also conjured up further missile contracts and hoodwinked Ferranti managers into believing that they were generating a sound cashflow. A complete analysis of the financial performance of what would become Ferranti International will be conducted in Chapter 6, when we shall link up with the discussions featuring in Chapter 1 concerning the mounting problems in a range of activities that would be enormously exacerbated by the Guerin fraud. Separating the two dimensions in this way allows a better understanding of the fraud, because just as with our analysis of the reasons why Derek Alun-Jones led his board into this merger, it is vitally important to differentiate between the objective facts of the situation and any subjective views based on hindsight or specific vested interests. Moreover, with such a mountain of data verified by some of the City's most prestigious firms it was by no means apparent that ISC was worthless. Another vital point to remember is that, as Michael Chance noted in his judgement on PMM's performance as the ISC auditors, Guerin's fraud was so cleverly constructed that it would have been extremely difficult to detect without some prior knowledge of the missile contracts and customers. This helps to explain why it took Ferranti management almost two years to discover the extent of the fraud, given the sophisticated nature of Guerin's network of front companies, secret bank accounts and the role played by the Proxy Board. But discover the fraud they did, with Alan Cooper, Ian Ball and Charles Scott playing the key detective roles in 1989, resulting in a divorce from Jim Guerin so soon after the apparently delirious honeymoon enjoyed after the formalisation of the merger in November 1987. It is a story of stubborn persistence and thorough analysis, in the face of lies and deception that would shock the British and American business communities; such is the impact that betrayed trust can have on business acumen and judgement.

4.1 The honeymoon

While the problematic relationship with ISC, and Jim Guerin specifically, was only to emerge at a later stage of the deliberations, it is clear that in the early months of the post-merger period Ferranti and ISC proved to be more than willing bedfellows. As we saw in the last chapter, the new board of directors had been agreed prior to the merger, with Basil de Ferranti stepping down as non-executive chairman, to be replaced by Sir Derek Alun-Jones as the new executive chairman and Jim Guerin as executive deputy chairman.[2] Many across Ferranti especially were rather bemused at the way Basil had been treated in these negotiations, because although he was given the nominal title of (non-salaried) company president,[3] he had not been privy to what had been agreed by Sir Derek and Guerin, only hearing of the deal when going up in the Millbank Tower lift to the board meeting that agreed the merger.[4] Alun-Jones clearly saw the merger as an opportunity to reinforce his position on the board, while it was also important to give Guerin a title that was warranted by his 4% stake in the new firm. At the same time, Charles Scott and Alan Shepherd retained the roles to which they had been elevated in August 1987, respectively, deputy managing director (finance and adminis-tration) and deputy managing director (operations), giving Ferranti people a powerful grasp of the decision-making processes. Indeed, seven of the new board were former Ferranti directors, while in addition the three non-executive directors who had worked with Ferranti for several years – Boyd, Broadley and Hoskyns – were also given a seat. In contrast, only six former ISC directors were appointed to the new board, two of whom (Fox and Heywood) had non-executive status.[5] While it is consequently apparent that Ferranti people dominated the new board, however, this discussion must also bear in mind the vital point that as CEO of ISC Jim Guerin continued to operate the Proxy Board, and consequently the allegedly lucrative overseas and US defence contracts, a fact of life over which Alun-Jones and his team could exert no control. On the other hand, at that first post-merger board meeting Alan Cooper started in his new capacity as company secretary,[6] an appointment that would later prove crucial in detecting aspects of ISC that in 1987 had not come to light.

The structure adopted by Ferranti International Signal[7] by the summer of 1988 was composed of two executive committees, each co-ordinating the activities across the respective divisions of Ferranti and ISC, while the Proxy Board also continued to run ISC Defence & Space (including Marquadt and several of the defence systems operations started by Guerin). This reveals further evidence of how in most respects Guerin was able to retain complete control over his former companies. Although a new logo was devised in 1988, as a symbol of the single identity which management was attempting to achieve, in effect it is difficult to see how significant progress had been made in absorbing ISC into the Ferranti organisation. In particular, the existence of two executive committees ensured that decision-making and scrutiny of contracts and finances could well be blurred. Even though Guerin justified the existence of the Proxy Board to the Ferranti International board as a means of providing access to lucrative US defence markets,[8] it was clearly going to be difficult to influence what was happening in that committee. Some executives – for example, those at Ferranti Defence Systems and Ferranti Computer Systems – were actually content with this situation, because this reinforced the basic philosophy of decentralised management, but clearly the most powerful divisional manager after the merger was James

Guerin. As deputy chairman of Ferranti International, as well as chairman of both the ISC executive committee and the ISC Proxy Board, he was able to exert considerable and unchallenged authority over most of what had formerly been ISC operations. In the detailed discussions prior to the merger, it had also been agreed that nobody from Ferranti would be appointed to watch over the newly acquired American and Italian subsidiaries, securing for Guerin valuable breathing space in his bid to blind his new partners to the fraud perpetrated in 1986–87. For example, at the first meeting of the new Ferranti International board in December 1987, nobody challenged him when he stated that ISC International's contracts were 'secret', because they accepted his argument that 'maintenance of secrecy is vital both with regard to retaining existing contracts and the winning of new contracts'.[9] In addition, of course, the reluctance to monitor ISC more closely was born of a long-held feeling within Ferranti that entrepreneurs like Guerin should be given as much freedom as possible, emphasising how the autonomous structure which had been so much a feature of Ferranti since the 1890s was perpetuated in the new era. In retrospect, though, while it would not have stopped the fraud, securing direct information from ISC would have cut short what was an embarrassingly long period before the full extent of Guerin's actions were discovered.

Regardless of the curious organisational nature of the new firm, just as with City commentators many within Ferranti expressed total confidence in the merger. Sir Derek was at pains to explain in the *Ferranti News* that as there was very little direct overlap in terms of products and processes, there were no plans to rationalise capacity in either firm, thereby reducing fears of any post-merger redundancies.[10] Indeed, he predicted that life for most Ferranti employees would continue much as it had done, with the acquisition strengthening the balance sheet and sustaining the security enjoyed since the mid-1970s crisis. Guerin reinforced this point in the same edition, but added that the merger offered rich promise, given both the plans to develop up to what he claimed were seven new businesses and the opportunities ISC could forge for Ferranti products in US and other markets. He went on to make the bold statement that: 'The history of mergers and their positive impact on the new corporation is not good. We are bucking the odds. We feel this thing will be very good, but it will require a lot of work on the part of all the people involved.' We now know, of course, that Guerin was certainly responsible for 'bucking the odds', but not in the way anticipated by many in 1987, when total confidence was expressed about the anticipated benefits. Hindsight views aside, though, it is fascinating to note that in explaining the qualitative benefits to be gained from merging together, both Alun-Jones and Guerin stressed the common entrepreneurial features of the companies, predicated on the decentralised modus operandi that had been a traditional feature of their evolution.

Although it was only in February 1988 that the new board decided to change the name of the combined firms to Ferranti International Signal plc (hereafter referred to as Ferranti International), at an early stage the senior management was heavily involved in extensive negotiations over how to achieve the synergy required in such circumstances. As we noted in the last chapter, very few of the enormous number of British mergers and acquisitions that took place from the 1950s to the 1980s had resulted in synergy – defined as '2+2=5', or simply making a greater whole out of the constituent parts – largely because of the failure to tackle the essential organisational challenges that accompanied this kind of activity. Apart from refusing to remove existing directors from senior posts, rarely would the predator impose its own organisational culture on the acquired operation, while replication of facilities and even competition between similar products was often sustained well after the merger.[11] Given the nature of the Ferranti-ISC arrangement, namely, a 60:40 share split, it was naturally incumbent on the former to take the initiative in both eliminating any unnecessary replication and harmonising activities, wherever possible. Of course, the curious organisational structure adopted by Ferranti International was always going to limit the extent to which Ferranti could absorb its acquired assets, allowing Guerin and his closest associates to continue to operate a substantial proportion of the overseas and US defence contracts. Nevertheless, other opportunities were available to the Ferranti management, resulting in some bold synergistic initiatives that offered rich rewards.

Board of Directors in November 1987
Sir Derek Alun-Jones (executive chairman)
James H. Guerin (deputy chairman and executive chairman of ISC)
Charles Scott (deputy managing director, finance & administration)
Alan A. Shepherd (deputy managing director, operations)
Phil E. Atterton (MD of Ferranti Defence Systems)
Albert E. Dodd (MD of Ferranti Instrumentation)
Peter F. Dorey (MD of Ferranti Computer Systems)
Nathan C. Blackwell (marketing director)
Joe H. Zilligen (ISC finance director)
R. Clyde Ivy (executive director)
Gavin Boyd (non-executive director of Ferranti plc)
Robin Broadley (non-executive director of Ferranti plc; MD of Barings plc)
Basil de Ferranti (company president; non-executive director)
James M. Fox (non-executive director; ISC)
James A. Heywood (non-executive director)
Sir John Hoskyns (non-executive director)

During the summer of 1987, in the build-up to the formal announcement of the merger on the London Stock Exchange on 21 September, Sir Derek Alun-Jones and Jim Guerin had started to discuss possible synergies, especially at senior management levels. The two corporate teams also met several times during September and October, when some plans were assessed and possible options considered. Once the merger had been accepted by both sets of shareholders in November, however, the intensity of the planning increased, with a conference of all divisional managers convened at Turnberry, in Scotland, using 'The Way Forward' as the theme. Arising from this event was a Co-ordinating Group, jointly chaired by Phil Atterton from Ferranti Defence Systems and a senior ISC executive, Joe Zilligen. Although this was largely an advisory body which reported its recommendations to the new board, it was essential if all the potential benefits of the merger were to be realised that such a body should consider perceived synergies. As Guerin had noted to the *Ferranti News*, by December 1987 this group had identified seven projects which promised significant rewards through the sharing of expertise and core technologies, including missiles, munitions, radar systems and educational computing.[12] Apart from having Atterton and Zilligen involved in this group, bringing their experience and ability to a complicated situation, Les Butler (Ferranti Defence Systems) was appointed operations manager, assisted by his colleague Les Butler, while on ISC's behalf Joan Beaton contributed to discussions from her Lancaster, Penn., base.

Having established this Co-ordinating Group, however, and even though Phil Atterton provided office space at the Crewe Toll facility in Edinburgh, it is in retrospect difficult to see much evidence of extensive synergy. Atterton reported regularly on the Co-ordinating Group's work to Ferranti International board meetings,[13] while at the first board meeting of the new firm Joe Zilligen offered up some thoughts on rationalising capacity across the two groups.[14] Nevertheless, the Co-ordinating Group would appear to have faded into obscurity by the summer of 1988, while thereafter much more attention was focused on acquiring accurate information on what was happening within ISC. Of course, for most Ferranti employees, as Sir Derek had predicted, the merger with ISC barely made any difference to their work, given that the four divisional managers were very careful about allowing their product offerings to be diluted by what many within Ferranti regarded as inferior technology. This was the main reason why the most immediate impact of the merger was a considerable amount of hyperbole concerning the *potential* benefits in the merger, rather than concrete evidence that it was resulting in synergy.

Irrespective of these views, it is vital to remember that a new subsidiary was planned and created from the early days of the merger. Crucially, this operation was set up as a separate company, rather than an adjunct to an existing division, because of the belief that if it ran into trouble, this would not affect other activities. It was also no surprise that this venture was linked with guided missiles, given that Ferranti Defence Systems had been acting as a subcontractor to ISC's PGM programme since early 1987 and Guerin had frequently offered the prospect of the substantial production contract to Alun-Jones during the pre-merger negotiations. The new venture was first discussed by the board in January 1988,[15] when Dr Shepherd presented a paper outlining the advantages of bringing together the various engineering teams in both Ferranti and ISC. Although it was envisaged that in the initial phase this new operation would be 'lean and mean', by bringing in what were described as 'heavyweight' staff from various parts of the two companies, it was anticipated that this venture could have a major impact in the UK, NATO and international missiles markets as a turnkey systems supplier. An announcement about the new firm was made in February 1988,[16] following which in April 1988 Ferranti International Dynamics Ltd was registered. Some later joked about the unfortunate coincidence linking this division's acronym – FIDL – and the fraudulent revelations of 1989. On the other hand, from its base at Signal House in Hanworth, Middlesex, the firm soon built up an order book worth £50 million, successfully linking together the technological and managerial capabilities of the two organisations to demonstrate the inherent possibilities in a well-planned merger. Progress in linking other operations would appear to have been less swift, however, and as the Lazards report had predicted,[17] acute difficulties were experienced by the Co-ordinating Group in gaining any access to Guerin's immediate empire run by the Proxy Board.

When the unfortunately named FIDL was created, it was immediately decided that the highly experienced Ian Ball would become MD, with Jim Guerin as executive chairman. Given the enormous successes achieved as MD of the Cheadle Heath division of Ferranti Computer Systems up to 1986, as well as his direct experience of working for ISC Electronic Systems since December 1986, Ian Ball provided that useful combination of direct knowledge of ISC activities and rigorous managerial abilities that would be required in co-ordinating the various activities into a cohesive business. To assist him, he was able to secure the services of Ken Goodwin as finance director of FIDL, having recruited him into ISC Electronic Systems early in 1987 from his former role as finance director of the Cheadle Heath division of Ferranti Computer Systems. Other former Ferranti managers brought into the FIDL hierarchy were Angus Sutherland (commercial director, based in Edinburgh) and Chris Boutell (technical director, based in Moston), while Alan Ford was seconded from ISC's European marketing section to take on this function. This core management team was also advised by several non-executive directors who sat on the board of FIDL, including Clyde Ivy and Sir

David Checketts of ISC, as well as Albert Dodd (MD of Ferranti Instrumentation), Ron Dunn (MD of Ferranti Defence Systems) and Bill Broekhuizen (MD of Ferranti Computer Systems). The Ferranti non-executives were chosen because of their existing contacts with the missile and weapons systems products that would be the mainstay of FIDL, because apart from the Hanworth complex formerly occupied by ISC Electronic Systems, the new company also occupied premises in Moston and Edinburgh. The latter, of course, had been involved in the PGM contract since the beginning of 1987, reflecting FIDL's aim of subcontracting a significant amount of any business secured to those parts of the Ferranti group that had the expertise. In August 1988, FIDL also took over the *Bloodhound* support business of Ferranti Computer Systems, based at the Derker Street factory in Oldham, providing not only a historic link with the company's earlier work on guided missiles,[18] but also a substantial production base for the PGM contract.

Apart from PGM, of course, Ian Ball and his team were confident that FIDL would become a significant competitor in the NATO weapons systems market, as well as contribute to the other programmes that Guerin and Ivy were allegedly managing from their American bases. Given that GEC and British Aerospace had dominated this market since Ferranti was excluded from guided missile work following the ramifications of the *Bloodhound* programme in the 1960s,[19] by offering an alternative source of supply FIDL felt that it was matching the spirit of the MoD reforms introduced by Michael Heseltine and Peter Levene.[20] Over its brief existence, however, FIDL would be heavily dependent on the programmes ISC had initiated, and in spite of an aggressive assault on potential NATO customers, no other missile contracts were secured. This placed an even greater reliance upon PGM, because as ISC Aerospace subcontracted all of the remaining development work to FIDL, as well as holding out the prospect of all of the production, Ian Ball recruited a team of approximately thirty engineers to sustain progress. While Guerin insisted that he would continue to act as the sole interface with the customer, the United Arab Emirates, on the patronising grounds that he felt it was vital not to confuse them with the change in corporate structure, effectively from April 1988 FIDL was in sole charge of PGM. As we shall see in the next section, however, Jim Guerin and Clyde Ivy must have sorely regretted this train of events, because having given Ian Ball and his team responsibility for pressing ahead with PGM, this inevitably meant that they would want to know more about the other missile contracts that ISC had included in its accounts at the time of the merger. It was while investigating these contracts that Ball started to uncover some of the fundamental inconsistencies in what Guerin and his closest colleagues were claiming, initiating a succession of related enquiries by Alan Cooper and Charles Scott that ultimately unravelled a fraud of monumental proportions.

4.2 Fraud uncovered

With FIDL by the spring of 1988 taking full responsibility for PGM, Ian Ball's workload was clearly going to increase significantly. Apart from putting together the managerial and engineering teams, as well as finding appropriate production and office facilities, he was also obliged at an early stage in FIDL's existence to deal with a highly delicate situation involving ISC's links with South Africa. As we noted in Chapter 2, since 1982 ISC had been acting as a sales agent for what was marketed as *Striker*, an anti-tank, laser-controlled missile that had been developed by Armscor. Although this kind of work was extremely sensitive, given the South African apartheid regime's continued presence on the United Nations embargo list, Jim Guerin claimed that the US government had approved the link. There were even apocryphal stories claiming that Mike Richards of ISC Aerospace had brought a model of the *Striker* missile into the USA, in a clandestine operation involving Gamma Associates, the front company used by ISC to ship equipment to South Africa and other countries. An even more bizarre story involved Clyde Ivy's attempt to import more *Striker* equipment into the USA by cargo ship, only to be foiled by the visit of a US Customs boat to that cargo ship, resulting in the covert material being ditched into the sea.[21] What did become evident, though, was the discovery early in 1988 by Alan Cooper that ISC had been supplying South Africa with high-frequency sonar equipment, revealing for the first time Guerin's role in building the CIA's South Atlantic monitoring system set up by Admiral Bobby Ray Inman.[22] After hearing of this information, Ian Ball decided to confront Clyde Ivy with the knowledge, claiming that it must be false, given the lack of any such sophisticated technical abilities in ISC. Agitated by Ball's discoveries, Ivy reluctantly admitted ISC's involvement as programme manager, using equipment supplied by US electronics corporations such as Loral. Furthermore, Ivy added that not only was Inman the key architect behind the programme, the whole scheme had been personally authorised by Henry Kissinger, US Secretary of State in President Nixon's regime. Even though, as we noted in Chapter 2, President Carter vetoed the South African link, it is clear that ISC continued to work under Inman's direction after 1977, providing the CIA with a highly sophisticated monitoring system that was regarded as essential to US security.

While Ball and Cooper were naturally amazed at these discoveries, as they had no evidence that the sonar programme still existed, they decided to discuss the situation with Sir Derek Alun-Jones. This prompted the Ferranti International chairman to seek a meeting with the most senior MoD civil servants, Peter Levene and Sir Michael Quinlan, at which ISC's South African trading was discussed in some detail.[23] By that time, the MoD had been tipped off (probably by US sources) about potential breaches of the UN

embargo, putting Sir Derek in a very difficult situation. Naturally, he reiterated the company line, that Ferranti International would never knowingly
break international law, a position the civil servants accepted. Following this
meeting, Sir Derek immediately rang Guerin to seek assurances on the allegation that ISC had been supplying military equipment to South Africa. These
were certainly forthcoming, Guerin stating that he was merely involved in
supplying personal computers to South Africa, as part of an educational
programme aimed at the black community. He also added that the US
government had given ISC 'a clean bill of health' on previous allegations,
points that were immediately reported back to Levene and Quinlan.

In spite of this flurry of activity, however, worries were continually
expressed about ISC's activities. This led to a further board discussion in
September 1988, when Guerin placed on record a false assertion that ISC had
not been involved in selling military systems to South Africa since the 1970s.
This seemed to persuade his new colleagues that there was no need to worry
about this issue, because no criticisms were voiced about ISC's past.[24]
Towards the end of 1988, however, after Clyde Ivy had approached FIDL with
a proposal that on behalf of Armscor they should sell a surveillance system
known as *Seeker* to the UAE, Ian Ball became alarmed that ISC's South
African links were pushing his business into dangerous territory.[25] Even
though this business could have been worth up to £30 million, Ball first
informed both Sir Derek Alun-Jones and Alan Cooper of Ivy's entreaties, and
then telephoned a senior civil servant at the Foreign & Commonwealth Office
(FCO) who was an expert on South African matters. It transpired from this
conversation that such a trading relationship was legitimate, leading Ball to
visit South Africa in January 1989, along with Wayne Radcliffe of ISC
Technologies Inc. A month later, Armscor sent engineers to visit the FIDL
team at Hanworth, resulting in agreement in principle that the *Seeker*
arrangement would go ahead. Before signing a contract, however, Ball wisely
sought further advice from the FCO, with a request for written approval of
the South African link. This prompted the FCO official to reassess his earlier
advice, probably because he was now being asked for a signed document,
convincing Ball that no part of Ferranti International should trade directly
with Armscor. After Sir Derek was fully briefed on these developments, this
became official corporate policy, thereby terminating all Ferranti links with
Armscor and South Africa. Although this was a difficult development for
Guerin and Ivy, as we shall see later this did not stop them from sustaining
their links with the apartheid regime, because these were essential to the
various missile programmes that they were anticipating.

While all this was happening, of course, given FIDL's role in prosecuting
the PGM contracts it was incumbent on Ian Ball to examine the funding base
for this work, activities that inevitably further aroused his curiosities about

the work of ISC executives. In relating this chain of events, it is vital to stress that others – especially Alan Cooper and Charles Scott – were undertaking their own investigations, but as the head of the PGM programme Ian Ball was at the sharp end of the detective work. One might also note that Clyde Ivy's ISC Aerospace operation in Westlakes, California, continued to control the missile development programme. It was in California that the first field trials of PGM were to be conducted in March 1988, witnessed by senior UAE officials, giving the impression to all within Ferranti International that this contract was being prosecuted effectively.

Once these trials had been conducted, of course, and even though they revealed some serious engineering problems that still needed to be overcome by Ivy's team, it was vital to consider full production of the first variant of PGM, by then known as *Hakim I*. This involved extensive discussions between Ian Ball, Jim Guerin and Clyde Ivy, most of which would appear to have been conventional in tone, with positive implications for the Derker St facility in Oldham the former had chosen. When it came to discussing financial aspects of *Hakim I*, however, Ball became increasingly confused about some of the comments made by Guerin. A key event in this respect was a telephone conversation Ball had with Jim Guerin on 27 April 1988. Prior to this, Ball had been totally preoccupied with putting FIDL together, finding appropriate staff and facilities, and compiling a cohesive, credible business plan. Of course, as a team at Ferranti Defence Systems' Edinburgh factory was working on the telemetry for PGM, nobody doubted the existence of the PGM contract, even though prior to the merger Ian Ball had been refused access to that part of the Hanworth factory that had been designated for PGM development.[26] The ISC accounts had also illustrated that substantial costs amounting to $130 million had already been incurred, mostly by Clyde Ivy's ISC Aerospace operation in Westlake, California, in developing what was a modular missile composed of a number of separate building blocks. As we noted in the last chapter, though, after widespread concerns had been expressed about the amount of profit ISC had extracted (see Table 4.1) from the development stage of PGM – Charles Scott estimated that this amounted to $20 million more than Ferranti would have extracted[27] – in the early months of 1988 Guerin and his finance director, Joe Zilligen, started to investigate ways in which this could be mitigated. Guerin explained this to Ball in their April 1988 telephone conversation as 'acquisition accountancy', while in June Zilligen gave a financial presentation to the ISC executive committee that claimed up to $130 million in PGM incurred costs had been transferred to other parts of the group balance sheet, thereby making available a larger profit which could be added to the 1987–88 results. This not unnaturally confused Ian Ball, because in claiming that he had used 'acquisition accountancy' to write off the costs against another contract, Zilligen was using a

Table 4.1 Profits claimed on Alpha and KP contracts by ISC, 1984–89 ($ m)

To March	Alpha	KP	ISC Group Operating Profit	Alpha/KP as % of total
1984	5.5	–	27.2	20.2
1985	10.3	–	41.8	24.6
1986	52.8	–	57.3	92.1
1987	21.1	25.2	68.2	67.9
1988	–	39.9	21.1	189.1
1989	–	20.1	62.1	32.3

Source: Chance Report, p. 4.

totally unfamiliar business vocabulary to the one in which Ferranti managers had been trained. When Zilligen also went on to talk about the stock being part of a 'hardwired' missile programme, as opposed to the 'modular' nature of PGM, Ball confesses to being completely confused.[28]

Given this strange terminology, the seeds of doubt had clearly been sown in Ball's mind by these two interactions with key ISC executives. Little came of this, however, because Ball was aware that as Guerin and Zilligen had made exactly the same presentation to the full Ferranti board,[29] as well as to PMM and a consortium of banks that had been supporting ISC for years, nobody else was voicing any criticisms of what Zilligen had done. Indeed, on 29 June Guerin went to some lengths to explain to the board what had happened to the PGM programme and ISC's recent use of 'acquisition accountancy'.[30] It was during this meeting that he claimed that initially PGM had been a 'hardwired' missile, but once Clyde Ivy had realised that this had limited sales potential he moved to a modular design, a decision taken around the time of the Ferranti-ISC merger. Moreover, Guerin was able to find a customer for the 'hardwired' equipment accumulated at Westlakes by Ivy's development team, supposedly allowing ISC Technologies to write off all of the PGM development costs. As we shall see later, Guerin would claim that it was through his Chinese contacts at Norinco that the 'hardwired' stock was offloaded,[31] but in June 1988 not a single voice was raised at the board meeting questioning what he was doing. Nevertheless, Ball had also secured a copy of the Zilligen presentation for his finance director, Ken Goodwin, who reinforced Ball's views that use of terms such as 'acquisition accountancy' and 'hardwired' terminology were confusing. Ball consequently decided that at his next meeting with Clyde Ivy, to whom he reported as Guerin's key missiles man, he would express his deep concerns about Zilligen's presentation. This meeting took place on 30 June, followed by further conversations on the following day, during which Ivy merely assured Ball that all was well with PGM and FIDL should continue with its development work.

As Ivy then returned to Westlakes, Ball was obliged to follow these instructions, even if he and Goodwin were never convinced about the explanations provided. When the company secretary, Alan Cooper, visited Hanworth to conduct an audit of all large export contracts, Ball took this opportunity to discuss his reservations. As Cooper had previously been head of the Ferranti patents and legal department, he had a comprehensive grasp of these highly complicated areas. His appointment as company secretary in December 1987 provided the board with direct access to extensive experience in legal matters, not to mention detective powers that were to prove invaluable. Not that his predecessor, Tom Grime, would ever have unravelled Guerin's tricks, but as he had recently been ill, it was decided that he should retire and leave Ferranti after a long and highly distinguished career. Cooper's visit to Hanworth was part of a brief received from the board, to investigate whether all ISC export contracts had the requisite licences, some external commentators (most likely, the MoD) having advised Sir Derek that concerns had been expressed on this issue. He had previously been to see Robert Shireman, finance director of ISC Technologies, who in spite of being extremely reticent about discussing the issue of export licences, provided Cooper with a contract for a 'hardwired' missile that dated back to 1984. After Ball raised his concerns about what Zilligen had said in June, Cooper decided to show him the contract Shireman had produced, exacerbating the worries mounting in the FIDL MD's mind. In particular, as his team had been involved in all PGM sub-assembly procurements, and he had inspected the development work conducted at Westlakes by Clyde Ivy's team, Ball was convinced that the 'hardwired' stock simply did not exist. Crucially, he refused to believe that ISC had access to the technology involved in the 'hardwired' contract revealed by Shireman, while Ball also noted that some of the PGM components such as gyro units and seeking equipment that were to be used in this missile had yet to be fully developed. Moreover, to achieve the basic specifications laid out in this new contract would require huge management and engineering teams that ISC had never possessed.[32]

It is now known that what Shireman had revealed to Cooper, and indirectly to Ball, was linked with what we referred to in Chapter 2 as the sham 1984 UAE and 1987 Norinco contracts, neither of which existed in anything other than paper form. The 1984 contract for a 'hardwired' missile had been concocted merely to dupe investors into believing that ISC was diversifying into the lucrative international missiles business, while the Norinco deal was the way that Guerin and Shireman transferred all the alleged costs accumulated from this programme to another sham contract purportedly signed with Norinco to supply the *Alpha* missile. Ball was shocked at the brevity of the contract Shireman had provided for Cooper, because such a document ought to have been voluminous, with all the technical specifications and legal material, as opposed to a few pages of typed script that offered superficial insights into a supposedly 'hardwired' missile programme. However, although Cooper and Ball exchanged written notes expressing their concerns, they did not pass these on to Sir Derek or any other member of the Ferranti board, leaving the rest of the company in the dark on a matter of crucial importance. On the other hand, in at least two telephone conversations with Guerin in November 1988, Ball strongly advised the ISC chief executive to confide in Sir Derek and explain his problems with the missile contracts. These suggestions were completely ignored by Guerin, revealing the arrogance that overlay the entire scam; the American entrepreneur felt he could continue to fool the Ferranti International board into believing that all was well.

At the same time, as we noted in Chapter 2,[33] by August 1988 Guerin must have been extremely concerned by the assassination of General Zia, given that the so-called KP missile contract had allegedly been negotiated personally with the Pakistani military dictator and nobody could predict with any certainty that country's future relationship with Western nations. Guerin was obliged to report to the board in November 1988 that Zia's death was a cause of much concern, at which point Sir Derek reported that no less than $180 million was outstanding on the KP contract.[34] Typically, Guerin was bullish about the prospects of recovering the situation, noting that the US government was planning to inject a major aid programme into Pakistan. Although much later Guerin was actually heard to muse that had Zia not been killed in that fatal air accident, then the KP contract would have come to fruition, as we shall see later this was sheer fantasy; KP was a sham. Extensive enquiries by the Pakistani Ministry of Defence in 1990 would later reveal that ISC Technologies had in 1987 secured two contracts for cluster bombs, worth £42 million. Moreover, it was also admitted that in the same year Lieutenant General Talat Masood, a senior Pakistani procurement officer, visited ISC plants in the USA. It must be emphasised that Masood was not linked with the bogus KP contracts, but Guerin was able to use this visit as part of the mirage he was building to convince the Ferranti International board that the missile contracts existed.[35]

It was also reported at that same board meeting that Guerin and ISC were going to be investigated by a Grand Jury, involving accusations that they had been involved in illegal arms shipments to Libya, Iran, Iraq and South Africa.[36] This first significant indication that ISC had for many years been involved in covert arms dealing had arisen as a result of other enquiries into the activities of Allivane, a British arms supplier that was being investigated for its links with Iran. This firm had been created in 1986 by Terry Byrne jnr, an economics graduate from Villenova University, Pennsylvania, who had joined ISC in 1979 and become one of Jim Guerin's protégés as a member of the crucial Middle East marketing team headed by Stu Pindell. Allivane's principal factory was at Cumbernauld, near Glasgow, where the 155 mm ERFB-BB long-range explosive shell was produced, using parts supplied by some of Europe's leading firms, including ICI, British Steel and Royal Ordnance. The key point about this highly sophisticated shell, which had a range that exceeded the NATO product by six miles, was that by 1987 Allivane had signed a contract to supply Iran with 150,000 units. Unfortunately for Allivane, though, with the Iran–Iraq war grinding to a halt by August 1988, the contract was terminated by the customer after a small proportion had been delivered, precipitating a severe liquidity crisis that bankrupted Byrne's enterprise. Given Guerin's role in helping Byrne to set up Allivane, not to mention its illegal trade with Iran, this consequently sparked investigations on both sides of the Atlantic into ISC's international contracting. This also coincided with the revelations from James B. Christian about the illegal activities perpetrated at United Chem-Con, another venture in which Guerin had played a leading role throughout its unfortunate history. As we saw in Chapters 2 and 3,[37] United Chem-Con had been formed by Guerin and his brother-in-law, Carl E. Jacobson, along with James B. Christian, a man widely lauded as one of the leading black American entrepreneurs of his era. In the next chapter, we shall also go on to examine how Christian's revelations about the way that Guerin and Jacobson ran Chem-Con were instrumental in persuading several agencies to delve further into their general business dealings. Although Guerin continually rejected Christian's accusations, both publicly through his attorney, Joseph Tate, and privately to his Ferranti International colleagues, as the summer of 1989 progressed it was increasingly difficult to deflect all of the mounting evidence.

These revelations naturally came as a major shock to the Ferranti International board, coming as they did at the same time that cashflow from the KP contract was causing major problems. Furthermore, Guerin was obliged to admit the arrest of Dr Ho, the head of ISC Datacom, the subsidiary that had been responsible for developing the data link equipment for PGM/*Hakim*. Even though the arrest was in connection with Ho's activities at another company, prior to joining ISC, his departure was causing severe problems on the data link project, extending delivery dates by a worrying margin. Once again, though, on the Grand Jury investigations Guerin assured the board that all of his exports had been fully licensed by the US Department of Commerce, calming any fears that the executive deputy chairman was about to be arrested. As we now know, this only delayed the inevitable, but at the time the board seemed once again content to accept his explanations, possibly because in a later item Guerin held out the prospect of what he called 'the big ticket – PGM 3 plus another country for a total of $600 million which looks hopeful'.[38] Such were the illusions that he was willing to conjure in order to cover up his tracks.

Why Cooper and Ball failed to take their concerns further remains a matter of serious conjecture, because over the course of 1988 no evidence emerged from either the documentation or conversations with Clyde Ivy and Jim Guerin to refute their feeling that as Ball noted in his private diary 'something was seriously wrong'.[39] At the same time, as part of the investigations Alan Cooper was conducting into ISC export licences, he also became increasingly concerned about the continued reliance on the South African links that Ivy and Guerin had nurtured since the 1970s. In particular, some of the PGM technology was licensed from Damarall, a subsidiary of Armscor, the state-owned South African defence conglomerate that had been one of the principal bulwarks against attacks on the apartheid regime. Although after an investigation by HM Customs & Excise, it was discovered that the South African licence had been taken out by ISC Aerospace, an American subsidiary, thereby exonerating all of ISC's British operations, Cooper was nevertheless concerned about this link with a country that was still on the United Nations embargo list. When added to the fresh knowledge that ISC had allegedly secured missile contracts with Pakistan (KP) and China (Norinco), Cooper was extremely nervous about the situation.

To understand fully what Ball and Cooper were beginning to unravel, it is essential to provide a swift recap of the various manoeuvres that Guerin and his senior executives had been perpetrating since 1984.[40] In the first place, although Guerin and Ivy vehemently denied any knowledge of these events, they later admitted that in May 1984 ISC Technologies (based in London) entered into a sham missile contract with the United Arab Emirates (UAE), allegedly worth $138 million, which was code-named *Alpha*. This missile was supposedly going to be 'hardwired', as in the contract that Shireman provided for Alan Cooper in June 1988. By 1988, fictitious costs of $100 million had been booked to *Alpha*, mostly involving subcontracting work by South African and Chilean front companies, while $116 million had allegedly been paid to these operations for components. To convince both PMM as auditors and the Ferranti management that this contract existed, Guerin himself paid $8.5 million from his private Swiss banking accounts to ISC Technologies, thereby providing a cashflow. It was only in April 1986 that ISC Technologies signed the genuine PGM contract with the UAE, worth $377 million, based on a modular design, rather than the 'hardwired' missile that featured in the *Alpha* contract. However, in order to account for the $8.5 million paid out for Alpha, Guerin created a false version of the PGM contract (later referred to as *Hakim* I) that had a price of $385.5 million, recouping his outlay at a stroke. Furthermore, and relating back to Zilligen's June 1988 presentation to the ISC executive on 'acquisition accountancy', Guerin had ISC Technologies enter into transactions with both the *Alpha* front companies and Norinco (the Chinese state-owned arms firm) to sell all of the fictitious components valued at $116 million in the accounts to the South African front company, for eventual onward sale to Norinco, using the code-name *Hakim* II. This was why Ian Ball was so confused after Zilligen's presentation: firstly because he was convinced that this 'hardwired' stock had never existed, and, secondly because of the flimsy nature of the contract with Norinco.

Of course, neither Ball nor Cooper could make the leap from expressing private misgivings to accusing Guerin of such monumental financial chicanery, given that they only had some pieces of the jigsaw. Furthermore, in the summer of 1988 they had no knowledge of the other fraudulent contract concocted by Jim Guerin, namely, the missile technology transfer contract worth $300 million signed in November 1986 with KP Industries Pty, of Pakistan, code-named KP (short for Khyber Pass). Operating through exactly the same front companies that were supposedly involved in the *Alpha* contract, this was yet another 'hardwired' missile that was going to make substantial profits. Indeed, as Table 4.1 reveals by 1987 ISC claimed to have made cumulative profits of $89.7 million on the *Alpha* contract, accounting for a significant proportion of ISC's group operating profit, especially in the crucial years prior to the merger. KP profits were of a similar order of magnitude, effectively keeping ISC in the black in 1988 and demonstrating in graphic form the contributions these fictions were making to public perceptions of ISC's commercial credibility.

4.3 The jigsaw pieces come together

As one might expect, what has just been related concerning the PGM, *Alpha* and KP contracts differs somewhat from the narrative provided in the previous chapter, largely because the latter is based on the reports produced by either Ferranti managers or various financial institutions, none of which knew the full story behind Guerin's activities. One can be quite confident, of course, that had Sir Derek and the Ferranti board possessed more accurate information, then the merger would not have happened. Unfortunately, however, while Ball and Cooper had developed a clear view on the 'hardwired' missile programme by July 1988, even then it was difficult for them to build a strong case against Guerin and Ivy. One should also stress that during the summer of 1988 the Ferranti board questioned Guerin about the *Hakim* II contracts, given that little cashflow would appear to have been generated from this business. Although it is now known that Guerin was recycling his own cash through both the front companies and private bank accounts in Panama and Switzerland, he reported back just three days later that Norinco had signed a contract worth $100 million, with a small progress payment made to ISC Technologies. This quite simply amazed the board, and especially Dr Alan Shepherd, deputy managing director (operations), because as a result of the extensive experience accumulated during long-drawn-out negotiations with Chinese government officials over semiconductor technology, he knew full well that such a contract would take months to negotiate and finalise.[41] Nevertheless, given the enormous trust placed in Guerin by the Ferranti board, they accepted his explanation that he had been working with Chinese officials on the *Hakim II* contract for some time, only revealing the full extent of the contract once it had allegedly been signed. Perhaps the prospect of securing business that had increased in value from the $375 million to what by November 1988 Guerin claimed was going to be worth $700 million blinded the Ferranti board to the conjuring tricks he was performing. Whatever the answer to this conundrum, one should also add that as auditors of ISC PMM verified the accounts containing these contracts, making them just as culpable as the Ferranti directors who voiced such confidence in Guerin's apparent achievements. Not even Sir David Checketts (MD of ISC Technologies) realised what he was signing away, because while it is glaringly obvious that he did not rigorously check the contracts, accepting Guerin's instruction that all was acceptable, he was merely a figurehead leader of a vehicle that was being used for a massive fraud.

Returning to our analysis of why Ball and Cooper did not take more decisive action concerning their discoveries about the 'hardwired' missile programme, another factor that must be considered is the availability of hard evidence. While they had been given a document by Shireman, the finance director of ISC Technologies, that seemed to be damning, it was only when other material became available that they began to fit more of the jigsaw together and saw the emerging picture. As we have frequently noted, both the *Hakim* and KP programmes were run through front companies, with ISC largely acting as merely the assembler of the end-product. We have also stressed that these front companies were figments of Guerin's fertile imagination, meaning that the subcontract documents did not actually exist. With terrier-like persistence, however, Alan Cooper was intent on harassing the ISC executive into providing these documents, because he increasingly realised as 1988 progressed that they were the key to understanding what was happening on these programmes. In retrospect, though, it is also patently clear that until the winter of 1988 these documents had not even been typed out; Guerin merely reported that they were part of the business of his Proxy Board, hiding the evidence from Ferranti sight. Only after continued requests from Cooper and the Ferranti board did Guerin relent and offer up the evidence. In fact, he asked his contracts lawyer, Greg Mansker, to produce a contract that laid out in fine detail all the various elements of the *Hakim* II programme, after providing him with all the data and technical specifications.[42] One should stress that Mansker was a totally innocent party in this transaction, because he was merely following the instructions of his client. At the same time, Ian Ball asked some of his team to investigate the subcontractors that Guerin was supposedly using, including Elverton and Navarino.

Clearly, the need for more information from ISC was mounting throughout 1988 and early 1989, especially when several key figures started to notice that some of ISC's contracts were failing to generate the cashflow anticipated prior to the merger. In time, of course, this would be the weak link in Guerin's grand scheme, because it would have been impossible for him to continue to churn his own money around the various front companies and Ferranti International without either setting off alarm bells in the accounts or draining his own wealth continually. Once again, though, while in January 1989 Cooper presented a thorough report on ISC's export licences, the Ferranti International board was content to accept Guerin's continued assurances that all was well with the various programmes (PGM, *Alpha* and KP). Crucially, although Cooper's report was distributed to all directors in January 1989, no board discussion ensued. Indeed, from 12 January to 14 March the only board action was sanctioning share transfers and sales through the various executive share schemes, indicating that the directors clearly had other things on their minds. Moreover, this failure to assess the implications of Cooper's findings coincided with Ball's conviction that no work was being done on the 'hardwired' missile that was at the heart of the *Alpha* contract. In January 1989, Guerin also made a serious error, allocating $20 million in cash to the KP and *Alpha* contracts, prompting Sir Derek and Charles Scott to fly across to Lancaster to discuss the situation with ISC executives. Guerin did admit that these contracts were causing his companies grave cashflow difficulties, blaming the political uncertainty caused by General Zia's death in August 1988 for a cessation of payments. He also accepted responsibility for having mistakenly allocated $20 million to these contracts, assuring Sir Derek and Charles Scott that the error would be corrected as soon as the Pakistani government recommenced their payments schedule. As this all seemed entirely plausible, Guerin was given more time to resolve the problems in Pakistan.

In the following month, however, further efforts were made to clarify the situation, when Sir Derek, Charles Scott and Ian Ball travelled to Lancaster to listen to Guerin's plans for 1989–90. Prior to meeting Guerin, over breakfast Ball decided to outline his deepening misgivings about the KP and *Alpha* contracts, explaining how Guerin had created a highly complex scam that would inevitably unfold in the following months. Even though later that same day he once again pleaded with Guerin to come clean to Sir Derek, Ball was singularly unsuccessful in convincing anybody on that trip that a crisis was imminent. Nevertheless, during the course of Guerin's financial presentation and in private conversations, the possibility of a leveraged buy-out was mooted by Guerin, all of which was shrouded in such terms as 'returning to my roots' or 'reinvigorating ISC'. Nobody would appear to have taken such sentiments seriously at that time, but clearly Guerin was already beginning to feel that it was essential to devise an alternative plan, on the grounds that the faith placed in him by the Ferranti International board could fade rapidly if categoric evidence of fraud ever came to light. Indeed, it is possible that ever since General Zia's assassination in August 1988 Guerin had been considering alternative means of keeping his scams a secret, with a leveraged buy-out emerging as his preferred option. Once again, though, an opportunity had been missed to unravel Guerin's scheme, because the February planning meetings between Sir Derek and Guerin passed off without incident, allowing the latter to continue with his grand scheme. Not even Sir David Checketts, the MD of ISC Technologies, could help Ian Ball and Alan Cooper build their case against Guerin, because the nominal head of this vital subsidiary was kept in a state of blissful ignorance by Guerin on both contractual and financial issues.

With his cover still in place up to the spring of 1989, Guerin and his closest associates were able to sustain the missile scams, ruthlessly exploiting the trust placed in him by senior Ferranti executives, as well as the privacy vested in the ISC Proxy Board. Even though Ball, Cooper and Scott had provided evidence that appeared to indicate some problems, not least with the 'hardwired' missile programme, as Guerin was continuing to move funds around his front companies, all seemed to be well. It was only when these sources started to dry up completely in March 1989 that Charles Scott really started to express serious concerns. Scott was especially concerned that two of the subcontractors, Elverton and Navarino, were no longer generating any cash on the Norinco contracts. It is useful to remember that both of these firms were registered in Panama, to which it now transpires Guerin would regularly make payments from his private banking accounts in Switzerland. Originally, a Belgian firm, Sestri Associates, had been the principal subcontractor on the mythical 'hardwired' missile programmes, but Guerin had transferred all of this work to Elverton and Navarino, front companies he set up at the end of 1986 to provide cover for his activities. When Alan Cooper eventually acquired copies of the contracts allocated to these Panamanian ventures towards the end of 1988, this immediately fuelled his suspicions further, because apart from slight differences in the sums involved, the KP and *Alpha* contracts were identical. Along with Charles Scott, he also worked out that Guerin had been using a payments loop that created the impression of a credible business, with his own money derived from accounts in Swiss, Panamanian and Bahamian banks creating the illusion that progress payments were flowing from the missile programmes, while subcontractors were paid for their work (using false invoices typed out by Guerin's associates in Lancaster), funnelling the money straight back into Guerin's bank accounts. As long as Ferranti International continued to receive the progress payments and they could pay the subcontractors' invoices, all was well; the problems started when these payments started to dwindle, then eventually stop altogether in the spring of 1989.

At the same time, another card Guerin could play in this game was to exploit the political repercussions of General Zia's assassination in August 1988, claiming in successive board meetings that this was the main reason why payments on the KP contract would appear to have stopped.[43] To verify this, Scott decided to investigate the situation for himself, setting up a meeting with the person Guerin claimed was the head of KP Industries. This person occupied an office in Rawalpindi, rather than the capital, Islamabad, from where he signed all contracts passed to him by Jim Guerin. In effect, though, and unbeknown to Charles Scott, this person was being paid by Guerin to cover up the fraudulent nature of the KP contract. Furthermore, he insisted on meeting Scott in Athens (Greece), rather than Rawalpindi, where he set up an office using $250,000 given to him by Guerin to rent space, equipment and support staff, giving the Ferranti deputy managing director the impression that he was meeting somebody with the status appropriate to a senior procurement officer. Although one might wonder why Scott did not make independent enquiries with senior Pakistani military officials in Islamabad, instead relying on contacts provided by Guerin, the Athens charade provided the reassurances required by Sir Derek and the Ferranti International board that the contracts existed and payments would be revived as soon as the political situation was clearer. Ball later quipped that Scott had been duped by what he described as 'Peter Sellers', alluding the way that the popular actor often imitated Pakistani people in films and on TV. It was a cruel jibe, but one that proved all too accurate.

Once again, the trust placed in Guerin had succeeded in securing the American valuable time in which to work out alternative means of covering up his earlier fraud. In March 1989, however, it was impossible to prevent the board from hearing about the continued problems with the delivery of *Hakim II* missiles. At this stage, it is pertinent to note that these missiles had been purchased for fitting to a French-made fighter, the Dassault *Mirage*, but as the aircraft manufacturer had been slow to perfect the appropriate software, Ivy had been unable to complete the development and trials stages. Dassault even refused to allow ISC Technologies to experiment with a *Mirage*, creating severe problems that could only be overcome if delivery, and hence payment, was further delayed. In typical style, Guerin assured the board that he had met UAE officials to confirm a clause in the contract that obliged the client to remunerate ISC for any delays caused by factors beyond their control.[44] Nevertheless, as Sir Derek reminded the board, this would have serious consequences for cashflow across the group, exacerbating what by then was becoming a serious problem for Ferranti International. We shall analyse the financial picture in Chapter 6, but it is clear that by March 1989 a considerable amount of evidence was being produced to bring into question the missile contracts that Guerin had brought to the table prior to and after the 1987 merger. How long he could rely on the board's patience on these matters was a matter of pure conjecture, forcing him to consider a radical solution.

It was at the end of this board meeting that Guerin revived the plan he had unofficially mooted in January 1989, to effect a leveraged buy-out worth $35 million of the former ISC operations.[45] He clearly realised that it would be only a matter of time before the frauds would become general knowledge. Sir Derek expressed his support in principle for this move, given that not only would it bring a healthy sum into the group's coffers, but also Guerin would continue to work closely with Ferranti International whenever possible. Guerin had already engaged the American financial conglomerate Drexel Burnham Lambert to consider his options, as well as negotiating a loan of $210 million with Citicorp that Parent Industries would use to purchase ISC from Ferranti International. Parent Industries was later prosecuted for fraudulently applying for this massive loan, because Guerin knew full well that ISC did not have the assets to cover such an amount.[46] Publicly, though, the buy-back was advocated as a means by which Guerin and his team of conspirators would be able to 'go back to where we started'. In essence, it was just another part of an elaborate cover-up, serving the invaluable purpose of keeping the Ferranti corporate team extremely busy. As we shall also see in the next chapter,[47] Guerin had actually transferred his ISC stock to his personal corporation, Parent Industries, in January 1987, shares that after the creation of Ferranti International were worth $67 million. This investment was then used in July 1988 to borrow $38 million from Citicorp in order to consolidate his borrowings and, more importantly, continue to fund the sham contracts. It is a deep irony that by this time Guerin was effectively using Ferranti International to fund his devious activities, compounding the hurt felt by many once this was discovered.

Detailed discussions about the buy-back were conducted in March–April 1989, during which all the options were considered by Charles Scott and reported back to the next board meeting.[48] By that time, as there was growing embarrassment over the Grand Jury investigations into Guerin's arms exports, the Ferranti International board was keen to distance itself from the American businessman. Moreover, Guerin was offering to take over all risks attached to the KP programme, as well as pay Ferranti International a fee worth 13% of all payments, providing the prospect of a significant injection of cash. While this would prevent the discovery of Guerin's fraudulent actions, it would also take the problematic contracts out of the company's balance sheet. In addition, as the Proxy Board would no longer exist, in organisational terms Sir Derek would then be able to bring all remaining parts of ISC into Ferranti divisions, create a single executive committee, and effect much greater control over the entire group. After listening to advice from senior executives at PMM, Baring Brothers and Herbert Smith (company lawyers), the board was consequently moving in favour of the deal, especially if Guerin agreed not to sell the significant tranche of Ferranti International shares he held for at least one year. Having agreed to remain outside of the meeting while the board discussed the issues, on being invited to return to his seat Guerin promised to meet all the commitments he had made privately to Sir Derek and publicly in the proposals tendered by Charles Scott.

With the board generally in favour of Guerin's offer, a three-man committee was established, composed of Sir Derek, Robin Broadley and Charles Scott, to pursue the negotiations. One should also add that a close associate of Guerin, Jim Fox, had just resigned from the board, ostensibly on the grounds of age and health.[49] By the time of the next board meeting, on 18 May, the triumvirate had clearly progressed matters to everybody's satisfaction, because it was reported that Guerin had left the company and moved all his assets into the holding company he had been running since the 1970s, Parent Industries.[50] In his place, Joe Zilligen was to take responsibility for reporting on ISC's US activities, while ISC Technologies was absorbed into FIDL. At the same time, Guerin issued a circular to all ISC employees explaining how the buy-back would work for those who would be transferred back into his business. Apart from outlining various aspects of the mission and business aims, the circular concluded by claiming that: 'Our future lies in our credibility in fulfilling our *commitments* to our customers ... maintenance of the reputation that we have established in the market area is *paramount* to ensure ongoing contracts in the future.'[51] In view of what had been happening within ISC from the mid-1970s, one can only regard such statements as total fiction.

While all this was going on, however, and of central importance to Ferranti International's finances, Charles Scott was compiling fresh corporate budgets that removed all of the fictitious missiles contracts from the corporate plan, minimising the possible impact total failure would have on performance. All seemed to be going well until at the next board meeting Sir Derek reported that the leveraged buy-out had failed,[52] largely because the banks refused to release former ISC assets which were after November 1987 fully accommodated in the much safer Ferranti accounts. This introduces a factor in the negotiations to which we shall return in Chapter 6, because the role played by the banks was to become central. More importantly, though, by May 1989 such deep suspicions had been aroused concerning both ISC's finances and the growing clamour for action against ISC for illegal arms trading that it was essential to terminate all links with the Lancaster entrepreneur. Consequently, Guerin and two of his associates (Fox and Ivy) were removed from the main board, and a single executive committee had been formed to bring the necessary level of co-ordination to the group's activities which had been sadly lacking over the previous eighteen months. Interestingly, Sir Derek had rejected Robin Broadley's suggestion, made as recently as January 1989, that the two executive committees ought to be combined into a single body.[53] As we also noted earlier, the board never met in that period to consider Alan Cooper's January 1989 report on ISC export licences, in spite of the company secretary's deep reservations about many aspects of these contracts. This revives our earlier discussion of one of the most serious weaknesses in the post-merger arrangements, because in allowing both the continued existence of the Proxy Board and a separate ISC executive committee, Ferranti had provided the vehicles on which Guerin could sustain the image of a viable business.

Of course, all of this activity was conducted under a heavy cloak of silence, with a press release issued on 8 May 1989 stating that even though Guerin and Ivy had resigned from the board: 'We are pleased that we shall continue to enjoy a close relationship in the future with Jim Guerin and Clyde Ivy.' It was also explained that FIDL would in future act as the principal link between Ferranti International and Parent Industries, while Guerin had promised not to sell any of his Ferranti International stock (amounting to 32 million shares) until July 1990. At the same time, the press release claimed that Parent Industries was going to buy back ISC Technologies and 60% of Electronic Systems Ltd (the Nigerian subsidiary), anticipating a satisfactory end to the negotiations. Removing Guerin, Fox and Ivy from the board, however, as well as creating a single executive committee, was the first major step in fathoming out exactly what had been happening at ISC, even if the discoveries were to prove extremely unpalatable for those who had spent the previous two years advocating the merger. As if to rub salt in the wounds inflicted on Ferranti International, in July 1989 it was reported that Guerin had sold 4,124,000 of his shares in the group, announcing publicly that he would offload his entire holding (of 31.8 million shares, accounting for 4.24% of the total capital) in the very near future, purportedly to fund the activities of Parent Industries.[54] Although it later transpired that Citicorp had been responsible for this share sale, in order to recoup some of the $38 million the bank had loaned to Guerin to fund the contract frauds, the board was extremely concerned at the impact this would have on the company's share price, which as we shall see in Chapter 6 (see Figure 6.1) was in any case falling precipitously at that time.

As well as the changes at board level, Sir Derek also took the opportunity to make two further modifications. Firstly, the company officially dropped the word 'Signal' in its name, becoming Ferranti International plc. Whether this could help to cast off the tarnish acquired as a result of the merger with ISC is highly doubtful, but it reflected a reality that he was keen to encourage. Secondly, in order to co-ordinate the Ferranti and ISC missile activities much more extensively, belatedly he brought all of the related subsidiaries into what was to be known as the Dynamics Group, wholly owned and managed by Ferranti International, with Ian Ball as MD. This Group combined FIDL, ISC Aerospace and those parts of ISC Technologies that had been involved in some aspects of the missile programmes, real or otherwise. Ball was instructed to take this action after yet another of his telephone conversations with Guerin on 8 July, during which it was made clear that the buy-back of ISC Technologies and ISC Aerospace was no longer possible, given the American's lack of funds. Poetically, Guerin was recorded as saying: 'I reckon this is a six-act play; we've seen Acts 1 and 2; Act 3 is just beginning.'[55] Whether others would have empathised with this rationalisation of what had and would be happening is highly unlikely, but it demonstrated to senior management at Ferranti International that Guerin was still trying to master-mind further manoeuvres, irrespective of the mounting evidence of a massive fraud.

Most importantly, having taken over these key subsidiaries with the ISC Group Ball was then able to acquire all of the surviving documentation – it later transpired that some had been shredded by Guerin and some colleagues – and summon for interview key individuals who in the past had hidden behind the customer confidentiality demands that Guerin had insisted on since negotiating the merger. It was at this stage that he discovered not only the original 1984 PGM contract with the UAE, but also some of the 'hardwired' subcontracts with the likes of Elverton and Damarall that had been signed well before the genuine PGM contracts agreed in April 1986. In his search for the full KP contract, which with technical specifications, subcontracts, delivery and installation details should have filled ten filing drawers, he found only a flimsy set of paperwork that had been 'childishly contrived'.[56] Moreover, just one person, Larry Resch, was in charge of the programme, compared to what Ball estimated would be a team of at least thirty highly qualified engineers. As Ball concluded from this foray into the bowels of ISC, 'the documentation I have seen, ostensibly in support of these contracts, and the circumstances of the "signing" of these contracts, should have caused any reasonably diligent auditing body to ask more searching questions, at least as early as 1985'.[57] This raises the vital question about how long Guerin was able to operate undetected by professionals who supposedly had privileged access to this documentation from the early days of the fraud.

While Ball was burrowing away in the filing cabinets and company safes at

ISC subsidiaries, and Alan Cooper was pursuing his own investigations, it is still fair to say that the summer of 1989 was still spent in considerable uncertainty, largely because the board was unable to ascertain the definitive legality of the contracts ISC had reported in its books prior to and after the merger. When Guerin had withdrawn from Ferranti International, the board even gave him an incentive contract to secure a regular cashflow from the KP contract, on the grounds that he knew the people involved in the procurement agency. Of course, the board was unaware of just how far Guerin had gone in bribing individuals to impersonate procurement officials, while the incentive contract provided him with another opportunity to shuffle money from his own private accounts in Switzerland and the Bahamas, blinding Ferranti International management to the crisis which was about to unfold. Just prior to Guerin's departure from the Ferranti International board, Greg Mansker provided Ian Ball with a copy of the memo from Wayne Radcliffe, Guerin's close associate, requesting advice on how ISC Technologies could 'invent' the sale of the Norinco stock that did not exist. Ken Goodwin, finance director at FIDL and Ian Ball's closest advisor, was also making enquiries into why the cashflow from Elverton and Navarino had stopped, only to discover that the addresses provided by Guerin on the invoices were false. These companies had actually been wound up by July 1989, arousing even greater suspicion across Ferranti International, while the reluctance of Guerin to provide any further information on the lack of any cashflow only deepened the concerns already expressed by Ball, Shepherd, Cooper and Scott.

By the summer of 1989, it was consequently becoming increasingly clear to senior Ferranti International executives that the KP and Alpha contracts were at best at a very early stage of development, and at worst a total fiction. Again, one can question why in view of what had been discovered by Cooper and Ball since the summer of 1988 that it took the board so long to act decisively. Ironically, after listening to Guerin's vacuous explanations, they could justify their caution on the grounds that precipitate action might kill off the contracts altogether, given the residue of trust which was still placed in Guerin. Nevertheless, Ball and Cooper continued their forensic analysis of both the contracts and the 'hardwired' technology that seemed to underpin KP and *Alpha*. This involved detailed questioning of not just Greg Mansker, Guerin's contracts lawyer, but also Wayne Ratcliffe and Stu Pindell. These interviews allowed Ball and Cooper to put the final pieces of the Guerin jigsaw together.

In August 1989, Charles Scott was also instructed by the board to make a second visit to Pakistan, to seek out incontrovertible evidence on the contracts. By that time, as Guerin was no longer bribing the alleged procurement official who had set up the false office in Athens to divert Ferranti International investigations, Scott was able to meet key civil servants, all of whom denied that any order for missiles had been placed with ISC. The MoD had also by then informed Sir Derek of some FBI inquiries into embargo-breaking by the American parts of ISC, news which prompted him to tackle Guerin once again. There followed a crucial series of board meetings between 6 and 10 September, to be described in greater detail in Chapter 6,[58] when the chairman formally informed the board that Guerin had finally admitted to fraud. By that time, of course, most were convinced that something serious was amiss, but there was general incredulity at the magnitude of Guerin's malfeasance. The 10 September board meeting was actually held at Barings Bank, when it was decided that an official announcement would have to be made, otherwise the board would have been knowingly trading when the firm was insolvent.

It is hard to imagine the atmosphere at that 10 September board meeting, as all the directors mused over the implications of the discovery. Some, like Joe Zilligen of ISC European Technologies, refused to believe that Guerin had perpetrated such an enormous fraud. Indeed, he had countered Ian Ball's accusations in July 1989 about Guerin's activities by arguing that the real cause of the group's financial woes was the overvaluation of computer systems stock in Wythenshawe. While there had been some serious problems with computer systems stock, however,[59] Ball retorted aggressively by arguing that 'there was a vast difference between taking an optimistic view of stock valuation and actually inventing contracts'.[60] It was by then crystal clear to Ball, after his conversations with Mansker, Ratcliffe and Pindell, that Guerin had created the KP and *Alpha* contracts to boost the size and profitability of ISC, using $8.5 million of the PGM down-payment provided by the UAE to convince auditors and Ferranti management that real cash was being generated. The extensive use of front companies as subcontractors, all controlled by Guerin and his most intimate of advisors, helped to cement the view that something credible was being built as a basis for FIDL's future. A puzzling feature of all this is why Guerin decided to claim that the KP and *Alpha* missiles would be 'hardwired', rather than using the modular design used on PGM, because when this became public knowledge across FIDL it immediately aroused deep suspicions, given that Ian Ball knew full well that the missile engineering team was fully committed to the latter. Another mistake was the inclusion of rocket motors in the 'hardwired' stock suppos-edly sold to Norinco, at the time of the 'acquisition accountancy' discussions with Zilligen in June 1988. The problem here was that the PGM rocket motors were at exactly the same time being bought from Norinco, leading Wayne Radcliffe to delete these from the second form of the contract seen by Mansker. However, only by August 1989 was all of this evidence available in such a form and matched up against other documents and the cashflow problems, preventing the board from coming to a definitive conclusion until

September. For example, they were unaware that for much of 1988 and the early months of 1989, Stu Pindell's main job for Guerin was inventing invoices from bogus subcontractors and writing fictitious progress reports on the KP and *Alpha* programmes.[61]

To the board as a whole, though, it would have been patently obvious that they had a duty to make a public announcement, otherwise they could have been regarded as having been a party to the crimes uncovered. Unfortunately, the annual report for 1988–89 had already been published in August, disclosing figures based on the financial picture available to the accountants at that time. This report had noted that, even though the pre-tax profits had fallen to £55.8 million (from £68 million in 1987–88), the profit attributable to shareholders had been given as £29.3 million (as opposed to £24.3 million in 1987–8) because extraordinary charges were much lower. Indeed, even though the UK defence and computer systems markets were proving difficult, with an order book supposedly totalling £1.6 billion and turnover increasing to £1.05 billion (compared to £822.1 million in 1987–88), Ferranti International seemed well set to maintain the profit levels recorded during the 1980s. This relatively rosy picture was, however, dashed completely at the company's AGM on 12 September, when the annual report posted on 11 August was withdrawn, trading in Ferranti International shares was suspended and the meeting postponed until Coopers & Lybrand had completed a full investigation. This was followed by a letter issued on 29 September, when the chairman wrote to all shareholders concerning the discovery of some suspect contracts. By the time a revised set of accounts had been announced on 16 November, the full scale of the disaster had become public knowledge.

4.4 Conclusions

While we must defer until Chapter 6 a full financial analysis of the financial crisis that in 1989 had struck Ferranti International, it was patently clear to all within the business and many outside observers that Guerin had done enormous damage to what since the mid-1970s had been a sound business. It is consequently essential at this stage to try to understand why Guerin perpetrated these crimes, misleading both Ferranti executives and highly qualified and experienced City professionals into believing that the ISC balance sheet was credible and promising.

A recurring feature of the views expressed by most contemporaries is that Guerin did not set out to commit fraud on this scale. Although in a moment of weakness he admitted to a reporter that in the early days of ISC he was willing to 'beg, steal or borrow' in order to put the business on a sound footing after its establishment in 1971,[62] this was mere hyperbole used to demonstrate that he had worked extremely hard to bring in contracts and generate profits. Some would describe this as a manifestation of his entrepreneurial instincts, because in using some outhouses linked to his own house he was acting out the classic start-up phase of an embryonic business. On the other hand, it was this desperation to succeed that in 1974 drove him to accept contracts from the US intelligence community, bringing him into contact with a world that was not only based on secrecy, but also engendered unconventional business practices. Working closely with Admiral Inman,[63] Guerin was absorbed into this culture, learning techniques that allowed him to build ISC through covert and illegal means. Having been allowed to set up front companies to avoid such niceties as export licences, it almost became second nature to circumvent the law, given that the bulk of his firm's business up to the early 1980s was covert, involving countries that were on the United Nations embargo list. Registering ISC on the London Stock Exchange in 1982 also provided the cover required for such activities, given that British corporate law permitted a lower level of revelation than its US counterpart. This also allowed Guerin access to a substantial pool of finance, because shareholders were persuaded to buy ISC shares, thereby providing the funds he could use to support both his philanthropic and business activities.

As we saw in Chapter 2, by the early 1980s Guerin was a veritable pillar of his home-town business community, Lancaster, Penn., where he distributed considerable sums to cultural and educational institutions, as well as becoming a significant employer in his own right.[64] This work also gave him an extremely loyal following, evidence of which was the reply Rev. Robert Bistline gave to a journalist when asked whether he was aware of Guerin's alleged criminality: 'Hogwash. You can put that in your newspaper.' As Rev. Bistline had been minister at Guerin's Church of God in Landisville, he was as close as most people to the Lancaster entrepreneur and refused to believe that he was anything other than 'a good man'.[65] Another Lancaster inhabitant was reported as saying in September 1989 that if the accusations against Guerin were correct, then: 'It would be like catching the Pope with his hands in the till.'[66] At the same time, it is fair to point out that Guerin was also on what might be described as the 'City treadmill', namely, he was obliged to assure his shareholders that ISC was capable of continuing to generate increased profits, or they would sell them to a potential predator. In addition, of course, even though British corporate law was relatively more lax, it was still essential to convince auditors that the balance sheet was credible, with contracts that actually existed. In this context, Guerin decided to invent export contracts that ostensibly appeared to offer rich potential, using the cash generated from one programme to persuade external observers that cashflow was assured. The ultimate prize, of course, was a merger with a profitable firm, because as long as he could persuade its management to allow him to continue to run various parts of his former business as if nothing had changed, this would bring in even greater wealth (by converting his ISC shares into those of the new partner). Although he was still faced with the challenge of convincing auditors and senior managers that the contracts existed, such was the image he had built up by the mid-1980s, as both an entrepreneur and philanthropist, that it seemed impossible he could be guilty of any crimes.

There was consequently a momentum factor involved in this scenario, a force that was building through the 1970s and 1980s as he continued to work directly with the US intelligence services in South Africa and the Middle East, culminating in the invention of substantial missile contracts for the purposes of generating even greater personal wealth. By imitating the covert activities and artefacts perpetrated by the intelligence community – front companies and bank accounts in countries such as Switzerland, Panama and the Bahamas, not to mention a conviction that the end justifies the means – Guerin convinced himself that he would always be the victor. How could anybody believe that such a person could commit such crimes? Why would Ferranti International executives not accept the validity of the missile contracts laid out in full before both auditors and colleagues? How would these same colleagues be able to discover that so-called Pakistani procurement officials were merely pawns in the game Guerin had been playing with such devastating effect for years? This bravado was one of the key reasons why it took Ferranti International executives so long to put all of the jigsaw pieces together and see the full picture. One should also stress that the executive team was heavily engaged in the process of combining two very different businesses, not to mention the enormous challenges associated with reviving divisions such as naval systems and telecommunications. In this context, it is clear that Guerin relied on the trust he had built up to compensate for any inconsistencies in what was either said or written down in the flimsy contract documentation.

It was only when Guerin's payments loop started to fall apart in the spring of 1989 that the charade became apparent. Although he used General Zia's assassination as the excuse to explain a cessation in payments on the KP contract, by that time it was becoming glaringly obvious to a small group of Ferranti International executives that something was fundamentally wrong. This payments loop – involving Guerin's private bank accounts in Switzerland, Panama and The Bahamas, mythical subcontractors in Panama, and the dubious missile contracts – was entirely reliant on money eventually flowing into Ferranti International, something which by March 1989 was just not happening; indeed, would never happen. His devious manoeuvre to buy back parts of ISC would have worked had the banks not resisted, forcing Guerin to admit some of his subterfuge to Sir Derek in May 1989. Even then, however, he was promising to pursue the KP contract and ensure that

Ferranti International received its anticipated profit, demonstrating that he was by then desperate to avoid total disclosure.

In outlining this chain of events, it is evident that as a clever manipulator Guerin succeeded in preventing Ferranti International executives from putting all of the jigsaw pieces together for what could well be regarded as an inordinately long period. As we have just noted, though, the trust factor was a major hindrance, while the organisational devices of separate ISC Proxy Board and executive committee allowed Guerin to prevent access to crucial documents, even if they existed at all. The Ferranti board had been well and truly duped, as had the auditors who were charged with the task of examining ISC's balance sheet. Although the ICAEW's 1993–6 investigations revealed that PMM were simply 'among those comprehensively deceived by a fraud which was designed and executed with extraordinary care and skill',[67] this was cold comfort to the many thousands of employees and shareholders who depended on Ferranti International for their livelihood. One might also add that the ICAEW was not the only body impressed by the scale of Guerin's web of intrigue, because a senior official in the US Internal Revenue Service, Gary H. Matthews, noted that: 'This is a classic case of incomprehensible fraud. Our agents were, frankly, stunned by the enormity of it.'[68] This could well help to explain why it was September 1989 before Ferranti executives unravelled the fraud, given the way Guerin had wrapped up each stage of it into a dense tissue of lies and deceptions. In the next chapter, we shall go on to examine the financial implications of these actions, as well as the various rescue packages devised by successive Ferranti International MDs, laying out in cold detail how Guerin had effectively ripped the heart out of the firm.

The conclusion to this chapter must consequently come back to our earlier discussion of merger synergies, because the Ferranti-ISC combination provides some deep insights into the lessons other managements might learn when engaging in this kind of activity. In the first place, reflecting the common problem with British mergers, there was a complete failure to integrate ISC into the Ferranti organisational structure, with Guerin being allowed to continue running his Proxy Board and a separate ISC executive committee. While the Ferranti International board of directors was charged with the task of making all decisions on strategy, resource allocation and legal matters, Guerin was steadfastly able to resist requests for essential information concerning various missile contracts, on the grounds of 'secrecy' or 'confidentiality'. Secondly, apart from the aptly named FIDL, there was hardly any integration of activities or rationalisation of capacity. This highlights the third defect, namely, a failure to exploit what in 1987 were heralded as the complementarities of linking ISC's marketing skills and the Ferranti engineering base; this just never happened. Consequently, as a direct result of these weaknesses Guerin was not only able to fool both Ferranti management and PMM auditors into believing that ISC was a financially sound business, but also hide his fraud for almost two years after the merger, resulting in the dire financial disaster to be outlined in the next chapter. While the whole point of merger and acquisition strategies is to achieve synergy, colloquially known as '2+2=5', in the Ferranti-ISC case it is difficult even to say that a '3' was achieved; many would argue that the end-result was '0', given the sad demise of Ferranti just over four years after trading in its shares were suspended in September 1989.

Notes

1 See above, pp. 60–1, for an analysis of this issue.
2 FBM 1, 25 Nov 1987.
3 FBM 3, 25 Nov 1987.
4 FBM 1, 25 Nov 1987. While the board minutes do not record this chain of events, I am assured by several sources that this was how Alun-Jones informed Basil of his demotion.
5 FBM 18, 25 Nov 1987.
6 FBM 4, 25 Nov 1987.
7 The board took until January 1987 before it decided on the company name, Ferranti International Signal plc. FBM 6, 26 Jan 1988.
8 FBM 6, 14 Dec 1987.
9 Ibid.
10 This section is based on reports in FN, Dec 1987.
11 See Wilson *British Business History*, pp. 208–11.
12 FN, Dec 1987.
13 FBM 7, 14 Dec 1987; 9, 26 Jan 1987; 6, 17 March 1988; 7, 11 May 1988; 5, 29 June 1998.
14 FBM 7, 14 Dec 1987.
15 FBM, 26 Jan 1987.
16 FN, Feb 1987.
17 See above, pp. 53–5.
18 See Vol. 1, pp. 399–417.
19 See Vol. 1, pp. 417–29.
20 See above, pp.44–6.
21 Ball FBI Report, and interviews with Ian Ball and Alan Cooper.
22 See Chapter 2, pp. 38–40, for a description of this work.
23 This meeting is recorded in a memo that Sir Derek sent to Alan Shepherd, Alan Cooper and Jim Guerin on 21 July 1988.
24 FBM 8, 7 Sept 1988.
25 Ball FBI Report.
26 See above, pp. 36–40.
27 Interview with Charles Scott.
28 This section is based on a report that Ian Ball wrote for the FBI in 1990, as part of the US investigations into Guerin's activities, hereafter referred to as 'Ball FBI Report'.

29 The term 'acquisition accountancy' first came up at board discussions in May 1988. FBM 4, 11 May 1988.
30 FBM 4, 29 June 1988.
31 See above, pp. 61–5, for a discussion of the Norinco link.
32 See earlier for Ball's initial views on ISC technical competencies, pp. 205–8.
33 See pp. 56–7.
34 FBM 5, 21 Nov 1988.
35 *Financial Times*, 16 Jan 1990.
36 FBM 6, 21 Nov 1987.
37 See above, pp. 33–4, for more information on Chem-Con and James B. Christian.
38 FBM 17, 21 Nov 1987.
39 Ball FBI Report.
40 See also pp. 165–7. for further insights into these activities, when the US courts started their actions against Guerin and his co-conspirators.
41 Interview with Dr Shepherd.
42 Court records.
43 FBM 17, 20 Nov 1987; 7, 11 Jan 1989.
44 FBM 6, 15 March 1989.
45 FBM 18, 15 March 1989.
46 *Financial Times*, 29 Aug 1990.
47 See below, pp. 178–80.
48 FBM 3, 27 April 1989.
49 FBM 1, 27 April 1989.
50 FBM 1, 18 May 1989. See above, pp. 138–40, for a description of Parent Industries' activities.
51 'The new company', Circular from J. Guerin to All New ISC (Private Company) Employees, 9 May 1989.
52 FBM 1, 19 June 1989.
53 FBM 13, 11 Jan 1987.
54 FBM 3, 5 July 1989.
55 Ian Ball's personal notes, 8 July 1989.
56 Ball FBI Report.
57 Ibid.
58 See below, pp. 168–70.
59 See later, pp. 165–80.
60 Ball FBI Report.
61 Court records.
62 Interview in *Independent on Sunday*, 16 June 1991.
63 Court records.
64 See above, pp. 32–6.
65 *Philadelphia Inquirer*, 13 Sept 1991.
66 *The Observer*, 24 Sept 1989.
67 Chance Report.
68 Reported in *Lancaster New Era*, 7 Nov 1991.

Investigations and court cases

THE DECISION TO suspend trading in Ferranti International shares at the AGM on 12 September 1989 was the kind of news story that would have extensive ramifications both within and outside the firm as a wide range of stakeholders and interested parties absorbed its implications. For the 26,000 employees, of course, nothing could have been worse than an announcement that seemed to place in jeopardy a large proportion of those jobs, while for investors who had sunk significant sums into the equity – including several thousand employees who thought they were building up a nice nest-egg for their retirements – could only wait for trading to be restored and a significant reduction in the value of their holdings. Similarly, customers were stunned at the news, not least the MoD officials who for many decades had placed considerable faith in Ferranti equipment. With the debate raging over who would supply key components to the *Tornado* programme, not to mention considerable consternation about the future of the UK defence budget as the Cold War seemed to be coming to an end, the firm's recovery prospects were under intense scrutiny. All of these factors will be analysed in detail in the next chapter, because before we can consider the corporate ramifications of the Guerin Scandal, it is first of all essential to understand what happened to the instigator and his co-conspirators. This chapter will consequently focus on the multi-agency investigation into Jim Guerin's activities that was building up substantial momentum from the summer of 1989, culminating in a succession of court cases that shocked many observers, especially once the state's role was revealed. Returning to a theme examined at the end of the last chapter, it is indicative of the scale and complicated nature of Guerin's fraud that as late as 2012 investigators were still searching for the money he squirrelled away as a result of his covert trading and fraudulent activities. Even though in 1991 James Guerin was jailed for a variety of crimes, including money-laundering through front companies, the fine details of all the fraudulent deals, arming embargoed nations and duping financiers and business executives into supporting ISC will probably never emerge. Furthermore, the trial of Clyde Ivy was suspended seven times, preventing the disclosure of crucial documents, while others proved to be equally evasive. Guerin has certainly never been completely open on these issues, a fact that explains why he was obliged to serve much of his fifteen-year sentence, obliging us to hypothesise about the career of a man who remains an enigma to all but his closest family and confidantes.

Before embarking on this analysis, however, it is important to explain why although ISC was registered in the UK and Ferranti International plc as the wronged party was British, all of the prosecutions arising from the Guerin Scandal were in American courts. Of course, several British agencies were involved in the investigations, including Scotland Yard's Serious Fraud Squad, HM Customs & Excise, and the Inland Revenue, as well as Ferranti International executives and accountants from Coopers & Lybrand and Grant Thornton. British courts also granted Ferranti International various writs to sue Guerin and key ISC employees for the amounts allegedly siphoned off since 1987. Nevertheless, as Guerin committed the bulk of his crimes either from Lancaster, Penn., or through his US-based subsidiaries, it was deemed essential that he should be prosecuted in American courts, not least because extradition proceedings were notoriously difficult to conduct. The US process was initiated by swearing in a Grand Jury, in this case in Philadelphia, an institution that in the American system is responsible for assessing whether a person or corporation can be charged with criminal offences. This Grand Jury, which is chosen from the same pool that provides trial juries, but only sits when evidence is presented by the investigating bodies, would in the Guerin case be busy from the summer of 1989 through to when formal charges were laid in November 1990. These charges were produced by a multi-agency team headed by Assistant US Attorney of the Eastern District headquarters in Philadelphia, Robert Goldman, and included representatives of the FBI, Internal Revenue Service, US Customs Service, and the Pentagon's Criminal Investigative Services. Goldman also consulted HM Customs & Excise and Scotland Yard's Serious Fraud Squad, but as we shall see later the US agencies were responsible for the bulk of the detective work and would lead the prosecution of Guerin and his closest colleagues, resulting in a plethora of court cases and legal decisions. Given the highly intricate nature of Guerin's business dealings, it was a brilliantly conceived and implemented investigation that provided even deeper insights into activities that had obviated international law for fifteen years.

5.1 Mounting evidence

While for good reason it had taken Ferranti International executives over two years to act decisively on mounting fears that Guerin had duped them into buying ISC, once trading in the firm's shares had been suspended on 12

September 1989 deep investigations by a host of agencies and reporters were initiated. By the end of that week, as a result of extensive briefings given to journalists in leading newspapers, reports were already being disseminated about what Guerin had done to the company's balance sheet. Figures ranging between £150 million[1] and $300 million[2] were bandied about, along with partial comments on ISC's missile exports to Pakistan, the UAE and China. As we shall see in the next chapter, this was part of the debate relating to the firm's future, because few were able to say with confidence that Ferranti International could withstand this scale of loss and survive as an independent body. Crucially as far as this chapter is concerned, though, while within Ferranti International Alan Cooper, Ian Ball and Charles Scott had by then gained an extremely good idea about what Guerin and his co-conspirators had been up to, it was now a matter of substantiating the accusations and, more importantly, recouping as much of the money as possible that had been siphoned off into bank accounts all over the world. It was the latter, of course, that was going to prove to be an impossibly arduous task, providing investigators and the courts with steady business for many years. To this day, Ferranti International investors and pensioners have been deprived of tens of millions of dollars, begging important questions about both Guerin's banking habits and the ability of certain countries to refuse access to accounts that are palpably full of ill-gotten gains. At the same time, as a result of the detective work conducted by several agencies on both sides of the Atlantic, detailed evidence of the nature and extent of Guerin's malfeasance was made available, resulting in a succession of court cases that meted out punishments of varying severity.

Of course, while the multi-agency investigations only moved into gear after 12 September, it is clear that Guerin and the Ferranti International board had been made aware of enquiries into ISC much earlier in the year. Indeed, the Ferranti International board had been informed as early as November 1988 that Guerin and ISC were going to be investigated by a Grand Jury over illegal arms shipments to Libya, Iran, Iraq and South Africa.[3] By that time, Alan Cooper had also discovered that ISC had been responsible for supplying highly sophisticated sonar equipment to South Africa, while a little later Clyde Ivy had unsuccessfully tried to persuade Ian Ball to undertake work with South Africa's Armscor on the importation of a surveillance system known as *Seeker* which would be sold on to the UAE. Although as we saw in the last chapter Guerin had been able to persuade his fellow-directors that there was no substance behind the Grand Jury investigations, placing on record a false statement that ISC had never sold military systems to South Africa,[4] by February 1989 Ball had persuaded Sir Derek Alun-Jones to make it official corporate policy that the firm would never trade with this embargoed country. Needless to say, though, as Guerin and Ivy continued to work with South African subcontractors on various missile programmes, the ISC chief executive completely ignored this ruling, providing the Grand Jury with an even greater incentive to sustain its investigations. Of course, these investigations would only result in prosecutions in 1991, but as we shall see later leaks from the Grand Jury allowed various newspapers to make startling revelations in September and October 1989 that were the prelude to even more dramatic stories involving Guerin and his confidantes.[5]

In addition to these Grand Jury investigations, more detail on which we shall reveal in the next section, another source of disturbing stories about Guerin was the trial of James B. Christian, the former president of United Chem-Con, the corporation the two of them had established in 1978 as a vehicle to exploit Defense Department policies aimed at placing contracts with minority-owned enterprises.[6] As we saw in Chapter 3, by 1987 Chem-Con had been closed down, directly as a result of the arrest of Christian and his vice-president (and Guerin's brother-in-law), Carl Jacobson, on charges relating to defrauding the government and the Meridian Bank of $16 million and bribing Navy purchasing officials.[7] These revelations were a part of the US government's *Ill-Wind* investigations into bribery of Pentagon officials, involving not only Chem-Con, but also the Marquadt subsidiary of ISC, fuelling further the growing belief that Guerin's business activities deserved much closer public scrutiny. It was also well-known that Guerin had tried to help his brother-in-law to avoid prosecution by arranging a clandestine flight to Chile, using his arms-trading partner, Carlos Cardoen, as the conduit. By the time Christian had been convicted in June 1989, however, Jacobson had been persuaded to return to the US, when he admitted his role in bribing US Navy officials to allocate contracts to Chem-Con and another firm, Wedtech. Christian was also willing to plead guilty to these charges, but at his arraignment and continuously over the following three years he sensationally accused his former mentor, Jim Guerin, of 'calling all the shots'.[8] Guerin's attorney, Joseph A. Tate, was instructed by his client to reject all of these insinuations, later arguing that: 'It boggles the imagination that Mr Guerin, who loaned and lost over $9 million to Mr Christian, is now the bad guy. If anyone was victimized, it was Mr Guerin.'[9] Of course, Guerin had chosen extremely wisely in hiring Tate to defend him. Described as the 'smartest guy in law school' at Villanova University, Tate's first job was in the anti-trust division of the US Justice Department, where he learned a good deal about the craft of prosecuting corporations, expertise he was later to put to good use in private practice in the 1970s, when he defended American giants such as RAC, General Electric and AT&T. By the 1990s, Tate was a partner at Dechert, one of the leading American corporate law firms, providing Guerin with all the legal support he would undoubtedly require over the following years.[10]

Of course, there is no surviving evidence that Guerin lost anything as a result of his links with Chem-Con; indeed, the converse is probably the case. Christian and Jacobson were eventually convicted on 6 June 1989, receiving sentences of, respectively, six years and two months (suspended for three years), while the former's accusations of extensive Guerin involvement in Chem-Con's illegal activities further fanned the flames that were by then licking at the ISC founder's boots. Christian later appealed against his sentence, partly on the grounds that it was discriminatory when compared to the relatively light penalty imposed on the white Jacobson, but mainly because he had provided the authorities with extensive insights into Guerin's business affairs. As he stated to one newspaper: 'I'm just a black, convicted felon trying to regain credibility, and the scales [of justice] don't tip the same for each, so I just have to do what I can, and hope that people will now believe that what I'm trying to do is genuine.'[11] Amongst the accusations he levelled against Guerin were that ISC drained Chem-Con of all its cash reserves just prior to the bankruptcy of June 1987, in order to support Guerin's arms-trading activities, while as we saw in Chapter 3 the transfer of the *Pestolite* business in 1982 had been effected as a means of enhancing ISC's profitabil-ity during the London flotation.[12] Crucially, Christian claims that it was Guerin who allegedly persuaded him to dispense illegal gifts and bribes to US Navy officials, as well as submitting illegal corporate accounts and attempting to defraud Meridian Bank of up to $16 million. Of course, Guerin denied all of these accusations, both in June 1989 and after Christian's appeal in March 1990, but when combined with the Grand Jury investigations into ISC's South African links it was clear to the authorities that something was seriously amiss at the Lancaster business. Christian was also released early from his six-year prison sentence, leaving the Camp Hill State Correction Institution on 24 July 1991, after serving less than two years. This reflected the widespread belief that his claims against Guerin had been accurate, leading him to sue Guerin for $93 million in damages.[13]

Not only was Guerin being accused by business associates such as James B. Christian of nefarious dealings, another sign that all was not well in ISC was provided by the fall-out with the corporation's chief counsel, William Clark. Clark had joined ISC in 1983, moving from his Washington law practice to Lancaster in order to oversee the expanding firm's legal work as a vice-president of ISC. By the beginning of 1989, however, his health had deteriorated to such an extent that he had decided to terminate the ISC contract and return to private practice. Apparently, such had been the pressures imposed on Clark by his boss, not least in obliging him to draw up contracts for work that just did not exist, that he could not continue to work for ISC. There were even hints that Guerin had threatened to sack Clark unless he completed all the dubious legal work necessary on the covert and fraudulent arms contracts. Clark had also been given evidence by two ISC executives, James Deitsch (financial controller of ISC Inc) and Michael Liddick (treasurer of ISC Inc), that Guerin was overstating the results on various contracts which did not appear to exist.[14] This had confirmed Clark's mounting suspicions that ISC accounts contained details that were increasingly difficult to substantiate, leading him to decide that it would be dangerous to continue working for the Lancaster corporation.

An agreement was negotiated in March 1989 between Guerin and Clark which would have given the latter $2 million, including $331,902 in unpaid salary and compensation for 'damages' to his personal and professional reputation, on condition that he would not reveal any details of his ISC career. However, no doubt because by that time he was running short of money, by June Guerin had only paid Clark $1 million, forcing the latter on 5 July to file a lawsuit against his former boss for $2.75 million. As this lawsuit also froze all of Guerin's assets, including those of his holding company, Parent Industries Inc, he was forced to deposit $2 million in an escrow account with the court, in order to resume trading. At the same time, Guerin also accused Clark of coercion and extortion, claiming that he had taped their conversations in order to protect ISC against false accusations. This forced the authorities to initiate further investigations into the situation, but undeterred by these delaying tactics on 9 January 1990 Clark sued Guerin for allegedly violating Delaware wiretapping law, forcing the latter to break cover for the first time since Ferranti International had suspended its shares.[15] By this time, of course, Guerin had also been accused publicly of violating US arms embargoes, money laundering and fraud, resulting in extensive interest in the wiretapping case. Not surprisingly, though, in a twelve-hour deposition Guerin exercised his Fifth Amendment right not to incriminate himself on no less than ninety occasions during Clark's inquisition. He also refused to answer any questions fired at him by British and American journalists waiting eagerly at the court entrance, resulting in a wide sense of frustration that was compounded by the court's decision to undertake further investigations.

It is clear that the Clark-Guerin case proved to be a vital stage in the multi-agency search for the truth behind ISC's activities, because the corporation's senior internal counsel proved to be an invaluable source of information for the investigating team. Even though the US Attorney's Office secured a federal court order freezing the $2 million deposited by Guerin, on the grounds that this money could have been earned illegally, Clark continued to co-operate with the authorities. The US Attorney was obliged to seek an extension of this freezing order in May 1990, during which FBI special agent Gerard O'Callaghan was able to confirm that Clark had provided intimate insights into the way Guerin had run ISC, even after the Ferranti merger. It was revealed, for example, that Clark had even replaced documents revealing illegal activities that Guerin and Michael Peck (president of Parent Industries Inc) had shredded. Some of these documents confirmed the claims made by James B. Christian concerning the way in which Guerin had used Chem-Con as a cover for fraudulent activities, while others assisted the Grand Jury investigations into ISC's trade with South Africa. More of Clark's revelations will also be discussed later in this chapter, when the full extent of the multi-agency report is examined, because his evidence did indeed prove crucial.

In spite of his total co-operation with the authorities, however, Clark was never able to recoup the money he claimed Guerin owed him. There were two reasons behind this failure: firstly, the court ruled that the money had probably been earned illegally; and secondly, when in February 1991 Ferranti International revealed the tapes Guerin had made of his March 1989 conversations with Clark, it was clear that the latter had been blackmailing his boss. Ferranti International, of course, was keen to secure as much of Guerin's money as possible, leading them to provide complete transcripts of the Clark-Guerin conversations in order to persuade the court that the $2 million should be paid over to the company. The transcripts revealed that Clark had created 'packages' of ISC documents that provided stark evidence of its illegal activities. As these 'packages' had been secreted away in various international locations, Clark promised that as soon as Guerin had paid over the full amount owed he would 'take a trip, and I don't mean a vacation trip .. And when I get back from that trip, I will tell you that I have been to certain places, and I have recovered the packages that are there, and I have destroyed them. I will take a book of matches and they will be done away with'.[16] Clark naturally challenged the legality of the tapes as evidence, because they had been acquired through an illegal wiretapping exercise, as well as claiming that Guerin had tampered with them. Ferranti International, however, had been careful enough to ask the FBI crime laboratory to check for any evidence of tampering, while the court ruled that the tapes did not contravene Delaware's wiretapping laws, ensuring that Clark was unable to win his case.

Coming at the same time that the ABC News show *20/20* had run an eleven-minute item entitled 'Made in America', explaining how Iraq had been supplied with cluster-bomb technology via Carlos Cardoen and ISC, the Clark-Guerin case provided further confirmation that the Lancaster-based corporation had been involved in activities of a highly dubious nature. Of course, nobody expressed much sympathy for Clark, especially as he had received $1 million from Guerin in June 1989, not to mention his role within ISC during the key years 1983–89 when all of the mythical missile contracts had been concocted. The employees and shareholders of Ferranti International were also extremely anxious to secure as much liquidity as possible in order to shore up the accounting 'hole' created by these contracts.

This case was strengthened by evidence from a US Inland Revenue Service official, who stated in court that at least $1.3 million of the $2 million deposited by Guerin in an escrow account had been derived from illegal trading, while the other $700,000 was illegally diverted from an ISC subsidiary.[17] The net was closing in on Guerin, while Clark was left to struggle on with his partial compensation package.

5.2 Grand Jury and multi-agency investigations

Having outlined some of the US investigations into Guerin's affairs that were being conducted from the end of 1988, it is now necessary to examine how the multi-agency team put together the case that would eventually result in his incarceration. Of course, this still leaves unanswered a host of questions discussed over the course of the last two chapters, especially those relating to the reasons why Ferranti plc merged with ISC, the management structure adopted after the merger, and the time taken to discover contractual infelicities. Indeed, it is apparent that in the flurry of legal activity few were willing to question the Ferranti board's culpability, especially once Sir Derek Alun-Jones was persuaded to stand down as executive chairman at the beginning of 1990, thereby deflecting all of the attention on to Guerin and ISC. As we have also already noted, while various British agencies and Ferranti International executives contributed to the investigations, the multi-agency team headed by Robert Goldman (Assistant US Attorney of the Eastern District headquarters in Philadelphia), and including representatives of the FBI, Internal Revenue Service, US Customs Service, and the Pentagon's Criminal Investigative Services, was primarily responsible for bringing Guerin and his co-conspirators to justice. They were also substantially assisted by the Grand Jury investigations into ISC's South African links that had been going on since the end of 1988, accumulating evidence that was leaked to newspapers in October 1989, just as the business and political worlds were trying to absorb the implications of Ferranti International's decision to suspend trading in its shares.

While this US team was starting to build its case against Guerin and ISC, the initial flurry of legal activity was in Britain, as the Serious Fraud Squad and Scotland Yard's Company Fraud Department announced a full-scale enquiry on 20 October 1989.[18] This decision had been reached after reading the report produced by Coopers & Lybrand, the prominent accounting firm that had been commissioned on 15 September by the Ferranti International board 'to undertake urgently a full investigation' into ISC, in the hope that this would provide sufficient evidence both to explain the fraud and secure the return of all moneys stolen by Guerin. To protect the interests of its shareholders and employees, Ferranti International had also subpoenaed all ISC documents at its US subsidiaries, sending a team of accountants from Coopers & Lybrand to implement this essential first step in the investigation. Not surprisingly, though, when the Coopers & Lybrand team visited ISC's Lancaster headquarters, not only had Guerin disappeared, but also some key documents were missing.[19] While ISC staff collaborated fully with the British accountants, and in spite of the noble efforts of William Clark up to March 1989 to replace all documents shredded by Guerin and his closest confidantes, it was apparent that the latter had done their level best to destroy a lot of incriminating information. A humorous note was at that time introduced into the proceedings, because after an ITN news crew had been tipped off by a US detective agency that a 'J. Guerin' had been seen flying into Britain, they forced their way into a Heathrow hotel room, only to discover a French salesman, Jean Guerin, 'quivering in his underpants as the cameras rolled and ITN's fiercest hounds confronted him'.[20] The news item never made it past the cutting-room floor.

The real 'J. Guerin' had, of course, disappeared from public view in August 1989, when he sold his Lancaster residence and moved to Naples, Florida, into what has been described as an 'elaborate bay-front Naples home at 3875 Gordon Drive', worth $1.65 million.[21] This house was in the heart of the Port Royal district of Naples, which the *Guardian* described as: 'Colonial-style homes stand alongside palatial mansions, a symbol of both the area's prestige and the money that goes with it.'[22] The report went on to note that Guerin's motor launch, *The Lady Theresa*, bobbed gently on the lake that fringed the estate, while a Lincoln Continental stood in front of the double garage, reflecting the quiet wealth that typified the area. Coincidentally, Carlos Cardoen owned a lot of property in that state, but it has not been possible to verify whether Guerin bought his new house from the Chilean arms trader. It is well-known, though, that Naples was regarded as a retirement centre for former members of the US intelligence community,[23] indicating how the former ISC chief executive was rekindling links which he had first made in the 1970s when working for the CIA in South Africa.

Just before he left Lancaster, Guerin sent a letter to the *Lancaster New Era*, the principal purpose of which was to reject all of the accusations James B. Christian had recently made about his role in Chem-Con's illegal activities, repeating the claim that this corporation's demise in 1987 had cost him $8 million. In coming to this conclusion, Guerin had evidently calculated that the 20% stake he held in Chem-Con was worth $8 million, a statement that can only be described as ridiculous, especially given the limited net worth of a business that was built on fraudulent trading and loss-making products. Nevertheless, as we have noted elsewhere, at that stage most Lancaster residents were willing to take his word over the convicted black entrepreneur.[24] The headline to Guerin's farewell letter – 'Farewell Lancaster: We're

Going to Miss You' – was also regarded as sincere, reflecting the esteem in which he was held after the estimated $2 million-worth of charitable donations he had made to a wide range of community activities.[25]

As summer turned to autumn, however, the attitude of Lancaster citizens was to change decisively as, firstly, Ferranti International and, successively, William Clark and the multi-agency investigative team started to mount a powerful campaign that not only corrected the sentimental views expressed, but also demonstrated in graphic form the extent of Guerin's nefarious activities. As we have already noted, leaks from the Grand Jury's work on ISC's South African links featured in newspapers on both sides of the Atlantic in September–October of 1989, while in the week following the suspension of Ferranti International shares on 12 September a barrage of accusations and unconnected evidence appeared, implicating Guerin directly in a range of criminal acts. The *Independent* was perhaps the best-researched report, because apart from mentioning the work of the Grand Jury, Christian's accusations concerning Chem-Con, and how Coopers & Lybrand had been commissioned to report urgently on ISC's financial situation, the newspaper revealed that ISC Technologies was also linked to the scandal associated with Banca Nazionale del Lavoro (BNL).[26] Others simply reported on the work of Coopers & Lybrand and the implications of the projected 'hole' in Ferranti International's accounts once the full extent of the fraud had been discovered.[27] By that time, the firm's publicity machine, headed by their publication relations agents, Fowlers of Stockport, and co-ordinated by the head of corporate publicity, Tony Thomas, had disseminated extensive publicity about the 'possibility' that Ferranti International had been duped out of up to £150 million. In the following week, the same team publicised the work of Coopers & Lybrand in both the UK and at ISC's headquarters in Lancaster,[28] but offering the figure of £200 million as the cost of working with Guerin.

The Ferranti public relations machine managed by Tony Thomas certainly did an effective job in cementing in the public's mind the view that Guerin was an international crook who had built his business on illegal foundations. Although as we shall see in the next chapter this did little to calm market fears over the damage this had done to the Ferranti balance sheet, it made it extremely difficult for Guerin to counter the accusations with convincing evidence. This to a large extent explains why between his departure from Lancaster in August 1989 and the Clark case of January 1990 it was impossible to find him and ask questions directly. In October 1990, photographs of his Naples house, complete with palm trees, high brick walls and personal motor-boat worth $150,000, featured in several newspapers, alongside interviews with a housekeeper who did not appear to know where Guerin had gone.[29] While his attorney, Joseph A. Tate, was frequently to be heard defending his client against any accusations levelled by a growing number of antagonists, it was January 1990 before he again appeared in public, at the second court case on Clark's compensation package, when as we saw earlier he used his constitutional right to silence as frequently as possible.

While Guerin's silence was in many ways understandable, it did nothing either to calm his critics or stem the flow of legal action against him. By far the most significant of these early actions was the issuance on 30 November 1989 of a civil writ by Ferranti International against Guerin and three of his colleagues, Robert Shireman, Lawrence Resch and Wayne Radcliffe, as well as five Panamanian companies (Sestri Associates, Technology Associates International, Elverton, Navarino Development and Lerwick Holdings). Although it was known that all of these companies had been dissolved, the writ alleged 'fraudulent misrepresentations during the period 1983–89, to the effect that sales and purchase contracts were genuine and payments made and received were made in the normal course of business'; in effect, that the accused 'knowingly participated in a dishonest scheme to extract funds from the plaintiffs'. This intricately researched document had arisen from a combination of the work of Ferranti International executives (Cooper, Ball and Scott) and the Coopers & Lybrand audit of ISC. It contained the first detailed breakdown of the accusations against the cabal that had brought Ferranti International to its knees, with the headline figure of $198.5 million (at current prices, £127 million) estimated as the sum they had siphoned off from a range of fraudulent contracts. The bulk of this money had been derived from $443.6 million churned by ISC Technologies and ISC London between February 1984 and July 1989 on three fictitious missile contracts:

- The first was signed by ISC Technologies and KP Industries Pty on 5 November 1986, to transfer missile technology, with an extension on 7 October 1987 to provide a technical facility and test range. This contract also involved four of the Panamanian companies as subcontractors.
- The second, signed on 12 May 1984, was a sham deal between ISC London (a subsidiary of ISC Technologies) to supply *Hakim* missiles to the UAE. This contract also involved another subcontractor, Bosque Rosa, details on which do not exist. [*It is vital to differentiate this contract from that signed in 1986 for the supply of* Hakim *missiles to UAE, because the latter actually existed.*].
- And the third was signed on 21 June 1988, when ISC Technologies and Elverton agreed to supply China North Industries Corporation (Norinco) with what came to be known as the *Alpha* missile system (which was actually the bogus *Hakim* missile that had allegedly been contracted to the UAE in 1984).[30]

The churning process involved the five Panamanian subcontractors related to twenty-nine bogus sales and purchase missile contracts, with Guerin and his co-conspirators orchestrating the various components in order to dupe all interested parties into believing that the contracts existed. This provides a succinct summary of the details that Ian Ball and Alan Cooper had been chasing since the Ferranti-ISC merger, involving both hardwired and modular missile systems, as well as the 'merger accounting' techniques devised by Guerin to cover up the way they transferred costs from the 1984 contract into the sales manifested in the 1988 China deal.

To delve further into what is generally referred to as a 'churning process', it is of crucial importance to understand the role played by Robert Shireman, ISC Technologies' finance director, because he was personally responsible for shuffling funds around the Guerin empire. As we noted in Chapter 2, Guerin had earlier been responsible for shuffling funds between ISC, United Chem-Con and Parent Industries, specifically in order to ensure that the 1982 London flotation was a success. This model was also used by Shireman, who operated from a sound-proofed, white-noise and magnetically protected office at the Handsworth facility owned by ISC Technologies, where he had encrypted fax and computer modems to move money from Guerin's Swiss bank accounts into Ferranti International. For example, if one takes the KP contract as an example, Guerin claimed that the Pakistani government insisted on paying ISC Technologies directly for the missile work, specifically into a Swiss bank account managed by a front company, Lerwick Holdings SA. ISC Technologies would then supposedly buy equipment from suppliers through the four front companies named in the Ferranti International writ, while Shireman shuffled the money around the accounts, convincing the firm's accountants that real transactions were happening. In fact, the money paid to the four front companies was simply returned to the Swiss banking account, boosting the net worth of Guerin and his collaborators and defrauding Ferranti International of millions of pounds.

At the same time that this writ was issued, Ferranti International also announced the resignations of several ISC executives. Most notable was Clyde Ivy, who had worked with Guerin since 1977 masterminding most of ISC's missile development work and acting as the key link with South Africa. Another long-time ISC employee who left at the end of 1989 was Carl Dreyer, the director in charge of product assurance who had moved from Hamilton Watch at the time Guerin had set up his own business in 1971. Two further departures were those of Joe Zilligen (chairman of the US and Italian arms of ISC) and Sir David Checketts (formerly managing director of ISC Technologies), reflecting Sir Derek Alun-Jones' desire to expunge all remaining links with Guerin's business affairs from the Ferranti portfolio. In total, twenty-three executives left ISC in this rationalisation wave at the

Lancaster headquarters of ISC. As one commentator noted: 'The web of coin-cidences and common associations with Guerin and many of his associates has slowly surfaced over the last several months.'[31] For example, it transpired that two of the ISC executives named in the 30 November writ had close links with United Chem-Con: Shireman's wife, Patricia, had been head of finance at the defunct corporation, while Resch had established a marketing firm with Carl Jacobson (who was also Guerin's brother-in-law).

Not surprisingly, though, neither Guerin nor his attorney, Joseph Tate, proved willing to comment on both the Ferranti International writ and the various connections commentators were making across the failing business empire. Of course, as we have noted earlier, former Lancaster neighbours and employees refused to believe that Guerin was capable of criminal actions. One person (most likely, Joe Zilligen, who had made similar accusations to Ian Ball[32]) even claimed that: 'Ferranti has skeletons in their accounting cupboard which the Ferranti board had been sitting on for some time. Now they've seen a convenient chance and they've decided to lump it all on the American. He's the odd man out, he's not part of the old boys' network here.' Few outside this closed community were willing to accept this kind of perverse interpretation of events, however, especially the US and UK teams that were relentlessly hunting down the evidence to build a water-tight case against Guerin and his co-conspirators.

In this context, the $198.5 million civil writ served by Ferranti International was but the first, albeit extremely significant, stage in a legal assault on Guerin and his co-conspirators. Indeed, the company stated publicly that further writs could be anticipated, given that within the first there were also claims for unspecified damages for the harm done to other operations within the group. According to the legal treaties between the UK and US, it would also provide the firm with access to any information generated in either country on Guerin and ISC. As we have already noted, though, given the difficulties associated with extraditing defendants to the UK, it was becoming increasingly clear that the balance of power moved to the Grand Jury investigations into the South African trade and the multi-agency team working on other aspects of ISC's activities, not least because they were also building up considerable momentum by that time. Indeed, the US and UK teams would appear to have coalesced by the end of January 1990, when personnel from the Serious Fraud Office and UK Customs & Excise travelled to Philadelphia, at the request of the MoD, to discuss sharing evidence with US Assistant Attorney Robert Goldman. One of the issues that the two teams discussed was the extent to which Ferranti was either the totally innocent victim of criminal acts or in some way culpable. As one source noted: '[Ferranti] is not the squeaky-clean bastion of British morals they would like everyone to think ... To think that they bought into Guerin's cloak of silence on a handshake just doesn't wash. There must have been a lot of winking going on when the merger documents were signed.'[33] It is not clear, however, whether this view was shared by many within Goldman's office, because it is clear that the focus of the multi-agency team's work was Guerin's activities. The sceptic's case was also not helped much by revelations in January 1990 that US Customs at the Port of Philadelphia had recently seized shipments of 'assorted military support equipment' that were being sent by Advent Marketing International Inc to ISC's agent in Singapore, Tony Stagg, for sale to various embargoed Third World countries. When it was also revealed that Advent Marketing was owned and managed by Guerin's son, also called James H. Guerin, this added further to the case being mounted against him.[34]

Indeed, any notion that Ferranti executives would be dragged into the US team's investigations were no more than a figment of the imagination of some former ISC employees and beneficiaries of Guerin's largesse, because after the meeting with the Serious Fraud Office and UK Customs & Excise in January 1990 the entire focus was placed on the Lancaster entrepreneur's business activities. Furthermore, Ferranti International executives contributed enormously to this detective work, offering transparent access to company documents and several wrote lengthy notes that summarised their work with Guerin and ISC subsidiaries. As a consequence of all of this work, on 29 March 1990 Goldman filed a seventeen-page document with the US District Court, Philadelphia, requesting that all of Guerin's assets should be frozen, under the Racketeering-Influenced Corrupt Organisations (RICO) Act. It was noted that not only had Guerin transferred the ownership of his Naples house to his wife, Helen, but also his holding company, Parent Industries Inc had been sold for $2.4 million dollars[35] in October 1989 to an associate, Michael Peck, who in turn had transferred its operations to Austin, Texas, and renamed it Urban Industries Inc. Peck, of course, had been a long-time business associate of Guerin's, and although there is no evidence that he had been involved in ISC's illicit arms trading, it is clear that in acquiring Parent Industries for one dollar he was trying to help his friend avoid the possibility that the court would seize all of his assets. Nevertheless, the District Court sided with Goldman's request, in that it agreed to freeze all of Guerin's assets, including those nominally held by his wife and Michael Peck. As the file explained that Guerin was being investigated for fraud that involved 'hundreds of millions of dollars',[36] Federal Judge Thomas N. O'Neill felt that the Justice Department had shown 'probable cause' that his money had been earned through racketeering. At the same time, he also extended the court's control over William Clark's $2 million compensation package, because ten days earlier Guerin and his former in-house legal counsel had come to a deal, whereby the latter received $1.7 million and Urban Industries $300,000.

Having secured this action in March 1990, Goldman's team returned to its meticulous search for categoric evidence of Guerin's illegal activities. Although they would have to return to the court within ninety days to continue the freezing order, it was by then clear that their work was sufficiently credible to persuade a judge that Guerin and his closest associates were going to be prosecuted for highly serious offences. As we noted earlier, some of this evidence had to be used in a continuance of the Clark-Guerin compensation case, when Goldman was obliged to return to court in order to ensure that the $2 million deposited by Guerin in an escrow account would not be paid out to Clark. At the May 1990 hearing, the court heard extensive evidence from Special Agent Amy Zelnik, a criminal investigator for the Inland Revenue Service who had looked into how Guerin had moved funds between ISC, Parent Industries and various overseas bank accounts. This was the first time that evidence on the latter had been presented, revealing that between 1984 and 1989 Guerin had used nine US bank accounts, thirty Swiss bank accounts, and various accounts in Belgium and Luxembourg to divert approximately $575 million to Parent Industries, which in turn funnelled the money back to ISC and a myriad number of shell companies, money which, firstly, artificially boosted the value of ISC prior to the November 1987 merger with Ferranti, and, secondly, duped Ferranti International executives into believing that the contracts existed. When referring to the various missile contracts that Guerin had fashioned, Zelnik replied decisively that: 'There was no product, technology, customers or vendors'.[37] FBI Special Agent Gerard O'Callaghan substantiated Zelnik's evidence, adding that Guerin had actually been manipulating his corporation's accounts since 1978.

Although it only lasted one day, the May court case demonstrated extensively that Goldman's multi-agency team had clearly by then built up a powerful case that reflected the intense research conducted into Guerin's business activities. Few could dispute the evidence being presented on what one contemporary observer described as 'an international charade of "cardboard" companies, secret bank accounts, [and] a non-existent contract'.[38] As a direct result of this assault, Parent Industries agreed to pay the government $2,376,000 and forfeit its share ($300,000) of the $2 million deposited by Guerin in an escrow account to compensate William Clark. This was effectively the first time Guerin had accepted any guilt for the multiple crimes of which he was being accused, albeit via his personal holding corporation, rather than as an individual, because Michael Peck had sold Parent Industries back to his associate in April. Indeed, the Justice Department was obliged to state that they would continue to pursue Guerin personally, as well as various other unnamed individuals, given the nature and extent of the crimes committed by ISC executives over the previous sixteen years.

While all this was occurring in the US, Ferranti International sustained its efforts to recoup the money Guerin had allegedly siphoned off directly from the company since the November 1987 merger. Not surprisingly, the November 1989 writ against Guerin and four other ISC executives had failed miserably to secure anything, leading Ferranti International to issue another writ on 18 June 1990 to recover the $189 million (£110 million) originally awarded by the courts. Justice Hoffman duly granted this writ, ordering Guerin in addition to pay all of the legal costs involved in the case, as well as provide information on the whereabouts of what the company now claimed was $450 million paid out to the five Panamanian firms mentioned in the November 1989 writ. Although Guerin refused to attend the hearing, he had provided a sworn statement through his US attorney, Joseph Tate, claiming that he had no documents to show Ferranti International, denying all knowledge of the Panamanian companies and stating that their managing directors did not exist. Justice Hoffman felt that this was simply not a credible defence, arguing that: 'If they were not genuine contracts, then the money must have been paid out for some ulterior purpose, and if it was, then Mr Guerin must know something about what happened'.[39] Indeed, Justice Hoffman felt that Guerin's response was 'contemptuous', not to mention 'illusory' and incomplete, stating that he had not given any evidence of being 'a litigant genuinely doing his best to comply with an order'. From the safe refuge of his Philadelphia office, Joseph Tate described this judgement as 'a sham', arguing that it was grossly unfair of Justice Hoffman to strike off Guerin's evidence. 'In the US', Tate incredulously stated, 'Mr Guerin's pleadings would have been sufficient and the parties would have been required to try the claims. The ruling by the British court was clearly biased in favour of its own citizens.'[40] How the attorney could have ignored the mountain of evidence on Guerin's illicit business activities which was already in the public domain is a matter we shall leave the reader to contemplate. Few could also believe Tate's claim that 'Mr Guerin had responded truthfully and fully to the papers served upon him'. Furthermore, all his pontificating about alleged bias did not prevent the courts from extending Hoffman's order on 27 July to Robert Shireman, Lawrence Resch and the five Panamanian companies, making them all liable for the $189 million mentioned in the 18 June writ. As he had acknowledged the November 1989 writ, Wayne Radcliffe was excluded from the July 1990 writ, but this still made him liable for the original sum and he would continue to be pursued by the courts. Two weeks later, though, Stuart Pindell was added to the writ, on the grounds that as president and marketing director of ISC International between 1983 and 1986 he had played a role in fabricating the first PGM contract with UAE.[41] Even though Pindell also secured the real *Hakim* contract in 1986, earning in the course of his duties a commission estimated in excess of $6 million, he had also been responsible for the fraudulent 1984 contract, worth a supposed $100 million.

In reporting these cases, *The Times* carried a highly amusing cartoon which represented two officials of the London Stock Exchange laughing about a caption which ran: 'Application from Ferranti for listing as a law firm'.[42] This reflected not only the company's mounting legal costs, but also the wide-spread interest in a case that had ramifications for a considerable number of people. Of course, few within Ferranti International were naive enough to believe that Guerin and his associates would immediately stump up the money they had extorted through the dubious missile contracts, but in the interests of shareholders, employees and customers it was imperative that they continue to harass them for appropriate compensation. This persuaded the board to file the next suit in the USA, when on 2 July a writ to recover $27 million in alleged losses from Technologies Associates International (TAI), one of the five Panamanian firms listed in earlier writs. Three individuals – Pablo Javier Espino (president), Adelina M. De Estribi (secretary) and Aida May (treasurer) – were mentioned in the writ as the key perpetrators who allegedly dealt in contracts 'TAI knew ... to be fictitious and the merchandise which [it] was supposedly supplying ... to be non-existent'.[43] While TAI had apparently been dissolved in February 1988, under US and Panama law it was possible for a US corporation to file suit up to three years after dissolution, justifying the expense of moving the legal action from London to Philadelphia. As this was a criminal case, Ferranti International was also obliged to provide more insights into how the fraud was perpetrated, with payments being 'looped' between ISC's subsidiary ESI Manufacturing (later ISC Technologies) on to TAI (and other Panamanian subcontractors) and back to ISC. This highlighted the elaborate nature of Guerin's scheme, involving phoney contracts, inventory and payments that TAI always knew existed purely to defraud Ferranti.

Within a week, however, Ferranti International was back in the Philadelphia courts, but this time it was defending itself against a writ issued by Clyde Ivy to claim his $198,000 annual salary. As we noted earlier, Ivy had been dismissed from the company in November 1989, charged with 'fraud, commission of a felony and dishonesty in the course of your employment', as well as 'failure to co-operate fully with the company's various investiga-tions'.[44] This action had summarily terminated Ivy's pension, as well as any right he had originally claimed to pay for his legal defence in the Grand Jury investigations into ISC's South African links. Ivy had made earlier fruitless efforts to persuade Ferranti International to restore his full pension, forcing him to sue the company and open up to full public exposition his personal role in ISC's expansion since the mid-1970s. In his defence, apart from refuting the base on which he was sacked, Ivy claimed he had provided as much help as possible to the company's investigation into ISC's illicit arms trading. These points were summarily dismissed by the US court, leaving Ivy without his pension, as well as a lot of international publicity that highlighted his extensive involvement in the Guerin Scandal. Indeed, given the weight of the evidence concerning his role in helping South Africa to build guided missiles, some commentators questioned why the British authorities had allowed him to take up his role as a director of one of Britain's leading defence companies.[45]

5.3 The net closes in

With this succession of court hearings on both sides of the Atlantic generating what to many people appeared to be amazing revelations about Guerin and his various business activities, by the summer of 1990 it was only a matter of time before formal criminal proceedings would be launched. The Ferranti International writs against Guerin and his associates had been civil cases, pursued in the vain hope that some of the fraudulent profits could be recouped. As we noted earlier, given the difficulties associated with extraditing US citizens to courts anywhere else in the world, the UK authorities investigating ISC (HM Customs & Excise, the MoD, the Serious Fraud Office and Scotland Yard's fraud investigators) had agreed at the end of 1989 that the criminal cases would be prosecuted in a US court. These were initiated in August 1990, when following the May 1990 revelations about the money-laundering aspects of the ISC fraud, the man leading the multi-agency investigative team, Robert Goldman (Assistant US Attorney) filed a thirteen-page list of charges against Guerin, ISC and Parent Industries in the Eastern District of Pennsylvania, Philadelphia. The file alleged that since 1978 Guerin had been involved in racketeering activity worth up to $700 million, including the creation of contrived contracts which were handled by numerous front companies of dubious origins, as well as laundering money through forty bank accounts, all with the intention of convincing auditors and investors that ISC was bigger than it actually was.

The Goldman team had consequently initiated a legal assault on Guerin and his co-conspirators that would eventually lead to the imprisonment of several ISC executives. The crucial point about the August case, however, was the announcement that Guerin's personal holding company, Parent Industries, had agreed to enter a negotiated guilty plea to one count of racketeering, with specific regard to defrauding Ferranti International of up to $1 billion. In January 1987, Guerin had apparently placed his 16 million controlling shares in ISC with Parent Industries, using this as the collateral for a $9 million line of credit with the Meridian Bank. Once the merger with Ferranti had been completed in November 1987, Parent Industries was by then holding $67 million worth of Ferranti International stock (amounting to 32 million shares), an investment that was used in July 1988 to borrow $39 million from Citicorp. This money was used by Parent Industries to consolidate all of its loans, cover Guerin's personal operating expenses (including his small fleet of jet aircraft), and fund 'new business acquisitions', the nature of which Goldman would not divulge.[46] When the value of Ferranti International stock started to slip, however, in the summer of 1989, Citicorp was able to use a condition of the loan to sell the shares, leaving Parent Industries with just $1.3 million. As this was the money that Guerin had deposited with the Fulton Bank in his case against William Clark,[47] Goldman argued that it must be seized under the RICO statutes because it had been gained as a result of defrauding Ferranti International. Goldman summarised the file succinctly, noting that: 'Parent Industries was an enterprise prepared to capitalise on a massive financial fraud conducted by itself, ISC and ISC employees.' Furthermore, although Guerin was not personally mentioned in the charges, given that he was the sole shareholder in Parent Industries and executive chairman, 'the former Lancaster businessmen and Parent [can be identified] as being one and the same', indicating that further charges would be presented to the court in due course.[48]

Another distasteful aspect of Guerin's stock sales was the court case involving Citicorp and the securities firm that bought the 32 million Ferranti shares (for £26 million, at 82p per share). After the suspension of trading in Ferranti stock on 11 September, this transaction attracted the department of the London Stock Exchange that investigated insider trading. It transpired that Guerin had pressured Citicorp's asset management division, Scrimgeour Vickers, into selling the Ferranti stock as quickly as possible, at the very least before the full implications of his ISC activities became public knowledge, resulting in a speedy deal with Smith New Court, another prominent asset management firm. By October 1989, however, Smith New Court was faced with a loss of at least £10 million on this purchase, after the suspension of Ferranti International share trading had been lifted, leading them to initiate a series of investigations that by January 1991 resulted in, firstly, the prosecution of a senior figure in Scrimgeour Vickers, Christopher Roberts, and secondly, the issuance of a writ against that firm for the return of the purchase price paid for the stock, as well as compensation for damage done to Smith New Court's reputation. At the first trial on 22 January, Smith New Court alleged that Roberts was not only fully aware of the impending collapse in Ferranti International share prices, but also misled them into believing that at least two other firms were interested in buying the 32 million shares at between 75p and 81p per share. This had persuaded Smith New Court to offer 82p, which Roberts had allegedly described as 'damned close' to the client's asking price.[49] Nevertheless, at the full trial in April 1991 Roberts was acquitted of making false or misleading statements, even though the two other bidders have never since materialised.[50] By March 1992, however, Citicorp had been ordered to pay Smith New Court £15 million in compensation. Even though the Court of Appeal later reduced this to just £1.4 million, on the grounds that the consequent reduction in the Ferranti International share price was irrelevant, these cases highlighted aspects of City activities that were poorly regulated. One should stress, though, that Ferranti International was unable to participate in these actions, because Guerin's agreement not to sell his shares was not legally enforceable.

While all this legal activity was happening, the US court cases were also continuing, generating widespread interest. Moreover, especially as the November 1989 civil writ had been signally unsuccessful, the Ferranti International board realised that this was an opportune moment to assert its right to full compensation from Guerin and his co-conspirators for the money fraudulently taken between 1987 and 1989. The company had always known that it had the right to pursue them through US courts, but it was safer to wait until the US Attorney had presented its damning evidence of embezzlement, money laundering and violation of anti-racketeering legislation before filing a writ in that country. As Clyde Ivy was still attempting to persuade a court that he had every right to the pension Ferranti International had denied him, on 21 September 1990 the company filed a civil writ that outlined the full extent of the alleged crimes committed by ISC executives. Crucially, Guerin was indicted alongside seven former ISC colleagues: Clyde Ivy, Robert Shireman, Wayne Radcliffe, Thomas Jasin, Terence Faulds, Anthony Stagg and Gerry Schuler. This was the first time that a US court had been given evidence, amounting to eighty-seven exhibits, on what was the full team of ISC conspirators.[51]

In the meantime, while Goldman was parading the charges against Parent Industries, and *de facto* against Jim Guerin, inevitably behind the scenes there was a considerable amount of activity involving his attorney, Joseph Tate, and the US Attorney office. Indeed, it was well known that apart from paying $4.4 million to the courts, Parent Industries was not going to be prosecuted further, while Tate was attempting a series of plea bargains on his client's behalf, as a means of avoiding a prison sentence. At the same time, a 'swarm of Federal agents are busy scouring some of the world's shadier offshore banking havens "to follow the money" and recover some of it from between 30 and 40 bank accounts'.[52] Other members of the team were looking into alleged arms shipments to South Africa and Iraq, as well as the fraudulent missiles contracts highlighted by the Ferranti International civil writ. This was probably why on 10 October 1990 Parent Industries pleaded guilty to the charges levied in August, in the hope that this could be used in a plea bargain to keep Guerin and the seven men mentioned in the Ferranti civil writ out of prison. Guerin even put his Naples house up for sale, at a price of $1.65 million, as well as his motor boat, while as early as 18 July he had entered into a mortgage with the US government guaranteeing that $600,000 from the sale would go directly to the state. Although by that time he had placed all of his assets in his wife's name, Helen Guerin was obliged to sign the mortgage, otherwise she would also have been prosecuted under the RICO legislation. The couple had also moved into a much more modest house, at 2144 Paget Circle, in Naples, worth $267,750, indicating clearly that he was beginning to feel the pinch effected by his prosecutors.[53]

While Ferranti International continued to pursue Guerin and others for compensation, it was clear that no money was going to change hands in 1990. Even though on 13 November Guerin agreed to a court order that not only obliged him to notify Ferranti International when his house had been sold, but also limit his household expenses to $4,000 per month and not to liquidate any other assets, this did not guarantee that a cent would be paid over to the company.[54] Moreover, the $600,000 fine imposed by the US Department of Justice on Parent Industries would take precedence over compensation to Ferranti International, leaving the firm with nothing more than a promise that its claims would be considered by the court.

Nevertheless, revelations of Guerin's alleged criminality continued to surface, for example when early in November 1990 federal prosecutors confirmed that Iraq was in possession of cluster bombs that had been made using technology transferred from ISC's Lancaster plant to Carlos Cardoen's Santiago facility.[55] By this time, of course, it was increasingly likely that as a result of the illegal invasion of Kuwait by Iraqi forces on 2 August 1990, US and allied forces would be engaging with Saddam Hussein's forces, subject to United Nations (UN) approval. On 29 November, the UN Security Council duly authorised the use of military force to eject the Iraqi army, unless they had withdrawn by 15 January, resulting in feverish diplomatic activity in the Middle East and across Europe. As Saddam Hussein refused to climb down, on 16 January 1991 the US launched an Apache helicopter raid on Iraqi forces, followed swiftly by an air raid by jet aircraft on Baghdad. In that first air raid, the factory known as Sahad 38 that was manufacturing the ISC-Cardoen cluster bombs was chosen as a key target, leading to its rapid destruction well in advance of the land war that started on 23 February. Such was the overwhelming might of the US-led coalition forces that by 27 February President Bush had declared a ceasefire, troops having liberated Kuwait and chased the Iraqi army deep into its own territory. For reasons that remain unclear, Bush refused to allow his generals to progress further and unseat President Hussein, allowing this particular problem to fester for another decade. Crucially, though, US Army sources were able to demon-strate that after inspecting Iraqi 155 mm shells fired from G-5 guns during

Desert Storm, they found power supplies originating in Lancaster.[56] This confirmed the role Guerin and Cardoen had played in arming Iraq during the 1980s, further substantiating the claims of US prosecutors that they had a case to answer. Guerin would later argue that as the technology underpinning this particular fuze was over thirty years old, anybody could acquire the expertise to manufacture it in bulk. Crucially, he denied categorically that ISC had ever been instrumental in providing Iraq with any goods or services that could potentially harm US citizens; he was a patriot and totally devoted to supporting US interests.[57]

With all the evidence presented during successive US court cases during 1989 and 1990, not to mention the discoveries made by the US Army after *Desert Storm*, by the beginning of 1991 many people were anticipating Guerin's imminent arrest and prosecution. For what politicians like to call 'strategic' reasons, however, it is likely that Robert Goldman's team was persuaded not to pursue their prey with alacrity, given the highly embarrassing revelation that a US defence corporation had been supplying Iraq with the technology to make offensive weapons. When one combines this evidence with what was also known about ISC's role in building sonar stations in South Africa, as well as Clyde Ivy's contribution to that country's guided missile programme and the various sham contracts ISC had entered into with Pakistan and China, it is clear that political priorities were going to take centre stage. Above all, President Bush and the Republican Party would not want highly embarrassing revelations being trumpeted in a Philadelphia court, as they would directly implicate President Reagan's two-term presidency, when as we saw earlier the US government embarked on its policy of 'active neutrality' and helped both Iraq and Iran to build formidable military machines.[58] Apart from having been vice-president during Reagan's presidency, George Bush had also been a director of the CIA in 1976–77, at exactly the same time that Admiral Inman had been planning the South African sonar stations to detect Russian nuclear submarines in the South Atlantic. Of course, while this is pure conjecture, one might accurately surmise that the prosecution of Guerin was consequently delayed for several months, mainly to allow the dust to settle on *Desert Storm* and deflect any accusations that the US government had been complicit in ISC's nefarious activities; no regime likes to be linked to criminality. Whatever the reasons for the delay in pursuing Guerin and his co-conspirators, it was clearly not for the want of evidence, because by the end of 1990 a plethora of material had been accumulated by the multi-agency team to support a prosecution of considerable conviction.

It was actually Halloween Day of 1991 when the US authorities finally presented the full range of the evidence they had been gathering for almost three years. Earlier that morning, all of the American defendants except

Guerin had been arrested at gunpoint, handcuffed and placed in a Philadelphia detention centre, indicating the importance of the accusations. By 11.30am, looking rather dishevelled and shocked, they had all been arraigned before Federal Magistrate Angell Faith, to whom they pleaded their innocence. She then agreed to release them, imposing strict conditions on their bail, including a $100,000 bond, a requirement to report weekly to the court, and a total limitation on travel outside Philadelphia. Curiously, Guerin was not subjected to the same treatment as his co-conspirators, partly because he was by then residing in Naples, Florida. Nevertheless, on 14 November he was obliged to present himself to the same court in Philadelphia, when he pleaded guilty to the eight counts listed in Table 5.1. Although no dates were set for the court cases, the state had made a decisive move against those who were regarded as responsible for what had happened at ISC since the early 1970s.

Table 5.1 List of accused and indictments filed in November 1991

Name and Address	Company role	Charges	possible prison sentence + fine
James H. Guerin, Naples, Florida	Founder of ISC; deputy chairman of Ferranti International	8 counts of contract fraud, illegal exporting, money laundering, and tax violations	86 years + $3.75 million fine
Robert Clyde Ivy, Lancaster, Pennsylvania	Director of Ferranti International	Illegal exporting, money laundering and contract fraud	515 years + $44 million fine
Wayne Radcliffe, Lancaster, Pennsylvania	Vice-president, special projects, ISC	Illegal exporting, money laundering, and contract fraud	150 years + $13.25 million fine
Terence Faulds, Holtwood, Pennsylvania	President of ESI	Money laundering, tax and export violations	461 years + $50.5 million
Thomas Jasin, Lancaster, Pennsylvania	President of ISC Technologies	Export violations	25 years + $2.25 million
Gerald Schuler, West Islip, N.Y.	ISC's freight forwarder	Export violations	165 years + $16.25 million
Robert Shireman, Marietta, N.Y.	ISC Technologies finance officer	Contract fraud and tax violations	10 years + $500,000

Lawrence Resch, San Clemente, Calif.	ISC business consultant	Contract fraud	15 years + $750,000
Anthony Stagg, Singapore	ISC Technologies sales and program manager	Export violations	15 years + $1.25 million
James Russell, South Africa	President of Canavco Inc, Westlake, Calif.	Export violations and money laundering	55 years + $3.2 million
William Randy Metelerkamp, South Africa	Freelance arms dealer	Export violations	5 years + $1.25 million
Vern Davis, South Africa	Freelance arms dealer	Export violations	15 years + $1.25 million
Brian Scott, South Africa	Kentron	Export violations	125 years + $1.25 million
Bert Quinn, South Africa	Kentron	Export violations	15 years + $1.25 million
Johan Lombard, South Africa	Armscor and Kentron	Export violations	15 years + $1.25 million
Jace Budricks, South Africa	Freelance arms dealer	Export violations	235 years + $23.25 million
Gerritt Pretorius, South Africa	Freelance arms dealer	Export violations	235 years + $1.25 million
Armaments Corporation [Armscor] of South Africa Ltd	ISC partner	Export violations	$11.5 million
Kentron Pty Ltd	ISC partner	Export violations	$3.5 million
Fuchs Electronics Pty Ltd	ISC partner	Export violations	$21.5 million

The public announcements about these indictments on 31 October were conducted with some fanfare, when at simultaneous press conferences in Philadelphia and Washington federal prosecutors from the US Attorney's Office unveiled the full extent of their case against a total of seventeen people and three South African companies who had worked for and with ISC, listing seventy-five counts of fraud, money-laundering, smuggling and export law violation. It was a masterly public relations exercise that involved a panoply of TV cameras, photographers and journalists listening to presentations complete with blown-up charts and photographs, as well as examples of the ISC fuzes supplied to Iraq, an ISC-made *Stryker* missile, and maps of the routes taken by both of these products from Lancaster and California and the 'money-looping' involved in allegedly phoney missile contracts. The Philadelphia press conference was perhaps the most impressive, because US Attorney Michael M. Baylson chaired an event in the ceremonial courtroom on the fifth floor of the US District Courthouse, where new federal judges are normally sworn in, with representatives of the SEC (James C. Kennedy), Department of Treasury (Henry J. Ballas), Defense Criminal Investigative Service (James J. Hagan), US Customs Service (David Warren), FBI (Wayne R. Gilbert), and Internal Revenue Service (Gary H. Matthews). Following a lengthy introduction by Baylson, each official spent a few minutes at the podium explaining the extent and nature of the fraud they had unravelled. Backing up a point made in earlier chapters,[59] all agreed that it was the most complex arms scandal they had ever investigated. Wayne Gilbert (FBI) even claimed that the case was 'one of the most significant cases of white collar crime that the FBI has investigated'.[60] Furthermore, as David Warren of US Customs concluded: 'It was done at the cost of this country and the lives of people everywhere',[61] linking the fraudulent activities with the illegal arms trading conducted with Iraq and other countries on the UN embargo list.

The complete list of people and firms included in the November 1991 indictments is provided in Table 5.1, which demonstrates that a total prison time of 2,122 years and $197.5 million in fines was expected by the Goldman team as a result of their three-year investigation. The inclusion of eight South African citizens and three corporations demonstrates the extent to which the team wanted to extend the coverage to Guerin's links with that regime, even though Nelson Mandela had been released from prison on 11 February 1990 and the apartheid system was being unravelled by the President, F.W. de Klerk.[62] At the Philadelphia news conference on 30 October 1991, US Attorney Michael Baylson was at pains to explain how as a result of seizing a shipment of household goods that Robert Shireman was returning to the US in July 1989, the Customs Service discovered a batch of papers that revealed ISC's extensive trade with South Africa, amounting to $30 million-worth of American-made weapon components. Having inadvertently given Alan Cooper key documents relating to ISC Technologies' sham missile contracts in the summer of 1988,[63] it is clear that the hapless Shireman was proving to be a major liability to Guerin and other ISC executives. Moreover, Baylson was also able to show that Fuchs Electronics had acted as the intermediary between ISC and Iraq in the supply of 380,000 power supplies that were fitted into the 155 mm shells used during *Desert Storm*, highlighting according to James J. Hagen, special agent of the Defense Criminal Investigative Service, how Guerin had 'put greed and the ability to make a buck above the well-being of our fighting men'.[64] The same South African firm also transferred the ISC-developed technology to Iraq for the manufacture of proximity fuzes in Sahad 38, demonstrating how Guerin had played a key role in arming the country against which the US and allied troops fought a bloody war.

While these exports naturally generated considerable publicity, the press conference also devoted a considerable amount of time, using numerous charts and graphs, to describing Guerin's financial manipulations. Specifically, it was alleged that he 'looped' $1.14 billion in and out of nine US front companies, thirty-eight phony Panamanian corporations and fifty-five Swiss bank accounts. In addition, Guerin was personally responsible for laundering $700 million, as well as falsifying corporate income tax returns to support three bogus missile contracts that were used to overvalue ISC. As Gary Matthews (Internal Revenue Service) stated: 'I would like you to visualize hundreds of thousands of these loops knitted together into an intricate, really enormous tapestry of fraud. This, we think, is a classic case of incomprehensible fraud. Our agents were stunned by the enormity of it'.[65] It was a highly impressive performance by the investigating team, creating the clear impression that, as John Hensley (Customs Service) noted, Guerin [and Cardoen] were 'major-league players in the arms-trading business'.

While through his attorney, Joseph Tate, Guerin issued a firm rebuttal of many of the allegations made by Goldman's team, the dual press conferences served the decisive purpose of convincing the general public that the three-year investigation had unearthed a mountain of evidence to support a comprehensive range of indictments (see Table 5.1). Even the formerly loyal people of Lancaster realised that 'Jim Guerin has ... been shown to be a liar [having] misled hundreds of people – people who befriended him and defended him; people who worked for him. In the end, Jim Guerin betrayed them.'[66] Interestingly, the same source also drew attention to the probable role of the CIA in directing at least some of Guerin's illegal arms exports, raising questions 'about the very soul of our government'. This comment arose from the claims made by Faulds, Jasin and Ivy that US intelligence agencies, high-ranking military, the former US Secretary of State Alexander Haig and even members of the Senate Intelligence Committee were fully aware of what since the 1970s ISC had been doing to support US strategic interests. Jasin even went as far as to say that General Haig facilitated ISC links with Sikorsky Aircraft, which wanted to use South African missiles on the helicopters it supplied to US Army covert units. In return for this favour, Guerin paid for ten ISC executives, at a cost of $500 per place, to attend a 1987 dinner held to raise funds for General Haig's run at the presidency.[67] Former CIA deputy director Bobby Ray Inman, who was instrumental in bringing Guerin into the secretive (and lucrative) world of illegal arms

dealing,[68] even went public in September 1991 with statements acknowledging the Lancaster entrepreneur's role in providing vital intelligence
information on the South African nuclear missile programme. Not surprisingly, US Attorney Michael Baylson refused to comment at the 30 October
1991 press conference on the CIA link, other than to agree that 'the CIA and
many other government agencies co-operated in this case'.[69] Indeed, the state
tried its level best to suppress any information on this highly sensitive issue,
even though at their own press conferences on 1 November 1991 Jasin, Faulds
and Ivy provided journalists with abundant information on the role of the
CIA, even mentioning the names of specific agents who worked closely with
ISC. As Ivy concluded: 'We believed that we had US government approval.'[70]

Of course, while these claims relating to South African sales were entirely
accurate, Inman having recruited ISC in the mid-1970s as the vehicle to
supply what the intelligence services regarded as essential equipment (worth
$200 million) to monitor Russian submarines in the South Atlantic, they
hardly justify the wide range of arms trading and fraudulent activities in
which Guerin and his co-conspirators indulged, on a scale that was truly
shocking. As we shall also see, in successive court cases little credence was
given to Ivy's conclusion and the claims of Guerin and others, as judges and
juries refused to accept that this justified what had been done. Crucially, in
spite of Inman's protestations, the CIA refused to provide any person or
evidence to refute or support such claims, significantly undermining the core
defence offered by the former ISC executives. Even though President Reagan
had bailed out Colonel Oliver North over the 'Iran–Contra Affair',[71] the US
government proved unwilling to come to Guerin's aid, in spite of his intimate
work with the CIA stretching back over nearly twenty years. Nevertheless,
when Guerin's trial eventually occurred, on 10 June 1992, after yet further
delays caused by his attempts to persuade the authorities that his actions had
been sanctioned by government agencies, he continued to appeal for mercy.
Although he pleaded guilty to the eight counts filed in October 1991, in an
incredible statement pleading for leniency he stated in mitigation to the US
District Judge, Louis Bechtle:

> I'm very sorry for what has happened and for what I have done. I never
> really appreciated the magnitude of what I did until the investigation
> began. I got carried away and felt our mission was above the law. It was
> misdirected patriotism.

Others preferred to describe him as a fantasist, one former ISC employee
stating that: 'He had these wild ideas that he was part of some sort of secret
operations that was an integral part of the national defense efforts.'[72]
Furthermore, nobody in the CIA or government circles was willing to
provide categoric evidence to support his claims, significantly undermining

the defence he consistently used, that all of his actions had been sanctioned at the appropriate levels. Indeed, Robert Gates, deputy director of the CIA in the early 1980s, stated in front of the Senate Intelligence Committee that his organisation had no knowledge of ISC's work in South Africa until informed by the FBI in 1986.[73] Of course, this does not explain why Guerin was allowed to continue to trade with South Africa until 1989, but the denial of CIA support was enough for the Senate to absolve the external intelligence agency of any culpability.

No less than twenty-one 'character letters' were also sent to Judge Bechtle, one of which was from Admiral Inman, who praised Guerin for displaying 'patriotism toward our country and a willingness to provide useful information even though it could have risked unfavourable publicity for his company'. Even though Inman was by that time one of President Bush's closest advisors on intelligence matters, however, his pleas for clemency were never going to influence the court. Among the other people to write to Judge Bechtle were Joe Zilligen, formerly a director of ISC up to 1987 and then of Ferranti International, who also wrote in glowing terms, stating that:

> Jim Guerin was an outstanding leader, a fair and reliable employer, a man of integrity, a man committed to his family, his God and his fellow man.. Jim's absence from our society will be our society's loss.[74]

Another former colleague, Carl Dreyer, claimed that:

> Mr Guerin was committed to the growth of ISC as a positive force in the community. He sought to create a stable employment opportunity for the community and directed special efforts to find and hire minority workers and handicapped persons.

Michael Peck, the former president of Parent Industries, also informed Judge Bechtle that 'Jim is a good person who made some serious mistakes and errors in judgement'. Similarly, the administrator of Guerin's charitable operation, Jean Spiese, reminded the court of his considerable donations to Lancaster social and cultural activities, concluding that:

> I know this will sound illogical, but I believe that Jim believed he was really doing God's will in all he did. I'll never understand how he got into the mess he's in now. But this I know – he is not a criminal.

Guerin's four children also wrote in glowing terms about his total dedication to them, Tom Guerin's letter proving to be the most incisive:

> They [Lancaster newspapers] would like you to believe that the focus of his life was to make money, and to do this at all costs. If this were true, he would have been more like the ordinary parent – the type that would have said he was too busy to spend time with us. He never did this.

Helen Guerin also pleaded with Judge Bechtle, requesting:

> Please put him to work by permitting him to start a new business. This will give people jobs. Let him teach and care for people. Put his talents to work and the Guerin family will be back in business and happiness will again be flowing in all our hearts. . Please, your honour, I beseech you. Have mercy on my husband. I need him so very much.

While few would deny the sincerity with which such statements were expressed, for those most directly affected by Guerin's activities since the mid-1970s they completely missed the key points, that he had committed crimes of such enormity that leniency was hardly an option. After all, the investigative team had proved that from the $958 million 'looped' through his maze of forty-two Panamanian front companies and fifty-three Swiss bank accounts, Guerin diverted $45.5 million to fund the contract frauds and smuggling expenses, as well as $18.1 million for himself.[75] Judge Bechtle also proved totally immune to such impassioned pleas, agreeing with the prosecution, headed by Robert Goldman, which had requested a fifteen-year sentence and $25,000 fine for the charge of laundering $958 million through Swiss bank accounts between 1983 and 1989, as well as shorter sentences which would run concurrently for contract fraud, tax evasion and weapons smuggling. In 1997, Guerin belatedly appealed against this sentence, on the grounds that his attorney, Joseph Tate, had misled him into pleading guilty.[76] This was rejected by Magistrate Judge Diane M. Walsh, who described the appellant as 'deceitful'.[77] Tate also stated publicly that Guerin was an 'habitual liar',[78] a point substantiated a day later when his client admitted that he had lied to his defence attorney continually throughout the period 1989–91.[79] The appeal failed.

5.4 Conclusions

Although Ferranti International refused to comment on the successful prosecution, especially as the civil suit aimed at recouping the money lost to Guerin's fraud was still extant, there was considerable satisfaction over Judge Bechtle's judgement. Of course, as we shall see in the next chapters, the board and remaining employees were much more concerned with the struggle to keep the group afloat and dealing with the enormous impact of the hole that had appeared in the firm's balance sheet. Nevertheless, seeing Guerin enter the Tallahassee State Penitentiary, where he spent twelve years of his fifteen-year prison sentence, at least demonstrated that the lead perpetrator could do no further damage either to Anglo-American business or world peace. As the *Intelligencer Journal* stated at the time of his indictment: 'Believed by many to be the American dream incarnate, Guerin epitomised the image of squeaky-clean success realised through what he often characterised as risk, hard work and a strong belief in God.'[80] Many others also rushed to his defence, pointing out how Guerin had donated hundreds of thousands of dollars to local charities and community activities. This image had, however, been dashed by not only the discovery of ISC-made components that had been used by Iraqi forces during *Desert Storm*, but also the litany of alleged crimes against both international and national laws, from contract fraud to tax evasion and money laundering.

As a consequence, few expressed any sympathy when at the end of December 1992 the *Lancaster New Era* carried an article reporting Guerin's predicament in jail, based on a three-page letter written by him to a reporter. This letter was built around the statement that: 'Prison is a hard experience coming on top of losing everything. It resembles nothing so much as a bad dream at the end of time.'[81] He was especially sad that he had missed Christmas with his family, because this had been the first time it had happened since serving in Korea in the early 1950s. Instead, he was compelled to share Christmas lunch with drug-dealers, burglars and white-collar criminals in what was a low-security penitentiary. Such are the penalties imposed on criminals. Many would have been shocked, however, at his revelation that he was 'teaching college-level business courses evenings, other Education Department duties afternoons, with mornings off'. One can only imagine what business techniques he was instilling in his students, given the kind of career he had pursued since the 1970s. Most would have preferred him to devote his spare time to cultivating the penitentiary farm, taking him back to his New Jersey roots. In addition, he also created a newsletter which was mailed out to a worldwide audience of former colleagues. This contained book reviews, religious messages and moral stories from life in prison, sustaining the image of a man who supposedly at heart was sincere, God-fearing and moral.

The successful prosecution of Guerin provided the US authorities with all the ammunition needed to pursue the others listed in the October 1991 indictment (see Table 5.1). While five of them – Anthony Stagg, Lawrence Resch, Robert Shireman, Gerald Schuler and Terence Faulds – had already pleaded guilty, and Wayne Radcliffe followed suit in July 1993, in November 1992 another high-profile case occurred, when Thomas Jasin was brought before the Philadelphia court. One should stress that after three trials the case against Jasin was eventually dismissed and in 2001 he moved into a top job at NASA, as director of the Robotic Lunar Exploration Program. Robert Goldman nevertheless pursued him throughout the 1990s, describing Jasin as 'a grovelling, corporate ladder-climber who ignored US export laws in hopes of garnering an opportunity for fame, fortune and his boss's admiration'.[82] The former chief executive of ISC Technologies was consequently obliged to endure a long court case that resulted in him being found guilty and sentenced to two years in prison. Jasin's legal team successfully appealed against this sentence, arguing that his client deserved a new trial on the grounds that he needed to read all of the classified documents made available by the CIA and FBI to the prosecuting team. This delayed fresh trials until 1998, indicating perhaps that after Guerin's successful prosecution the US state was less than committed to pursuing other ISC executives. In July 1998, however, Judge Jan E. Dubois reimposed Jasin's two-year sentence, arguing that the classified documents revealed nothing to change the 1992 court's decision. Once again, though, Jasin appealed against the judgement, delaying his imprisonment until December 2000, at which point all legal processes had been exhausted. By August 2001, all charges against Jasin had been dropped, because after an appeal based on the failure of his attorney to provide effective assistance, a court dismissed the earlier indictment.[83] Further substantiating our claim that the state had by that time lost interest in pursuing the ISC executives, the US Attorney's office chose not to contest this decision, not least because Jasin had already served most of his term.

The most significant of Guerin's co-conspirators, of course, had been Clyde Ivy. Apart from his substantial role in developing the South African missiles link, it had been Ivy who had participated in the sham missile contracts with the UAE, Pakistan and China, making him a major target for Goldman's multi-agency team. Ivy was even described by one federal prosecutor as 'a Wal-Mart of weaponry', such had been his role in international arms trading, especially with South Africa.[84] For over six years, however, his legal team successfully avoided a court case, variously pleading a tissue of false reasons that prevented the state from pursuing the October 1991 indictment. His principal claim was that the CIA had authorised ISC's work with South Africa, forcing Judge Jan E. Dubois to read all of the classified documents assembled by the prosecuting team. Finally, after being arraigned in April 1997, Judge Dubois jailed him on fifty-two counts of corporate crime, including contract fraud, money laundering and illegal arms trading, having found no evidence to support Ivy's claims of CIA complicity. However, while the nominal sentence for these crimes was 515 years in jail and a $44 million fine, after intense plea bargaining Ivy's legal team managed to negotiate this down to six months in jail and six months home detention.[85]

The leniency of Ivy's sentence again raises questions about the extent to which the state was by then willing to press the case against those cited in the 1991 court papers. Moreover, when it came to the sentencing of Stagg and Resch in 1998, Judge Dubois argued that Ivy's sentence ought to be regarded as the benchmark against which others should be measured, because the missiles man had not only been Guerin's closest advisor, but also less co-operative than the others.[86] As Table 5.2 indicates, Stagg and Resch were given extremely light sentences, especially if one considers the gravity of the offences committed, while the others served sentences that barely reflect their role in one of the biggest corporate scandals of the late twentieth century.

Finally, it is important to note that while the South African individuals listed in Table 5.1 were never brought to court, the three South African firms were in February 1997 successfully prosecuted and fined $12.5 million for weapons smuggling. Of course, the United Nations embargo on trading with South Africa had been rescinded in 1994, but because of Armscor's relationship with ISC, resulting in the pirating of American missile technology for onward sale to China and Iraq, US prosecutors refused to drop the indictments issued in

Table 5.2 Jail sentences and fines imposed on former ISC executives

Name and address	Jail sentence (date imposed)	Fines or compensation	Prison sentence served
James H. Guerin, Naples, Florida	15 years (July 1992)	$25,000	12 years
Robert Clyde Ivy, Lancaster, Pennsylvania	6 months (Feb 1999) + 6 months home confinement (Oct 1999)	0	6 months
Wayne Radcliffe, Lancaster, Pennsylvania	6 months + 3 years probation (Oct 1999)	$7,500	6 months
Terence Faulds, Holtwood, Pennsylvania	3 months + 3 years probation (Oct 1999)	0	3 months
Thomas Jasin, Lancaster, Pennsylvania	2 years (Nov 1992)	0	18 months (but in 2001 was exonerated after three trials)
Gerald Schuler, West Islip, New York	6 months (July 1999)	0	6 months
Lawrence Resch, San Clemente, California	3 months + 3 months home confinement + 3 years probation	$10,000	3 months
Anthony Stagg, Singapore	3 months home confinement + 3 years probation	$16,000	3 months

October 1991. This was clearly a source of some embarrassment to the new South African regime headed by the massively popular Nelson Mandela, resulting in detailed negotiations between his Deputy President Thabo Mbeki and US Vice President Al Gore. Finally, in 1997 an out-court settlement was reached that resulted in all charges against the individuals being dropped, while Armscor, Kentron and Fuchs (see Table 5.1) agreed to face the same US court that had dealt with Guerin and his associates.

This result again demonstrates clearly that having secured Guerin's 'scalp', the US prosecutors would appear to have been less than committed to ensuring that the others indicted in October 1991 should serve anything resembling the possible sentences outlined in Table 5.1. Of course, politicians were much more concerned with rebuilding the US's links with Nelson Mandela and South Africa from the early 1990s, making it almost inevitable that court cases against those indicted would never materialise. Moreover, continually publicising ISC's activities in South Africa, Iraq, China, Pakistan and Chile in a succession of high-profile court cases did not serve US interests very effectively, especially as this reinforced the growing impression that the CIA and senior military strategists and politicians had been encouraging covert arms trading and flouting international law. Even though in 1993 George Bush Snr was replaced as President by the Democrat Bill Clinton, bringing to an end twelve years of Republican rule, it was still felt impolitic to allow prosecutors to trail information on the last two decades of illicit governmental support for a host of regimes and terrorist groups that were widely regarded as alien to the interests of Western democracy. Indeed, few US politicians wanted to read more revelations about how the Iraqi military used American technology against allied troops during the First Gulf War, or how the US funded the Mujahadeen terrorists of Afghanistan, laying the foundations for the rise of the Taliban (against whom the Allies conducted a bloody and frustrating war since 2002). It was also argued that while the ISC defendants would serve minuscule sentences, they had all been severely financially embarrassed by the indictments, not to mention suffered psychological damage from which they would never recover. On the other hand, this would have generated very little sympathy from the many thousands of Ferranti International employees and investors whose careers and resources were devastated by what happened to the company consequent upon the suspension of share trading in September 1989. It is to this issue that we shall now turn, examining in detail how senior management approached the enormous challenge facing them after discovering ISC's net worth was virtually nil and the Ferranti International balance sheet had been severely dented. Whether this was a fatal 'holing', or merely a serious 'graze', remains a matter of considerable conjecture.

Notes

1 *Daily Telegraph*, 18 Sept 1989; *The Times*, 18 Sept 1989.
2 *Lancaster New Era*, 23 Sept 1989.
3 FBM 6, 21 Nov 1987. See above, pp. 72–5.
4 FBM 8, 7 Sept 1988.
5 See *Sunday Observer*, 8 October 1989, and *Sunday Correspondent*, 24 Sept 1989.
6 See above, pp. 55–60, for a fuller description of Chem-Con's ill-fated history.
7 Jacobson later pleaded guilty of paying $255,000 in bribes between 1982 and 1985 to the Director of the US Navy's Office of Small & Disadvantaged Businesses. *Intelligencer Journal*, 10 June 1989.
8 This was reported in *Observer*, 24 Sept 1989.
9 Reported in *Lancaster New Era*, 8 March 1990.
10 *Philadelphia Inquirer*, 4 Nov 2005.
11 *Intelligencer Journal*, 23 May 1990.
12 See earlier, pp. 31–6.
13 *Intelligencer Journal*, 6 Sept 1991.
14 This section is based on reports in *Lancaster New Era*, 17 May 1990.
15 *Lancaster New Era*, 17 May 1990.
16 Reported in *Lancaster New Era*, 7 Feb 1991.
17 *Lancaster New Era*, 7 Feb 1991.
18 *Independent*, 21 Oct. 1989.
19 *Lancaster New Era*, 25 Sept 1989.
20 *Sunday Correspondent*, 15 Oct. 1989.
21 *Intelligencer Journal*, 11 Oct 1990.
22 *Guardian*, 20 Sept 1989.
23 *Intelligencer Journal*, 3 April 1990.
24 See above, pp. 31–6.
25 *Lancaster New Era*, 8 August 1989. See above, pp. 35–6, for an outline of Guerin's charitable donations.
26 See above, pp. 89–92, for information on how BNL had funded the illegal arms exports to Iraq.
27 See, for example, *Daily Telegraph*, 18 Sept 1989, *The Times*, 18 Sept 1989 and *Financial Times*, 18 Sept 1989.
28 See reports on 24 and 25 Sept 1989 in *The Observer*, *Sunday Telegraph*, and the *Intelligencer Journal*.
29 *Intelligencer Journal*, 11 Oct 1990.
30 The writ was extensively reported in newspapers on 1 December 1989, including *Lancaster Intelligencer Journal*, *Financial Times*, *The Times*, *Independent*, and *Lancaster New Era*.
31 *Lancaster Intelligencer Journal*, 1 December 1989.
32 See above, pp. 40–4.
33 *Intelligencer Journal*, 8 Jan 1990.
34 Ibid.
35 The deal was composed of a single payment of one dollar plus twenty-four interest-free payments of $100,000, providing Jim and Helen Guerin with a nice

pension for their retirement to Florida.

36 This case was reported in, for example, the *Observer*, 1 April 1990, *Independent on Sunday*, 1 April 1990, and *Lancaster New Era*, 30 March 1990.

37 Reported in *Intelligencer Journal*, 16 May 1990.

38 *Lancaster New Era*, 29 Jan 1990.

39 Reported in *Daily Telegraph*, 19 June 1990. See also *Independent*, 20 June 1990

40 *Independent*, 20 June 1990, also reported in *Daily Telegraph*, 20 June 1990.

41 *Lancaster New Era*, 11 August 1990.

42 *The Times*, 27 June 1990.

43 *Lancaster New Era*, 3 July 1990.

44 Reported in *Lancaster New Era*, 6 July 1990. See also FBM.

45 *Lancaster Sunday News*, 6 April 1997.

46 *Intelligencer Journal*, 29 Aug 1990. This case was also reported in the *Daily Telegraph*, 29 Aug 1990, *Financial Times*, 29 Aug 1990, and the *Guardian*, 29 Aug 1990.

47 See above, pp. 35–41.

48 *Intelligencer Journal*, 29 Aug 1990.

49 *Financial Times*, 23 Jan 1991.

50 *The Times*, 26 March 1992.

51 *Intelligencer Journal*, 22 Sept 1990.

52 *Financial Times*, 30 Aug 1990.

53 *Intelligencer Journal*, 11 Oct 1990.

54 *Intelligencer Journal*, 15 Nov 1990.

55 *Intelligencer Journal*, 8 Nov 1990.

56 *Intelligencer Journal*, 1 Nov 1991.

57 *Intelligencer Journal*, 1 Nov 1991.

58 See above, pp. 41–3, for a review of this policy.

59 See above, pp. 44–7.

60 *Lancaster New Era*, 1 Nov 1991.

61 *Intelligencer Journal*, 1 Nov 1991

62 South Africa did not hold its first multi-racial elections until 27 April 1994, reflecting the difficulties experienced during the lengthy negotiations between Mandela and de Klerk.

63 See above, pp. 48–50.

64 *Intelligencer Journal*, 1 Nov 1991.

65 Ibid.

66 Ibid.

67 *Intelligencer Journal*, 5 Feb 1990.

68 See above, pp. 72–4.

69 *Philadelphia Inquirer*, 11 Nov 1991.

70 Ibid.

71 See above, pp. 53–5.

72 Comments of a former ISC executive, quoted in *Lancaster Intelligencer*, 3 Oct 1989.

73 *Intelligencer Journal*, 1 Oct 1991.

74 *Lancaster New Era*, 8 June 1992.

75 *Lancaster New Era*, 25 Aug 2000.
76 *Lancaster New Era*, 26 June 1999.
77 *Intelligencer Journal*, 27 June 1999.
78 *Intelligencer Journal*, 16 Sept 1999.
79 *Intelligencer Journal*, 17 Sept 1999.
80 1 Nov 1991.
81 *Lancaster New Era*, 29 Dec 1992.
82 *Intelligencer Journal*, 17 Nov 1992, 30 Nov 1992, 2 Dec 1992.
83   *Intelligencer Journal*, 10 Aug 2001 and *Legal Intelligence*, 27 Feb 2001.
84 *Intelligencer Journal*, 28 Feb 1997.
85 *Lancaster Sunday News*, 6 April 1997.
86 *Lancaster New Era*, 16 Oct 1998.

6

The rescue strategy

WHILE THE LAST chapter has outlined the exhaustive nature of the multi-agency investigation into the fraud and other crimes perpetrated by Guerin and his closest associates, culminating in a fifteen-year jail sentence for the former ISC chief executive, we now have to analyse how those left with the horrendous task of effecting a recovery of Ferranti International coped with this enormous challenge. The fraud had created a huge hole in the company's accounts, estimated at approximately £400 million, while the acquisition of bank debt totalling £660 million in October 1989 was only going to add substantially to the financial burden. On top of these difficulties, there was also an emerging credibility gap, in that both customers and suppliers proved far less willing to trust Ferranti International. This credibility gap was felt especially by Sir Derek Alun-Jones, because as the chief executive of the firm that had entered into the merger, not to mention being executive chairmen of the joint enterprise, there were many demands for his resignation. To his considerable credit, while agreeing that he should resign, Sir Derek felt it was incumbent on him to put in place a rescue package, before giving way to a new chief executive, the search for whom started in October 1989. Whether or not this person was ever going to effect a full recovery from the ISC-induced crisis will be a major preoccupation of the next chapter, providing a fascinating insight into the way in which employees at all levels struggled with the many challenges facing Ferranti International. Certainly, there was little chance that a 'White Knight' would come to the firm's rescue,[1] because ironically having merged with ISC to forestall a take-over bid, it was highly unlikely that Sir Derek could persuade anybody to provide the much-needed capital injection. In this chapter, we shall be principally concerned with the crucial six months following the announcement that trading in Ferranti International shares would be suspended. For those who had endured the traumatic mid-1970s crisis, it was a case of *déjà vu*, yet with the even more frightening implication that this time the government was not ideologically disposed to step in with a bail-out. Times had changed decisively in this respect, placing much greater emphasis on senior management's ability to re-engineer the firm and save thousands of jobs in the crucial high-technology sector.

In focusing on the rescue strategy enacted by Sir Derek Alun-Jones and his fellow-directors, we shall see how the senior management team and employees at every level of the organisation invested considerable efforts to overcome the crisis. As we have just noted, the political environment was radically different from that which had resulted in the 1974 government-led rescue package, because since the election of a Conservative government in 1979 that was committed to market solutions to macro- and micro-economic problems, the firm could not anticipate a bail-out from the taxpayer.[2] This placed Ferranti International at the mercy of its bankers, with consequences that were to rip the heart out of the business, not to mention making it increasingly unlikely that Sir Derek's successor would be able to effect a full recovery. At the same time, although the ISC-induced financial crisis played a fundamental role in precipitating the demise of Ferranti International, one should also include the wide range of other problems besetting the firm from the mid-1980s, especially the decline in demand for defence equipment and the deep problems besetting several divisions that arose from other decisions taken in the 1980s. Although the crisis that engulfed Ferranti International in September 1989 was initiated by Guerin's nefarious activities, there is little doubt that a range of other factors, both internal and external, exacerbated the tasks faced by senior management, resulting ultimately in the firm's demise by December 1993.

6.1 The crisis strikes

Prior to certain board meetings at the beginning of September 1989, it is apparent that the previous years had been challenging for various divisions across Ferranti International. As we related at the end of Volume 2 and in Chapter 1,[3] by the mid-1980s the firm was struggling to sustain the profitability levels recorded earlier in the decade. The key internal factors that lay behind this deteriorating performance were analysed in Chapter 1, focusing especially on changes to the defence market, failings in various civil activities and troubles in some American acquisitions.[4] In addition, a major external pressure was the threat of a take-over from predators such as Plessey, forcing the Ferranti board to increase dividend payments as a proportion of net profits (see Table 1.1), in order to maintain shareholder loyalty. Crucially, the acquisition of ISC failed to boost corporate performance; indeed, Sir Derek was obliged to accept under intense questioning from a financial journalist in June 1989 that it was difficult to claim total success on this front.[5] This questioning was prompted by the firm's announcement of a profits warning, amounting to a 20% shortfall on the 1988–89 results. As Ferranti had already

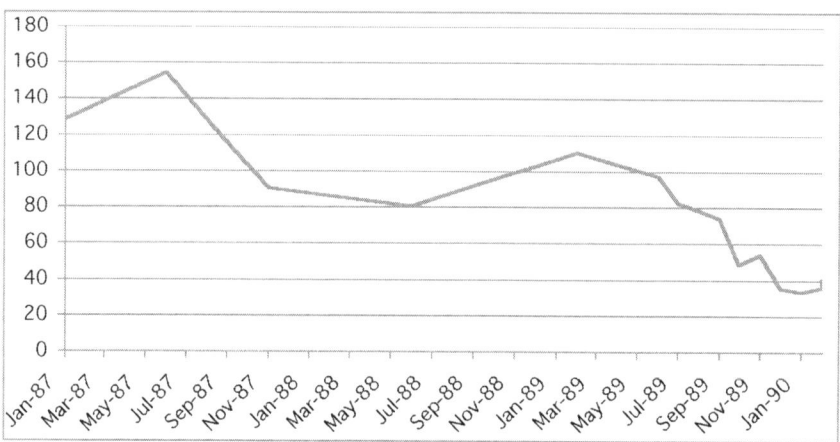

Figure 6.1 Ferranti International share price, 1987–90

reported in March 1989 that 1,000 jobs had been cut in its commercial computer division (at Wythenshawe),[6] commentators were beginning to express severe reservations about holding on to Ferranti International equities.[7] Moreover, even though Ferranti Defence Systems Ltd (FDSL) had secured a contract to supply the *Tornado* pilot display panels,[8] considerable uncertainty surrounded discussions over which company would be awarded the production contract for onboard radar equipment to be fitted to the next generation of European military aircraft.[9] It was also in August that the naval systems department (Bracknell) lost the Type 23 frigate command and control computer systems orders,[10] undermining the commercial credibility of another key component of the Ferranti portfolio. Not surprisingly, Ferranti International shares had since June 1989 been falling in value on the London Stock Exchange (see Figure 6.1), having already slipped significantly from their post-merger high in February 1989 of 110p.

Given this context, it is apparent that the Ferranti International board was already wrestling with serious problems by the time a series of decisive board meetings was called between 6 and 10 September. After intense debate about both the nature of the contractual issues at ISC Technologies and the most effective immediate responses, as well as taking advice from representatives of Barings Bank, Herbert Smith, Grant Thornton and PMM, it was decided to suspend trading in the company's shares, to take effect on 11 September. By that time, as we saw in Chapter 4, it was clear to senior Ferranti International executives that the KP and *Alpha* contracts were a total fiction. As we also noted in that chapter, one can question why it had taken the board so long to act decisively, especially in view of the information generated by Alan Cooper and Ian Ball during their investigations of ISC Technologies' overseas contracts.[11] While the report produced by Cooper for Sir Derek on this subject had been delivered on 5 January 1989, it was September before the rest of the board were given copies, a development about which Robin Broadley expressed considerable surprise.[12] Not only did Sir Derek miss this opportunity to involve the board in these investigations, there had also been several other occasions when senior executives could have decided to act decisively on the mounting suspicions concerning ISC Technologies' activities. Charles Scott's meetings with various Pakistani officials stand out in this respect, while the failure of Guerin to raise enough funds to buy back parts of ISC ought to have set warning-bells ringing. There had also been clear warnings from the MoD that ISC was being investigated by the FBI over various embargo-breaking contracts, news that should have obliged the Ferranti International board to pursue a forensic enquiry into these allegations. Instead, Sir Derek in particular, as well as others in senior management positions, chose to accept Guerin's denials and categoric statements of innocence, preferring to place more emphasis on the potential profits to be made from even larger missile contracts. Above all, it was this total trust in Guerin that overcame all of the insinuations and overt evidence, leading to the delay in making crucial decisions until early September 1989.

The crucial board meetings started on Wednesday 6 September, when the chairman invited advisors from Barings Bank, the leading law firm of Herbert Smith, two accountants from Grant Thornton, a representative of PMM (the firm that had conducted the audits of ISC in 1986–87), and as many of the directors who were available at what was short notice. With the firm's annual general meeting planned for 12 September, at which shareholders would be asked to approve the accounts for 1988–89 that had already been published in August, it was incumbent on the board to decide just exactly what they would reveal. As Charles Scott had by then ascertained more accurate information on the Pakistani contract, and it was also evident that the *Alpha* contract was barely credible, the legal advisors were clear that the board had no choice but to admit that previously published accounts contained false information. Inevitably, the discussions went on for some time, Sir Derek adding during a period when the advisors had been asked to leave the room that 'making a statement [on the fraudulent contracts] would be extremely damaging in seeking ultimate recovery in Pakistan and in prospective sales such as EFA [the radar contract for the latest generation of European military aircraft]'.[13] Such were the extant uncertainties that the advisors were brought back into the meeting and asked to consider a range of options, from going ahead with the accounts as they stood, deferring a dividend announcement, or full revelation of the situation.

The failure to come to a decision at that meeting resulted in another board meeting on the following day, when the same group of advisors attended in order to guide the board through the various options. By that time, Charles Scott had reformulated the financial forecasts for 1989–90 and 1990–91, as a prelude to recasting the published accounts for the previous two years. It was also increasingly accepted by the board that in the circumstances not only should the AGM be adjourned, but also the much more drastic step ought to be taken of suspending all trading in Ferranti International shares. Once again, though, the final decisions were deferred on both fronts, because Sir Derek wanted firstly to discuss the situation with the firm's bankers, while the Barings Bank representative, James Lupton, was asked to initiate discussions with the London Stock Exchange concerning the suspension of share trading.[14] This work had been completed by Sunday 10 September, including a meeting between Sir Derek and NatWest on the evening of 9 September, leaving all concerned in no doubt about the unusual nature of the situation. Furthermore, the 10 September board meeting was convened at Barings Bank, at which all the formalities were approved and Scott's forward projections analysed in minute detail. The latter also included the creation of an Asset Disposal Programme, in recognition of the need to fill the gap created by the false missile contracts, while Coopers & Lybrand was commissioned to conduct a full-scale investigation of the merger and consequent financial situation, to be delivered by 2 October. Crucially, and with a heavy heart, the board had initiated processes which in retrospect marked the beginning of the end for Ferranti International. While it was another four years before bankruptcy proceedings were started, it is clear that the momentous decisions of 10 September were to have dramatic consequences for all who had any links with the firm.[15]

Once again, one must return to the image conjured up by that board meeting. As some of those who were in attendance remembered,[16] it was an atmosphere that combined abject misery at the inevitable implications of their decisions with continued disbelief at the scale and nature of Guerin's activities. Indeed, privately Joe Zilligen of ISC European Technologies refused to believe that Guerin had perpetrated such an enormous fraud. Of course, he had been steadfast in this position, having countered Ian Ball's accusations in July 1989 about Guerin's activities by arguing that the real cause of the group's financial woes was the overvaluation of computer systems stock in Wythenshawe. While Ball had successfully disproved this accusation,[17] to the board as a whole, though, it was patently obvious that they had a duty to make a public announcement, otherwise they could have been regarded as having been party to the crimes uncovered. Of course, the annual report for 1988–89 had already been published in August, disclosing figures based on the financial picture available to the accountants at that time. This report had noted that, even though the pre-tax profits had fallen to £55.8 million (from

£68 million in 1987–88), the profit attributable to shareholders had been given as £29.3 million (as opposed to £24.3 million in 1987–88) because extraordinary charges were much lower. Indeed, even though the UK defence and computer systems markets were proving difficult, with an order book supposedly totalling £1.6 billion and turnover increasing to £1.05 billion (compared to £822.1 million in 1987–88), Ferranti International seemed well set to maintain the profit levels recorded during the 1980s. This relatively rosy picture was, however, dashed completely at the company's AGM on 12 September, when the annual report posted on 11 August was withdrawn. The suspension of trading in Ferranti International shares had also occurred at 8 am on 11 September, pending a full investigation of the firm's accounts by Coopers & Lybrand.

Having had a hectic schedule of formal and informal meetings in the previous week, from 11 September Sir Derek and his senior colleagues were then involved in an even more intense period. As MD responsible for operations, Dr Shepherd convened a meeting of all subsidiary heads at 8 am on 11 September, while Sir Derek and Charles Scott met with senior people at NatWest, Barclays and Chase Manhatten that morning, followed by discussions with Sir Peter Levene at the MoD and his equivalent at the DTI, Alistair MacDonald. At another board meeting on 12 September, reports were tabled on all of these discussions, leading to the general belief that the crisis could be controlled, both financially and in terms of customer expectations. Of course, nobody was complacent, especially as the Coopers & Lybrand investigations would produce definitive evidence on the extent of the financial 'hole' created by Guerin. It was consequently unclear whether in issuing a public announcement to shareholders the board should give a specific figure, given that it was impossible at that stage to be definitive.[18] On one issue, however, they were all agreed, namely, that: 'In general terms we have to accept that any short term recovery [from Guerin and his associates] of any money is unlikely. We must plan on that basis and have started by asking the Banks to support the Company on this basis.'[19] At the same time, the chief corporate publicity officer, Tony Thomas, was obliged to quash a rumour that the company's troubles originated with a £50 million naval electronics contract with Iraq.[20] While ISC's Italian subsidiaries had certainly been involved in contracts of this kind, Thomas was at pains to explain that these had not contributed to the emerging crisis. Such was the degree of uncertainty in those hectic days that Thomas and his team were obliged to keep a careful watch on the rampant speculation emanating from journalists and other commentators.

Of course, it was inevitable that speculation was rife, given the reluctance of the board to release much information to explain why the shares had been suspended. The extremely brief AGM held on 12 September at the Millbank headquarters failed to satisfy the small number of shareholders who attended, Sir Derek specifically stating in answer to a request for details by stating forcibly: 'I would discourage speculation and I do not propose to take any questions'.[21] This prompted some fierce exchanges, especially with individual shareholders who could not muster the kind of financial backing of the institutional fundholders present. For example, Douglas Gordon not only questioned the board's lack of judgement, but also 'looked in vain for a single statement of regret in any of your letters'.[22] Warming to his brief, Gordon went to state: 'Sir Derek must have been a babe in the woods to get swindled that way.' The lack of information disseminated to shareholders was another cause of widespread concern, making Tony Thomas's job no easier, as well as stretching the patience of those who had been loyal to Ferranti since the 1978 refloatation,[23] leading to the fabrication of rumours and half-truths concerning the cause of the crisis. This obliged the board to devote a considerable amount of time to drafting a legally defensible, yet circumspect, letter to shareholders that adequately explained the reasons why trading in Ferranti International shares had been suspended.

At the same time, Sir Derek's primary concern was retaining the bankers' support; if they withdrew any facilities, it would have been calamitous. Consequently, considerable efforts were made to negotiate a rescue package that would ensure the short-term survival of Ferranti International, the consequences of which we shall assess over the next chapters. At the next board meeting, on 19 September, apart from reporting on these negotiations Sir Derek admitted that he had been talking to various companies – British Aerospace; GEC; Siemens; STC – which might invest in Ferranti International, in order to shore up the weakened balance sheet. While a preference was expressed for British Aerospace, on the grounds that they 'need us as much as we need them because of our electronics expertise', especially in relation to the ongoing debate about the next generation of European military aircraft,[24] the board wanted to keep open its options on this type of rescue.[25] At that same meeting, it was also agreed to enter into a facility agreement with a group of banks (NatWest, Barclays, Chase Manhattan and four others[26]) for a loan of up to £70 million, secured on the company's assets. With Barings Bank acting as underwriters of this loan, the banks proved to be sufficiently supportive of Ferranti International, thereby pre-empting a short-term liquidity crisis while the investigations continued. On the other hand, as we shall see over the course of this chapter, the conditions imposed by the banks were to prove especially arduous; not only were they able to exact a significant rate of return on their lending, the banks also demanded that up to £100 million of the company's assets must be sold in order to cover the increased loans. As the *Financial Times* headline put it, this represented a 'Multi-million pound car boot sale', with particular emphasis placed on the disposal of ISC's divisions.[27] It soon became clear, however, that as we shall see later this was going to prove extremely problematic, given their association with fraud and illicit trading. This forced the board to consider other disposals, the consequences of which were to create different yet equally troublesome challenges for the recovery strategy.

As these challenges were only to emerge slowly from mid-September 1989, the board felt that securing the £70 million facility at least provided the liquidity to maintain the business, not to mention calming the growing fears expressed in the City and several newspapers concerning the company's future. By that time, a figure of £150 million was being widely used to indicate the size of the financial problem, while some commentators feared that major customers would baulk at placing substantial contracts with a firm that had been so fatally holed.[28] With the West German defence ministry expressing considerable scepticism about the ability of Ferranti Defence Systems Ltd to complete what could be a £2 billion radar contract for the EFA radar system,[29] those employed in the much-maligned ISC divisions feared that they would never be able to secure another government contract. Such was the publicity surrounding the company's plight that on 18 September the BBC's *Nine O'Clock News* covered the story, quoting Sir Derek's plea that: 'The company will survive because it's a great company. It employs an enormous number of people. It does a lot of turnover and it's technically a very fine company.'[30] While accepting that mistakes had been made with respect to the acquisition of ISC, he was at pains to stress the continued viability of an enterprise that had existed for over a century. At that time, however, it was impossible to stop newspapers like *The Times* carrying editorial comment about 'Ferranti in crisis' and quoting unattributed hindsight opinions that the board of directors had not only failed to conduct due diligence on ISC, but also avoided all of the alleged warnings about Guerin and his business practices.[31] The *Sunday Times* even carried one story claiming Sir Derek had 'lost his temper and defended his new deputy chairman [Guerin] as a fine businessman and good friend', after having been summoned to the MoD by Sir Peter Levene once the merger with ISC had been announced.[32] Although the MoD was obliged later to issue categoric denials that it had warned Sir Derek off the merger, observers continued to use hindsight as a means of questioning the motives and actions surrounding this decisive event.

Inevitably, this situation agitated the board considerably, with the directors' workload showing no sign of easing as September progressed: Sir Derek and Ian Ball travelled to Abu Dhabi to discuss the PGM contract with Sheikh Mohammed; Dr Shepherd met the ISC proxy board; and Nathan Blackwell visited Pakistan to pin down both General Masood (head of Pakistani military procurement) and Mr Ehtisham (managing director of KP

Industries) on the exact state of the KP contract. With regard to the latter, of course, as Guerin was no longer in a position to bribe people, it was easier to ascertain the truth from officials, while sufficient assurances were received from Sheikh Mohammed about PGM to satisfy the board that these contracts would continue.[33] Nevertheless, as there was still too much uncertainty about the financial situation, when discussing the circular letter to shareholders the board was still reluctant to make bold statements about the extent of the fraud and possible losses. This delayed its publication even further, resulting in considerable unease amongst shareholders.[34] Indeed, the board seemed to be paying more attention to its banking supporters, rather than those who actually owned the firm. On the other hand, it is only fair to point out that as PMM were objecting to any specific reference to a fraud, given the legal implications of such an admission for ISC's auditors, the exact wording had to be very carefully phrased to avoid unnecessary legal action.

Another key issue with which the board wrestled at that time was what to do with the ISC businesses located in the USA. Since Guerin's resignation in May 1989, Joseph Zilligen (formerly, the ISC finance director) had been chairman of Ferranti International USA, reporting to the board on all US activities. By early October, however, it was apparent to the board that it was essential to take a firmer grip of the ISC subsidiaries, Robin Broadley having noted that 'there was a tremendous management weakness there'.[35] In these circumstances, Sir Derek turned to Albert Dodd, the MD of Ferranti Instrumentation who had built an extensive reputation as a 'safe pair of hands' capable of dealing with corporate crises. Dodd was immediately despatched to Lancaster, Penn., where he set about acquiring as much information on the beleaguered ISC subsidiaries and imposing much stronger control of the deteriorating financial situation.[36] To Zilligen, however, this presented a challenge to his credibility, because while Ferranti International presented this managerial change as part of the integration of ISC into the group, and he remained a director, it was clear that his links with Guerin had tarnished his reputation.[37] Indeed, by November Zilligen had been suspended from all executive duties and invited to resign from the board, after several of the potential partners that Sir Derek had been courting commentated unfavourably on his continued presence.[38] Zilligen eventually resigned at the end of the year, but not after making strident demands for extensive compensation which were strongly resisted by the board.

While Albert Dodd's initial role was to replace the devolved style of management that had characterised the way in which the ISC businesses had been run since 1987 with a much tighter set of controls, another key role would be to investigate how quickly Ferranti International could offload these activities. Particular emphasis was placed on selling Marquadt, given that Zilligen was confident of a price in excess of $115 million for the

California-based advanced technology firm. As we shall see later, this view proved far too optimistic, even though Albert Dodd engaged the prominent investment bank Morgan Stanley to advise on the sale.[39] When one remembers that Dodd was also running Ferranti Italia at that time, not to mention continuing in his roles as MD of Ferranti Instrumentation and a main board director, this was exhausting work. It was consequently decided in the summer of 1990 to relieve him of the US responsibilities, replacing him with the finance director of Ferranti International USA, James Shinehouse, who became president and chief executive officer. A graduate of West Chester University, Virginia, Shinehouse had worked for six years for Peat Marwick Main & Co as an auditor. He joined ISC in 1986 as director of internal audits,[40] but it is clear that he had never been a party to the frauds perpetrated by senior ISC people. Indeed, he was trusted by Albert Dodd to continue the diligent management of the US operations and ensure that as much was sold at remunerative prices. These roles he played extremely well over the course of the following three years, building a reputation as a highly talented financial manager.

6.2 Public announcements and Sir Derek

It was finally on 29 September 1989 that the chairman issued a seven-page circular to all shareholders concerning the discovery of a major fraud, based on some suspect ISC contracts that predated the 1987 merger. Sir Derek explained in some detail 'that the company has been the victim of a serious fraud', mostly located in ISC Technologies and involving 'sales contracts and sub-contracts which did not in reality exist'.[41] Although admitting that this had 'significantly weakened' the company, he also stressed that not only had its bankers provided adequate liquidity to sustain the business, there was every prospect of a robust recovery based on the group's 'great strengths in selected areas of defence and civil electronics'. Indeed, a supportive memo issued by the MoD was included in the circular, while Sir Derek outlined how Coopers & Lybrand was conducting a detailed investigation that would provide much greater clarity on the extent and impact of the fraud. This also acted as the prelude to relisting the company's shares on the London Stock Exchange on 3 October, an issue to which we shall return in the next section.

At the board meeting when this letter was approved, apart from further debate about the varying dimensions of the perceived fraud, there was also discussion of another key issue, namely, the position of Sir Derek Alun-Jones. This item had been placed on the agenda by Sir Derek himself, leading him to state that he only held the position of chairman as a result of the board's wishes. It was left to Charles Scott to note that 'the board has total confidence in the way in which Sir Derek is handling matters', a statement that was approved unanimously by the board.[42] Sir John Hoskyns also reiterated the board's total support for Sir Derek, when responding to questions at the reconvened (but hastily adjourned) AGM on 10 October, stating that it would be 'foolish' to suggest that the chairman should resign at this crucial stage in the company's history.[43]

While this would have reassured Sir Derek of his board's support, one should stress that externally there was mounting pressure on him to resign and allow the appointment of somebody whose reputation was not tarnished by the ramifications of a failed merger.[44] Throughout September and October the leading newspapers carried often extensive analysis of the company's predicament, frequently featuring photographs of Sir Derek alongside Jim Guerin at 1987 meetings when the merger was announced.[45] Headlines such as 'A major force snatches disaster from the jaws of success',[46] '"Sloppy" management attacked by institutional shareholders',[47] or 'American rocket man who rolled Ferranti',[48] instilled widespread fear amongst shareholders and employees, with most commentators latching on to the figure of £150 million as the scale of the losses. As one commentator noted of Sir Derek:

> He used to brag that he was brought into Ferranti to save the company from the Ferrantis, the extraordinary and talented [founding] family ... But Sir Derek Alun-Jones, the personable and urbane chairman of Ferranti International Signal, has managed to produce a version of horrors which rivals any past errors of the Ferranti family.[49]

Many other highly critical comments were especially made about the decision to embark on this merger, with both implicit and explicit views expressed in abundance concerning the alleged warnings given to Sir Derek and his fellow-directors about Guerin's business activities.[50]

These attacks inevitably employed a good deal of hindsight, especially when it came to claims that Sir Derek and his board had been warned off ISC, allegedly by the MoD.[51] Publicly, Sir Derek shrugged off such attacks with his usual aplomb and self-confidence, denying that any warnings of substance had been given by either the MoD or financial institutions. Having spent the previous fourteen years at the head of Ferranti, he had carefully nurtured the image of being in total command of his brief, speaking regularly with journalists and City people about corporate strategy and general industry developments. He was consequently 'liked and respected' in the most influential circles,[52] even if he had never enjoyed the best of working relationships with MoD officials. On the other hand, apart from the widespread concerns expressed about the ISC merger, some commentators were beginning to question aspects of the Alun-Jones era. For example, in spite of both market trends and an avowed preference for building up the civil side of the Ferranti portfolio, throughout the 1980s he had overseen a growing dependence on defence orders. The sale of the electronic components division to Plessey in 1987 was regarded as decisive in this respect, providing a major challenge to those charged with the task of engineering a recovery in Ferranti International fortunes, an issue to which we shall turn in the next chapter.

Another criticism that one hears voiced in the late 1980s was an accusation that Sir Derek was no longer as committed to the brief he had been given in 1975. The *Scotsman* even claimed that he had 'lost his edge', quoting the 1987 sale of what had once been the world-leading electronic chip business to Plessey as a clear sign that Ferranti under Sir Derek was no longer capable of sustaining key competitive positions. With 'Skeletons ... emerging from the [ISC] cupboard', the same source went on to argue that while Sir Derek was widely liked in City circles, this 'raises serious questions about his judgement and his grip on the organisation'.[53] Few denied the considerable achievements of, firstly, rehabilitating the company's fortunes after the mid-1970s liquidity crises, earning him a considerable reputation in the City of London. Secondly, by the early 1980s Ferranti was generating both improved dividend returns and healthy premiums on the equity, adding significantly to his reputation. In turn, this also brought him several invitations to join the boards of other prestigious firms, distracting him from the full-time job he had at Ferranti. For example, in 1986 he was made a non-executive director of GKN, and although he resigned from this post in May 1988, this role was replaced by similar positions in Mason Best International (a privately owned US bank) and Consolidated Gold, one of the world's leading mining conglomerates. In typical fashion, however, Sir Derek robustly refuted any explicit or implicit attack on his commitment to Ferranti International, preferring to devote his considerable energy and ability to the challenges in hand.[54] At the same time, it was clear to many that he was under considerable pressure; even if photographs taken at the time frequently showed him smiling and continuing to act as if this was just another business exercise, there is no doubt that he was totally devoted to correcting the problems that had emerged on his watch.

Given the long history of conflict that had characterised their relationship, the irony of this situation was not lost on Sebastian de Ferranti, who seized the opportunity to make a series of statements both to the board[55] and in the press,[56] outlining his distaste for the way in which Sir Derek had managed the company. As soon as the crisis broke, he immediately leaked to the press the contents of the Lazard Brothers report he had commissioned in 1987, stressing the level of uncertainty that surrounded Guerin and ISC.[57] Apart from attacking the alleged financial orientation of Sir Derek's strategies, Sebastian suggested that a committee composed of major shareholders should be convened, a representative from which ought to be appointed to the board. This rekindled the former chairman's early 1980s plan to oust Sir Derek and regain family control of the group,[58] because even though by 1989

Sebastian only held 1.8% of the Ferranti International equity, after having sold off a substantial number of shares to fund the construction of his splendid new house at Henbury Hall, he still felt very close to the firm that had once been his life. Sir Derek consequently agreed to meet Sebastian to discuss these issues, but the board firmly rejected all of his arguments about culpability and managerial changes,[59] leaving him fuming on the sidelines as the scenario unfolded.

Several newspapers also carried extensive comment on the situation in which Ferranti International found itself, placing the blame firmly on Sir Derek's shoulders.[60] Although some of this commentary was objective and reflected City expectations, there were also several crude attempts at character assassination which were in poor taste. One especially vitriolic article was penned by *The Times* journalist Bernard Levin, who while admitting his total ignorance of City matters chose to question Sir Derek's decision to lead Ferranti into the merger with ISC. Entitling his article, 'Off target but ready for firing: Bernard Levin gives Ferranti's Sir Derek Alun-Jones a timely rocketing', using a range of anecdotal evidence based on hindsight claims that Sir Derek had been extensively warned that 'Mr Guerin was not quite 16 annas to the rupee'. Levin went on to claim: 'The list of people who, having taken a look at Mr Guerin, decided to have nothing to do with him could scarcely be contained in an entire volume of the London telephone directory.'[61] Using a cartoon depicting Sir Derek tied to a guided missile that was about to be despatched, the journalist demanded his resignation and the appointment of a more professional manager who would act responsibly. This prompted the beleaguered Ferranti International chairman to reply vigorously, using that newspaper's famous letters column to decry Levin's propensity to 'base his opinions on … fiction'.[62] While accepting the quality of Levin's comedic writing, Sir Derek forcefully denied the claims that abundant warnings had been given about the credibility of ISC's accounts. Alluding to the report produced by Lazard Brothers for Sebastian de Ferranti,[63] he also mentioned that the former owner's trusts did not vote against the ISC merger,[64] while Basil de Ferranti as chairman of Ferranti plc was 100% behind his managing director.

Another key agent in the discussions surrounding the immediate crisis facing Ferranti International was the government, not least because the MoD was the firm's principal customer, and the DTI had extensively supported other activities. This was why Sir Derek personally met with the leading figures in those ministries, extracting promises from Sir Peter Levene at the MoD that all contract payments would be settled promptly, in order to provide the essential liquidity. Sir Peter was also extensively consulted over the course of the following three months about the potential alliance with either a leading British firm or one of the major European and American conglomerates that expressed an interest in an investment. While discussions of this kind were essential, however, not least because of the extreme sensitivity of negotiations over the EFA contracts,[65] the incumbent Conservative government refused to countenance any direct state involvement in Ferranti International. This *laissez-faire* attitude was born of an ideological commitment to market solutions; even though the DTI especially had been heavily involved in regional economic activities throughout the 1980s,[66] with the abolition of the National Enterprise Board by Margaret Thatcher it was clear to all parties that the state would not be investing directly in private enterprise. Of course, Donald Dewar and a group of Scottish Labour MPs lobbied the Scottish Secretary, Malcolm Rifkind, on behalf of the Ferranti operations around Edinburgh, while other prominent Labour politicians such as Bryan Gould and Martin O'Neill met with DTI and MoD ministers and officials.[67] While the Defence Secretary, Tom King, was willing to make supportive statements, however, there was never any realistic chance of a taxpayer bail-out along the lines of the 1974–75 rescue.

It was consequently apparent from a very early stage in this crisis that Sir Derek and his board were regarded as the principal architects of their own destiny,[68] with the MoD and DTI adopting a watching brief that rarely extended to much more than rhetorical support. This political environment served to reinforce the firm's total commitment to finding a way out of the crisis, ignoring their critics in the interests of an objective analysis of the various options available to Ferranti International by that time. In this respect, relisting the company's shares on 3 October was, of course, an important move in restoring market confidence, even if they had lost 35% of their value, falling from the suspension price of 73.5 pence to just 48 pence (see Figure 6.1). Much depended on what would be revealed in the revised accounts that would be announced on 16 November, given that this would give a truer indication of the firm's market value and the extent of the damage done by its merger with ISC. Specifically, shareholders, employees and other stakeholders were anxious to know what proportion of ISC's net worth calculated by PMM of $320 million still existed. Of course, there were some valuable assets in the ISC group, especially the defence and space group and Italian operations. Similarly, Ferranti International Dynamics – FIDL! – was still heavily involved in the development and production of the PGM missiles, *Hakim I* and *Hakim II*. On the other hand, both Ferranti and its advisors had been duped into believing that ISC was worth the money paid out in 1987, when in fact an elaborate tissue of lies and deceit had been devised to inflate ISC's market value.

The true extent of the financial crisis was finally revealed to the board on 2 October, when the head of Coopers & Lybrand's investigations team, James Truscott, delivered their much-anticipated report. This exercise had been

conducted with such alacrity and accuracy by a thirty-strong team of
accountants that the Ferranti International board had no option but to heed
all of its conclusions at yet another vital meeting on 4 October.[69] Although
delving into considerable detail, which was condensed into a ten-part report
of just eighty-five pages, the most vital piece of information generated by
Coopers & Lybrand was $385 million, denoting the extent to which ISC's
assets had been inflated at the time of the 1987 merger with Ferranti. In
addition, they also calculated that the balance sheet had been exposed to a
fraud worth £215 million Linked to these key pieces of data were two conclusions: firstly, that Guerin and his closest associates had deliberately inflated
the value of ISC by creating a range of false contracts; and secondly, the
implication that PMM had failed in their due diligence duties. While the
former merely confirmed what all directors had by then accepted, the latter
led to concerns that if the full document was passed to the firm's bankers then
the defamatory comments could create further problems. It was consequently
decided that Coopers & Lybrand should be asked to produce a summary
report for the banks and prospective partners that revealed only the bare
financial data. On the other hand, the board agreed that if the Serious Fraud
Office (SFO) wanted to see the full report, then this would be made available,
in the interests of pursuing the alleged criminals and possibly recouping
some of the money defrauded from Ferranti shareholders. The SFO duly
made a request for a copy of the report, leading to its immediate transmission, while the DTI was also provided with the full document. Coopers &
Lybrand were asked to conduct further investigations into ISC's trading
activities, given that some prospective partners expressed a reluctance to
invest in Ferranti International until it was crystal clear that further problems
did not exist.[70]

Providing assurances of this kind was, of course, an essential component in
the emerging rescue strategy devised by the board, in that considerable
efforts were made to interest a range of potential partners in taking an equity
shareholding, thereby avoiding the necessity of extending the firm's fixed
debt. Sir Peter Levene at the MoD had also sanctioned this strategy, on
condition that as the most dominant defence supplier in the UK, GEC was
not the chief partner, leading Ferranti International directors to work extensively on British Aerospace. At the same time, two leading financial
institutions were collaborating on an alternative proposal that would have
split Ferranti International into two groups. The initiative for this had come
from senior executives at Ferranti Defence Systsems Ltd, based in Edinburgh,
who persuaded the leading Scottish fund management firm of Murray
Johnstone to work with the prominent merchant bankers Hill Samuel on a
scheme to separate what had been the four major Ferranti divisions from the
ISC subsidiaries.[71] Having conducted this exercise, they were also advocating

the combination of Ferranti core activities with another major electronics firm, possibly Thorn EMI, in order to protect existing contracts from the possibility that customers would either withdraw their business or refuse to place new commissions. When discussed by the Ferranti International board, however, it was clear that they were much less interested in this option than a British Aerospace involvement, especially if Thomson was also involved on the sonar side of the business.[72]

The strategy of finding a partner to invest in an ailing company was frequently referred to in the City of London as finding a 'White Knight', in that it was expected that a firm would come riding to the rescue, endowing it with the resources that were required in order to stave off bankruptcy. Indeed, entreaties were being made to several other sources, including Lockheed, the Singapore Investment Bank and Daimler-Benz. In October, Dr Shepherd also made a series of presentations to potential partners such as AEG Telefunken, Westinghouse, Sagem, Dowty, and Finmeccanica, while spending even more time with British Aerospace and Thomson. Following what Sir Derek described as this 'beauty parade',[73] a Second Stage Information Package was distributed to all of these firms, while discussions were held with existing shareholders, most noticeably the leading institutional investors that had stuck with the firm since the refloatation in 1980, to ensure that they were happy with the possibility of a major investment.

While considerable optimism was being expressed both within and outside the company that a 'White Knight' would take a major equity holding, it was still necessary for Barings Bank to engage in more detailed negotiations with a syndicate of thirty banks, in order to supplement the £70 million facility provided in September. Barings' ability to perform this kind of role was widely acknowledged, given its esteemed status in the City of London – Sir John Baring sat on the Court of the Bank of England – and its links with a substantial number of other leading financial institutions.[74] These revised banking arrangements would need to be concluded before Ferranti International could publish its revised accounts, given that prospective partners were never going to buy an equity holding until they received cast-iron assurances that the firm was still liquid.[75] This inevitably involved Charles Scott's team in a considerable amount of work, alongside the firm's auditors, PMM and Grant Thornton, because it was essential to give the clear impression that the firm remained a sound investment. In the interim, Barings Bank brokered detailed negotiations with the banking syndicate, headed by NatWest, ANZ Grindlays and Chase Manhattan, leading to an agreement signed on 14 November that had enormous implications for the future of Ferranti International.

On the one hand, the agreement itself gave out a strong signal to the financial markets that leading institutions had enough faith in the firm to provide liquidity of up to £300 million. Indeed, the agreement when announced publicly was extremely well received, even if few were sanguine enough to interpret this as the end of the firm's problems. On the other hand, it is vital to assess the conditions imposed by the bank syndicate, because apart from all the usual clauses dictating that repayment of the loan would be the first charge on Ferranti International assets, they also stipulated that Ferranti International would have to sell off assets to the value of £100 million, as well as consider an equity issue of up to £150 million. While the latter had already been considered by the board as an essential part of the rescue operation, the stipulation that the firm would have to sell up to £100 million worth of assets imposed a serious constraint on the firm's longer-term viability. Put simply, given the firm's financial status by that time, its bargaining position was so poor that predators were reluctant to pay full market prices for any product range that was up for sale, while such were the liquidity issues affecting certain parts of the group that only the most profitable would be placed in the shop-window. One might consequently argue that the banks had imposed such harsh conditions on their support that it is difficult to see how Ferranti International would be able to engineer a robust recovery, especially as the most profitable divisions would be stripped out of the group. We shall return to this debate at several junctures in the next chapter, questioning whether the attitude of the firm's bankers proved sufficiently supportive, at a time when its bargaining position was weakening significantly.

Having come to this agreement with the banks, it was then possible to produce a revised set of accounts for 1988 and 1989, laying bare for all to see the full impact of Guerin's action. Of course, a considerable amount of preparation had been done by Charles Scott's team on this exercise, involving PMM and Grant Thornton extensively in recasting figures that had accommodated the fraudulent contracts devised by Guerin and his closest associates. The key dimensions of the revised accounts were debated in minute detail at a board meeting on 3 November, resulting in the decision to reveal that the 'bottom line' was an accounting loss of £400 million, made up of £215 million on the false contracts, added to which was a write-down on ISC's assets of £185 million.[76] This reflected the depth of the crisis in a company whose market value in September 1989 was just £230 million. The gross profits for 1988–89 were reduced from the £55.8 million registered in August to £13.1 million, while the 1988 gross profit of £68 million had been cut to £54.5 million. Crucially, the net worth of ISC at the time of the 1987 merger had been nil, with further investigations by Coopers & Lybrand demonstrating that in the previous four years the firm had significantly inflated its value by incorporating contracts that patently did not exist.[77] As Appendix A reveals, the board was consequently obliged to dig deep into its reserves over the following years, whittling away the accumulated total of £159.2 million recorded in 1986–87. This again reinforces the vital importance of the financial package negotiated with the company's bankers, even if arguably the conditions imposed exacerbated what in essence was a desperate situation.

The AGM of 16 November was not surprisingly an extremely tricky event for Sir Derek and the board, because for the first time they were obliged to face their harshest critics and explain why investments in Ferranti International had fallen so drastically. Of course, considerable emphasis was placed on the nature and scale of the fraud perpetrated by James Guerin, in an attempt to deflect some of the criticism, with descriptions of non-existent arms deals, the web of Swiss and Panamanian front companies, and cash outflows to Guerin enlivening the atmosphere at that fraught meeting. Shareholders were assured that legal proceedings would be initiated against 'undisclosed parties' to recoup some of the £215 million lost as a result of the merger, although it was impossible to say when any of this money would be repaid.[78] At the same time, Sir Derek categorically denied any claims that the board had been informed of any irregularities in either ISC's accounts or trading, arguing that Ferranti conducted intensive discussions with as many people as possible. On the other hand, he was ready to implicate PMM as ISC's auditors in the crisis, proclaiming that: 'We had no reason to doubt the validity of ISC's audited accounts and reliance was placed on the last set of accounts presented by PMM.'[79]

Although the legal ramifications of this statement ran well past the time covered by this chapter, it is appropriate at this point to delve further into the way in which PMM had conducted its audit of ISC. Earlier sections have highlighted how question marks hang threateningly over this exercise, for example the failure to oblige ISC executives to provide more concrete evidence on the secretive overseas contracts that accounted for such an enormous proportion of the firm's sales and profit. Simply allowing Lawrence Resch to show PMM staff a bonded warehouse in Belgium hardly resembles the pursuit of 'due diligence', leading the *Financial Times* to ask 'one wonders the extent to which [the say-so of management] was identified as a risk by the Peats audit team, and to what lengths the firm went to establish third party verification of the figures from the sensitive contracts'.[80] This article arose out of 'damning statements' made by Sir Derek Alun-Jones in the revised set of Ferranti International accounts published in November 1989, when he concluded that:

In summary ... the audited accounts of the ISC group at 31 March 1987 did not show a true and fair view of that company's assets and liabilities; as a result Ferranti was induced to enter into a merger it would not otherwise have contemplated and paid far too much for ISC.[81]

One should remember that auditing was at that time conducted according to the ICEAW's 1985 Auditing Guidelines, which placed the ultimate responsibility on management to ensure that all of the accounting information was accurate. Moreover, in 1986–87 PMM had insisted that Guerin should pursue much more conservative accounting policies on the substantial overseas contracts, given his earlier propensity to extract much higher levels of profit than would be conventional in other publicly traded companies.[82] Nevertheless, as we shall see in Chapter 7, important questions remained concerning both the quality and nature of the auditing work conducted by PMM, resulting in a legal case that would prove to be instrumental in changing City practices.[83]

While these issues were being discussed both privately within the Ferranti International board and publicly in many leading newspapers, crucially the continued support of the firm's bankers was used as clear evidence that the financial world shared the board's confidence that a sound recovery could be effected. This deal meant that Ferranti International had a gearing ratio of almost 200%,[84] forcing Sir Derek to placate anxious shareholders by noting that ongoing negotiations with as many as fifteen potential partners reinforced the message that Ferranti International had a future. As he stated at the rearranged AGM: 'We have adequate resources to carry out current plans and carry them out energetically. The company is trading almost normally in every aspect of its business.'[85] He consequently resisted the demands of some shareholders to resign, on the grounds that continuity of leadership was essential if Ferranti International was to be steered successfully off the rocky ground on which it had found itself. As he said to a reporter from *The Times*: 'The pilot doesn't eject the moment a bomb goes off in the cabin. We are trying to hang on to the joystick and get the plane safely down.'[86] Having been given the unanimous support of his board, as well as most of the firm's institutional shareholders, he also felt confident enough to continue as executive chairman. Nevertheless, the AGM had clearly been a traumatic experience for the board as a whole, following which the share price fell 2.5p to 53.5p (see Figure 6.1), reflecting the widespread concern at the scale of the balance sheet revisions.

Another reason why the share price fell after the AGM was the announcement that the company was going to split its 10p Ordinary shares into one 9p Ordinary share and one Special 1p share, with the latter benefitting from any net proceeds from litigation against the perpetrators of the fraud. Most commentators regarded this ruse as a means by which an outright bid for the entire group could be avoided, thereby ensuring the firm's continued independence.[87] As we noted earlier, the board was investing considerable time in courting potential partners, with British Aerospace regarded by most as the obvious partner. Indeed, BAe and Thomson CSF built up a holding that represented 1.7% of Ferranti International equity by 20 October 1989, at 56p;[88] the Dowty Group had also allied with the private German firm of Bosch, appointing Rothschild to examine a possible investment;[89] and others such as GEC and Daimler-Benz continued to build up a presence.[90] In view of the significant profit reductions publicised at the AGM, this activity was also vital, in that City of London analysts were convinced that a realistic market price for the company's shares was in the vicinity of 25–30p,[91] as opposed to what was an expected bid price of between 56p and 70p.[92] As Figure 6.1 reveals, since the post-merger peak of 110p in February 1989, Ferranti International shares had been on a vicious downward slope, highlighting its extremely vulnerable state as negotiations continued with potential partners.

While various firms continued to build up a stake in Ferranti International, one should also stress that this coincided with a process of concentration across both Europe and the USA, as leading firms attempted to assimilate the implications of recent and perceived future trends in defence markets. These trends will be assessed in greater detail when we come to analyse Ferranti International's prospects in the 1990s, but it does help to explain why so many potential partners engaged the board in discussions and requested a presentation.[93] In spite of the efforts made by Dr Shepherd, however, to satisfy this demand, not to mention the publication of revised accounts for the previous two years, there was growing dissatisfaction with the failure to provide more detailed information on the troubled components in the Ferranti International group. Although at the reconvened AGM on 16 November it was admitted that severe problems were being experienced at Ferranti International Controls with its *Ranger* energy management system, leading to adjustments totalling a further £14.4 million to the originally reported 1988–89 profit, predators were concerned at the possibility that other divisions were struggling.[94]

Above all, though, splitting the shares was regarded as a major deterrent to would-be bidders,[95] leading to the successive withdrawal of almost all of the likely contenders in the latter weeks of November. Of course, the company's precarious financial situation did not instil great confidence amongst the predators, especially with the gearing ratio racing past 200% as a result of the deal Barings Bank had brokered with the syndicate of thirty banks. During November, Barings Bank and the Ferranti International Board also devised a standby equity underwriting facility, by which through a rights issue of 748 million 10p Preferred Ordinary Shares at 25p the firm would raise £187 million.[96] Underwritten by eight of the firm's major institutional investors,[97] in return for double voting rights and preferential treatment should Ferranti International be wound up, this rights issue was partially regarded as a means of forestalling negative action by the banking synidcate. As well as reassuring the bankers that the board was thinking positively about financial strategies that did not rely totally on debt, though, in delaying the rights issue until February 1990 this provided the remaining predators time either to prepare a bid or withdraw from the situation. Given the growing concern over the share split announced in November, however, not to mention the continued concerns expressed about the company's financial credibility, most were choosing the latter option. Indeed, by early December the company's preferred partner, British Aerospace, had announced that it was no longer interested in taking an investment in Ferranti International.

While this decision was heavily influenced by British Aerospace's recent acquisition of the troubled Rover Group,[98] in October it had also merged its missiles division with that of Thomson-CSF,[99] the leading French defence contractor, providing management with a plethora of organisational challenges. At the same time, others speculated on British Aerospace's refusal to take on Ferranti International, especially in view of the financial information they had seen.[100] Whatever the cause, as Figure 6.1 illustrates this decision had a dramatic impact on the ailing company's share price, exacerbating the fears of and pressures on shareholders and employees alike. When in January 1990 Thomson-CSF also withdrew from the negotiations with Ferranti International, the shares fell even further, to just 1p above the proposed 25p rights issue price. As we shall see later, Thomson-CSF continued to express significant interest in acquiring a share in the successful sonar business of Ferranti Computer Systems Ltd, leading to the formation of what would be a viable joint venture company in 1990.[101] Sir Derek also rejected City rumours that his firm would consequently be obliged to conduct 'a fire sale', arguing that: 'We're not up with our backs against the wall'.[102] Nevertheless, with all the potential partners having left the negotiating table, few were willing to express optimistic sentiments about the firm's future prospects.

While all of this was happening on the financial front, the company's legal advisors, Herbert Smith, were preparing actions on two fronts. Firstly, as we saw in the last chapter, on 30 November the firm issued writs against Jim Guerin, Robert Shireman, Lawrence Resch, Wayne Radcliffe and the five Panamanian companies that had acted as supposed subcontractors to the KP and *Alpha* contracts. This writ was based on the allegation that there had been 'fraudulent misrepresentations during the period 1983–89, to the effect that sales and purchase contracts were genuine and payments made and received were made in the normal course of business ... [and] knowingly participated in a dishonest scheme to extract funds from the plaintiffs'. Ferranti International was seeking damages to the tune of $198.5 million (at current prices, £127 million), the sum that Guerin and his associates had allegedly siphoned off from a range of fraudulent contracts. Although the board recognised that there was only a remote possibility that any of this money would be recouped, it was essential to demonstrate to the company's backers that efforts were being made to seek compensation, even if the multi-agency US investigation would always take precedence in the courts.[103]

The second legal action that Herbert Smith had been preparing was equally tricky, in that it involved PMM as auditors of ISC. In their first report on the financial crisis, Coopers & Lybrand had alluded to possible negligence by PMM, an issue that the board chose to shelve until more detailed investigations had been conducted. By the end of December 1989, however, it was becoming clear from both Coopers & Lybrand's enquiries and preparatory work by Herbert Smith that a negligence case could be pursued.[104] At this stage, Herbert Smith was only suggesting a claim in the region of 'at the very least in the low teens of millions of dollars'. Interestingly, PMM had just agreed to reduce its auditing fee from £175,000 to £100,000, a gesture that the board accepted 'in view of the circumstances'.[105] However, as the House of Lords was currently considering another case with strong similarities to the PMM-ISC situation, Herbert Smith suggested that a decision on liability should be delayed until a judgement had been passed. This case involved another well-established auditing firm, Touche Ross, which had been accused by Caparo Industries of failing to notice that the stocks of a firm it had acquired in 1984, Fidelity, were allegedly overvalued. It was clearly vital that the legal responsibilities associated with auditing should be resolved through this case before Ferranti International could move forward, even if many in the City felt that PMM had a case to answer.

These discussions also raised another issue, because with the board consulting a battery of professional advisors, not to mention relying even more on Barings Bank for guidance, Ferranti International's legal expenses were rising enormously. Apart from the £100,000 fee paid to PMM, Coopers & Lybrand would demand a payment of £250,000, Herbert Smith's bill exceeded £300,000, Cazenove & Co was paid £200,000 for underwriting services, and in December 1989 Barings Brothers received £1,000,000 (plus VAT and sundry expenses).[106] At a time when the interest payments on bank loans were escalating rapidly, it is clear that the firm's finances continued to suffer as the crisis unfolded. Irrespective of these pressures, however, the board felt compelled to continue both to use these professional advisors and pursue compensation through the courts, otherwise they could have been accused of 'going soft' on the real culprits. With further court cases pending, not to mention the planned rights issue and need to renegotiate the standby facility with its bankers, the company was clearly going to be saddled with these additional costs for some time, exacerbating the crisis and placing even greater emphasis on the need to dispose of assets as a means of improving the liquidity situation.

6.3 Asset disposals

An asset disposal programme, of course, had been on the board's agenda since early September, when the crisis first broke, with various parts of the former ISC group identified as the most obvious contenders. Specifically, Marquardt was regarded as the first business to go under the hammer, even if there remained a strong whiff of scandal associated with this operation, arising from the 'Operation Ill-Wind' investigations of the FBI.[107] Although nobody at Marquardt was ever prosecuted as a result of these investigations, they highlighted the general aura surrounding ISC operations, namely, that few people were willing to trust anything associated with Guerin's former business activities. As we shall see later, these sentiments waned after 1990, to such an extent that former ISC subsidiaries were eventually sold to rivals. Nevertheless, such was the attenuated nature of all negotiations concerning ISC assets that Ferranti International was unable to shore up its short-term liquidity problems through these sell-offs. Even though Marquardt management had several meetings with potential purchasers such as Rocketdyne,[108] it proved extremely difficult to persuade this American defence company to meet the estimated value of the Californian firm of £70 million. Indeed, by January 1990 Albert Dodd was reporting that even though he had reduced the offer price to £65 million, few buyers were willing to come forward.[109] This thwarted the board's original plan to raise a considerable amount of money from asset sales, placing much greater emphasis on an alternative programme that had much deeper implications for the future of Ferranti International.

While the board struggled with the challenges associated with disposing of tainted ISC assets, it became increasingly apparent that the focal point of this programme would not be one of Guerin's businesses but what to many was the 'jewel in the Ferranti crown', Ferranti Defence Systems Ltd (FDSL). Having since the 1950s been consistently the largest contributor to Ferranti output and profits, building on the sound foundations laid by Sir John Toothill, Sir Donald McCallum and the highly inventive engineers recruited into the Edinburgh operation,[110] it was apparent to both Ferranti International directors and MoD officials that at the core of any rescue strategy was the future of this vital division. Indeed, at the first meeting between Sir Derek and the MoD's Head of Procurement, Sir Peter Levene, immediately after the firm's shares had been suspended, intense discussions were held about the future of the EFA radar contract. The background to these discussions was the protracted negotiations between the various partners who were planning to build the next generation of joint European military aircraft, code-named EFA (European Fighter Aircraft, or 'Eurofighter'). This project had been initiated as long ago as 1984, but while the MoD had signed up for the development phase in 1986, by 1989 West Germany still remained sceptical about the British contribution. As we have already noted, while FDSL had in 1986 been assigned the development contract for the onboard radar to be fitted to the next generation military aircraft being designed by a European consortium, at stake was a production contract worth well in excess of £1 billion.

Both politically and economically, the Eurofighter contract consequently had enormous implications, with the MoD extremely keen to sustain a major British presence in the EFA project and FDSL anxious not to lose its reputation as one of the world's leaders in this field. Using the highly innovative 'ring laser' system developed by a team headed by John Rawlston, FDSL was widely regarded as the best equipped to complete this part of the highly advanced project, sustaining employment in Central Scotland at a time when industrial employment was declining rapidly in that politically sensitive region.[111] Ferranti engineers were inevitably confident of eventual success, having been working on this ring laser system since 1979, a position fully supported by the MoD throughout these delicate negotiations. Although the Ferranti International financial crisis certainly did not help strengthen the MoD's case, Sir Peter Levene assured Sir Derek that technically FDSL was still in an extremely strong position.[112] Having provided these assurances, however, progressively over the following months considerable pressure was put on the Ferranti International board to consider selling the Scottish defence business, given the political implications of failing to secure these enormous contracts. It is worth noting, though, that publicly and in conversations with Ferranti International directors the MoD strongly encouraged a partnership with British Aerospace, as opposed to GEC, given the latter's increasingly dominant position in UK defence markets.[113] As the weeks passed, on the other hand, and West German lobbying over the Eurofighter radar intensified, the MoD switched its position, making it difficult for the board to resist the pressure to sell FDSL to GEC. This inconsistency exacerbated the tensions felt by the board while conducting these negotiations, and although the situation was eased by the withdrawal of British Aerospace in December 1989, it was still difficult to see a way forward on the asset disposal programme.

Of course, the enormous uncertainty created by all these highly confidential negotiations did nothing for the morale of FDSL employees at all levels, because rumours in abundance circulated in newspaper reports and even television news bulletins. As we noted earlier, it was unlikely that the Conservative government was going to intervene, because in spite of being extensively lobbied by Scottish MPs, its preoccupation with market solutions, as opposed to taxpayer bail-outs, resulted in nothing more than rhetorical support for FDSL from the Secretary of State for Scotland, Malcolm Rifkind, and Minister for Defence, Tom King. John Rawlston and his team were, nevertheless, confident that they had the engineering edge over their German and American rivals, providing FDSL's chief executive, Phil Atterton, with a decisive negotiating card in the ongoing discussion with the Eurofighter syndicate. On the other hand, as one potential partner after another withdrew their interest in taking a substantial equity holding in Ferranti International, and the board devoted enormous amounts of time to preparing for the proposed rights issue, the firm's financial weaknesses gave its rivals for the Eurofighter radar production contract a powerful reason to refuse to place such a large amount of business with FDSL. This forced Atterton and key members of the FDSL management team such as R. Dunn to ponder on alternative strategies, leading in January 1990 to discussions with Sir Derek about the possibility of teaming up with GEC. Although Sir Derek was initially sceptical, recognising that FDSL provided a substantial contribution to the group's output, profits and cashflow, he was persuaded on 9 January to telephone the formidable chief executive of GEC, Sir Arnold Weinstock.[114]

It transpired that Lord Weinstock had actually been considering just such an alliance, giving this telephone conversation real momentum that set in train a series of meetings which by 23 January resulted in the announcement of a major deal. The preliminary negotiations were actually conducted with Simon Weinstock, the son of Lord Weinstock who as GEC's commercial director with specific responsibility for defence markets put everything in place. Apparently, GEC's City advisor, Hambros, recommended a joint venture between Ferranti International and GEC, but this was rejected by Sir Derek, on the grounds that he would lose control to the much larger firm.[115] As *The Times* reported, there ensued a fascinating set of negotiations, in that Sir Derek had little to lose in pressing Lord Weinstock for the in-house valuation of £300 million. While GEC was only willing to offer £150 million, Sir Arnold knew that FDSL would prove to be a major asset, both in securing the EFA radar contract and other opportunities in global defence markets.[116] There was consequently a series of face-to-face meetings between the two executive chairmen, resulting in GEC agreeing to pay £270 million, subject to any future adjustments arising from a full audit of the subsidiary's assets. This was heralded by the firm as a significant victory for Sir Derek over the redoubtable Lord Weinstock, even though others felt that the very lifeblood of Ferranti International was being allowed to seep away,[117] undermining its chances of recovering fully from the ISC-induced crisis. GEC publicists were also ecstatic about this deal, in that the MoD's implicit involvement meant that it was unlikely the Office of Fair Trading would become involved, cementing further its grip on the European airborne radar business. Indeed, even though the Office of Fair Trading expressed concerns about the decline in competition in this sector, in February 1990 the DTI minister, Nicholas Ridley, sanctioned the deal, on the grounds that it was 'in the public interest'.[118] While this decision inevitably generated some critical comment, not least because it would appear that the Office of Fair Trading was heavily lobbied by the MoD and market control concerns were ignored in favour of the UK securing the EFA radar contract, it reflected the sense of urgency affecting defence stocks at a time when the market was contracting sharply.[119]

Of course, the negotiations were not as trouble-free as this narrative makes out, while in the following year considerable difficulties were experienced in reaching a final settlement figure.[120] Crucially, for many FDSL employees this marked the end of an era, while the transfer to GEC was like being sold as a commodity without any consideration given to their feelings on the matter. Few anticipated a conducive future as a GEC employee, especially in view of the stark contrast this represented to life as a Ferranti employee, with its free-booting culture and happy environment. One might also question whether this deal was as 'stunning' as Sir Derek Alun-Jones claimed when making the announcement on 23 January.[121] Of course, for GEC this virtually guaranteed the Eurofighter radar contract, reinforcing its increasingly dominant position in European defence markets. On the other hand, while an injection of £270 million in cash was extremely welcome to a firm with bank debts amounting to £300 million, for Ferranti International the medium-term benefits were not as obvious, given FDSL's overwhelming importance to the group's commercial viability. When discussing the implications of losing this 'jewel in the crown', the board was informed by Charles Scott that apart from reducing group turnover from £1.1 billion to £600 million, the other divisions, and especially computer systems, were undergoing such traumatic market conditions that profitability would be even more severely dented.[122] Moreover, although the FDSL sale made the planned rights issue unnecessary, Barings Bank was still advising in February 1990 that not only would further disposals be required, but additional loans of £62 million were essential to maintain liquidity.[123]

This advice came as a great shock to the board, because apart from the cash payment of £270 million received for FDSL, GEC also bought 50% of Ferranti Italia for a further £40 million, while a further £17 million was raised in December 1989 by the sale to ServiceTec of the computer service and maintenance division of Ferranti Computer Systems Ltd (FCSL). While some City analysts were critical of the ServiceTec deal, on the grounds that at 6.5 times historic earnings (of on average £3.9 million per year) this was much lower than the norm in software sectors,[124] the move was seen as essential to the asset disposal programme. Withdrawing from the former ISC activities in Italy was also regarded as strategically sound, not least because since the 1987 merger it had been extremely difficult to integrate these businesses into any other part of Ferranti International. As GEC was actually buying only the defence activities within Ferranti Italia, efforts were also made to sell the civil businesses to the Italian industrial conglomerate Finnmeccanica, giving the asset disposal programme significant momentum.

The final stage in the asset disposal programme engineered by Sir Derek was the sale of 50% of the FCSL sonar business, based in Cheadle. As we saw in Volume 2, since the late 1960s Ferranti engineers had been highly success-ful in developing a range of sonar equipment, mainly for the Royal Navy's submarine fleet, building a business that by 1990 was selling £40 million annually. Indeed, in February 1990 this division announced a £20 million order from the Royal Navy for ten sonar systems, providing potential buyers with a major incentive to buy into the business. Although in December 1989 Thomson CSF had withdrawn its interest in buying a substantial stake in Ferranti International, this did not prevent its management from continuing to negotiate a deal on the sonar business. These discussions continued into 1990, resulting in an announcement on 8 February that Thomson would pay £32 million for a 50% stake in a new joint venture, Ferranti-Thomson Sonar Ltd. As FCSL had been reluctant to sell off this division, given its profitability and market reputation, this represented an excellent deal for both parties.[125] Ferranti-Thomson Sonar, under the energetic management of Gerry Bentley, also continued to perform well in the 1990s, sustaining its reputation for advanced engineering to such an extent that it dominated that market.

6.4 Sir Derek's departure

The asset disposal programme initiated in September 1989 had clearly been a major success, if one judges it purely in terms of the quantity of money raised from selling FDSL (£270 million), the sonar division (£32 million) and computer maintenance activities (£17 million). On the other hand, while raising £319 million in this way resulted in the cancellation of the £187 million rights issue, Ferranti International was still obliged to arrange a further £63 million standby facility with its bankers, given persistent liquidity concerns. Crucially, in his final weeks as chairman of Ferranti International Sir Derek could well be accused of presiding over the rapid break-up of the group he had run since taking over from the family in 1975, selling off the most profitable businesses and jeopardising its long-term future. As we have already seen, while he enjoyed the total support of his board of directors, external commentators and some shareholders expressed deep reservations about his tenure of office. 'For God's sake, go!' was perhaps the harshest of the headlines on this issue,[126] prompting vigorous responses from Sir Derek to the inaccurate and biased series of accusations. However, even his stoutest apologists recognised that it was only a matter of time before he stood down as chairman. Indeed, Sir Derek was powerless to resist the demands from the larger institutional shareholders that the chairman should resign, while at the same time accepting the moral argument that he really did not have any alternative.

Of course, as some employees have speculated since September 1989, even though Sir Derek's departure was inevitable, there was a strong case for the entire Ferranti board to resign, given its unanimous support for the 1987 merger. On the other hand, this could well have done more damage to the divisions, while in the circumstances Sir Derek was regarded as a sufficient sacrificial lamb. He consequently left Ferranti International on 13 February 1990, having initiated the rationalisation programme imposed by the banks. Many employees (especially those who were about to lose their jobs through much-needed rationalisation programmes) were disgusted at the size of his remuneration package, including a £491,000 payment to recompense him for premature retirement from a contract that still had two-and-a-half years to run.[127] It is important to stress that Sir Derek had signed a rolling three-year contract in the summer of 1978, the review of which occurred every year. The most recent review had been in July 1989, several months prior to the ISC revelations, making it extremely difficult for the company to wriggle out of its contractual obligations, even if the board had wanted to pursue this course of action. Indeed, the board consulted their legal advisors on the contract, as a result of which the £491,000 compensation was agreed.[128] Not surprisingly, Sebastian de Ferranti led the protests at this payment, issuing a statement through the trusts that still owned a considerable number of Ferranti International shares that described it as 'really a rather rude gesture to shareholders who have lost so much money under his chairmanship'.[129] Even though Sir Derek was widely praised for not selling his considerable holding of Ferranti International equity, amounting to almost 400,000 shares (plus options to buy a further 737,000), and others accepted that this kind of deal was common in the British corporate community,[130] the compensation package left a bad taste in the mouths of many employees and small shareholders who were coping with either the threat of redundancy or massively reduced earnings on their investments.

Whatever one might think of this deal, it is essential to conclude this chapter by offering an objective view of Sir Derek's contribution to the development of Ferranti since his arrival as chief executive in November 1975. In particular, one must remember that he had taken the helm at a time when the firm could well have been sold off to predators such as GEC, Plessey or Racal, having suffered a severe liquidity crisis as a result of the eponymous owning family's reluctance to take hard decisions on major loss-making divisions. Even though Sebastian de Ferranti later publicly claimed that Alun-Jones was only interested in extracting maximum financial value from the firm's assets, probably in the interests of fattening them up for a sale, Alun-Jones stuck with Ferranti for just over fifteen years. Moreover, not only did Ferranti secure a successful flotation on the London Stock Exchange in 1978, but over the next ten years its shares were generally regarded as worthwhile investments. The crucial point, though, is that far from undermining what we have labelled the 'Ferranti Spirit' – namely, the commitment to an engineering-led strategy in the context of an organisational environment based on extensive devolution of control – Alun-Jones encouraged this culture just as vigorously as the de Ferranti family had done up to the 1970s. Indeed, the firm's improved financial strength was based primarily on the development of products and technologies that gave Ferranti a competitive edge in what were highly challenging markets, leading to the decisive conclusion that by 1987 Ferranti was a much stronger business than it had been in 1975, an achievement that can be attributed to the management style of its chief executive throughout that period

Of course, this was not a linear process; there were failures as well as successes. For example, some of the investments in US subsidiaries proved extremely troublesome after 1987, while Ferranti failed over the period 1975–87 to reduce its reliance on defence markets, in spite of statements at successive AGMs that the board wanted to boost civil-based divisions. Above all, though, Sir Derek will be remembered for taking Ferranti into a merger with ISC that would ultimately result in bankruptcy and the loss of many jobs and significant reductions in shareholder value. As the *Sunday Times* observed, 'his reputation as the man who had taken Ferranti from being a problem-laden group controlled by the state into a group with a worldwide reputation, has disappeared overnight'.[131] One might regard this judgement as unfair, given the plethora of advice Ferranti sought from sound City institutions at the time of the merger; equally, though, it is fair to conclude that business executives can only be judged by the legacy they offer their successors; and in the case of Sir Derek Alun-Jones, this was a company on its knees, saddled with enormous debts and its most profitable division sold off to a major competitor. It was the task of Sir Derek's successor to seek a viable route through this disaster, offering a conundrum that many felt in 1990 was impossible to resolve.

Notes

1   A 'White Knight' in British business circles was a person or firm that would rescue an enterprise from bankruptcy.
2   *Independent*, 22 Sept 1989.
3   J.F. Wilson (2007), *Ferranti: A History*. Vol. 2. *From Family Firm to Multinational, 1975–1987*, Crucible Books, pp. 365–78.
4   See above, pp. 15–22.

5   *Financial Times*, 16 Sept 1989.
6   For details on this division's 1980s performance, see Vol. 2, pp. 219–28.
7   *The Times*, 12 Sept 1989 and 16 Sept 1989; *Sunday Times*, 24 Sept 1989.
8   *Sunday Times*, 17 Sept 1989.
9   This story will be covered below, pp. 153–5.
10 This story was related in Vol. 2, pp. 237–45.
11 See above, pp. 35–41, for coverage of this work.
12 FBM
13 FBM 6 Sept 1989.
14 Ibid.
15 The author should report that within a month of this board meeting he had been obliged to relinquish his contract as a consultant archivist to Ferranti International, resulting in the return of a computer and various devices to the Publicity Department.
16 Interviews with Charles Scott, Albert Dodd and Dr Alan Shepherd.
17 See Vol. 2, pp. 234–6 , and below, pp. 41–3.
18 FBM 4, 12 Sept 1989.
19 Ibid.
20 *The Times*, 13 Sept 1989. Similar comments were also made in *Financial Times*, 13 Sept 1989.
21 *Daily Telegraph*, 13 Sept 1989.
22 *Intelligencer Journal*, 11 Oct 1989.
23 *Independent*, 13 Sept 1989.
24 *Financial Times*, 20 Sept 1989.
25 FBM 1, 19 Sept 1989.
26 The National Bank of Abu Dhabi, the National Bank of Kuwait, Credit Lyonnais and HSBC were the other banks.
27 *Financial Times*, 22 Sept 1989.
28 *Financial Times*, 20 Sept 1989.
29 *Independent*, 22 Sept 1989.
30 Reported in *The Times*, 19 Sept 1989.
31 *The Times*, 19 Sept 1989.
32 *Sunday Times*, 24 Sept 1989.
33 FBM 1, 25 Sept 1989.
34 FBM 1, 29 Sept 1989.
35 FBM 8, 4 Oct 2010.
36 Interview with Albert Dodd.
37 *Wall St Journal*, 14 Oct 1989.
38 FBM 5, 15 Nov 1989.
39 FBM 13, 3 Nov 1989.
40 *Lancaster New Era*, 3 August 1990.
41 Circular to Ordinary and Preferred Shareholders of Ferranti International Signal plc, 29 Sept 1989.
42 FBM 4, 29 Sept 1989.
43 *The Times*, 11 Oct 1989.
44 *Sunday Times*, 24 Sept 1989.

45   For example, *The Times*, 19 Sept 1989.
46   *Financial Times*, 19 Sept 1989.
47   *The Times*, 16 Sept 1989.
48   *Sunday Times*, 24 Sept 1989
49   *Observer*, 17 Sept 1989.
50   See for example *Sunday Times*, 17 Sept 1989.
51   *Sunday Times*, 24 Sept 1989.
52   *Guardian*, 20 Sept 1989.
53   *Scotsman*, 14 Sept 1989.
54   Interviews with Sir Derek Alun-Jones.
55   FBM 2, 29 Sept 1989.
56   *Sunday Times*, 8 Oct 1989.
57   See *Independent*, 16 Sept 1989.
58   See Vol. 2, pp. 58–67.
59   FBM 2, 29 Sept 1989.
60   *The Times*, 7 Oct 1989.
61   *The Times*, 9 Oct 1989.
62   *The Times*, 10 Oct 1989.
63   See above, pp. 104–6.
64   The family trusts abstained in the crucial vote.
65   See later, pp. 234–6.
66   See, for example, its support of Japanese investments in automobile production.
     T.R. Whisler (1999), *The British Motor Industry, 1945–94*, Oxford University Press.
67   *Independent*, 22 Sept 1989; *The Times*, 19 Sept 1989.
68   *Financial Times*, 20 Sept 1989.
69   This section is based on FBM 1, 4 October 1989, which outlined the main details
     in the Cooper & Lybrand report and discussed their implications.
70   FBM 2, 10 October 1989.
71   *Sunday Times*, 24 Sept 1989.
72   FBM 5–6, 4 October 1989.
73   FBM 10, 3 Nov 1989.
74   *Observer*, 21 Jan 1990.
75   FBM 5, 10 Oct 1989.
76   FBM 5–6, 3 Nov 1989.
77   FBM 3, 15 Nov 1989.
78   *Financial Times*, 18 Nov 1989.
79   *Observer*, 19 Nov 1989.
80   *Financial Times*, 18 Nov 1989.
81   Ferranti International Signal plc revised annual report, Nov 1989.
82   See earlier, pp. 60–5.
83   See P. Howson (2004), *Commercial Due Diligence*, Gower, Ch. 1.
84   The gearing ratio is the relationship between debts and equity.
85   *Observer*, 19 Nov 1989.
86   *The Times*, 11 Dec. 1989.
87   *Observer*, 19 Nov 1989.
88   *Electronic Times*, 20 Oct 1989.

89 *The Times*, 17 Nov 1989.
90 GEC already had a 2% holding in Ferranti International, shares it had acquired when buying Plessey in July 1989. *Electronic Times*, 20 Oct 1989.
91 *Observer*, 19 Nov 1989.
92 *Financial Times*, 18 Nov 1989.
93 *Financial Times*, 30 Oct 1989.
94 *Financial Times*, 18 Nov 1989.
95 *Observer*, 19 Nov 1989.
96 FBM 2–3, 30 Nov 1989.
97 These were British Coal Pension Fund, Electra Investment Trust, Globe Investment Trust, Guardian Royal Exchange, Legal & General, Philips & Drew, Postel, and Prudential Assurance. For comment, see *The Times*, 2 Dec 1989, and *Independent*, 2 Dec 1989.
98 See Whisler *British Motor Industry*, pp. 367–8, for an analysis of this episode.
99 *The Times*, 17 Oct 1989.
100 *Independent*, 2 Dec 1989.
101 See below, pp. 269–70.
102 *The Times*, 19 Jan 1990.
103 See above, pp. 160–1.
104 FBM 3, 20 Dec 1989.
105 FBM 7, 20 Dec 1989.
106 Ibid.
107 See above, pp. 143.
108 FBM 2, 25 Sept 1989.
109 FBM 1, 8 Jan 1990.
110 For more details, see Vol. 1, pp. 322–34, and Vol. 2, Ch. 7.
111 See Lovering 'Opportunity or crisis?'.
112 FBM 4, 12 Sept 1989.
113 FBM 5, 4 Oct 1989.
114 FBM.
115 A. Brummer & R. Cowe (1998), *Weinstock. The Life and Times of Britain's Premier Industrialist*, HarperCollins, pp. 214–5.
116 *The Times*, 27 Jan 1990.
117 *Financial Times*, 25 Jan 1990.
118 *Guardian*, 10 Feb 1990.
119 *Independent*, 10 Feb 1990.
120 See later, pp. 234–6.
121 *The Times*, 24 Jan 1990.
122 FBM 2, 23 Jan 1990.
123 FBM 14, 2 Feb 1990.
124 *The Times*, 12 Dec 1989.
125 *The Times*, 9 Feb 1990.
126 *The Times*, 20 Sept 1989.
127 In addition, it was agreed that Sir Derek should be given use of the 'rod' on the River Test, allowing him to continue his beloved salmon fishing. FBM 10, 8 Feb 1990.

128 *Independent*, 27 Feb 1990.
129 Quoted in *Independent*, 27 Feb 1990.
130 Sir Ralph Halpern received compensation of £2 million on leaving the Burton
    Group. *Financial Times*, 1 Nov 1991.
131 *Sunday Times*, 24 Sept 1989.

7

The 'New Ferranti International'[1]

W HILE THERE IS always a tendency to write history as if all paths lead to a
specific destination, in the case of Ferranti International's final three
years as a trading operation it is difficult to see it as anything other than a
forlorn rescue operation. Indeed, analogies such as 'Clearing out the Augean
stables' come to mind when analysing the efforts expended to rebuild the
business. Even though in June 1990 the new chief executive sustained the
equine analogy by stating that 'having cleaned out the stable, there is still a
horse in there',[2] the following years demonstrated that Ferranti International
just did not possess any of the key characteristics – financial muscle, sheer
scale and market domination – that would have facilitated a total recovery. Of
course, one must not denigrate the Herculean efforts made by employees at
every level of the organisation; even though morale had inevitably been badly
dented by September's revelations, there was still a widespread feeling in
1989–90 that a viable business could be salvaged from the wreckage. The
appointment of an expert 'company doctor' in February 1990 also signalled
that the board was confident of effecting a Phoenix-like recovery that in
September 1989 had seemed impossible to many. This new chief executive,
Eugene Anderson, would also go on to perform a series of minor miracles,
not least in sustaining good relations with the firm's bankers, thereby keeping
the firm afloat longer than some had anticipated. Nevertheless, not only had
the balance sheet been fatally holed by Guerin's fraud, but Sir Derek Alun-
Jones had also been obliged by the MoD to sell off the most profitable
division, Ferranti Defence Systems Ltd (FDSL). Moreover, high interest
payments, losses on other businesses and the need to put aside enormous
sums for exceptional items in the balance sheet, sapped the lifeblood from
Ferranti International, resulting in a litany of asset disposals that made long-
term survival increasingly unlikely.

In addition to these challenges, one must also add that Ferranti
International was facing an extremely difficult marketplace: in the first place,
with the end of the Cold War, governments across Western Europe and North
America were reassessing their military budgets, leading to significant

changes in the defence industry; and, secondly, a major international recession resulted in both higher interest rates and lower demand for a wide range of electronic products. This combination of factors would prove just too much for Ferranti International, leading to its eventual demise in December 1993, when liquidators were finally called in to salvage a few worthwhile activities.

In investigating how this scenario unfolded, over the next two chapters we will focus especially on the general corporate story, and especially how Sir Derek Alun-Jones' successor, Eugene Anderson, tried to forge a 'New Ferranti International'.[3] The key to understanding this radical new approach was Anderson's desire to centralise decision-making as far as possible, especially in financial terms, providing an enormous contrast with the highly decentralised nature of the firm under both the de Ferranti family and Sir Derek. Even though in 1975 the latter had introduced financial planning techniques to the way Ferranti was managed, it was always accepted by the powerful divisional 'barons' that these targets remained indicative, rather than forcefully imposed on the engineering-led strategy that dominated the corporate culture. By February 1990, however, it became crystal-clear to every manager, at whatever level, that Anderson was in total control of the business, imposing an iron will on decisions and actions of whatever magnitude. Whether even this style of management would prove successful is, of course, another matter of conjecture, given the internal and external challenges facing Ferranti International, providing yet another fascinating insight into corporate strategy and structure. Nevertheless, Anderson and his team of senior managers pressed on with their 'New' agenda, working harmoniously with the contracting labour force to build a fresh business capable of surviving the rapidly changing environment.

7.1 Eugene Anderson and organisational change

Even though at successive press conferences and company meetings Sir Derek Alun-Jones had rejected all proposals that he should resign as executive chairman of Ferranti International, throughout the latter months of 1989 it was always apparent to the board that he would have to stand down. As we noted in the last chapter, not only did the board express 'total confidence in the way in which Sir Derek is handling matters',[4] at the reconvened AGM on 10 October Sir John Hoskyns also stated that it would be 'foolish' to suggest that the chairman should resign at this crucial stage in the company's history.[5] Throughout this difficult period, Sir Derek insisted on two conditions for his departure: firstly, a suitable successor should be available; and, secondly, he felt it was incumbent on him to put in place a short-term recovery strategy that ensured the firm's survival.[6] Cynics might also add a third condition – a suitable retirement package, details of which were examined at the end of the last chapter – but above all Sir Derek was anxious to lay the foundations for a recovery, even though he came under intense pressure from shareholders to leave this job to somebody else.

When assessing Sir Derek's departure from Ferranti International, there are some remarkable similarities with the way that he replaced Sebastian de Ferranti in 1975. In the first place, the same firm of headhunters, Spencer Stuart, was used to find a suitable chief executive. More importantly, just as Sebastian's tenure as chief executive was terminated as a result of demands made by the company's new owners (namely, the state),[7] it was the institutional shareholders who were going to underwrite the rights issue who insisted that their money should be managed by a fresh face. The task of finding this person fell principally to Sir John Hoskyns and Robin Broadley, whom the board asked to use their extensive networks across British and international business to find a suitable replacement. They started working with Spencer Stuart in December, inevitably sparking extensive rumours in the City of London, and resulting in several prominent businessmen being paraded past a nervous board.[8] Just as he had done in 1981,[9] Sebastian de Ferranti lobbied aggressively in favour of Sir John King, the redoubtable chairman of British Airways who had impressed the business and political communities in bringing the privatised carrier into profit. Patrick Gillam of British Petroleum was also an early contender, as well as Donald Peterson (chairman of Ford UK) and Lord Sharp (chairman of Cable & Wireless). At one stage Sir John Cuckney was touted as the favourite, given his formidable achievements in nursing the crippled helicopter company, Westland, back to health, not to mention his close connections to Thomson CSF's British merchant bank, Lazard Brothers.[10] For reasons which remain confidential, however, by January 1990 none of these candidates was still being considered,[11] leading the *Sunday Telegraph* to speculate that 'a well known businessman with good links with the City' had been found.[12] This person turned out to be Eugene Anderson, somebody with whom Hoskyns and Broadley had been talking since Spencer Stuart had first been commissioned.[13] Considerable confidence was by January 1990 being expressed concerning this Texan's impeccable academic qualifications and renowned experience as a 'company doctor', providing the board with some reassurance that they had alighted on the kind of manager who would be capable of taking over from Sir Derek.

Born in August 1938 in Pampa, Texas, and raised on a cattle ranch, the young Gene (as he was always known) Anderson was materially affected by the experiences of his parents during the 1930s Depression. As he later noted: 'My parents were college educated but the depression changed their lives drastically and it coloured a lot of my childhood. Security became very important and we were careful about money for luxuries'.[14] This upbringing sustained him throughout his life, although at no stage has he ever aspired to returning to the land. Having acquired a first degree in chemical engineering from the University of Texas in Austin, after earning an MBA at Harvard Business School he moved into the chemicals industry, working for the Tenneco Oil Co, a Texan speciality chemicals corporation. After short spells as a process engineer in New Orleans, then an operations analyst at the Houston plant, in 1966 he was sent to the UK to trouble-shoot the problems experienced by Globe Petroleum, based in Lincolnshire, at which he orchestrated a financial recovery and significant expansion. After returning to Houston in 1969 as a director of supply and transportation, rising to vice president of Tenneco International by 1973, he was seconded to Albright & Wilson, the British chemicals giant, to resolve problems at its Newfoundland phosphorous factory. His appointment in 1981 as president of Celanese International, the overseas subsidiary of the US rayon giant, reflected his growing status, although what really brought him to everybody's attention was his role in masterminding the recovery in Johnson Matthey's fortunes.

Anderson took over as chief executive of Johnson Matthey in the spring of 1985, at a time when this precious metals processor had recorded losses of £165 million. This appalling situation was largely attributable to the collapse of its subsidiary, Johnson Matthey Bankers, one of only five gold bullion dealers in the UK. This banking operation had during the early 1980s indulged in some high-risk lending to Middle East traders, the bulk of which proved to be worthless, resulting in the accumulation of debts totalling £400 million. Given the importance of bullion dealing to the City of London's activities, the Bank of England stepped in to stem Johnson Matthey Bankers' losses of £250 million.[15] Such was Anderson's rigorous management style, by 1989 Johnson Matthey was able to record a profit of £60 million, with debts down to a minimal £4 million,[16] earning him a formidable reputation on both sides of the Atlantic as a veteran of corporate turnarounds.[17] It was also extremely serendipitous that in December 1989 Anderson resigned as chief executive of Johnson Matthey, principally because his preferred strategy of reducing the firm's dependence on platinum clashed with the vested interests of a major shareholder, Harry Oppenheimer's Anglo-American Corporation. In addition, as Anderson wanted to acquire a rival, financed by a share swap deal, this would have diluted the 38% stake in Johnson Matthey held by Charter Consolidated, the British investment house in which Anglo-American Corporation had a 36% interest. Realising that his strategies would consequently never be implemented, Anderson decided to resign from Johnson Matthey, ostensibly to 'pursue other business interests', but undoubtedly linked to the overtures extended by Spencer Stuart about the Ferranti International job.

During the early weeks of 1990, Gene Anderson and the Ferranti International board were involved in a series of detailed negotiations that seemed to promise much. Inevitably, one of the key sticking points was salary, Anderson having earned £588,537 (including bonuses) in his last year at Johnson Matthey, substantially more than Sir Derek's remuneration package of £195,000 per annum. Nevertheless, Anderson persisted with the negotiations, telling one journalist that: 'If there was no hope, we wouldn't be talking. The damage is not irreparable and the company can be saved and improved.'[18] Commentators were certainly encouraged to read that Anderson continued to express an interest in the Ferranti International job, seeing this as distinctly 'good news' for a firm that had been put on the road to recovery by its existing management.[19] Typifying the kind of comment secured from City experts, Robert Sassoon of the leading brokerage firm County NatWest stated that: 'I rate him very highly. He has charisma and respect. He's a very good selector of people. He's able to harness the talents within a company, and he's a man of vision.'[20] It was especially noted that while he had taken the hard decisions to close or sell loss-making divisions at Johnson Matthey and the other firms at which he had worked, Anderson had also preserved the research and development programmes that lay at the heart of the firm's future expansion. This is resonant of the 1974 negotiations between Sebastian de Ferranti and Derek Alun-Jones, when exactly the same characteristics were being sought by Spencer Stuart for an executive to replace the chairman and managing director, indicating once again how history has a habit of repeating itself. Above all, though, Anderson was described as 'a problem-solver with a fertile mind', pursuing results in a stubborn, yet challenging, style that made him 'a good man in a crisis'.[21] These were characteristics that would be tested to the absolute limit in running Ferranti International.

While the Ferranti International board was unable to offer Anderson a comparable salary to that which he had earned at Johnson Matthey, a compromise was reached, whereby a basic annual remuneration package of £300,000 (including a £25,000 bonus) was offered, plus 9.3 million share options priced at 36.8 per share (compared to the prevailing market price of 40p). On joining Johnson Matthey, Anderson had purchased £412,500–worth of shares at 65 pence each,[22] as a means of demonstrating his commitment to the ailing firm. By the time he had left, the shares were trading in excess of £4 each, giving him a healthy profit on the initial investment.[23] While he could not anticipate the same kind of return on any investment in Ferranti International, he nevertheless bought £250,000–worth of its equity,[24] a gesture that went down extremely well with his fellow-directors, not least because many of their share options were languishing in loss-making territory. Sir Derek was consequently able to announce his resignation as chief executive on 23 February 1990, leading to predictable headlines such as 'Ferranti move to lasso the Texan'[25] and 'A Texan tough guy rides in at Ferranti'.[26] Anderson followed this up with a round of interviews with financial journalists to outline his commitment to undertaking 'a complete strategic review', expressing total confidence in both his ability to manage this turnaround and the company's innate technological resources. Even though he was often described as being quietly spoken, and physically as far from the image of a Texan cowboy portrayed in newspaper headlines as one can imagine, he did not pull his punches:

> Any dispassionate observer would see that you need to enhance the performance of the company over the next year or two, even forgetting the ISC problems. If you look at the profits over the last five years, they have been flat and declining. In the first six months of this financial year the company lost £115 million.[27]

This indicated very clearly to the Ferranti International board, and perhaps more specifically to his immediate predecessor, that he was not interested in saving reputations; there was a job to be done and he was going to perform this task as rigorously as possible, whatever damage that would do to Sir Derek's record. One might also mention that Anderson spent only three hours in conversation with Sir Derek, when the change-over was being finalised, indicating that the new chief executive was not interested in listening to extensive explanations for past mistakes.[28] While Anderson went on to express public support for the compensation package awarded to Sir Derek, he had made it known that he was fully aware of the many reasons why Ferranti International was in trouble, providing a shot across the bows of anybody still with the company who might have resisted his reforms.

Of course, just as Derek Alun-Jones had discovered when joining Ferranti in 1975, Gene Anderson was in an extremely strong bargaining position. After all, the incumbent board of directors was almost exactly the same as that which had agreed to the 1987 merger with ISC and taken almost two years to discover the fraud. As we have also just hinted, several other internal problems were beginning to give serious cause for concern, placing the directors very much on the back foot when confronted by Anderson at the initial meetings. Although all of the legal niceties were completed by the board meeting on 23 February, when Anderson officially replaced Sir Derek as chairman, chief executive and managing director, it was 26 February before he actually chaired a full meeting.

One of the first impressions that the new chief executive gained of the group was that in certain senses Ferranti International was heading towards serious financial difficulties even before the ISC fraud had been revealed. Anderson was especially critical of the strategic plan he was shown, reaffirming our earlier comments about the optimistic nature of these documents.[29] Similarly, it was also apparent that as a result of overvaluing assets, cost overruns (on, for example, the *Ranger* system), over-costed defence contracts, excess stocks, weakly priced civil contracts, and excessive productive capacity, it was possible to calculate that in the 1987–88 accounts it could be predicted that a £200 million hole was about to appear. Furthermore, he was also very critical of the firm's accountants, Grant Thornton, in allowing management to hide these problems for so long. Of course, his colleagues rejected such notions, arguing that not only was Ferranti International fundamentally sound, but also Grant Thornton was not guilty of any cover-up. We shall see, however, that as the early 1990s progressed almost all of Anderson's predictions would come to pass, while the ISC fraud added massively to the challenge he faced. In the short term, though, he was convinced that the combination of his 'American can-do' attitude and track record would produce the right results. He was also provided with a great opportunity to imbue in the organisation and employees a radical new approach towards the business, because the senior management especially was convinced of the need for change.

This opportunity was grasped with alacrity by the new chief executive to launch a radical revision of the organisation, describing in a document entitled 'The "New" Ferranti International' how he wanted to centralise decision-making and override the formerly devolved style of management that had prevailed at Ferranti since the 1890s. There were eight dimensions to this fresh philosophy:

1 Review the strategies of all businesses and develop a coherent centrally administered strategy for the company.
2 Analyse the performance of all businesses to determine the scope for further rationalisation, efficiency improvement and better organisation.
3 Emphasise profit and cash generation, satisfactory returns on investment and growth.
4 Complete the disposals which have been agreed so as to fulfil commitments to bankers.
5 Renegotiate debt, reduce number of banks to a limited number of relationships banks, and reduce borrowing costs in line with improved financial status.
6 Pursue litigation and secure recoveries of past losses.
7 Ensure employees have proper incentives and are committed to first quality performance.
8 Communicate programme to employees, the City, customers, suppliers and governments.[30]

Although Sir John Hoskyns noted that 'the general pattern [in British business] was away from a central administration', he accepted the need within Ferranti International for much stronger central co-ordination. This was supported by the rest of the board, even though Dr Shepherd noted the difficulties of 'putting together two very decentralised companies' which had traditionally drawn up their own long-term strategic plans.[31] Anderson responded by stating that in future the group as a whole would operate on the basis of a single plan that would be managed from the centre, leaving the board in no doubt as to the way he intended to run things.

When considering this decisive episode, no doubt many would have reminisced that Anderson's desire to introduce much tighter central control of the company's finances had been tried before – witness the initial moves by both A.W. Tait in 1903 and Derek Alun-Jones in 1975. However, there is no doubt that as a matter of some urgency Anderson was able to introduce a completely new kind of organisational structure to Ferranti International, abandoning at a stroke what had been one of the most consistent features of the company for many decades, departmental autonomy. As deputy managing director with specific responsibility for this area, Charles Scott was instructed by Anderson to enhance the accounting systems and disciplines, introducing new reporting mechanisms that left managers at every level in little doubt that their actions would be monitored in minute detail. At the same time, the rigorous planning mechanisms introduced by Sir Derek Alun-Jones were sustained, albeit with much stronger central direction, as the 'New' strategy outlined in its first three points. To reinforce these developments, in August 1990 Charles Scott was moved to the post of commercial director, while David Shipley was seconded from Coopers & Lybrand Deloitte to 'oversee the financial function'.[32] Although some might have regarded this appointment as undermining Scott's position, Anderson had brought in Shipley because of the need to produce much more detailed accounts to board meetings, indicating how the new chief executive was changing management's emphasis at a time when liquidity issues were paramount. Moreover, Scott was reassigned to a role that proved central to the firm's recovery, making a major contribution in streamlining the commercial activities across Ferranti International and using his extensive grasp of the business to assist Anderson in achieving the revised strategy.

Linked with the introduction of these tighter, central financial controls, Gene Anderson was also struck by the need to change attitudes within the group, and especially in those divisions which had been heavily reliant on the cost-plus pricing system associated with defence contracts.[33] Just like his predecessor, he was enormously impressed with the creativity on show across the product range, praising the firm's consistent ability to 'punch above its weight', in that Ferranti International had been able to achieve a competitive advantage in advanced technologies against much larger electronics conglomerates. On the other hand, it was apparent to the new chief executive that pricing was based on attitudes that were resonant of a previous age. Moreover, while a cost-plus culture was most prevalent in the naval systems department at Bracknell and what remained of the avionics business in Edinburgh, the group as a whole had developed a dangerous habit of what he felt was a practice of 'sweeping costs' into defence contracts, thereby allowing overheads to expand at an alarming rate. Charles Scott had been highly critical of the rapid expansion in capacity during the 1980s, especially by Ferranti Computer Systems Ltd at Wythenshawe, and the failure to take a radical view of production needs.[34] In that buoyant period, of course, these views barely made an impact on board discussions, especially when powerful divisional 'barons' such as Peter Dorey or Donald McCallum used their enormous influence to effect expansion after expansion. By 1990, however, Anderson was extremely keen to terminate both the expansionary tendencies of divisional 'barons', as well as adopt a much more ruthless costing structure that fully accommodated the much-changed internal and external environments. Times had changed decisively, a message he hammered home at every opportunity.

The most effective way of dealing with this anachronistic culture was to introduce both a contracts review committee and internal audit department, both of which imposed much greater discipline on the allocation of overheads and costing processes generally. These instruments were both controlled by an audit committee composed of board members and chaired by Robin Broadley. Ironically, of course, Baring Brothers was brought down by a lack of auditing controls over its speculative activities, but at Ferranti International Broadley was trusted to keep a careful watch over these processes. Only slowly, however, did the firm's accounting policies adapt to the new environment, reflecting the residual legacy of a defence-oriented culture that had dominated since the 1930s.

Another of the effective ways of changing the corporate culture at Ferranti International, apart from radically changing the financial reporting system, was to institute a weekly Monday morning assembly of senior managers, impressing on all concerned that a new sense of urgency was being introduced to corporate affairs. It was a most traumatic time for everyone, especially those whose traditional independence had been preserved even after the mid-1970s crisis. Some felt that the new culture was imposed too quickly and without sufficient time for a process of blending together of the various styles. Similarly, senior managers resented the inference that they had not previously been working to the best of their capacities, creating an awkward climate at the outset. Anderson, on the other hand, saw himself as a catalyst, waking people up to the central responsibility of recreating a commercially viable organisation, overriding the concerns of other managers in the belief that a change in management style was essential. He also provided exemplary leadership, in the sense that for the following six weeks he did not take a single day off (including weekends), committing himself totally to dealing with the challenges he faced.[35] As somebody with total confidence in his ability to effect the required turnaround, he was frequently 'out there pumping hands like an American politician', reassuring employees at all levels that their jobs were safe. This was part of a positive programme aimed at preserving the tremendous loyalty that staff had for Ferranti, a culture that had been imbued by the de Ferranti family and sustained by divisional managers for decades. Above all, Anderson realised that the firm's greatest assets were a workforce replete with highly creative talent that had been able to build a competitive product range, even if they would be expected to work in a much-changed corporate culture.

This clear message was disseminated as widely as possible in Anderson's first weeks as chief executive, firstly through personal visits to as many company outposts as possible, and secondly by making himself available to journalists of every ilk. In addition, the EGM on 26 February 1990, called to ratify the sale of FDSL and 50% of Ferranti Italia, also provided an opportunity to hammer home the clear message that 'a new broom' was sweeping through the organisation. Although hidden away in the document announcing the EGM was further bad news for the group, that the DTI was attempting to recoup £4.3 million from Ferranti Electronics Ltd, a sum arising from the levy imposed on the MESS programme,[36] the City expressed its favourable opinion on Anderson's appointment by boosting the firm's share price by 3p (see Figure 7.1) on the day of his appointment. As if to reward them for this loyalty, Anderson also drove through the issue of 77.5 million special 1p shares, allotted as fully paid to all existing shareholders on the basis of one special share for every ten ordinary shares held. This bonus issue had actually been devised by Sir Derek Alun-Jones, as a means of distributing any funds recouped from the legal cases against Guerin and PMM. While few held out much hope that these special shares would ever produce a dividend, it was a gesture that was exploited by the group as a means of sustaining the loyalty of its hard-pressed shareholders, none of whom had received a dividend payment for the previous year.

While these public relations exercises were being conducted, Anderson was conducting his own appraisal of the firm he had joined. As the statement quoted earlier indicates, of course Anderson was well aware that Ferranti International was facing not only the financial implications of Guerin's massive fraud, but also some systemic problems arising from either poor acquisitions or deteriorating market conditions. While the systemic problems will be analysed in greater detail later, it is worth noting that when the revised

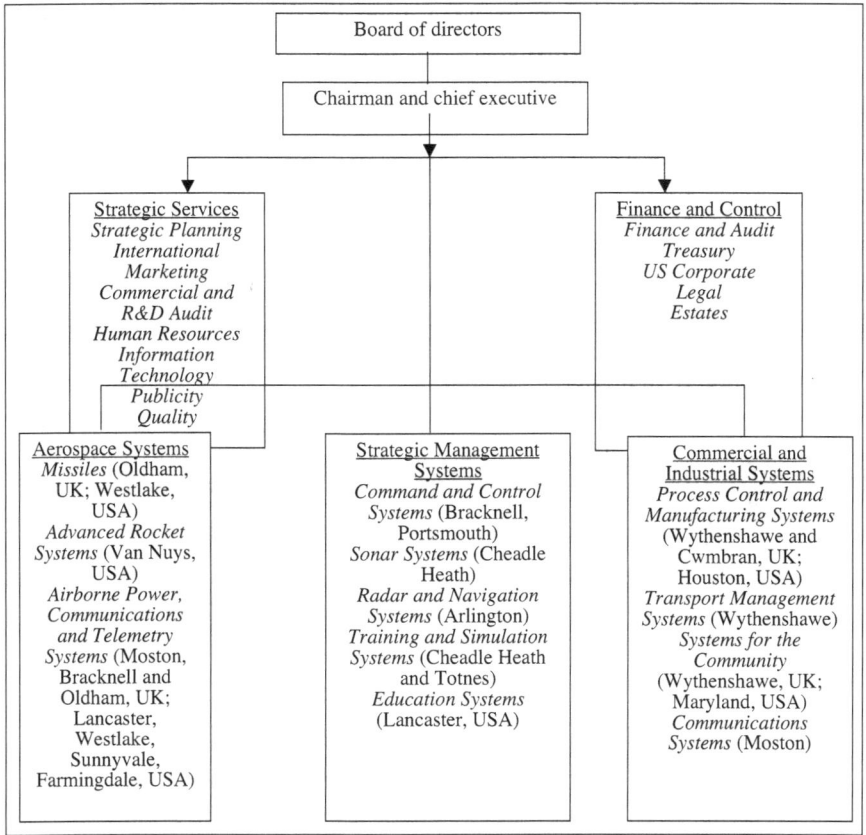

Figure 7.1 The structure of Ferranti International by the summer of 1990

accounts for 1988–89 were published in November 1989, in addition to accommodating the ISC-induced losses the finance director Charles Scott was also obliged to add an adjustment totalling £14.4 million related to the severe problems experienced at Ferranti International Controls with its *Ranger* energy management system. As we shall see later, the *Ranger* contracts continued to cause major difficulties over the following two years, indicating how the balance sheet was being holed from several directions. Further bad news came in November 1989, when the US Army rejected the first proto-types of an electronic fuze, FMU-139/B, developed by Ferranti International Defense Systems Inc, based in Lancaster, Pennsylvania. As this had been the first fuze contract (worth $23.9 million) for which the Lancaster plant had been prime contractor, as opposed to being a sub-contractor to another defence supplier, this decision did enormous damage to its long-term prospects. Moreover, the US Army had provided $1.8 million in progress payments on this contract, creating the possibility that this subsidiary would have to repay this money unless the development programme proved more successful.[37] The Lancaster plant continued to struggle with this project until the beginning of 1991, when production was finally approved by the US Army, providing yet another hammer-blow to the prospects of ISC generating any positive cashflow, with the multi-agency investigations into Guerin's illegal arms trading making it increasingly unlikely that any of its subsidiaries would be awarded significant US defence contracts.

Of course, not all of the news stories about Ferranti International were dominated by doom-and-gloom. After all, the 1989 order book was worth £900 million, and some divisions were considered to have great prospects. One of the major success stories, building on the well-established technological competitive edge developed since the 1960s, was the sonar division at Cheadle Heath, which in 1988–89 secured export orders worth £6 million from navies in New Zealand and West Germany. By that time, Cheadle Heath's annual sales had exceeded £45 million, generating healthy profits of £5.6 million. This was why Thomson CSF had been so interested in forging a joint venture with Cheadle Heath, leading to the formation of Ferranti-Thomson Sonar in February 1990 and bringing £32 million into Ferranti International coffers. This success was also sustained in the following years, for example through the acquisition of a £120 million contract to develop and supply the new generation of the Sonar 2057 towed array equipment, to be fitted to the *Upholder* class of submarine over the period 1992–99.[38]

On the other hand, the process control computer division at Wythenshawe had lost 700 jobs in the spring of 1989. Similarly, failure in August 1989 to secure the £150 million computer contracts for the Royal Navy's Type 23 frigate severely dented the prospects of the formerly robust naval computers division at Bracknell, while by January 1990 over 300 redundancies had been announced at the Moston plant of Ferranti Instrumentation. Crucially, none of these difficulties could be attributed to the ISC-related issues revealed in September 1989, indicating clearly the extent of the challenges facing Ferranti International. Indeed, again as we shall see later, perhaps the biggest challenge facing the firm by 1990 was the combination of dramatic changes in international political rivalries that precipitated the end of the Cold War with a severe economic recession, materially affecting the markets in which Ferranti International competed against much stronger corporations.

While as a widely acknowledged 'company doctor', Gene Anderson was naturally familiar with the circumstances in which he found himself, in settling into his new role as chairman and chief executive of Ferranti International it is unlikely that he had ever been faced with such a challenging scenario. It was consequently inevitable that in the first two months he would conduct a comprehensive strategic review, hiring the management consultancy division of Coopers & Lybrand Deloitte, along with its affiliate, Outram Cullinan, to conduct a fundamental reappraisal of how Ferranti International should be configured. Of course, Coopers & Lybrand had developed an intimate understanding of how Ferranti International operated, given its recent work on the financial crisis. It was also accepted that with several important components of the group having been sold off (FDSL, Ferranti Italia and the computer maintenance division), merged into a joint venture (sonar), or closed down (parts of ISC), the strategic shape was taking on a different form. Moreover, the group was shrinking at a rapid rate, with turnover down from £1.05 billion (1988–89) to £795 million (1989–90). This process continued in March 1990, when the laser and electronic components businesses at Dundee were sold off to local management buy-outs, for a total consideration of £7.7 million.[39] In addition, Melton Medes Ltd purchased Ferranti Resin Ltd (for £1.2 million), and the ceramic seals division of Ferranti Instrumentation was bought by Normec (Manchester) Ltd (for £380,000). Although the board had little choice in accepting the need for this process, especially the loss of FDSL, and the sales brought in valuable liquidity, it was increasingly imperative that the board needed to convince its shareholders and bankers that the rump was commercially viable.

It was this discipline which led Coopers & Lybrand Deloitte and Outram Cullinan, working intimately with senior management, to draw up a report entitled 'Rebuilding shareholder value'. Although only discussed by the full board on 18 May 1990,[40] a month earlier the executive committee had been comprehensively briefed by the consultants, providing Gene Anderson and his closest colleagues with time to absorb its implications. A key feature of the report was the consultants' advice that the group should pursue a much more focused product strategy, 'moving out of businesses unless they are connected with other core businesses', thereby leading to an extensive rationalisation of factory occupancy and significantly reducing both overhead and direct costs. As Anderson later noted when reviewing this strategic exercise, 'it has been all about finding out what unites this company', and especially bringing a greater degree of integration and synergy to what by 1990 was still a highly disparate group of businesses.[41] We have noted in previous volumes of this history that as a direct result of both divisional autonomy and geographical dispersion, Ferranti management had struggled to achieve these aims in the past, resulting in excessive replication of both engineering and marketing activities and limiting the ability of overlapping business units to exchange invaluable resources.[42] This was a situation that Anderson abhorred, forcing management at all levels to think about integration and communication. The board also expressed its total support for the plan, Sir John Hoskyns stating that it was 'a tremendous step forward', because it provided for both a broad overview of priorities and the basis for iterative changes to the product base.

At a conference attended by sixty divisional and sub-divisional managers on 22 May, this consensus was further ratified, after Gene Anderson and Dr Shepherd provided presentations on the report.[43] Similar presentations were also made to Sir Peter Levene at the MoD and at meetings with three of the firm's major banks, NatWest, Barclays and the National Bank of Abu Dhabi.

'Rebuilding shareholder value' had consequently been a major success in offering what in future was referred to as the Strategic Review & Recovery Plan, persuading both senior management and Ferranti International's key stakeholders that the firm was moving in the right direction. Crucially, the principal focus of the plan (see Figure 7.1) was an extensive reconfiguration of the group into what were described as three 'customer orientated' divisions, aerospace systems, strategic management systems and commercial and industrial systems. While some of the titles used to label the sub-divisions were familiar to Ferranti employees, it is clear that by the summer of 1990 Ferranti International had been dramatically restructured. The key emphasis, however, as the divisional and most of the sub-divisional names indicate, was on the company's ability to provide systems, ending any pretence that it would be involved in some of the components and service sectors which had survived the merger. Crucially, the realignment of core activities had been undertaken on a much more rigorous basis than ever before, indicating how, with strategy and structure having been fundamentally reassessed and reoriented, Ferranti International emerged from the initial stages of the crisis a much-changed firm. It is especially noticeable that authority revolved totally around the chairman and chief executive, with both the functional services and operating divisions reporting directly to him, who in turn reported to the board. As the 1990 annual report noted:

> Central control has been enhanced to serve the new structure. A focussed and effective corporate organisation will set strategic direction, formulate top-down quality objectives, provide specialist and international marketing support, co-ordinate and monitor business unit performance, set information technology strategy and implement strong financial controls.

Nothing like this kind of hierarchical control had ever been attempted at Ferranti, indicating the extent to which Gene Anderson was imposing his management style on an organisation that was still reeling from the September 1989 revelations and subsequent rationalisation. In order to support this supervisory work, Anderson also appointed a personal assistant, Jon Parker, a lawyer who had worked closely with him at Johnson Matthey.[44] While this reduced the formidable workload he had given himself, there was never any doubt who ran the company at a time when decisive leadership was required.

It was very much to the credit of Gene Anderson and his fellow-directors that the organisational revolution affecting Ferranti International was pursued with such alacrity. It is interesting to note, though, that while the new chief executive was given *carte blanche* to implement his strategic and structural changes, the board remained much the same, if not in actual composition, certainly in character. Of the directors in post at the time of the fraud revelations, only Sir Derek Alun-Jones and J.H. Zilligen (formerly of ISC) had left the board by January1990. Perhaps most surprising was Anderson's reluctance to appoint new directors to the board. While one might add that in the circumstances it was difficult to persuade prominent people to join the Ferranti International board, it was clear that Anderson was happy with the quality of his senior management team and their total commitment to rescuing a firm to which most had a life-long connection. Indeed, in order to reinforce the organisational changes linked to the creation of three divisions, Anderson elevated Bill Broekhuizen (managing director of commercial and industrial systems) and Ian Ball (managing director of aerospace systems) to the position of director,[45] sustaining the tradition at Ferranti of populating the board with divisional managers. The third divisional managing director, Albert Dodd (managing director of strategic management systems) had retained his directorial status, having more than proved his worth as a key member of the senior management team by resolving various problems at the ISC subsidiaries. On the other hand, Anderson was never going to allow divisional managers to represent only their sectional interests; after 1990, all interests would be subjugated to the broader corporate aim of recovering from a difficult position. This became apparent in consequent board meetings, because while each divisional managing director was expected to provide a report on their respective activities, the discussions were always dictated by overall corporate goals, rather than sectional interests.

While senior managers were clearly going to witness the imposition of some dramatic changes to their *modus operandi*, for the rest of the company's employees the announcement of this radical restructuring of the business marked a period of significant flux. Of course, as we noted earlier, there had been several hundred redundancies in 1989, as divisions came to terms with the changing financial and market environments in which they were operating, from June 1990 the restructuring involved a considerable movement of resources and people. Worst affected were those who had worked at the sites in Cwmbran, Cheadle Heath, Bracknell, Portsmouth and Wythenshawe, as parts of the old Ferranti Instrumentation and Ferranti Computer Systems divisions were reshuffled into the new configurations. Although redeployment packages were offered to most employees, for 350 staff at Cwmbran it was especially difficult to be expected to move to Oldham. For another 200 people at Bracknell, Portsmouth, Bridge House at Gatley, and the Moston Training Centre, it was only possible to provide redundancy terms as the firm struggled to cut costs and improve corporate productivity.[46] These were tricky times for all concerned, creating a climate of fear across all three divisions that failed to dissipate over the ensuing months. Even though Gene Anderson encouraged senior managers to express total commitment to the Recovery Plan and all of its implications, and extensive discussions were held with trade union officials, as Albert Dodd noted there remained considerable difficulties in transmitting this enthusiasm down the hierarchy,[47] highlighting a human resource challenge that would not be resolved over the next three years.

7.2 Recovery chances: the internal perspective

With the reorganisation launched and decisions on the composition of his senior management team resolved, Gene Anderson was by May 1990 in a position to focus more on implementing the core strategies devised for each of the three divisions. Of course, he had already been working on these strategies with the respective divisional managing directors, each of whom were asked to work within the overall corporate strategy of operating as a systems company. Specifically, all future corporate publicity devised by Tony Thomas's team at Bridge House stated that:

> The mission of Ferranti International is to improve significantly and materially the performance of the Company through greater customer orientation, total quality, better organisation and enhanced employee commitment; in short, to develop a performance culture that will provide satisfaction to our shareholders, our customers and our employees.

As we noted earlier, it was felt vital that the three divisions should be much more 'customer orientated', avoiding past mistakes that had seen Ferranti staff focus much more on the technologies they were developing. Another key element was the much greater focus on systems, as opposed to the former emphasis on providing a considerable proportion of the components internally. In a sense, this represented an extension of the decision made in 1987 to sell Ferranti Electronics Ltd to Plessey, terminating over fifty years of electronic component production. In the new structure, however, as represented in Figure 7.1, the aim was to rationalise the distribution of both people and plant in a much more integrated manner, thereby increasing the efficiency of the group as a whole. Of course, as we noted at the end of the last section, given the enormous logistical and personal factors involved in implementing this ideal, the strategy worked better on paper than in practice, especially as moving people around a highly geographically dispersed organisation presented challenges that could frequently not be overcome. Nevertheless, this was the aim as espoused in Anderson's Strategic Review & Recovery Plan, offering the prospect of reviving the firm's fortunes through a much more imaginative use of available resources.

In one sense, the Strategic Review & Recovery Plan proved to be an instant success, because with the help of Robin Broadley and Barings Brothers Anderson used this document to place the company's banking arrangements on a more conventional footing. We saw in the last chapter that Ferranti International had entered into two standstill agreements with its bankers, on 14 November 1989 and 2 February 1990, the immediate consequences of which had been to dispose of assets and repay all of the lending provided by the syndicate. As one can see from Table 7.1, even though the quantity of cash held in the bank by Ferranti International had risen appreciably by 1990, firstly, this was the result of massive disposals, and, secondly, as the company's bankers insisted that 95% of this should be placed on deposit as collateral for contingent liabilities, little of this money was available to support the further development of core activities. Moreover, the costs of rationalisation and reorganisation, including a growing number of redundancies, had reached £122.3 million in 1989–90, while that year's interest payments on its bank borrowings (totalling £275.5 million) were almost £50 million. Of course, the two standstill agreements with its banking syndicate had provided the essential liquidity to survive the immediate impact of the ISC-induced financial crisis, but consequent upon the asset disposal programme that had seen over £400 million come into the firm, Anderson was in a good position to renegotiate this lending and place it on a longer-term basis. This third agreement with its bankers, eventually signed on 18 July 1990, provided a £10 million overdraft facility, a cash advance facility of up to £60 million, as well as various bonding facilities for those divisions with substantial overseas contracts (for example, FIDL), all of which were provided on terms which reflected Ferranti International's growing financial credibility.

While it is vital to remember that this financial credibility had been

Table 7.1 Ferranti International finances, 1985–93 (£ m)

Year to March	Bank loans/overdrafts	Cash in bank	Net borrowings
1985	72.3	46.9	25.4
1986	65.1	35.6	29.4
1987	41.6	17.7	23.9
1988	190.5	44.9	145.6
1989	226.6	67.0	159.6
1990	275.5	166.7	109.8
1991	98.9	4.1	94.8
1992	90.4	23.9	66.5
1993	99.5	8.9	90.6

achieved as a result of substantial asset disposals, the third bankers' agreement graphically demonstrated that in financial terms there was mounting evidence Ferranti International was coming through its ISC-induced traumas. Apart from the much more favourable terms of these facilities, it also meant that the need to issue £62.38 million in loan stock could now be dropped. At the same time, the board realised that it was still necessary to generate some cash to keep the company afloat, resulting in both further asset disposals (to be described later) and securing a loan of $35 million from Progress Credit Corporation on the land owned by Marquadt at Van Nuys, California. More importantly, instead of the fixed-interest loan stock, it was decided that a rights issue should be used, providing a much more flexible form of capital generation that would better serve the interests of Ferranti International. The rights issue would be on the basis of one new ordinary share for every four ordinary shares held, generating £45.5 million (net of all underwriting and legal expenses, which would total £1.3 million). It was also possible to secure sixteen firms as underwriters of this rights issue, with Barings Brothers heading a syndicate that included some of the City's leading investment houses, such as Philips & Drew, GRE, Globe Investments, Prudential Assurance and Guardian Assurance.[48] This was fortuitous, because by the time the deadline for accepting the rights issue had expired on 14 August a total of 98,524,873 shares had not been taken up.[49] Indeed, in the week prior to the deadline for shareholders to take advantage of the issue the *Sunday Times* was predicting 'a widespread revolt by investors', with several institutions refusing to buy shares in a company that was making such heavy losses.[50] Nevertheless, the underwriters mopped up these shares, ensuring that the firm received all of the £45.5 million as a means of funding the Strategic Review and Recovery Plan.

Having placed the firm's borrowings on a sounder, long-term footing, and as Table 7.1 reveals at the same time significantly reduced bank borrowings for 1990–91, Anderson and Broadley had given Ferranti International a much better chance of surviving the rapidly changing market environments experienced by its operating divisions. Although in the 1990 annual report Anderson accepted that the firm would 'not be operating at peak effectiveness until the new organisation finds its feet', he was confident enough to predict that it was in a stronger position than in February 1990, providing a conducive organisational and financial environment in which its innate technological resources could be extensively exploited. In stark contrast to the previously vague way in which the organisation achieved synergy across multiple technological capabilities, the new structure and its highly integrated and centrally co-ordinated management system offered richer possibilities, for example in making available software packages that could improve the performance of different types of equipment. When combined with the extensive introduction of total quality management techniques across the three divisions, latching on to what in British manufacturing industry was an increasingly popular means of improving productivity, this reinforced the drive towards integration and the achievement of unprecedented levels of synergy in pursuing the systems approach that lay at the heart of the Strategic Review & Recovery Plan.

Armed with the revised banking agreement, a £45.5 million injection of capital from the August 1990 rights issue, and a refocused strategy and structure, by autumn Ferranti International was consequently given a major opportunity to return to what could be described as normal trading, especially compared to its experiences since the previous September. Inevitably, though, and in spite of consistently optimistic statements emanating from Gene Anderson, who used every opportunity to build greater confidence in and across the firm, resolving the internal and external challenges facing Ferranti International was by no means straightforward. In this context, it is essential to address some of the other internal problems facing senior management, leaving an assessment of the external environment to the next section.

In embarking on this exercise, it is highly appropriate to start by examining the principal business acquired as a result of the merger with ISC, guided missiles. Although Guerin had falsely claimed to have secured missile contracts from China and Pakistan, the PGM project conducted on behalf of the United Arab Emirates was very much a reality, forming the *raison d'etre* for the creation of Ferranti International Dynamics Ltd (FIDL), based at Hanworth, Middlesex, but with the main production facility in Oldham. As managing director of FIDL, Ian Ball had been driving the PGM project as effectively as possible, given the problems he inherited from the chief designer of the *Hakim* missile, Clyde Ivy. These problems revolved around the failure to design a robust system that would both satisfy the customer and act as the basis for second and third generations of the missile. It was consequently March 1990 before the first production model of *Hakim I* rolled out of the Derker St factory in Oldham, by which time FIDL had been absorbed into the new aerospace systems division run by Ian Ball. By that time, however, because the UAE had provided substantial progress payments in 1987 and 1988 of £129.4 million and ISC had taken almost all of the profit on this contract, missile production was causing severe cashflow difficulties which would not be resolved until completion of the contract in 1991, at which point a settlement figure would be paid. Moreover, the contracts carried substantial performance bonds worth £134 million which exacerbated the liquidity issues, especially as the French aircraft manufacturer, Dassault, which was to supply the *Mirage* jets to which the PGM were to be attached, could only promise delivery in 1992.

While Ian Ball was able to persuade the UAE to modify the bonding requirements, and even though deliveries of *Hakim I* were ahead of schedule by July 1990, this business represented the group's biggest single source of cash outflow. Indeed, an operating loss of £8.9 million was made on the missile business in 1989–90. A further factor that complicated matters considerably in the summer of 1990 was the discussions concerning *Hakim III*, the award of which was looking increasingly likely. Indeed, a contract price of $275 million had been agreed by March 1990 for the supply of 330 missiles, offering the prospects of further expansion at Derker Street. On the other hand, Robin Broadley offered the view that aerospace systems should forego *Hakim III*, given the enormous liquidity implications of taking business that would only start producing significant profits in 1992, or even 1993.[51] Both Gene Anderson and Ian Ball rejected this argument, on the grounds that as *Hakim I* and *II* were progressing well, producing the third generation would be much easier and potentially more profitable. Nevertheless, big question marks were placed over the future of this business, reflecting the group's continued financial weakness, even after the rights issue and renegotiated bank agreement.

By September, however, Ball was obliged to report that due to inflationary effects on inputs, projected total production costs had increased by $7 million, reducing the anticipated profit on the fixed-price contract of $275 million by that amount, exacerbating the board's hesitancy. With mounting military tension in the Middle East, it was also difficult to meet General Khalid, resulting in the expiry of the tender at the end of October. The board decided to extend the tender another two weeks, in the hope that General Khalid could be contacted.[52] However, as neither *Hakim I* nor *Hakim II* could be tested by the client, owing to the failure of the French aircraft manufacturer to deliver the *Mirage* aircraft until 1992, the UAE proved reluctant to commit itself to *Hakim III*. It was consequently March 1991 before Ian Ball was able to sign the *Hakim III* contract

A second major source of illiquidity that was causing severe consternation at both board level and in the commercial and industrial systems division was the continued difficulties of completing development work on the *Ranger* energy management system. This business had been acquired at a cost of $10.7 million from TRW as long ago as 1984, largely in the hope that its supposedly radical new computerised energy management system could be sold in significant numbers to American and other electricity suppliers. Operating as Ferranti Industrial Controls Corporation (FICC), and reminiscent of the organisational problems besetting the parent company's relationship with ISC, as we saw in Volume 2 the major issue would appear to have been the failure to impose adequate project management controls on the subsidiary's activities, with its former owners being allowed to continue to manage the firm just as they had done prior to the acquisition.[53] Even though several major customers such as the Carolina Power & Light Corporation and Utah Power & Light Corporation had placed orders, providing substantial progress payments to support the *Ranger* development programme, by 1989 losses totalling £14.4 million had been made by FICC. To deal with these problems, in 1989 Paul Reynolds was seconded from Ferranti Computer Systems to impose stronger technical management on the *Ranger* project. By the spring of 1990, however, customers continued to complain of attenuated delivery dates, with several in the position that penalty payments exceeded the agreed price of the system.[54] This situation failed to improve over the course of the following year, with two customers demanding the return of their progress payments. The board was consequently obliged to set aside £40 million as an exceptional item in the 1990–91 accounts to cover these demands, while FICC continued to make losses totalling another £10 million. In total, by the time FICC had been placed into Chapter 11 of the US Bankruptcy Code in August 1992, it had cost the group over £45 million, massively undermining the credibility of the initial decision to acquire TRW in 1984.

Faced with this scale of cash outflow on the *Hakim* and *Ranger* businesses, Anderson and the board were obliged to ask serious questions about the firm's ability to invest in new, high-risk ventures. The 1989–90 annual report certainly highlighted this danger, noting that while a total of £16 million had been spent on R&D across the group that year: 'We are reassessing these expenditures to determine their appropriate level for the future.' In this context, one must assess the continued commitment to mobile telephony, because while this venture had been in existence for several years, it was certainly high-risk and extremely expensive. Of course, given the massive expansion of mobile telephony since the 1990s, creating some of the world's most profitable and powerful corporations, it is important to stress that Ferranti International was moving into a high-growth sector that promised considerable rewards for the first-movers. On the other hand, in 1990 not only was the market still embryonic, but also the costs involved in developing both the basic equipment and communications network required an enormous initial investment. Moreover, as Ferranti Instrumentation had discovered when working with the GTE Corporation to establish Ferranti GTE Ltd, their foray into telecommunications brought them into confrontation with much larger corporations such as British Telecom and AT&T, making it extremely difficult to build market share and generate a positive cashflow.

The move into mobile telephony had started in March 1987, when Albert Dodd (then managing director of Ferranti Instrumentation) was introduced by John Pickin (the Ferranti technical director) to Libera Developments Ltd, a firm that had been developing what at that time was known as CT2 technology (or, digital cordless technology). This was perhaps the firm's bravest attempt to expand its civil business, while many predicted significant growth in a sector that was being deregulated. By May 1987, Ferranti had taken a 25% stake in Libera Developments and signed a licence to manufacture and market its products,[55] leading to greater progress in perfecting the technology. Although it is interesting to note that users were only able to make (but not receive!) calls on the system known as *Zonephone*, it offered a highly novel form of communication through a portable handset within what was known as a *Telepoint* zone in a network of base stations. To market *Zonephone*, in December 1987 a £10 million-venture Ferranti Creditphone Ltd was formed, with Ferranti taking a 60% stake and the remaining funds provided by venture capitalists from the City of London, Electra Investments. Prophetically, at the board meeting when setting up Ferranti Creditphone was ratified, Sir Donald McCallum noted that to succeed Ferranti Creditphone would require 'great determination and a dedicated team', otherwise it would be 'killed by the competition'.[56] Indeed, just at that time all of the world's leading telecoms firms were venturing into mobile telephony, providing a stern test of Ferranti Instrumentation's ability to convert the technological capabilities bought in from Libera into positive commercial results.

Although one must stress initially that Ferranti Creditphone was by no means a major cause of the group's liquidity problems in the 1990s, the whole episode demonstrates the challenges associated with taking risks on new ventures that had extended gestation periods. Launched with considerable publicity in the spring of 1988, *Zonephone* was marketed as the 'must-have' product for the 'Yuppies' that appeared to be running the British economy by the late 1980s, as well as people who lived a peripatetic lifestyle. It was February 1989, however, before the DTI agreed to licence the *Telepoint* network, repeating problems that Ferranti GTE had experienced earlier in the decade when launching its range of telephones and business communications equipment.[57] Considerable optimism was nevertheless expressed about the prospects for growth, especially when powerful supporters such as Hanson Industries were recruited to back the Ferranti Creditphone syndicate that was going to bid for a licence for the next generation of mobile telephony, known as PCN (personal communications networks).[58]

It is also important to stress, however, that a year later the network only extended to Greater London, using Esso petrol stations as the *Telepoint* bases. Indeed, the authoritative journal *Cellular Business* claimed in 1991 that *Zonephone* was both too expensive and extremely limited in its service. Moreover, in making calls many users experienced interference from other wireless systems, while the inability to receive calls further prohibited wider use by those who were constantly mobile.[59] Particular criticism was also voiced about the handset, which apart from costing £200 was christened the 'Ferranti brick' because of its bulk; it certainly did not fit into either a suit pocket or handbag.[60] In addition, subscribers had to pay an annual fee of £100, while usage rates were 30 pence per minute, making the service inaccessible to all but the wealthiest.[61] As by that time Ferranti International had invested £8 million in developing *Zonephone*, it came as a big surprise to the board to hear that only 200 customers had been connected. Although Ferranti Creditphone was predicting an increase to 20,000 customers by March 1991, Gene Anderson described this as 'wildly optimistic'.[62] External commentators were also highly critical of the minimal amount of marketing conducted by Ferranti Creditphone, leading some to believe that by autumn 1990 'Telepoint has all but blown it in the UK.'[63]

The board was consequently sceptical about supporting the next phase of development, which was predicted to cost at least £40 million in total, with Ferranti International having to contribute £25 million. Ironically, because he had been sceptical of the commercial prospects of Ferranti Creditphone, at the end of 1988 Albert Dodd had tried to sell this venture for £25 million to one of its major rivals, Hutchison, the firm which went on to develop the *Orange* mobile telephony business.[64] This proposal was never actually pursued energetically by the board, largely because at that time both the company's venture capital partners and the board rightly regarded cellular telephony as a fashionable civil technology which was about to expand dramatically, while Sir Derek was also keen not to project a negative image to an increasingly sceptical City community. In very different circumstances, however, by March 1990 the board was looking to sell off one-half of its holding in Ferranti Creditphone, on the grounds that Ferranti International had assumed a market position in cellular telephony which was never justifiable; it was a luxury the group could no longer afford. Unfortunately, though, it proved impossible to find a buyer, even though Albert Dodd engaged GTE in extensive discussions,[65] leading Gene Anderson to insist that unless a sale had been completed by 30 September then the subsidiary would be closed.[66] This move was only prevented by the direct intervention of the minority investors in Ferranti Creditphone, Electra Investments, because they agreed to take over all of its liabilities in return for the 60% held by Ferranti International for just £1.8 million. While one might argue with the benefit of hindsight, and specifically the knowledge that by the early twenty-first century the bulk of the developed world seemed to live by communicating via mobile 'phones, that the Ferranti International board was taking an excessively short-term view of this business's prospects, it was clear by the summer of 1990 that the group just could not afford to sustain such a major source of negative cashflow. In simple terms, financial constraints had taken precedence over the technology-led strategy which had dominated the firm's outlook throughout its history, begging the more fundamental question, namely, whether Ferranti International would ever be capable of recovering fully from the traumas of 1989.

By providing these insights into *Hakim, Ranger* and *Zonephone*, or what were potentially three key future elements of a revived Ferranti International, it is apparent that by the latter months of 1990, and in spite of the renegoti-ated financial structure, the group was still struggling to present a viable base to its stakeholders. In addition to these three episodes, it is also important to mention other liquidity challenges that continued to warrant careful attention, not least the cash required to pay for redundancies and plant closures arising from the rationalisation programme instituted by the Strategic Review. Furthermore, throughout 1990 the Lancaster plant that had formerly been the headquarters of ISC was continuing to struggle with the FMU-139/B electronic fuze,[67] arousing concerns that it would have to repay all of the progress payments provided by the US Army, amounting to over $2 million. Much to the relief of the Lancaster team, the US Army persisted with the contract for much of 1990, even though the fuze failed a third test in June,[68] leading the board to consider closing the plant. Although by December there were unofficial reports that the fuze had finally passed these tests, by that time development costs had eaten up virtually all of the profit on this contract, doing irreparable damage to the Lancaster business's chances of becoming viable.

As the 'New Ferranti International' strategy had outlined, another key dimension of Anderson's plans was to sustain the sale of non-core divisions. In this context, he set up a Disposals Task Force, composed of himself, Charles Scott and other senior managers where appropriate,[69] that met weekly from September 1990. Its initial task was to compile a 'Disposal List', the bulk of which was ISC or US-based. Top of this 'List' was the much-troubled FICC, while Marquadt, Venus, Sciaky, Cardion, Ferranti Eastman Survey and Ferranti ORE featured as priorities. In the UK, the team wanted to sell Ferranti International Engineering, fuel dispensing systems (at Dalkeith), Ferranti Business Communications, satellite communications (at Poynton), and the land no longer used at the Wythehshawe factory. Similarly, they were also keen to dispose of the remaining 50% stake in Ferranti Italia (hopefully, to Finmeccanica, the state-owned Italian electronics and defence conglomerate). These plans were further complicated when after extensive negotiations with the GEC accountants charged with resolving the difference between the £270 million paid by that company for FDSL and the actual valu-ations reached after almost eight months' work, a major disagreement started. These negotiations had inevitably been extremely protracted, with accusations from both sides that the wildly differing valuations had been reached unfairly. At one stage, GEC was demanding a repayment of up to £70 million, but by October this had been significantly reduced to £30 million. As this was still a substantial amount of cash, however, accounting for two-thirds of the funds generated by the August rights issue, GEC was persuaded to take a Ferranti division as payment in kind, leading to further negotiations over exactly which part of the group would be sacrificed in the interests of retaining the agreed £30 million.[70] As we shall see later, it was finally decided that the missiles business would best fit this bill, leading to even further negotiations that would drag on for months.

Such were Gene Anderson's fears over the liquidity situation by the end of October that he resurrected a plan that Sir Derek Alun-Jones had initiated in September 1989, namely, the purchase of the entire group by a firm such as GEC, BAe or Thomson.[71] Even though the Disposal Task Force was working hard to sell off various non-core activities, these were relatively small businesses that would not generate much more than £5 million by the end of the year. Moreover, if GEC refused to take payment in kind for the agreed £30 million, then Ferranti International would be faced with imminent bankruptcy, given the negative cashflow experienced by almost every other part of the group. Albert Dodd felt that after all the effort put in by staff at every level of the organisation, this solution would be extremely unpopular, arguing that continued asset disposals ought to be pursued as a means of sustaining the core activities. Anderson, however, was adamant that even though he had been impressed with the degree of commitment expressed by most Ferranti International employees, from the senior management down to the shopfloor staff, it was necessary to consider a sale. This was reluctantly accepted by the rest of the board, resulting in more work for Barings Brothers in preparing a document that could be touted around various possible purchasers.

The decision to revive the sell-off strategy was naturally kept top-secret, only to be discussed at board and executive committee levels until positive interest could be generated from a potential purchaser. In the document drawn up by Barings and at the next board meetings, these firms were consequently referred to in code, as either 'Bronze' or 'Silver', in order to limit the possibility that news of this sell-off panicked the City, thereby leading to further reductions in Ferranti International's share price (see Figure 8.2). It was clear to all concerned, however, that the likely candidates were GEC and BAe in the UK, Finmeccanica and Thomson in Europe, and Marion Marietta and Raytheon in the USA. Gene Anderson also kept the MoD and DTI fully informed of these developments, as they represented the group's major customer base. By December 1990, both BAe and GEC had signed confidentiality agreements, allowing Baring Brothers to release the sale document, while meetings were being arranged with the European firms. Of course, as the board had been through all of this at the end of 1989 and earlier in the year, there was little enthusiasm behind these presentations, given that the initial entreaties had been received with such scepticism. Indeed, by February 1991 all but Finmeccanica had withdrawn from these negotiations, while even this Italian conglomerate was only interested in a strategic alliance on computerised control systems that at best would bring in a loan of £50 million.[72] The other potential investors were not surprisingly scared off by the widespread feeling across the City of London that the Ferranti International recovery would be extremely protracted, especially as in December 1990 it announced a £20.4 million loss for the six months to September 1990, compared with a loss of £15.4 million in same period of the last trading year. Even though the order-book was reported to be £628 million, which seemed respectable in the deteriorating economic conditions, the exceptional costs associated with disposals, closures and redundancies were expected to eat significantly into future profits as Ferranti International came to terms with its much-changed status.[73]

Although an injection of £50 million from Finmeccanica would have been extremely helpful at that stage, the board was naturally extremely reluctant to add yet more fixed-interest borrowing to the balance sheet. Finmeccanica also later withdrew this offer, having had access in April 1991 to Ferranti International's three-year plan, the details in which made for very bad reading. It is also relevant to note that although Finmeccanica was state-owned, it had made heavy losses in 1990–91 as a result of major investments in its core defence and electronics businesses.[74] The board was also given a cashflow report by David Shipley, who was at pains to emphasise how the group was rapidly running out of cash, not least because the Disposals Task Force was experiencing significant delays in achieving its goal of between £39 million and £44 million in asset sales, while continued vacillation by the UAE over the award of the *Hakim III* missile contract and significant cash outflows from FICC exacerbated the situation.[75] Another mounting cause of concern was the main board's difficulty in imposing more stringent management controls on those US subsidiaries that were still subject to the ISC proxy board's jurisdiction. Even though Albert Dodd, and then Jim Shinehouse, had been able to establish a degree of order across the bulk of the former ISC business activities in the USA, given the statutory requirement that all American defence contracts should be controlled by an American-based board of directors, the ISC proxy board was still responsible for substantial operations such as Marquadt and ISC Defense Systems (see Figure 2.1). This resulted in the removal of the proxy board by the spring of 1991, finally bringing to an end one of the trickiest aspects of the organisation introduced by Jim Guerin.

With cashflow difficulties causing increasing concern, in March 1991 the board was obliged to resort to what was a highly desperate measure of borrowing £15 million from the Ferranti Pension Fund.[76] This naturally shored up the finances in the short-term, but with bank borrowing rising to £73 million and projected losses for the group as a whole for 1990–91 of £25 million, even such a desperate measure failed to stem the cash outflow. By June, David Shipley was also reporting that overdue creditors had risen to the unsustainable level of £43 million, with little prospect that this figure would fall in the near term; indeed, it would probably rise over the summer, unless substantial asset disposals could be made. This obliged the board to consider whether it should cease trading, a debate on which the views of Herbert Smith and Barings Brothers were sought.[77] This once again placed a heavy premium on Gene Anderson's ability to persuade the banks that Ferranti International was viable, highlighting the crucial role the new chief executive played in keeping the firm afloat. Indeed, it is probable that had Anderson failed to nurture such a positive relationship with Baring Brothers and the banking syndicate that supported the firm, by the summer of 1991 Ferranti International could have been made bankrupt. When the 1990–91 results were being discussed by the board in July 1991, accountants from Grant Thornton also questioned whether the firm was a going concern,[78] providing Anderson with yet more challenges at a time when external commentators were beginning to doubt whether the firm would ever move into profit.

In addition to sustaining a healthy relationship with the bankers, Anderson also forced his board to address two key issues that could make or break the group: firstly, GEC's demand for compensation over its £270 million purchase of FDSL; and secondly, the legal case against PMM. Of course, efforts to dispose of what were regarded as non-core businesses continued, but as this process was being attenuated by the understandable desire of purchasers to exploit Ferranti International's widely known financial difficulties and continually reduce offer prices, the board recognised that this strategy was not going to solve immediate cashflow problems. For example, while in September 1989 the board had anticipated raising up to $150 million from the sale of Marquadt, in April 1991 it was sold off in three packages (the land, propulsion systems, and ordnance) for $40 million, with the respective purchasers (Wilshire Towers, Atlantic Research, and Ordnance Products) exacting a hard bargain for what were sound assets. Although some disposals were going through the books with commendable speed – in March 1991, the *Autocourt* fuel-dispensing business was sold to Siemens for £16 million, after just a couple of months of negotiations – it was extremely unlikely that the 1990–91 target of £72 million worth of disposals would be reached.

The negotiations between GEC's auditing team and Ferranti International over the £270 million paid for FDSL had been extremely protracted, with claim and counter-claim continually being passed between the two parties over the exact nature of the business's true worth. As we noted earlier, by

October 1990 a final compensation figure of £30 million had been reached, but negotiations dragged on another six months over exactly how Ferranti International was going to pay what was a substantial sum for a cash-strapped firm. Rather than pay out such a huge amount of cash, Charles Scott would eventually suggest that GEC should be remunerated in kind, for example by taking the missiles business. As we saw earlier, Ian Ball had already informed the board that as ISC had already taken all the profit on *Hakim I*, missile production would swiftly move into loss, while Ferranti International was also still servicing bonds amounting to £134 million. A complication arose in June 1991, when the MoD expressed a preference for Thomson CSF as the purchaser of FIDL, rather than GEC (which already had a strong position in the UK missiles market).[79] Although Thomson was willing to make a cash offer of £30 million for FIDL, however, this still meant that GEC would have to be paid exactly that sum, making a deal with the French firm much less attractive. This resulted in Anderson terminating the negotiations with Thomson, giving GEC a clear run at acquiring the missile business.

In spite of these developments, negotiations between GEC and Ferranti International dragged on interminably. At one stage, the entire deal was thrown into doubt because after talking to the UAE, GEC imposed various financial conditions on *Hakim III* that proved to be totally unacceptable. This also prompted the Abu Dhabi Bank of Commerce, which had been central to the many deals involving the *Hakim* contracts, to suggest that the UAE ought to purchase FIDL. While this alternative offered rich possibilities, not least in the proposed price of £50 million, as it would have been extremely difficult for the UAE to acquire export licences, once again GEC was left as the only possible purchaser. Having resolved its differences with the customer, partly through the intervention of Ian Ball, who worked hard to persuade General Khalid that this was a good deal, by the end of August GEC was ready to sign the agreement. This was to prove extremely beneficial to Ferranti International, because not only was the firm released from the enormous bonds securing the contracts, but also GEC offered to pay £38 million for FIDL and various parts of Ferranti Aerospace Inc that had been involved in the missiles contracts.[80] The board was consequently very grateful to Ian Ball for making such a success of the missile business, not to mention the negotiating skills of Charles Scott in completing the complex discussions with GEC,[81] given the prime importance of offloading an activity that was causing the group acute liquidity difficulties.

On exactly the same day that the Ferranti International board agreed to this deal, Gene Anderson reported the receipt of £30 million from PMM.[82] As we saw earlier, the company had issued a writ claiming £530 million in damages from PMM in February 1990, after considering the various reports drawn up by Coopers & Lybrand on the way that PPM had conducted its audits of ISC in 1986–87, as well as taking extensive legal advice from Herbert Smith. By April 1991, Ferranti International was spending £100,000 per month on legal work by Herbert Smith,[83] indicating how zealously the board pursued a deal on this claim. As we saw in the last chapter, even though in February 1990 the House of Lords had ruled in favour of Touche Ross in a five-year-long case brought by Caparo Industries, arguing that auditors cannot be sued for negligence,[84] Ferranti International felt that they had such a solid case against PMM that it was worth spending so much on the case. PMM naturally publicised its role in persuading Jim Guerin to adopt a much more conservative accounting policy in 1986–87, while the prevailing auditing guidelines placed the onus of responsibility for ensuring that accounts were accurate firmly on management's shoulders. Nevertheless, Sir Derek Alun-Jones was adamant that ISC's accounts had been inadequately audited, leading to headlines such as 'Figures did not show true and fair view.'[85] There was also growing concern across the City that auditors ought to accept much more responsibility for the data that they verified, building momentum for the adoption of what in the 1990s came to be known as commercial due diligence.[86]

In spite of its public rebuttal of the claims made by Ferranti International, by the beginning of 1991 privately PMM was willing to enter into negotiations on a possible compensation payment. A significant factor in persuading them to adopt this conciliatory stance, apart from the obvious desire to limit the adverse publicity associated with the case, was Gene Anderson's success in securing £50 million from Arthur Young over its audit of Johnson Matthey Bankers. Inevitably, there was little consensus between the parties on the amount that PMM would pay, with PMM initially offering as little as £15 million. After a long series of meetings, in July 1991 PMM finally offered £40 million, as long as the case never came to trial. As Herbert Smith had consulted the prominent barrister D. Oliver QC on this issue, they were confident of a settlement in the region of £300 million if the case went to court. However, not only was there no trial date set for the case, it was clear to the board that PMM could also drag it out for several years by appealing against any negative judgements.[87] With liquidity issues currently causing the board considerable concern, specifically the rapid growth in overdue creditors, such delays just could not be countenanced, forcing the board to agree with the greatest possible reluctance to PMM's offer. PMM put a gloss on the settlement by insisting that far from being an admission of negligence, it merely ended what could have been a lengthy legal case. Moreover, as their professional indemnity insurance covered the payment,[88] it did no damage to the balance sheet, especially as it was spread over two instalments, of £30 million and £10 million (payable in February 1992).

While some surprise was expressed by external commentators at the scale of the pay-out, given that Ferranti International had initially asked for £530 million and had sued Jim Guerin for $189 million,[89] for a cash-strapped firm the injection of £30 million in August 1991, with the promise of another £10 million in six months' time, was very well timed. Dragging the case through the courts, possibly on to the House of Lords, would have been far too protracted, while it was by no means certain that in view of that body's decision over the Touche Ross-Caparo case, success was guaranteed. In this context, it is worth considering the judgement of Michael Chance, the executive counsel who in May–June 1996 conducted a lengthy investigation into PMM's audit of ISC accounts on behalf of the Institute of Chartered Accountants in England and Wales. As a former deputy director of the Serious Fraud Office, Chance was well versed in this kind of investigation, while access to extensive documentation, much of which had been generated by the multi-agency investigation into Guerin's crimes in the USA, ensured a thorough analysis of what had transpired. Although the report highlighted some of the deficiencies in contemporary auditing practice, especially when confronted with the use of front companies, Chance came down firmly in support of PMM. His conclusion was categoric:

> There is no scope for the suggestion that PMM were faced with clear evidence of dishonesty and failed to pursue it because, for example, they had allowed themselves to become too close to their client's senior management and were unwilling to confront them. The reality is that PMM were among those comprehensively deceived by a fraud which was designed and executed with extraordinary care and skill.[90]

Of course, it is impossible to say whether the House of Lords would have produced the same conclusion, but in view of the breadth and scope of Chance's investigation it is unlikely that they would have been able to avail themselves of the 'clear evidence of dishonesty' to which Chance alluded. One can only agree that the board had made the correct decision in accepting a £40 million payment, not least because it provided a lifeline at a time of acute illiquidity.

As we saw earlier, the GEC compensation deal was also resolved at the same time, providing a further £5 million and relieving to some extent the liquidity fears reported by David Shipley at successive board meetings since the spring. Another source of cash was provided by the settlement of the Clark-Guerin case in Philadelphia,[91] resulting in a payment of $1.2 million by the US authorities to Ferranti International, the courts having decided that this money had been earned from the frauds perpetrated by Jim Guerin. Most attention, however, was paid by commentators to the PMM settlement, with the implication that the auditors had come out on top. Indeed, Anderson was willing to accede publicly that Ferranti International's 'desperate need for cash' prompted the low settlement with PMM, at a time of 'toil, trouble and trial' for the firm.[92] These admissions also coincided with the announcement of its 1990–91 results, which revealed pre-tax losses of £98.1 million, placing in jeopardy the agreements Anderson had negotiated with its bankers in the summer of 1990. By that time, the net worth of Ferranti International had fallen to just £130 million, compared to an estimated £230 million when the summer 1990 banking agreement had been negotiated, giving cause for widespread concern about the level of indebtedness being incurred.[93] The chief executive was consequently obliged to utilise his widely acknowledged skills in persuading the syndicate to sustain its support, even though privately the board was being advised that there were growing doubts as to its status as a going concern.[94] This instigated negotiations on a fourth standstill agreement between Ferranti International and its bankers, with the latter insisting that both the PMM and GEC compensation cases should be resolved as a condition of their continued support.

With a fourth standstill agreement in place by 9 November 1991, giving the firm liquidity cover until the end of March 1992, as well as having safely banked the GEC and PMM cheques, the board could anticipate a less troublesome period. The various changes to the group were duly ratified by shareholders at the AGM on 27 September and an EGM on 6 December, again reflecting the trust placed in Gene Anderson's management skills by a financial community that was still waiting for its first dividend from Ferranti International since the spring of 1989. As the headline to Andrew Alexander's influential column in the *Daily Mail* trumpeted, 'Ferranti clings on',[95] indicating how by then it was widely accepted that Anderson was performing minor miracles in keeping the business afloat. As we shall see in the next chapter,[96] however, in the early months of 1992 liquidity concerns re-emerged, leading to serious consideration of the firm's legal status. At the same time, Ferranti International was also obliged to cope with an external environment that proved far from conducive to any recovery strategies the board might consider. This analysis of the external environment will also highlight the difficulties of ensuring a total alignment of corporate resources with the rapidly changing context in which defence firms were operating by the early 1990s.

7.3 Recovery chances: external–internal alignment?

Of course, there were many critics who had lambasted Sir Derek Alun-Jones for selling off FDSL, given its role as consistently the most profitable division within the group since the 1950s. Similarly, the missiles business was regarded as a potentially profitable business that could have sustained the group during the 1990s, especially if *Hakim III* had been awarded. In evaluating these decisions, as we have just noted financial exigencies had persuaded the board to dispose of these assets, bringing in cash in order to bail out the rest of the business. At the same time, another consideration uppermost in their minds was the state of the British and world defence markets, because while both had remained buoyant for much of the 1970s and 1980s, from 1985–86 especially considerable concern had been expressed about the nature of this business. This was a major issue for a firm that had relied excessively on defence markets for over forty years, with the acquisition of ISC reflecting Sir Derek's desire to reinforce this strategy. After all, as he rightly argued in public and private,[97] Ferranti had never been able to generate much profit from civil ventures, apart from electricity meters and power transformers, while even in those departments severe problems had been experienced in the 1970s. In spite of a moratorium imposed on defence spending by a new Conservative government in 1979–80, the defence market had also increased in size, from almost £22 billion in 1978–79 (at 1991 prices) to £25.7 billion by 1984–85, with the Falklands War of 1982 sparking a significant surge.[98] Thereafter, however, British defence spending levels declined by fourteen per cent in real terms, to £22 billion in 1992–93, falling to less than 4% of GDP, the lowest level since the 1930s. As we also saw in Volume 2, in 1985 procurement policies and contract conditions had been dramatically changed, leading to the imposition by the MoD's new head of procurement, Sir Peter Levene, of competitive tendering and a dramatic reduction in the old system of providing progress payments for work underway.[99] Dubious claims by the mid-1980s defence secretary, Michael Heseltine, that this would 'galvanise British industry' was simply political rhetoric which attempted to hide the real reason why the Conservative government introduced these new rules, namely, as part of its assault on the general levels of government expenditure aimed at funding income tax reductions.

Over the late 1980s and early 1990s, the domestic defence market was consequently both contracting and open to much more intense competition from American and European firms, leading commentators to warn investors that companies committed to this market would perform poorly.[100] A worrying indication of these trends was the failure of Ferranti International's naval systems to secure the contracts to supply computerised control systems to the Royal Navy's new generation of Type 23 frigates, because in 1988 a French firm was awarded this lucrative business.[101] GEC's acquisition of Plessey also provided this conglomerate with even greater market power, while by focusing resources on its Marconi subsidiary Lord Weinstock was able to create a major international defence supplier. This strategy also reflected wider trends in the European and North American defence industries, because once Mikael Gorbachev and George Bush had in 1989 signed the protocols that effectively ended the Cold War, this forced politicians to think about how they might convert 'guns into ploughshares'.[102] A succession of defence reviews followed in most Western nations, further reducing the size of the international defence market, while just as in the 1960s, government ministers worked actively to encourage concentration in the defence industry, on the grounds that this would create firms capable of competing for the remaining business. Of course, some export markets such as the Middle East remained buoyant, especially after the 1991 Gulf War, when the USA and its allies stepped in to repel Iraqi forces from Kuwait. As a result, BAe was able to secure the first stage (worth £5 billion) of the multi-billion pound Al Yamamah contract with Saudi Arabia to supply forty-eight *Tornado* military aircraft, the benefits of which were spread across several British firms, including past and current parts of Ferranti. Nevertheless, competition from American and West European firms intensified in these sectors, as US defence spending also fell victim to the same kind of pressures felt in the UK, leading experts such as John Lovering to conclude that: 'The defence industry is in crisis.'[103]

Whatever the moral implications of these debates about defence spending in the 1990s, it was clear to Gene Anderson and his team that Ferranti International could not anticipate the same kind of returns from what had been its staple business since the 1950s. Given the financial implications of retaining both the onboard radar and missiles businesses, with their enormous liquidity requirements, disposing of these activities could well have been extremely judicious. One might speculate that the board would also have been happy to offload the naval systems business, because once a wholesale review of the company's accounting procedures had been conducted by Charles Scott, it was realised that this division had an extremely unfortunate legacy. Few could have anticipated the severe problems which this exercise would reveal, because Peter Dorey had built a business that had consistently contributed significantly to Ferranti profitability. Nevertheless, it transpired that naval systems had always placed a value on its technical development contracts, putting this under the heading of stocks in the balance sheet. It was a ruse which, with the MoD providing generous progress payments for work-in-progress, would always mean that the division was able to generate healthy profits. Once the provision of progress payments was terminated in 1985 by the MoD, however, it was discovered that substantial write-offs had to be effected to many contracts. The contract profits problem would appear to have been most acute at the Cairo Mill plant of what had been Ferranti Computer Systems, where the cost of developing a new generation of naval systems was causing major difficulties. As the managing director of the strategic management systems division, which from the summer of 1990 encompassed Dorey's former empire, in 1991 Albert Dodd was instructed by Gene Anderson to restore some order to its accounts. It was at

this stage, though, that while this helped improve the division's ailing relationship with the MoD, it also discovered that £20 million would have to be
written off against stock adjustments. Dodd's revelations also sparked off a
company-wide review of its government contracts, as a result of which over
the two trading years 1989–91, Ferranti International was obliged to charge
over £110 million as 'Exceptional Items' for this purpose. This indicates how
the firm's accounting systems proved to be totally unprepared for the
changing defence market conditions of the late 1980s, reinforcing the belief
expressed by Gene Anderson that the whole system would have to be revolu-
tionised if Ferranti International was ever going to be a profitable firm in the
radically different post-1985 climate.

In addition to these problems, as operations director Albert Dodd was
also dealing with the challenge of reviving what had been the automation
systems business at Wythenshawe, demonstrating how one of the firm's
former powerhouses was struggling to survive in an extremely difficult
market. These difficulties highlight yet another feature of the contemporary
trading environment, because with defence markets contracting domesti-
cally and internationally, the situation was exacerbated by the onset of a
major international recession that severely affected demand for capital
equipment. Of course, the 1980s had started with an international recession
induced by a combination of yet further oil price increases imposed by the
Organisation of Petroleum Exporting Countries (OPEC) and the introduction of monetarist policies by the UK, USA and several international
economies. This resulted in two extremely difficult years in the UK, with
Gross Domestic Product (GDP) falling by 2% in 1980 and 1.2% in 1981,
precipitating the collapse in British manufacturing output. A service-sector
boom in the 1980s provided the basis for a robust recovery, with annual
GDP growth averaging over 4% in the mid-1980s. In 1990, however, the
international economy experienced one of its periodic downturns, with UK
GDP growth falling to just 0.8%, followed by negative growth in 1991 of
−1.4% and a slow recovery over the following two years. In response to this
deteriorating economic environment, the government took the usual step
for that period of increasing Bank of England interest rates; while in the late
1980s they had averaged 9%, by 1990 they stood at 14.5%, only falling back
to the 1980s norm in 1992. For a firm that was heavily reliant on enormous
bank borrowing, this exacerbated the problems associated with sustaining
output and generating a positive cashflow, especially with the markets for its
staple products in steep decline.

There was consequently a growing realisation that Ferranti International
was not only dealing with a massive fraud, it was also being forced to re-
evaluate its position in the marketplace. During the mid-1980s, as a defensive
response to the mid-1980s take-over threats, the board had been preoccupied

with a merger and acquisition policy which was regarded as central to its strategic vision. To a significant extent, absorbing ISC had also taken up excessive amounts of management time, limiting the opportunities for a radical reassessment of the changing market. Ironically, though, while acquiring ISC had been a defensive response to the threat of a take-over by Plessey, in buying a firm riddled with problems it made Ferranti International totally immune from this possibility of being bought by a rival. After the fraud had been discovered in 1989, executives were again kept extremely busy dealing with both corporate and divisional implications, limiting the chances to conduct the much-needed strategic exercise. Indeed, by the 1990s the board was involved in what can only be described as a 'fire-fighting' exercise, reacting to such problems as the enormous losses on *Ranger* and the rationalisation or sale of other divisions. Furthermore, because of the group's much-changed financial status, there was a growing reluctance to do business with Ferranti International divisions, in spite of the agreement with its bankers in November 1989. Morale across the group was also much depleted, giving the distinct impression to an outsider like Anderson that radical change was required.

The first move along these lines had, of course, been the Strategic Review and Recovery Plan, reshuffling what had formerly been five divisions into three 'customer-oriented' divisions. As he noted in the 1990–91 annual report, when describing these changes to shareholders, 'it is clear that while technically the company has been innovative and successful, it has needed for some time to move aggressively to address its competitive position, given the radical changes in the marketplace'. This statement highlighted once again Anderson's criticisms of his predecessor's regime, because as we noted earlier he had stated publicly that profitability had been poor since the mid-1980s.[104] Moreover, in his annual report for 1991–92 Anderson returned to this theme by claiming that senior management had been responsible for 'the failure to respond quickly to the new competitive defence environment in the late 1980s'. The discovery of enormous accounting problems in the defence-oriented divisions during 1990–91 provided decisive evidence of these deficiencies, while the product range continued overwhelmingly to favour defence markets.

Having sold off a considerable proportion of the defence-related divisions, however, activities that had taken up an enormous amount of management time, in the 1991–92 annual report Anderson was able to state that they were going to devote much more time to securing profitable business. In order to achieve this, in the latter months of 1991 he had instituted another reorgani-sation of the group, largely because with the aerospace systems division gutted by the loss of the missile and US aerospace activities, it was necessary to reshuffle the remaining activities.[105] Instead of the three divisions (see

Figure 7.1), it was decided that eight business units would be created. These business units (and their primary product markets) were:

- *naval systems* (naval and maritime command and control systems);
- *systems integration* (ground-based and airborne management systems);
- *simulation and training* (naval, airborne and land training and simulation systems);
- *industrial systems* (real-time control and monitoring systems for industrial and energy applications);
- *commercial systems* (real-time computer control systems for air transport and civilian emergency services);
- *satellite communications* (microwave systems for civil and military applications);
- *components* (specialist hardware and sub-systems, ordnance and avionic equipment);
- *USA operations* (ordnance, power supplies, telemetry tracking and advanced welding systems).

As the new operations director, Albert Dodd was responsible for overseeing these business units, while the central staff at Bridge House provided support for marketing, purchasing and other functional activities.

Inevitably, this reorganisation also involved several senior management changes. The most notable was Ian Ball's resignation from his position as managing director of aerospace systems, to become a non-executive director with specific responsibility for advising Gene Anderson on trends in the defence industry. Alan Cooper, the other person alongside Ian Ball who had been primarily responsible for unravelling Guerin's fraudulent activities, also decided to retire as company secretary in November 1992. Although Cooper continued to advise the board on legal matters over the following thirteen months, his resignation brought to an end a highly distinguished career at Ferranti that most recently had proved pivotal. Bill Broekhuizen had already resigned as managing director of industrial and commercial systems in June 1991,[106] having decided that the difficulties associated with running this declining business were simply too burdensome. Indeed, at that stage he decided to retire to his home in the Lake District, after thirty years' service with Ferranti during which he had contributed extensively to especially the computer systems business. As we have just seen, the third divisional managing director, Albert Dodd, had already moved to become the operations director, giving him an even more influential role in fashioning corporate strategy. Finally, in November 1991 Gene Anderson persuaded R.J. Davies to join the firm as group finance director,[107] replacing David Shipley in this post, who in any case had only been on secondment from Coopers &

Lybrand. As a former finance director at Ford Motor Co, Waterford Wedgwood and Coopers & Lybrand, Davies was an extremely useful acquisition for the board, bringing extensive experience of both corporate finance and general City activities, at a time when Ferranti International's credibility continued to deteriorate.

By aligning strategy and structure in this way, as well as freshening up the board, Anderson was attempting to bring even more focus to management efforts than he had done in the summer of 1990 when driving through the Strategic Review. Linked with this new approach, from the summer of 1991 every manager and over 50% of other employees were trained in quality improvement methods associated with the Total Quality Management (TQM) techniques that were being disseminated across British industry. The guiding principles behind this strategy were 'Conformance to requirement' and 'Getting it right first time', not only sustaining and enhancing what had been a Ferranti tradition of high-quality engineering, but also eliminating waste and errors that added to cost.[108] Whether in the context of a contracting group this was ever going to make much of an impact is debateable, but at least Ferranti International made an effort to introduce what was potentially a significant means of improving performance. At the same time, having failed to upgrade the group's IT system for several years, which in itself was a startling admission for a company of this type, by the autumn of 1991 an IT Strategy Group had been formed to assess this situation. However, when the group reported that the net cost of an upgrade would cost £13.6 million, this persuaded the board that the new systems should only be introduced in a piecemeal fashion.[109] While this was understandable in the context, there is little doubt that failing to introduce the latest computer software inhibited organisational improvements, at a time when their rivals were investing massively in what was by then accepted as essential support services.

It is possible to hypothesise that given both the agreement on a fourth standstill agreement with the firm's bankers and a second restructuring of the operating activities, the board could well have anticipated a period of steady recovery. Indeed, Robert Davies drew up a Near-Term Financial Strategy that was based on a progressive move back to profitability and viability. In the prevailing market conditions, however, such optimism was barely possible, because with severe cutbacks in both defence and civil markets it proved extremely difficult to boost turnover and generate profits. Typifying the group's problems in microcosm was Ferranti Healthcare, a US subsidiary based in Baltimore which had been formed in the summer of 1988, after Ferranti International had acquired the healthcare division of Pentamation Enterprises for $15.7 million and absorbed it into existing diagnostic data handling capabilities. Although it was able to secure some high-profile contracts for its *Leadership* hospital management system, for example to

Roswell Park Memorial Institute in New York and the Monmouth Medical Center in New Jersey, just like its *Ranger* counterpart at FICC the business failed dismally to generate enough business to cover development and production costs. Moreover, irregularities were discovered in Ferranti Healthcare, resulting in the dismissal of the general manager, compounding the subsidiary's difficulties in securing more business. With a monthly cash outflow by December 1991 of $700,000, and predictions that by March 1992 the subsidiary would have cost the group $37 million, it was decided to placed the corporation into Chapter 11 of the US Bankruptcy Code and look for a purchaser.[110] After persuading Keane, Inc to buy Ferranti Healthcare for just $1.8 million, on condition that they took over the subsidiary's liabilities, this brought to an end yet another disappointing American venture.

While the acquisition of this business at the height of the late 1980s boom had been an astute piece of business, seizing new opportunities in computerised management systems that were becoming increasingly popular, with the onset of a major international recession in 1990 demand for such expensive equipment had fallen markedly, making it increasingly difficult to sustain profitability. This is why Ferranti Healthcare can be regarded as typifying the group's problems in microcosm, because the product range was dependent on the availability of customers willing to invest substantially in increasingly sophisticated systems that involved both high capital costs and ongoing maintenance and upgrades. What had been the commercial and industrial systems division was especially badly affected by the reduction in demand for this kind of equipment, forcing Bill Broekhuizen to sell off the two cripplingly expensive Wythenshawe sites and concentrate all production in the much smaller Concord complex just next door. Charles Scott had been highly critical of the decision in 1986 to expand the activities of automation systems from its original Wythenshawe factory into the neighbouring Ciba Geigy site, arguing that the business could not justify this enormous increase in overheads. Such was the precipitous collapse in orders by 1990 that Scott's predictions were proving all too accurate, leading to the closure and sale of the Wythenshawe/Ciba Geigy site and occupation of the Concord facilities.

This retrenchment was a clear reflection of market trends, placing in jeopardy the division's future. Of course, continued product development ensured that its range of process control, communications and transport systems remained highly competitive, resulting in the acquisition of some highly prestigious contracts. For example, in 1991 the division supplied the eleventh offshore system to Shell for its Gannett computer-aided platform operations, while Nuclear Electric purchased an £8 million upgrade to its software controlling the advanced gas-cooled reactors. On the other hand, not only was commercial and industrial systems dogged by the ongoing *Ranger* saga at FICC, over the period 1988–89 to 1991–92 sales fell by over

20%, from £153 million to £121 million, at a time when inflation averaged almost 10% per year. Even more worryingly, over that period the division reported operating losses of £92 million, and while both FICC and Ferranti Healthcare had been offloaded by the beginning of 1992, its future was very much in question. Significant contracts continued to come their way, for example, flight information systems for Amsterdam's Schiphol Airport and Manchester Airport's new terminal, but these by no means covered the development and production costs incurred. Above all, this system required a much higher level of orders in order to justify the product development costs, something which in the context of a major international recession was simply not forthcoming.

With civil markets proving to be extremely competitive throughout the early 1990s, placing in jeopardy a significant proportion of the business, it is vital to stress that as a result of both disposals and closures, not to mention a significant contraction in the size of the UK and international defence markets, Ferranti International was unable to turn to its traditional bolthole. While various divisions continued to sell equipment to defence customers on both sides of the Atlantic, there was no core business on the scale of Ferranti Defence Systems in Edinburgh capable of generating substantial profits from an expanding portfolio of highly regarded onboard radar and communications equipment. Even the naval systems business based at Bracknell was but a shadow of its former self, having fallen victim to a combination of the MoD's competitive tendering system and a significant reduction in Royal Navy expenditure on sophisticated onboard computerised control systems. Much of its business by the 1990s was consequently focused on upgrades of older systems, such as the CACS 1 command system supplied to the Royal Navy's Type 22 frigates, improvements to the ADAWS system installed in the *Invincible* class of aircraft carrier, and a refit of *HMS Southampton*, a Type 42 destroyer that had been damaged while on duties in the Arabian Gulf. Although these fixed-price contracts were completed on time and to budget, and significant export contracts were secured in the USA, Jordan, Korea and Brazil, concerns were expressed at board level about the future of a division that was heavily dependent on a contracting market.

Ironically, though, by far the most profitable component of the Ferranti International group during the early 1990s was Ferranti-Thomson Sonar Systems (FTSS), the joint venture formed in February 1990 with Thomson CSF to exploit the two firms' renowned expertise in this market. Under Gerry Bentley's creative management, over the course of the following three years this subsidiary continued to win significant contracts from defence ministries in several countries. Orders for the 2050 batch 4 sonar to be fitted to the *Trident* class of submarines and active dipping sonar for the *EH101 Merlin* helicopter provided the foundations for a successful business that was sustained throughout the 1990s. The irony here revolves around the nature of this business, because both Sir Derek Alun-Jones and Gene Anderson had devised rescue strategies that were predicated on a major competitor taking a substantial stake in Ferranti International. Another joint venture that proved to be extremely successful was Ferranti-Bendix Power Generation Ltd (FBPG), which brought together the two firms' widely regarded expertise in power supply systems. This firm was able to win large contracts to supply the power units for the European Fighter Aircraft, providing a highly profitable foundation for a business that prospered over the next decade. While one might stress that FTSS and FBPG were operating in two of the few defence markets that were actually growing at that time, it is interesting to speculate whether a comparable move by the entire group would have resulted in a much more viable future. Indeed, the failure to ally more positively with either an American or European corporation with the market presence of a Bendix or Thomson significantly undermined the group's recovery prospects, because, firstly, the board was obliged to continue its reliance on bank borrowing, and secondly, Ferranti International's credibility as a viable operation was deteriorating as the 1990s progressed. Moreover, as both defence and capital equipment markets were severely depressed at that time, the prospects of a robust recovery remained poor. One should also stress that management was so busy fire-fighting and dealing with short-term issues that it was difficult to find the time to think strategically. Such were the challenges imposed by the 1989 crisis that any dynamism left within Ferranti International was atrophying as a direct result of a crisis mentality that cascaded from top to bottom in the organisation.

A final issue to discuss in this section is whether Ferranti International had been able to realign its core strategy and competencies with the highly challenging external environment, an exercise that goes right to the heart of any assessment of strategic credibility. In this respect, it is pertinent to note that in the 1992–93 trading year defence business still accounted for 63.5% (amounting to £155.6 million) of the total (£244.7 million), while 67.2% (£97.7 million) of the firm's net assets (£145.2 million) were focused on this sector. In view of the acute difficulties in this market, both at domestic and international levels, this could well be regarded as extremely dangerous. While civil markets were no easier after 1990, sustaining the company's traditional dependence on defence was indicative of a highly conservative approach towards realigning corporate strategy. It could well be that the board and business unit managers were desperate to secure any contracts that would help the balance sheet recover from its ISC-induced crisis and other internal shocks. Indeed, as we shall see in the next chapter, by 1993 the near-term financial strategy was built on the award of an order to supply a major computerised communications system (*Delmon Eye*) to Saudi Arabia, indicating that the realignment of corporate priorities was subsumed by the need to rebuild the business in whatever markets proved responsive to Ferranti International technologies.

7.4 Conclusions: a 'New Ferranti International'?

There is, of course, much more that could be said about the many aspects of even a slimmed-down Ferranti International. After all, even in 1992–93 the eight business units were still involved in a myriad range of product markets, employing over 5,000 people across a geographically dispersed network of facilities that covered the UK, USA, Korea, Singapore, Australia, Brazil, Chile, Belgium, Germany and Switzerland. Most importantly, and in spite of the deep economic recession and cuts in defence spending, the business units were still based on the core strategy devised by Gene Anderson in 1990 which emphasised the need to offer advanced systems that built on the remaining technological competencies associated with computerised command and control, communications and integration. Apart from R.J. Davies, who had joined the board of directors in November 1991, there was also tremendous continuity at that level of management, a move that was interpreted publicly as vital to the recovery process. Crucially, the financial institutions seemed to be quite content with this board, because Gene Anderson was able to use his negotiating skills to manoeuvre them into providing a series of short-term borrowing facilities that maintained liquidity at a crucial time. Although one might well regard this financial support as a just reward for the generous dividends shareholders had received from Ferranti throughout the 1980s, more realistically these facilities were a major vote of confidence from the City in the rescue strategy devised by Gene Anderson and the Ferranti International board, leading to some confident expectations that the firm would soon turn the corner.

Of course, this sanguine picture hides a terrible reality, namely, that by 1992 Ferranti International was much-changed from its 1989 incarnation. In one sense, this had been very much the aim of Gene Anderson's 'New Ferranti International' paper for the board of February 1990,[111] when he outlined the principal features of what would be a dramatic reorganisation focused on much greater central control of strategy and finances. Never in its history had the firm been so dominated by senior management, and especially compared to the previous thirty years, when divisional 'barons' had fashioned their own strategies in the full knowledge that the board was content to give them extensive freedom to pursue new technologies. By the 1990s, these freedoms had been banished to the realms of history, indicating how something 'New' had been forged through the imposition of strong financial and managerial controls. At the same time, Anderson had encouraged the divisional (and later, the business unit) managing directors to pursue much more customer-oriented strategies, forcefully aligning structure and strategy at Ferranti International.

On the other hand, these distinctively 'New' features of the way in which the group was managed should also be contextualised, specifically with reference to the all-embracing disposals programme that had partially been imposed by the banking syndicate, but which continued into 1993 as a means of providing the funds required to keep the firm afloat. As one shareholder complained at the 1991 AGM, 'a swarm of corporate locusts was draining Ferranti of resources',[112] an accusation that was difficult to defend, given the loss of both highly talented staff and businesses that had contributed the bulk of the group's profits over recent decades. Crucially, by the early 1990s Ferranti International could never aspire to achieving any of the key characteristics mentioned in the first paragraph of this chapter – financial muscle, sheer scale and market domination – that would have provided the foundations for a total recovery from the crisis that struck the firm in 1989. Whether this weakness was caused primarily by the ISC fraud or other factors we shall go on to analyse in Chapter 8, where the litany of disposals will be placed in a broader context composed of an extremely difficult trading environment and the presence of several problematic divisions within the Ferranti International portfolio. In concluding this overview of Gene Anderson's first two years as chief executive, however, while one can state boldly that he had succeeded in creating a 'New Ferranti International', it is not entirely clear whether this was by design or as a result of responding to pressures that had been both inherited from the previous regime and imposed on him by factors beyond his control. It is these issues that we shall now go on to assess, while at the same time describing how the group slipped into bankruptcy and lost its fight for survival.

Notes

1 This was the title of a document submitted by Gene Anderson at FBM 11, 26 Feb 1990.
2 *Guardian*, 20 July 1990. This story was entitled 'Time to saddle up'.
3 FBM 11, 26 Feb 1990.
4 FBM 4, 29 Sept 1989.
5 *The Times*, 11 Oct 1989.
6 Sir Derek asked Albert Dodd to draw up some plans for a restructuring of the firm, but these were dropped once the new MD was found.
7 See J.F. Wilson (2000), *Ferranti. A History*. Vol. 1. *Building a Family Business 1882–1975*, Carnegie Publishing, pp. 35–45
8 FBM 3, 8 Jan 1990.
9 See J.F. Wilson (2007), *Ferranti. A History*. Vol. 2. *From Family Firm to*

Multinational, 1995–1987. Crucible Books, pp. 65–66.
10 *Scotsman,* 11 Jan 1990.
11 Ibid.; *Observer,* 21 Jan 1990.
12 *Sunday Telegraph,* 7 Jan 1990.
13 FBM 3, 8 Jan 1990.
14 *The Times,* 31 Oct 1992.
15 *Observer,* 21 Jan 1990.
16 *The Times,* 31 Oct 1992.
17 *Wall St Journal,* 6 Feb 1990.
18 *Intelligencer Journal,* 7 Feb 1990.
19 *Financial Weekly,* 9 Feb 1990.
20 *Lancaster New Era,* 23 Feb 1990.
21 *The Times,* 31 Oct 1992.
22 *Engineer,* 15 Feb 1990.
23 *The Times,* 31 Oct 1992.
24 FBM 6, 27 March 1990.
25 *Daily Mirror,* 23 Feb 1990.
26 *Daily Mail,* 24 Feb 1990.
27 *Financial Times,* 24 Feb 1990.
28 Interview with Gene Anderson.
29 See earlier, pp. 87–9, and Vol. 2, pp. 365–78.
30 FBM 11, 26 Feb 1990.
31 Ibid.
32 FBM 9, 12 July 1990.
33 Interview with Gene Anderson.
34 See Vol. 2, pp. 365–78.
35 Interview with Gene Anderson.
36 See Vol. 2, pp. 171–4, for more details on this programme.
37 *Lancaster Sunday News,* 6 Nov 1989.
38 FBM 4, 7 Feb 1991.
39 FBM 1, 9 March 1990.
40 FBM 1, 18 May 1990.
41 *The Times,* 31 Oct 1992.
42 See Vol. 1, pp. 533–7 and Vol. 2, pp. 24–31.
43 FBM 5, 31 May 1990.
44 FBM 9, 12 July 1990.
45 FBM 14, 3 July 1990.
46 Report to employees, No. 27. July 1990.
47 FBM 10, 31 May 1990.
48 The other underwriters were Postfund Nominees, Legal & General Assurance, Mineworkers Pension Scheme, BriTel Fund, Electra Investments, Murray Johnstone, British Coal Staff Fund, and Mercury Asset Management.
49 FBM 2, 16 Aug 1990.
50 *Sunday Times,* 29 July 1990.
51 FBM 4, 27 March 1990.
52 FBM 8, 2 Oct 1990.

53 Vol. 2, pp. 223–4.
54 FBM 5, 1 May 1990.
55 FBM 6, 28 May 1987.
56 FBM 10, 14 December 1987.
57 Vol. 2, pp. 135–44.
58 *The Times*, 15 Sept 1989.
59 *Cellular Business*, Jan 1991, p.14
60 *Sunday Times*, 9 Sept 1990.
61 *Cellular Business*, Jan 1991, p.14.
62 FBM 3, 27 March 1990.
63 *Sunday Times*, 9 Sept 1990.
64 Interview with Albert Dodd.
65 FBM 10, 31 July 1990.
66 FBM 8, 2 Oct 1990
67 See earlier, pp. 123–5.
68 FBM 4, 3 July 1990.
69 FBM 9, 10 Sept 1990.
70 FBM 4, 31 Oct 1990.
71 FBM 9, 31 Oct 1990.
72 FBM 6, 7 Feb 1991.
73 *The Times*, 12 Dec 1990.
74 For further information on Finmeccanica, see E. Felice (2010), 'State ownership and international competitiveness: the Italian Finmeccanica from Alfa Romeo to aerospace and defense (1947–2007)', *Enterprise and Society*, Vol. 11, No. 3, pp. 594–635.
75 FBM 7–8, 7 Feb 1991.
76 FBM 5, 4 April 1991.
77 FBM 6, 6 June 1991.
78 FBM 3, 22 July 1991
79 FBM 4, 6 June 1991.
80 FBM 3, 9 Aug 1991.
81 FBM 5, 5 March 1992.
82 FBM 5, 9 Aug 1991.
83 FBM 9, 4 April 1991.
84 See above, p. 197, for a discussion of this case. *Daily Telegraph*, 9 Feb 1990.
85 *Financial Times*, 18 Nov 1989.
86 Howson, *Due Diligence*.
87 FBM 4, 1 Aug 1991.
88 *Accountancy Age*, 15 Aug 1991.
89 *The Times*, 13 Aug 1991
90 Chance Report, 1996.
91 See above, pp. 162–3.
92 *Daily Telegraph*, 15 Aug 1991.
93 FBM 5, 5 Sept 1991.
94 FBM 6, 6 June 1991.
95 *Daily Mail*, 13 Aug 1991.

96 See pp. 269–77.
97 Interview with Sir Derek Alun-Jones.
98 Lovering 'Opportunity or crisis?', p.101. See also Vol. 2, pp. 372–4.
99 Vol. 2, pp. 372–4.
100 *Wall St Journal*, 15 Feb 1990.
101 Vol. 2, pp. 237–45.
102 Interview with John Lovering, *Independent*, 6 Jan 1990.
103 *Independent*, 6 Jan 1990.
104 *Financial Times*, 24 Feb 1990. See above, pp. 34–8.
105 FBM 11, 9 Dec 1991.
106 FBM 11, 14 June 1991.
107 FBM 3, 6 Dec 1991.
108 *Ferranti International. Review of Operations, 1992–93*, p.7.
109 FBM 4, 3 Oct 1991.
110 FBM 9, 5 Dec 1991.
111 FBM 11, 26 Feb 1990.
112 *The Times*, 28 Sept 1991.

8

Demise and epilogue

IT IS DIFFICULT to convey on paper the traumatic nature of those early 1990s years for Ferranti International, with newspaper stories aplenty announcing either mounting financial losses, possible take-overs or factory closures and redundancies, not to mention corporate missives revealing rationalisation exercises, management changes and two major reorganisations in as many years. By March 1990, Ferranti International had already slipped almost forty places in the *Sunday Times* Top 250 British companies, from 212th to the 'wooden spoon' position at the bottom,[1] indicating how the September 1989 announcements had affected its financial health. Over the course of the following three years, it proved impossible to improve on this record; indeed, one might argue that performance deteriorated significantly, undermining the claims made at successive AGMs and EGMs that there was light at the end of the tunnel.[2] After all of the disposals and closures, by the end of 1990 the group was also described as 'a ragbag of businesses', few of which were capable of generating the profits required to alter dramatically the group's bottom line.[3] These views persisted into 1991, when in August the *Observer* noted that 'the City cannot see the rationale of the Ferranti rump',[4] while by autumn of 1992 commentators were noting that Gene Anderson had been physically affected by the rigours of his two years at the helm.[5] As we noted in the last chapter, one can only admire the perspicacity of those who survived this onslaught, because throughout that era staff at every level of the organisation committed enormous amounts of effort and imagination in coping with the various challenges. Above all, though, acute illiquidity arising from the ISC fraud significantly limited management's ability to pursue more ambitious strategies, because not only were the divisions/business units starved of development funds, but also customers proved reluctant to place substantial contracts with Ferranti International. As the board was constantly reminded, debts owed to unsecured creditors grew to dangerous levels in the early 1990s, highlighting the constant danger of bankruptcy at a time when politicians were reluctant to interfere with the free play of market forces and use taxpayers' funds to bail out ailing firms. Indeed, government apathy to the plight of one of Britain's major electronics firms was a prominent feature of the early 1990s environment, highlighting an issue to whch we shall return in the conclusions to this chapter.

While in the last chapter we initiated the debate concerning the reasons why after four years Ferranti International was unable to rebuild its finances and project a positive image to both shareholders and customers, clear conclusions have yet to be reached on this issue. Of course, one must accept that the ISC fraud created an enormous hole in the balance sheet, resulting in massive bank lending that restricted strategic decision-making and resulted in extensive asset disposals. It is also fair to note that the single most important source of Ferranti profits since the 1950s was one of the first disposals, limiting the restructured group's ability to generate anything like the same returns as it had done in the 1980s. On the other hand, many of the later asset sales arose from the desire to offload businesses that were either already making losses or would soak up scarce financial resources in further product development. This once again highlights the questions asked in the last chapter about the credibility of the decisions on strategy and structure made either side of 1989. Even if the severe early 1990s economic recession and deep defence expenditure cuts exacerbated the challenges facing the board, it could well be the case that the demise of Ferranti International was the product of a combination of massive fraud and an awkward product legacy. Whatever the case, by December 1993 Ferranti International had succumbed to 'a long fight against the inevitable',[6] providing a tragic end to 111 years of innovation and excitement.

8.1 Deteriorating finances

It was noted at the end of Section 7.2 that by the beginning of 1992, with the PMM and GEC cheques totalling £45 million safely banked and a fourth standstill agreement negotiated with the banks, Ferranti International's finances looked stronger than they had done a year earlier. This sanguine view, however, could not have been further from the truth, because such were the board's concerns about liquidity that in February 1992 a meeting was held with representatives of Herbert Smith, Slaughter & May, Barings Brothers and Coopers & Lybrand to consider some brutal truths. After a lengthy discussion Gene Anderson and Charles Scott were able to provide sufficient assurances to the external advisors.[7] Nevertheless, as the board was still anticipating a loss of £40.4 million for the 1991–92 trading year, compared to the forecasted figure of £34.4 million notified to the banks, and the accounts department was receiving in excess of 150 writs per month from overdue creditors,[8] it was apparent that Ferranti International was once again teetering on the edge of bankruptcy, prompting Robin Broadley to ponder on its chances of securing a major contract in the near-term future.[9]

Just as David Shipley had done in 1991, throughout 1992 Robert Davies was consequently obliged to maintain a vigilant watch on overdue creditors and liquidity. By that time, of course, given the scale of the asset disposals (see Table 8.1), the former were no longer as large as they had been in 1991. On the other hand, as one can see in Table 8.2 and Figure 8.1, Ferranti International was still struggling to generate any profit on its regular trading. This persuaded the board to resurrect for what was the third time the possibility of entering into a joint venture with another major electronics corporation, especially as the Italian state-owned electronics conglomerate Finmeccanica had recently expressed an interest in merging its computer activities with naval systems and systems integration. At the same time, given the recent successes of Ferranti-Thomson Sonar in securing contracts worth over £100 million, the board was considering a sale of its 50% stake in this venture for what could be up to £50 million.[10] It rapidly became apparent, however, during the negotiations conducted by Albert Dodd that if the sonar joint venture was sold, then the Italian conglomerate might lose interest in buying a major stake in Ferranti International.[11] At the same time, a major dispute with Finmeccanica over its acquisition of Ferranti Italia emerged, creating tension between the two parties that dragged on until the early months of 1993. Even though Finmeccanica was proposing to pay £56 million for a 29% stake in Ferranti International,[12] the latter was reluctant to agree to the former's demands over Ferranti Italia, which amounted to £21.8 million in compensation. These issues were clearly deep-rooted, but what really forced Finmeccanica to terminate discussions about a joint venture was the highly complicated arrangements that would have to be put in place in linking the two firms' civil businesses. The Italian conglomerate was also undergoing a major reorganisation at that time, creating major challenges to its absorption of Ferranti International into what was already a highly diverse business.[13] As we shall see later, detailed negotiations with GEC were also being conducted from the autumn of 1992, with Lord Weinstock making a series of derisory offers for the company that added to the sense of gloom descending on the board. By June 1993, Finmeccanica had formally withdrawn its interest in acquiring a stake in Ferranti International. Even though their respective naval systems businesses continued to talk about a strategic alliance, effectively by the summer of 1993 the British firm was at the mercy of GEC, a prospect that did not fill many people with much optimism.

With the prospects of recruiting a major investor once again shelved, and the banks insisting that a sale of the 50% stake in Ferranti-Thomson Sonar would be unacceptable, it was consequently necessary for Gene Anderson, Robert Davies and Robin Broadley to negotiate what was a fifth amendment to the bank standstill agreement first agreed in November 1989.[14] Liquidity

Table 8.1 Asset disposals by Ferranti International, 1990–93

Year/month of sale	Subsidiary	Purchaser	Value of deal (£ m)
Dec 1989	Computer maintenance	ServiceTec	17
Feb 1990	50% of Ferranti Italia	Finmeccanica	77
Feb 1990	Ferranti Defence Systems; 50% of Ferranti Italia[a]	GEC	270[a]
Feb 1990	Dundee component and laser business	MBO[b]	7
Feb 1990	50% of sonar	Thomson CSF	32
Dec 1990	Fuel dispensing	Dresser UK Ltd	16
April 1991	PABX communications systems	Siemens	6.8
April 1991	Ferranti International Engineering Ltd	Bridgetest Ltd	
April 1991	Ferranti ORE	Geoacoustics Ltd	3
May 1991	Voice Systems	Brite Voice Systems Ltd	3
July 1991	Road traffic systems	Peek Traffic Ltd	3
July 1991	Ferranti Creditphone	Electra Investments	1.8
Aug–Dec 1991 (with land disposals in early 1993)	Marquadt	MA Acquisitions Corp; Kaiser Aerospace; ARC	41.2
Sept 1991	Cardion Electronics	Siemens	17
April 1992	Ferranti Healthcare	Keane Inc	1.8
April 1992	Ferranti Infographics and metrology service and maintenance	ServiceTec	3
Sept 1992	Dalkeith Industrial Components	MBM Technology Ltd	3
Dec 1992	Ferranti International Controls Corp	Elsag Bailey Inc	1.8
June 1993	Ferranti Venus; Ferranti Sciaky; Ferranti Bendix	Eldec Corp; Flow International; Allied Signal	3.6; 1.8; £1
TOTAL			£509.8 million[c]

Notes: [a] Ferranti International was later obliged to accept a revaluation of this asset, resulting in the sale of the missiles business and some of the US aerospace activities for £38 million.
[b] MBO: management buy-out by local team.
[c] This includes the £5 million net gain on the sale of the missile business to GEC.

Table 8.2 Profits, dividends and retained earnings at Ferranti International, 1986–87

Year to March	Profit (loss) pre-taxation (£ M)	Capital employed (£ M)	Return on CE[a] (%)	Net[b] profits/ (losses) (£ M)	Dividend payments[c] (£ M)	Dividends as a proportion of net profits (%)
1986	41.1	217.0	18.9	28.0	7.5	26.8
1987	50.2	233.5	21.5	31.5	8.5	27.0
1988	54.4	354.1	13.8	15.5	8.5	54.8
1989	13.1	477.1	2.7	(0.8)	5.8	(74.2)
1990	(161.7)	342.2	(47.2)	43.2	0	–
1991	(98.1)	208.1	(47.1)	(165.2)	0	–
1992	(39.6)	141.2	(28.1)	(44.1)	0	–
1993	(12.6)	147.3	(8.5)	(22.7)	0	–

Notes: [a]The return on capital employed (CE) is calculated by dividing the pre-tax profit/loss by the capital employed.

[b] Net profits are defined in the balance sheet as the funds attributable to the ordinary shareholders, having deducted taxation, minority interests and extraordinary charges from the figures given in column 2.

[c] This sum includes both preference and ordinary share dividends, but it is important to emphasise that the former never cost the company more than £100,000 per annum.

Source: Ferranti Annual Reports 1986–93.

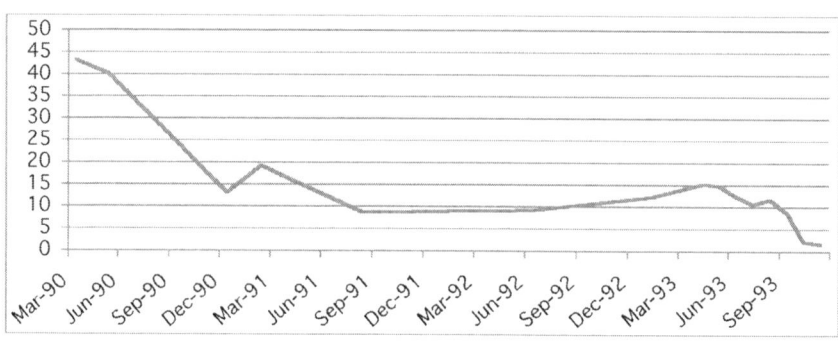

Figure 8.1 Ferranti International share price, 1990–93

was so tight by that time that no less than 187 writs had been received in September 1992 from unsecured creditors. While the chief executive was able to persuade the banks to sign this amendment, once again demonstrating his outstanding skills in this respect, at the same time Robert Davies reported that 'there had been a clear change in the tone of the negotiations with the banks who, recognising the forecast fall in the Company's net worth, were intent on minimising their exposure'.[15] Crucially, the lack of working capital was causing several business units major problems in meeting contract milestones, while in tendering for contracts managers had been obliged to raise their prices, in order to boost liquidity. Albert Dodd confirmed this to the board, reporting that of the sixty contracts for which the company had tendered over the previous two years, forty-nine had been lost on price alone.[16] Above all, customers were increasingly nervous about placing significant orders with Ferranti International, given the intensifying rumours of either its impending break-up or complete closure.

Another emerging problem was the loss of key staff, for example at highly successful activities such as simulation and training. As Ian Ball stated, 'either by redundancy, transfer or re-organization ... [it] had lost many of its key staff, who were acknowledged international experts in this field, and might therefore have seriously eroded its previous expertise'.[17] This situation was compounded by the failure to invest in an upgrade to the group's computer software in the autumn of 1991, which was limiting the contracts review committee's ability to estimate costs accurately.[18] While the latter was only partially resolved in the following months, it was the former that would continue to occupy senior management; even though overdue creditors were by no means as large as they had been in 1991, it was still essential for Robert Davies to channel scarce cash to those suppliers who were vital to the completion of major contracts.

With the negotiations over an investment from either Finmeccanica or GEC unlikely to produce swift results, Gene Anderson consequently decided to reinstitute the disposals taskforce that had largely been in abeyance since the end of 1991.[19] Much of this activity was focused on disposing of the remaining US (land owned by Marquadt, Sciaky and Venus) and Scottish operations (Dalkeith), providing Robert Davies with the challenge of securing a fair price for assets that were not exactly the most attractive to potential purchasers. The major problem with the land owned by Marquadt was a health and safety issue, in that extensive testing of propulsion systems created concerns that the property was heavily polluted. These reservations were eventually overcome, resulting in the sale of the land to a property development firm, while Sciaky and Venus were offloaded later in the year, bringing in vital liquidity that was used almost immediately to satisfy unsecured creditors. Indeed, just as in 1989–90, the disposals strategy remained at the heart of Ferranti International's planning, an issue we shall assess in the next section. The 1993–96 Corporate Plan actually stated that its success hinged on 'three critical transactions': disposing of the sonar activity; entering into a strategic partnership; and securing the *Delmon Eye* contract.[20] As the bank syndicate approved this plan in March 1993, it was consequently vital for the respective business unit managers and board directors to pursue these as vigorously as possible.

It is indicative of the state of Ferranti International finances that one of these 'critical transactions' was a single contract, the *Delmon Eye* air defence command and control system that was intended to be installed in Bahrain to support the *Falcon Eye* system purchased by Saudi Arabia. While one should stress that if secured this would be worth £122 million over the following three years, the banks were nervous about the £20 million advanced payment guarantee that the firm would have to provide, accentuating the short-term liquidity pressures. Nevertheless, the contract would have been sufficiently profitable to resolve these problems over the medium term, reinforcing its vital importance to corporate planning. The board was also confident of winning this order, because in 1989 Ferranti Computer Systems had supplied what was code-named *Falcon Eye*, a highly sophisticated computer-controlled communications system that covered all air and sea activities across Saudi Arabia. Furthermore, as BAe and Saudi Arabia had already signed the multi-billion Al Yamamah II deal, which involved supplying not only *Tornado* military aircraft, but also a comprehensive command and control network, in offering *Delmon Eye* Ferranti International was anticipating a major piece of business. It later transpired, though, that due to unhelpful movements in the sterling/dollar exchange rate, BAe had been obliged to submit an even higher price for *Delmon Eye* than Ferranti International had tendered as a subcontractor, amounting to an increase in price of almost £20 million.[21] This alienated the Saudi Arabian Ministry of Defence, and in spite of lobbying by the UK Minister for Defence Procurement, Jonathan Aitken MP, by the spring of 1993 it was clear that the customer was losing interest. Albert Dodd was only able to report in July 1993 that it was possible Saudi Arabia would award the contract by Christmas, while a £40 million extension to the *Falcon Eye* system was also being delayed.[22] As Anderson commented to one reporter, this business 'keeps receding into the future like a desert mirage'.[23]

While Davies was pursuing the disposals strategy, as operations director Albert Dodd was responsible for a rigorous policy of rationalising productive capacity, especially in the North West of England where the firm had traditionally occupied a lot of premises. The most important step was persuading Oldham Borough Council to purchase the Cairo and Orme Mills for £620,000 and lease them back to the company.[24] This allowed the firm to close its Moston factory, bringing to an end over fifty years of Ferranti activity in that town,[25] but significantly reducing overhead costs on a facility that had always been inordinately expensive to run. Similarly, capacity in the USA was reduced significantly, with the switch of all ordnance production to a single Lancaster plant. This move was temporarily halted after a fire on 2 December destroyed part of the Lancaster factory,[26] but Jim Shinehouse (head of the ISC businesses in the USA) and Ivor Kelly (director of planning

operations) pressed ahead with the transfer, as well as continuing to rationalise activity in all of the other US subsidiaries.[27] At the end of 1992, the
board even decided to close the company's head office at Bridge House, relo-
cating the much-reduced central services to the Concord Business Park,
Wythenshawe. While this did not create any serious logistical problems for
the staff involved, by 1993 the central services was composed of only one-
third of the staff who had been employed at a bustling Bridge House in 1989,
providing yet further evidence of the way in which Ferranti International was
contracting.

By the time Ferranti International had revealed its results for the 1992–93
trading year at the end of June, headlines such as 'Ferranti still in the
doldrums' typified the response of commentators that remained unim-
pressed with the prospects of a swift return to profitability.[28] The failure to
bring in the *Delmon Eye* contract, rumours of growing numbers of writs from
angry suppliers, and a pre-tax loss of £24.5 million all contributed to dismal
reports that further depressed the share price.[29] Above all, it was apparent that
unless another firm provided a significant capital injection, most were
predicting imminent bankruptcy, even if a sixth standstill amendment
provided bank support up to June 1994. Such were the firm's difficulties that
under the 1989 Companies Act the board was obliged to convene an EGM on
5 October, because at £48 million the net assets amounted to less than one-
half of the company's called-up share capital (£96.8 million).[30] This was
extremely humiliating for Ferranti International,[31] having made bullish
comments since 1990 about a return to profitability and rebuilding shareholder value. Moreover, at the EGM Anderson was obliged to report that
losses for the first half of 1993–94 would be higher than the commensurate
period of 1992–93, with the amount owed to unsecured creditors rising by
the month. The firm's bankers were consequently 'keen to draw a final line
under the travails of the past few years', pressuring Anderson and his board
into decisive negotiations with GEC about buying the entire group at
whatever price Lord Weinstock offered.[32] Some speculated that 'something
has gone wrong',[33] but clearly the bankers' patience had simply expired,
leading to the enforced negotiations with GEC which effectively signalled the
beginning of the end for Ferranti International.

8.2 Tracking performance, 1990–1993

Before assessing the final denouement of Ferranti International, it is worthwhile considering why the firm ended up at the mercy of GEC. Firstly,
though, it is vital to stress that given his extensive and successful negotiations
with the banking syndicate, there is no evidence that Gene Anderson had
been brought in to carve up Ferranti International and ensure that the bank

debt was repaid at any cost. Over the period February 1990 to December 1993, the new chief executive clearly made every effort to rationalise the activities of Ferranti International with the specific aim of giving the group a more viable core which might survive as an independent entity. The funds raised from extensive asset sales was also a major contribution to clearing the company's debts, while reducing overheads and implementing a series of economy measures would have further assisted the recovery programme instituted at the end of 1989. Nevertheless, in spite of all this industrious work by Anderson and his management team, after 1989 Ferranti International proved incapable of recording a gross profit on its operations, eating up the cash accumulated from asset sales. Figure 8.2 illustrates clearly the nature of the problem, because with turnover plummeting as a result of both disposals and deteriorating market conditions, losses totalling £195 million dominate the period 1989–93. Although a net profit of £43.2 million was recorded for 1989–90, this was only possible after including the sale of FDSL, which brought in a net sum of £222 million. Why, after over four years had passed since the fraud, had matters deteriorated, rather than improved? Why was Ferranti International incapable of generating a net profit over that period? Was it simply a matter of blaming Jim Guerin and the £215 million fraud?

One of the first issues to discuss in this respect is the asset disposal programme, and specifically the early loss of the most profitable component of the Ferranti group since the 1950s, FDSL. One can only hypothesise about what would have happened had the MoD not forced Sir Derek Alun-Jones to

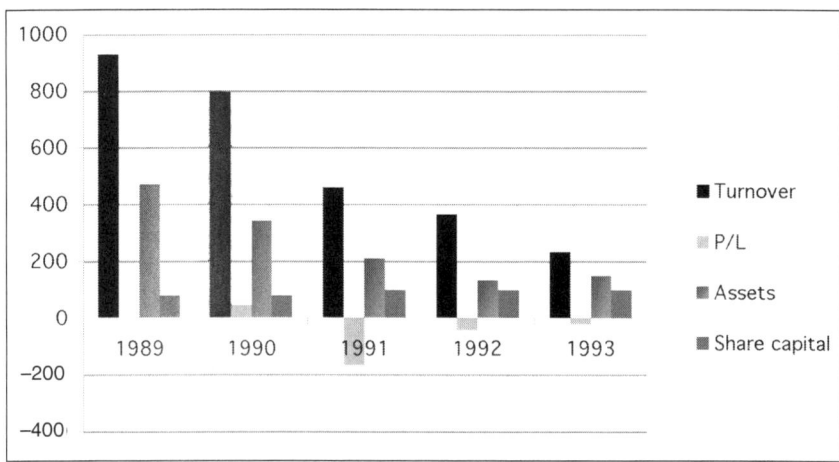

Figure 8.2 Ferranti International financial performance,
1989–93 (£ m)

sell this 'jewel in the crown', because having secured the £2 billion contract to supply the onboard radar for the EFA, GEC was assured of a highly profitable business that has continued to prosper since the early 1990s. Of course, the disposal strategy had initially been imposed by the banking syndicate in 1989, as an essential condition of its standstill agreement which helped to cover the ISC-created hole in Ferranti International's balance sheet. On the other hand, it is important to remember that this agreement insisted on asset sales of just £100 million, rather than the £300 million generated by the sale of FDSL, emphasising the key role played by the MoD in this disposal. One might go as far as to say that having disposed of this 'jewel', the board was obliged to sustain this programme over the next three years (see Table 8.1) because it lacked the funds to support such a diverse and capital-intensive range of businesses. This point is reflected in the sale of Ferranti Creditphone, Ferranti Healthcare and FICC, because in different circumstances the group would have sustained these subsidiaries, given their considerable market potential. As a cash-strapped firm, however, it was hardly likely that scarce funds would be diverted to supporting high-risk ventures at a time when the economic environment had deteriorated badly.

The complete litany of disposals is provided in Table 8.1, providing remarkable testimony to the liquidity needs of an ailing company. In addition, one should remember that as well as these disposals, which brought in £515 million gross, Ferranti International was paid £40 million by PMM to settle the impending court case over that firm's audit of ISC, as well as £1.2 million by the US authorities once the Clark-Guerin court case had been resolved, making a gross total of £556.2 million. The net figure, however, was much lower, because Ferranti International was obliged to use a significant proportion of the proceeds either to compensate aggrieved customers or pay for plant closures and redundancies arising from the changes in location. Indeed, while up to 31 March 1991 a net injection of £232.6 million was provided by the asset disposals, in the next two years a net loss of £7.6 million was made as a result of this activity. While the PMM and Clark-Guerin payments were entirely available for internal use, as well as the £45.5 million raised in the August 1990 right issue, in effect the net injection of capital into Ferranti International as a result of disposals, compensation payments and the rights issue was £311.7 million between 1990 and 1993.

While this looks like a substantial amount of money that could be used to sustain the operating divisions through the tricky early 1990s economic environment, the bulk of it was used either to reduce bank exposure or meet the losses made by ventures such as FICC and Ferranti Healthcare. Furthermore, we have tracked how over the course of the 1989–93 period Ferranti International was obliged to sign a succession of standstill agreements, principally because the group simply could not sustain its financial

commitments. In this respect, Gene Anderson had provided decisive negotiating skills in persuading the banking syndicate to maintain its support,
leading many fellow-directors to believe that without this relationship
Ferranti International would have disappeared much earlier. Bank exposure
stood at the remarkable figure of £689.4 million at its peak in the early
months of 1990, at a time when the net worth of Ferranti International fell
drastically from approximately £200 million in September 1989 to just half of
that figure a year later. As we saw in Table 7.1, while in 1990 Ferranti
International was holding a lot of cash in the bank (£166.7 million), it was
not allowed to use this because the banks insisted that the money should be
held on deposit as collateral for loans. While bank exposure fell drastically
over the following three years to £100.9 million, by 1993 net borrowings
(£90.6 million) were rising again (from £66.5 million in the previous year),
by which time net worth had fallen to just £54.2 million. Moreover, with
interest rates increasing over this period, not only was Ferranti International
obliged to use funds generated by asset disposals to reduce bank lending, the
firm was also paying a high price for this capital: interest payments exceeded
£80 million over the two trading years 1989–91, while even though net
borrowings fell over the next two years (see Table 7.1) this bill amounted to
£40.6 million, almost equalling the August 1990 rights issue (£45.5 million).

Assessing the contribution of bank indebtedness to the performance of
Ferranti International is naturally a difficult issue. On the one hand, without
the support of Barings Brothers, NatWest Bank and the thirty other banks that
agreed to the November 1989 standstill agreement, Ferranti International
could well have been subsumed by the £215 million ISC fraud. Even though
bank debt rose to the frightening figure of £689 million in the early months of
1990, this was crucial to survival. On the other hand, one must assess the
conditions imposed on this lending, because not only did the syndicate of
banks enforce asset disposals, it also insisted that all of the cash generated
from this exercise should be used to repay the bank lending, limiting the
prospects of boosting performance. While the later asset disposals arose from
the need to offload loss-making subsidiaries that drained scarce resources
from the group, the lack of funds to invest in profitable business units acted as
a major constraint on performance as the 1990s progressed.

Having mentioned the existence of loss-making subsidiaries, however, one
is inevitably switching the analysis from an attack on the nature of bank
lending to the composition of the Ferranti International group. As we have
seen in both earlier chapters and Volume 2,[34] significant question marks hang
over either the decisions to acquire certain businesses or the way in which
new ventures were managed. The most notable of these problem areas, of
course, was FICC, which because of over-ambitious technological plans for
the *Ranger* system and poor project management acted as an enormous drain

on group finances. Its estimated losses of £45 million also coincided with the announcement of the ISC fraud, while the publicity associated with demands from customers for compensation further undermined the group's reputation, especially in the USA. Ferranti Healthcare also experienced similar problems, due largely to the collapse in investment in hospital computerisation across the USA during the early 1990s. By the beginning of 1992, this subsidiary had lost almost £5 million, in spite of an investment programme costing £2.5 million in new facilities and equipment, forcing Ferranti International to file for protection under Chapter 11 of the US Bankruptcy Code.[35] Similarly, other US subsidiaries (including former parts of the ISC group) failed to move into profit after several years of investment. This reinforces a claim made in Volume 2, that the 'US Strategy' fashioned by Sir Derek Alun-Jones was a commercial failure of significant proportions, adding significantly to the ISC-induced balance sheet problems.

This damning indictment of what was a key component of the Ferranti corporate strategy during the 1980s was one of the legacies to which Gene Anderson alluded when first moving into the post of Ferranti International chief executive.[36] At the same time, he was also obliged to wrestle with severe challenges in some of the UK-based divisions, compounding the overall nature of the managerial role. These problems were most acute at Ferranti Creditphone, which we noted in the last chapter was a highly ambitious venture into mobile telephony that in the hands of a cash-rich firm would have produced long-term rewards. In the context of a depressed economic environment, though, not to mention the need to invest much more in a rapidly developing technology, there was little prospect that in the early 1990s the group would recoup its outlay. The severe recession of that period would also materially affect the ability of other civil businesses to generate remunerative orders, most notably what had been automation systems division at Wythenshawe which specialised in the development and production of computerised command and control equipment for a wide variety of customers, from manufacturing industry to emergency services such as the police. With declining order books and increased competition from European and Japanese conglomerates, this exacerbated that division's traditional problem of accommodating the high level of engineering that went into each contract into a contract price that would prove profitable. As we noted earlier, the failure to upgrade the software used by the contracts review committee added to the problems, because it was increasingly difficult to estimate accurately how long each contract would take to complete, placing the group in danger of having penalty payments imposed by customers. With FDSL no longer cross-subsidising other civil activities in Scotland, it was also vital to sell these business units (either to management buy-outs or to competitors) before they became a drain on group finances.

With the various civil businesses struggling to produce any profit by the early 1990s, it is also clear that some of the defence-oriented units were faring no better. Apart from the significant damage disposing of FDSL did to the group's profitability, this sale also coincided with a significant downturn in the fortunes of the other division that up to the late 1980s had been a mainstay of the group, namely, naval systems, especially after it failed to secure the contract to supply command and control systems for the next generation of Type 23 frigates for the Royal Navy. The discovery of significant accounting difficulties in this business unit, resulting in a write-off amounting to £20 million, also highlighted how the group's internal systems had failed to adapt to the changes wrought by Sir Peter Levene to the MoD's contractual arrangements.[37] Ironically, the most profitable defence business unit was Ferranti-Thomson Sonar, in which Ferranti International had a 50% stake after going into partnership with the French defence conglomerate in 1990. We have also emphasised how defence markets in both the UK and internationally proved extremely difficult after 1990, making it impossible to rebuild the other defence businesses. Furthermore, as in 1992–93 defence accounted for 63.5% (amounting to £155.6 million) of total business (£244.7 million), as well as 67.2% (£97.7 million) of the firm's net assets (£145.2 million), Ferranti International was still heavily dependent on a market that was both highly challenging and contracting.

While one should not forget that within Ferranti International there were several extremely successful businesses, including simulators and training equipment, flight information systems and emergency services information systems, the severe economic recession of that period, combined with deep defence expenditure cuts after 1990, made it extremely difficult to acquire the scale of order throughput that would have helped to drag the group out of its financial quagmire. One highly prestigious contract was the supply in 1993 of an advanced flight information system to Manchester International Airport's new Terminal 2, using two IBM computers to run the sophisticated software that serviced 250 screens, from check-in through to baggage claim.[38] While the system was highly regarded and worked extremely well, this was the only contract of its type awarded at that time, limiting the advantages of developing such advanced software. This loss-making theme dominated the early 1990s, with the three divisions (see Figure 7.1) recording total trading deficits of £213.3 million in just two years (1989–90 and 1990–91). Compounding this harsh market environment was the existence of loss-making businesses within the three divisions, with FICC, Ferranti Creditphone and Ferranti Healthcare the worst offenders. Table 8.2 provides even more detailed information on the group losses, illustrating that what to many financial commentators was the decisive indicator of performance, return on capital employed, was negative throughout the period 1989–93. This poor performance also inevitably resulted in zero dividend payments, giving the over-whelming impression to observers of a dying company. Just to add insult to injury, in April 1993 the DTI insisted that Ferranti International should repay £1.5 million of the grant support it had received from the Micro-electronics support scheme (MESS) programme.[39] Although the DTI agreed to take this sum in thirteen monthly payments of approximately £115,000,[40] this added further to the liquidity crisis enveloping the firm by that time.

This liquidity crisis was not difficult to detect, because apart from the publicly available data presented in six-monthly and annual balance sheets, internally the accounts department was receiving at least 150 writs each month from unsecured creditors. Although David Shipley and Robert Davies were successively able to ensure that suppliers of vital components were paid regularly, and the various divisional managers often worked through their weekends to ensure that cashflow issues were addressed, by 1993 some suppliers were beginning to refuse to offer credit, insisting on cash payments. When rumours of this situation started to circulate more broadly, Ferranti International was also affected by potential customers stating that they were reluctant to place contracts with a firm that might disappear imminently. Moreover, as we noted earlier, essential staff with highly scarce skills were leaving the firm in droves, either as a result of closure and redundancies or disposals, creating severe difficulties for those who remained. Cutting staff costs and reducing overheads were, of course, essential features of the corporate strategy enacted from September 1989, when the ISC-induced crisis first hit the group. Nobody could have predicted, however, the scale of the cuts that would be implemented over the following four years, with 1993 providing little relief for a workforce that by then was battle-scarred and totally demoralised. Similarly, given the group's historic commitment to an engineering-led strategy, Table 8.2 reveals how the board was obliged to cut R&D expenditure to a level that would barely have kept any of the eight business units up to the standards expected of a high-technology firm. Indeed, while the extensive disposals programme cut the heart out of the group and facilities were either closed or sold in significant numbers, the inability to invest in products and processes for the future begged the vital question, namely, whether there was a future for Ferranti International.

One can consequently discern a downward spiral of decline, starting with the September 1989 announcement of the ISC fraud, accelerating as a result of the FDSL sale and discovery of heavy losses in various business units, and culminating in acute illiquidity that sustained the firm's dependence on bank borrowing. Of course, this downward spiral was significantly exacerbated by external problems in both civil and defence markets, making it extremely difficult to boost turnover and secure profitable contracts. Above all, though, Ferranti International's financial situation was deteriorating rapidly, with the

1993 decision to borrow £15 million from the Ferranti pension fund illustrating graphically the depths to which the group had plunged. Even though in June 1990 the British courts had demanded that Guerin and his most immediate associates (Robert Shireman and Larry Resch) should pay $189.8 million in compensation to Ferranti International, it was highly unlikely that anybody would ever live to see any of that money returned to its rightful owners. In the meantime, by spring 1992 Ferranti International had spent over £22 million in legal costs chasing various cases, outgoings that would have significantly undermined the most profitable of firms, but to Ferranti International was invaluable cash that could have been invested in rebuilding the firm's product base.

The significant reduction in the size of Ferranti International can be tracked decisively in Figure 8.2, which outlines how in terms of turnover and assets the 1989–93 era was characterised by a considerable slimming exercise. At a time when inflation averaged over 7% per annum, it was especially alarming to record a decline in turnover from £927 million to £231 million, while total assets fell from £469 million to £147 million. Of greatest concern to the banking syndicate that sustained its support for Ferranti International up to the autumn of 1993 was the collapse in the group's net worth, because having been approximately £200 million in September 1989, by the summer of 1993 it was as little as £48 million (or, less than one-half of its issued capital). Running in parallel with these trends was the failure to generate any net profits over this period, losses amounting to what was an extremely disturbing £195 million.

Another graphic indication of what had happened across the group is featured in Table 8.2, which reveals how the workforce declined markedly after reaching its all-time peak of 24,818 in 1987–88. The worst year for job losses was clearly 1990–91, when the workforce was reduced by almost 52%, as the rationalisation programme, disposals and redundancies took their full impact. The process also continued over the following two years, with the workforce standing at 4,690 in March 1993, or just 18.9% of the peak in 1987–88. By 1992, sixteen of the company's sites had either been closed or sold, giving the very clear impression to many demoralised employees especially, not to mention shareholders deprived of dividends since the summer of 1989, that prospects seemed bleak. Interestingly, this slimming exercise was also reflected in the reduction in the size of the board, because as directors retired it was decided that they should not be replaced. In 1990, there were eleven directors, and while Robert Davies joined in November 1991 to take over the finance function formerly performed by Charles Scott and David Shipley (who was never a full member of the board), after the retirements of Phil Atterton (July 1992), Charles Scott (September 1992) and Nathan Blackwell (March 1993) the board contracted to just eight. This further reflected the depressing image projected by Ferranti International by that time, with no self-respecting executive wanting to be associated with a business that seemed to many to be doomed.

8.3 GEC's penny

The data in Figure 8.2 and Table 8.2 provide graphic proof of the financial woes experienced by Ferranti International after 1989. Desperate measures such as the £15 million loan from the Ferranti Pension Fund reinforced the feeling that the board was struggling to keep the firm afloat. Even though the 1992–93 accounts anticipated a £2 million refund from the Inland Revenue as a result of over-payments in the previous two trading years, this only covered a small fraction of one month's writs from unsecured creditors which were demanding immediate payment for goods supplied. Indeed, there was intense discussion at board level throughout May and June 1993 over the nature of the accounts. One issue was whether the company should immediately adopt the accounting regulations, known as FRS-3 and arising from the 1989 Companies Act, a debate that was resolved in favour of restating the previous three years' results on this basis, because it made them look slightly more favourable. Crucially, though, the auditors Grant Thornton was questioning whether the 1992–93 accounts were acceptable. For example, they wanted to know if all of the write-offs built into the accounts were realistic, while as the sale of Ferranti-Thomson Sonar was critical to continued bank support, they needed to be assured that this could be achieved at a remunerative price.[41] This delayed publication of the results for at least another month as the board worked through the dozen queries raised by Grant Thornton, while Gene Anderson and Robert Davies were obliged to negotiate a sixth amendment to the bank standstill agreement as an essential condition of financial credibility. It was consequently only at the end of June that the accounts were approved by the board, and even then they were based on a series of anticipated events that were based on a combination of wishful thinking and intense negotiations with customers and potential investors.

While the firm was able to publish its results, however, mostly to the satisfaction of its auditors and bankers, it was still not clear whether the firm should continue trading. By that time, a vicious Catch-22 situation had emerged, in that the firm desperately needed to boost turnover as a means of improving its financial credibility, but as customers were increasingly reluctant to place orders with its business units because of extensive rumours of illiquidity, contracts were simply not forthcoming. Indeed, in September 1993 the board was informed that for the sixth consecutive month the firm had failed to match the projections offered in Robert Davies' near-term financial strategy devised at the end of 1992.[42] The sale of two US subsidiaries, Venus and Sciaky, brought in a small amount of capital (see Table 8.1), whereas disposing of the 50% stake Ferranti International held in Ferranti-Bendix generated a grand total of £1 (in return for Allied Signal taking over all of its liabilities).[43] Although selling the firm's shares in ServiceTec brought in another £571,000, this was nowhere near enough to convince either the board or the firm's bankers that Ferranti International was able to trade legally, leading to further intense discussions at the October board meeting.[44] Once again, much of this debate was predicated on an intervention by GEC, in the hope that this would provide sufficient liquidity for the remaining business. This intervention was also made even more urgent when Finmeccanica revived its claim for compensation over its acquisition of Ferranti Italia as long ago as 1990, resulting in an agreement to pay £4 million to the Italian conglomerate. Although Finmeccanica agreed to accept this sum in phased payments – £400,000 in October, £1.6 million in January 1994, and £2 million in March 1994[45] – these were liabilities that few directors felt Ferranti International could ever afford.

With liquidity problems mounting almost by the day, a crucial board meeting was convened for 12 October 1993, with representatives from Cazenove & Co, Baring Brothers and Herbert Smith invited to offer their views on the various options available to Ferranti International.[46] Of course, these options were also narrowing by that time, not least because by then the *Delmon Eye* contract looked like an extremely remote possibility, the other business units were struggling to generate profits on contracting order-books, and many suppliers were refusing to extend any further credit. The firm's continuing financial difficulties also continued to feature in the financial columns of most newspapers throughout the early 1990s, while by the time of the September 1993 EGM City analysts were spreading rumours that an imminent break-up of the group was being planned,[47] precipitating a further decline in Ferranti International share values. As Figure 8.1 reveals, the share price had been falling since the spring, but when the EGM announced that net assets were only valued at £48 million, or under 50% of the £97 million share capital (see Appendix B), they were trading at just 8.5p. In these circumstances, few were able to predict a credible recovery,[48] while internally the total preoccupation with liquidity constraints severely impaired management's ability either to think about strategic issues or secure much new business.

At the decisive 12 October board meeting, the board was left in no doubt that unless an equity injection was forthcoming, then within a month Ferranti International would be in breach of its covenants with the banking syndicate. Indeed, Robert Davies was anticipating that at his next meeting with the banks on 19 October they would declare a default on an anticipatory breach of the standstill agreement, specifically in relation to the net worth of the group.[49] With little or no prospect of existing shareholders subscribing for another rights issue, especially as a minimum of £50 million would be needed to keep the firm trading, this obliged the board to consider the sale of the business. Gene Anderson had recently been approached by a Malaysian firm, Time Engineering Berhad, a major Far Eastern IT services provider, but as this only related to a minority holding, not to mention the inevitable delays associated with pursuing due diligence exercises, nobody felt that this was a realistic alternative. There was consequently nothing else to consider but an offer from GEC that had been tabled in private conversations between Lord Weinstock and Gene Anderson.

As we noted in section 8.1, while Albert Dodd was conducting negotiations with Finmeccanica about a strategic alliance between September 1992 and February 1993, throughout that period Gene Anderson and Robert Davies were also meeting Lord Weinstock and senior GEC managers about either an equity injection or outright purchase of Ferranti International. Acquiring Ferranti International, of course, was an extremely attractive proposition for GEC, because apart from the highly regarded engineering and software competencies that were distributed across the remaining business units, the group had over £200 million of losses that could be written off against tax liabilities, not to mention a surplus on the pension fund of approximately £130 million. On the other hand, the well-known liquidity problems detracted from these advantages, making Lord Weinstock extremely wary of committing himself to the purchase. In spite of having accumulated a cash-mountain of £1.6 billion in GEC's balance sheet, his attitude could well be summarised in a reply to one of his project managers at GEC-Marconi, who had just provided information on Ferranti International's deteriorating financial situation: 'Thank you for telling me. I'll buy them when they go bankrupt.'[50] Of course, this tactic was never revealed to Gene Anderson, who pursued a deal with GEC for almost fifteen months in the forlorn hope that Weinstock would agree to resolve the group's problems. A major presentation was made to GEC's senior management on 24 November 1992, while over the following months Robert Davies met several divisional managing directors to discuss complementarities in key areas such as defence systems, simulators and training, and sonar.[51] This prompted an offer from Lord Weinstock for the entire Ferranti International equity, on condition that the share price (currently trading at 12p; see Figure 8.1) was heavily discounted by up to 60%, up to 20% of the bank debt would be written off, and the pension fund surplus was transferred to GEC. Although the board rejected this offer, partly because it was highly unlikely that the banks would agree to such a write-down, Robin Broadley argued that this could well be the best deal available to Ferranti International shareholders.[52]

With Broadley's prophetic statement ringing in their ears, the board felt obliged to focus its attentions on the faltering negotiations with Finmeccanica, soliciting a variety of offers from the Italian conglomerate that, as we noted earlier, never materialised into formal agreements. Robert Davies also met with Roy Gardner, a GEC director, to discuss how they had reached their disturbingly low valuation of Ferranti International, but it was impossible to persuade them to offer improved terms, other than paying a maximum of £20 million for the 50% stake in Ferranti-Thomson Sonar.[53] In the meantime, of course, the sixth standstill agreement with its bankers provided further short-term support for the group, in the expectation that the *Delmon Eye* contract would soon be awarded.[54] As we noted earlier, however, this proved to be a classic case of wishful thinking, while over the summer the banks clearly regretted their complicity in Gene Anderson's requests as cashflow continued to deteriorate and new business failed to materialise.

By the end of July, negotiations with GEC had consequently been revived, given that this seemed to offer the only realistic chance of mitigating the worst effects of the mounting liquidity crisis. While Gene Anderson had also held some talks with BAe at that time, this group was only just emerging from its own financial difficulties, caused mostly by overextending itself in the late 1980s,[55] providing little encouragement of a realistic alternative to GEC. Not that the board was enthusiastic about succumbing to the GEC bid, given that Roy Gardner would only go as high as 7.5p per share, factoring in the tax losses and pension surplus.[56] Nevertheless, in the circumstances it was clear that 'beggars cannot be choosers'; with group losses amounting to £2 million per month, the board had little option but to allow GEC accountants to conduct a detailed examination of the accounts.[57] In subsequent meetings between Gene Anderson and Lord Weinstock, however, the failure to secure the *Delmon Eye* contract proved to be a major stumbling block to a formal bid, in that GEC calculated this single order to be worth 3p per share.[58] When Weinstock combined the results of the GEC due diligence exercise with this calculation, he also argued that the various legal liabilities and bank standstill agreement amounted to at least another 2p per share, leading him to the dismal conclusion that GEC could only offer 1p per share, valuing Ferranti International at just £10.1 million.[59]

When this offer was first discussed by the board at what we described earlier as the decisive meeting of 12 October, while there was naturally general disgust at such a derisory valuation, all recognised that with cash flooding out of the group at an alarming rate, there was little else they could do but accept. Gene Anderson was also convinced that the bank syndicate would approve of this change in ownership, because the group was in breach of its covenanted level of losses by £5.6 million and GEC was cash-rich. Indeed, as GEC would be taking on approximately £110 million in bank debt, this effectively made its offer worth £150 million, which would certainly ease the concerns expressed by the bank syndicate about Ferranti International's liquidity problems. In addition, GEC also agreed to pay £1.3 million to the preference shareholders,[60] bringing the total cash offer to £11.4 million. Some accused Weinstock 'of becoming too generous in his old age',[61] and clearly his attitude had softened when compared to the response he had given to his GEC-Marconi manager about buying the group when it had gone bankrupt. Although a problem arose when Thomson CSF objected to GEC taking over one-half of Ferranti-Thomson Sonar, this was resolved through intervention from the MoD, which promised to mediate over the issue of how this lucrative subsidiary should be managed.[62] The biggest worry, however, would be the response of Ferranti International shareholders to such an offer, given both the lack of a dividend since the summer of 1989 and the dramatic collapse in the market value of their stock (see Figures 6.1 and 8.1). There was also the added complication of the special shares created early in 1990, the specific aim of which was to distribute any funds recouped from the ISC fraud to those who had owned Ferranti International stock in September 1989. As 90% of shares had to be voted in favour of the GEC offer, the board was naturally concerned that a significant number of shareholders would not even bother to vote, thereby compromising the deal.[63] Nevertheless, the board encouraged Anderson to persuade Lord Weinstock to make a formal offer for 100% of the stock at 1p per share, while an extensive advertising campaign was launched to persuade shareholders that this represented a credible deal.

Following further discussions between Gene Anderson and Lord Weinstock, by 28 October a firm offer of 1p per share had materialised, conditional upon GEC (acting through Touche Ross) conducting a full due diligence exercise on Ferranti International and the conversion of the special shares into ordinary shares.[64] To quieten the City rumour mill, on the evening of 26 October Gene Anderson conducted a round of press interviews announcing to the financial community that an offer of 1p per share from an unnamed suitor was imminent. As by that time it was common knowledge the two companies had been in detailed discussions, every newspaper reported the following day that GEC was the suitor in question.[65] There was also widespread recognition that the 'long agony' suffered by Ferranti International since September 1989 was finally to come to an end,[66] a fate that was confirmed on 29 October when press releases from Baring Brothers and S.G. Warburg (the merchant bank acting for GEC) formally announced the 1p offer. In the ensuing publicity campaign, which cost the company almost £300,000,[67] Gene Anderson made it crystal clear that this offer was 'the only alternative to receivership', primarily because the banks had exhausted their patience and customers were refusing to award new contracts.[68] As The Times commented, though, the announcement was 'nothing short of a disaster' for shareholders who had seen the price plummet (see Figures 6.1 and 8.1) and dividends passed,[69] confirming the board's fears that they were faced with a major fight to persuade this group to back the deal.

By the time Ferranti International shareholders had received a comprehensive document drawn up by Barings and Warburg to outline the nature of the bid on 12 November, the battlelines between the board and various groups had been drawn. The biggest problem facing the board was the ownership structure, because while 8,000 institutional shareholders owned 90% of the issued capital, 40,000 individuals owned the other 10%. Secondly, the special shareholders had to be convinced that they should accept 1p per share, when technically they were entitled to a dividend arising from the £41.2 million – £40 million from PMM and £1.2 million from the Clark/Guerin case – generated from the proceeds arising from the company's attempts to recoup the money lost as a result of the ISC fraud. As one electronics analyst noted: 'Someone who is only being offered a penny a share does not have much to lose'.[70] John Katz, who set up a Ferranti Shareholders Support Association (FSSA), also argued forcefully that administration was 'a better route' for the assets that GEC had so badly undervalued.[71] Although he later denied that he had advised anybody to vote against the penny bid, arguing that he had merely lobbied for more information from GEC about its intentions,[72] there is little doubt that his actions contributed to the general unease about the real value of the Ferranti International rump. The board was also concerned that by the end of November only 28.6% of the institutional investors had voted in favour of the GEC bid,[73] while the FSSA continued to demand a better deal that reflected the true market value of the remaining assets. Even though powerful institutions such as Prudential, Philips & Drew, and the Co-operative Insurance Society supported Anderson,[74] and many City commentators recommended shareholders to 'Take the penny from heaven',[75] there was little likelihood that the required acceptance level would be achieved.

Regardless of all this lobbying, however, summarised in a *The Times* headline as 'Fighting Katz and dogs',[76] there is no doubt that the key factor would be the results of the due diligence exercise being conducted by a team of fifty accountants, lawyers and managers from GEC and Touche Ross. This was an extremely thorough investigation involving GEC managers visiting business units and challenging contract estimates, while Touche Ross accountants pored over as much corporate documentation as possible, including the highly revealing board minutes.[77] Given the extensive information made available to this team, they were able to conduct a forensic analysis of Ferranti International's financial state, producing a report for the GEC board on 29 November. After reading this report, on the following day Lord Weinstock presented it to the full board, the outcome of which was the decisive view that it demonstrated 'a very considerable deviation from our own understanding of Ferranti's financial condition and prospects'.[78] They consequently decided that under condition 1(d) of the offer, GEC had no option but to revoke all offers. As some commentators hypothesised, while there was no suggestion of a 'black hole' in the accounts, 'it appears that a lot of small deficiencies in the Ferranti figures added up to sufficient cause to withdraw'.[79] This view was immediately conveyed by Lord Weinstock in a telephone call to Gene Anderson, who convened a board meeting that day at the unusual time of 6 pm to report GEC's decision. By the next day, when the Ferranti International board met for the penultimate time, a letter from Lord Weinstock had been received confirming the bid's withdrawal, obliging Gene Anderson to request the Stock Exchange to suspend trading in the company's shares.[80]

Although the board debated whether GEC was simply playing a tactical game, expecting Ferranti International to offer different terms, a consensus emerged that the tone of Weinstock's letter was that the firm should go into receivership.[81] Baring Brothers was consequently instructed to inform the Take-Over Panel that GEC had withdrawn its offer, while in recognition of its default under the standstill agreement it was agreed that the banks should be invited to appoint receivers. Put simply, Ferranti International was no longer able to trade lawfully. It was still necessary to hold shareholders' meetings on 8 December, to conform with the 12 November circular announcing GEC's bid, on which day the board met for the last time, principally to note that as a result of the receivers' appointment none of the directors had any executive responsibilities. John Talbot and Murdoch McKillop, corporate recovery partners at Arthur Andersen, had been appointed as receivers on 2 December, a move that prompted *The Times* to state: 'The battle for survival by Ferranti, one of the most illustrious names in British industrial history, ended abruptly yesterday'.[82] At the same time, as we shall see later, Lord Weinstock was by then in a position to pluck the most promising businesses from the corpse, demonstrating once again his renowned ability to negotiate the best deal for GEC.

Coming just three weeks prior to Christmas, these developments were clearly devastating for the 3,600 people who still worked for Ferranti International. Of course, another 20,000 employees (see Table 8.3) had been directly affected by the group's financial difficulties since September 1989, suffering either redundancy or transfer to another firm as a result of asset disposals, indicating the scale of this crisis. Nevertheless, for the 3,600 people still on the books in December 1993 the timing was both truly appalling and regarded by all as a poor reward for the enormous effort put into rescuing the firm. In addition, of course, suppliers owed up to £30 million were in danger of bankruptcy, possibly leading to a further 2,000 redundancies. Nevertheless,

Table 8.3 Ferranti International expenditure on R&D (£ m) and workforce, 1988–93

To 31 March	R&D spend	Workforce (at 31 March)
1988	36	24,818
1989	58	24,549
1990	16	21,299
1991	7.9	10,325
1992	3.4	7,311
1993	1.9	4,690

the board had little alternative but to acquiesce to the inevitable, because neither the banks nor the law would allow the group to continue to trade. It was also clear from the initial efforts of the receivers that large-scale redundancies would not be announced, because they were primarily concerned with selling the business units to other firms. In fact, 630 jobs were cut in December, mostly from the Cairo Mill production unit and at the headquarters at Concord Business Park,[83] as the receivers started the monumental task of assessing the real worth left in the group. They also distributed a letter to all employees explaining that it was essential to reduce the workforce to levels that were 'appropriate to existing levels of business',[84] demonstrating to all concerned that in the circumstances there was little option.

Having just completed work at Leyland-DAF, Britain's largest manufacturing receivership since Rolls-Royce in 1973, the two receivers, John Talbot and Murdock McKillop, were extremely well-equipped to cope with the Ferranti International crisis. They lost no time in despatching teams of accountants and lawyers to every business unit and the headquarters, seizing control of the finances and management systems. Their first task was to 'launch an assault on the purchasing managers whose bargaining skills caused Ferranti to under-price its work and slump into loss and, ultimately, receivership'.[85] In view of the Catch-22 situation highlighted earlier, this might be regarded as excessively critical, while we have also reported that many contracts had been lost because of the high prices tendered. Nevertheless, Talbot and McKillop were anxious to impress on both the business units and customers that contracts would be terminated unless they were going to generate a reasonable return. Although all of the business units continued to trade over the following six months, closure remained an imminent threat, putting enormous pressure on the remaining managers and staff.

In spite of the group's perilous financial state, there were of course several business units that were regarded by predators as of considerable value. The most significant of these was Ferranti-Thomson Sonar, with a flourishing order-book that included equipment to be supplied to the UK's *Trident* class of nuclear-powered submarines and other navies around the world.

Although it had recently lost some highly prestigious contracts, the naval systems business at Bracknell was similarly highly regarded, not least because it was in line to perform significant upgrades to the command and control systems previously installed on Royal Navy warships. Linked to naval systems was the systems integration unit which had supplied the *Falcon Eye* warning system to Saudi Arabia as part of the first stage of the enormous Al Yamamah deal. Another successful adjunct to these activities was the design and production of simulators for a wide variety of military and civil customers, while airport information systems, control equipment for utilities and communications systems were all attractive businesses that the receivers could package up and sell to a range of predators. Above all, though, it was vital for the receivers to move swiftly on this 'fire sale', because otherwise 'the highly skilled teams of scientists, who are Ferranti's most valuable asset and the main attraction for any potential bidder' would leave for more secure jobs elsewhere.[86]

Reflecting the quality of the personnel that still worked for Ferranti International, it is perhaps no surprise that the receivers attracted several expressions of interest from managers keen to acquire the businesses they had spent a long time developing. Of course, one of the core Ferranti traditions had always been to encourage high levels of 'intrapreneurship' across the organisation, with senior management devolving considerable autonomy to divisional and departmental managers.[87] This had instilled a high degree of loyalty to what we have previously labelled 'The Ferranti Spirit', namely, an engineering-led ethos which lay at the heart of the firm's growth since the 1880s. Consequently, in December 1993 what the *Daily Mail* labelled as the 'Magnificent Seven' attempted to put together a consortium to buy the entire group, what in general terms was called a management buy-out (MBO). Headed by the person who had been director of strategic sales and marketing, Phil Burton, seven managers that had operated just below board level approached Coopers & Lybrand, BAe and several venture capital firms with a view to acquiring what they felt was a fundamentally sound business.[88] Given the scale of the resources needed to refloat the business, Burton and his colleagues recognised that a conventional management buy-out was not feasible, persuading them to create a consortium that would prevent the break-up into a myriad range of small businesses. While Talbot and McKillop welcomed this move, however, significantly raising morale within the stricken group,[89] these hopes were soon dashed as the consortium struggled to generate the kind of support required to persuade the receivers that they could salvage a viable business.

Although Burton and his MBO team continued to work on the consortium idea until the spring of 1994, it became increasingly obvious that the receivers would have little option but to sell off business units as individual packages.

There was even a feeling amongst the MBO team that the receivers used their presence as a means of persuading GEC to bid for the group.[90] There were also widespread suspicions that the only reason why Lord Weinstock had agreed to consider making an offer for the equity was the access this gave his team and Touche Ross to every part of the group, allowing him to build up an intimate understanding of which parts he might 'cherry-pick'.[91] Inevitably, GEC sources denied these rumours, arguing that Lord Weinstock had been genuinely interested in acquiring Ferranti International, for the reasons we outlined earlier. Nevertheless, given what we heard of the conversation he had conducted with a GEC-Marconi manager, it was clear that Lord Weinstock was ready to 'cherry-pick' assets. Moreover, he had a responsibility to GEC shareholders to secure the best deal, undermining any claim that he could be accused of Machiavellian tactics. On the other hand, when in March 1994 the receivers announced that GEC was the preferred bidder for the defence businesses of Ferranti International, Weinstock had clearly played a very clever and patient game. Not only did GEC acquire several potentially profitable activities, at a price of £60 million, but also these units were not saddled with the bank debt that he would have been obliged to pick up in November 1993. These deals were completed by May, while in the following month Marconi acquired the US munitions activities, and in September the satellite communications and microwave components units were sold to GEC. By the end of the year, the 50% stake in Ferranti-Thomson Sonar had also been purchased by GEC, creating a £400 million sonar business.

Apart from effectively killing off the manager-led consortium, it is clear that Lord Weinstock had confounded his critics and pulled off a superb deal for GEC. As Brummer and Cowe also argue, both the DTI and MoD had been complicit in this strategy, accepting Weinstock's argument that in view of global political trends they should be supporting the creation of a 'UK defence champion' that was capable of matching the US and European conglomerates that were also pursuing aggressive merger and acquisition strategies.[92] Although he was never able fully to achieve this aim, because BAe remained independent of the GEC-Marconi empire, in acquiring the key assets within Ferranti International at a much cheaper price than anticipated in November 1993 Weinstock demonstrated his characteristic ability to negotiate worthwhile deals. One should also remember that in 1990 he had been asked by the MoD to buy FDSL, virtually guaranteeing the enormous contract to supply the ECR-90 onboard radar systems to the European Fighter Aircraft worth up to £2 billion. Ironically, the ECR-90 had successfully passed its first flight trials by the time Ferranti International had been placed in receivership, while what by then was called GEC Ferranti Defence Systems had also secured contracts to supply inertial navigation systems and other equipment to the next generation of RAF trainer aircraft.[93] It is also notable that the Edinburgh operation had by then shed almost 2,000 jobs, once the GEC accountants had taken over and rationalised FDSL's activities into the expanding Marconi defence empire.

Of course, GEC did not acquire all of the business units that were still trading in December 1993. It is especially noticeable that while the manager-led consortium did not succeed in defeating GEC, the Cairo Mill components unit was sold to a management buy-in engineered by a consultant, Trevor Tuckley, as well as several managers (Angus Mincher, Peter Davis, Hugh Middleton and David Platt). Tuckley had been brought in by the receivers to restructure the components business into four units – avionics, design engineering, electronic assembly, and repair and maintenance. As Cairo Mill still had outstanding orders worth £17 million, Tuckley was able to persuade the managers to work with him in raising funds from venture capitalists Murray Johnstone to back his bid to buy these activities and sustain approximately 450 jobs. Another firm that was outmanoeuvred by GEC, Thomson CSF, purchased the industrial systems division in the summer of 1994. While this ostensibly saved 285 jobs, however, the Ferranti International business was absorbed into that of Thomson, leading to the closure of the Wythenshawe plant that had been a mainstay of the group since the 1950s, when the *Bloodhound* guided missile was designed and manufactured.

The closure of Wythenshawe was symbolic of the trauma that had struck Ferranti International so decisively in the early 1990s. Although it took until May 1995 before the receivers were able to sell off the command and control systems, and September 1995 before information systems was sold, Ferranti International was effectively broken up in the six months after GEC had withdrawn its 1p-a-share bid. By that time, the only surviving remnant of the Ferranti name was its pension scheme, valued at almost £363 million when the company was placed into receivership. There were some fears that Ferranti pensioners would not receive the full benefit of their contributions, because the £15 million loan granted to Ferranti International in February 1993 was never going to be repaid. Furthermore, because Barings Bank provided advice on the Fund's investment strategy, considerable concern was expressed when as a result of another massive fraud, this institution collapsed at the end of 1994. Fortunately, though, neither of these factors materially affected pensioners' prospects, because in the first place the scheme had only lent £15 million to Ferranti International (or less than 5% of its assets), while the acquisition of Barings by a Dutch concern meant that all the assets were secured.

As a postscript to this whole sorry story, it is worthwhile noting that the Ferranti Pension Fund has been a significant success story. When the receivers were appointed, although nominally the Fund was valued at almost £400 million, a highly cautious evaluation that considered the impact of the company's demise and the need to pass control to an insurance company resulted in the conclusion that there was a deficit of £25 million. This naturally alarmed both trustees and pensioners, leading to energetic negotiations that resulted in a dramatic turnaround. As he was the last director still in post, Albert Dodd was appointed chairman of the Ferranti Pension Scheme at the end of 1993, providing the kind of leadership required in ensuring that the Fund flourished. The first decision was to ask Law Debenture to act as independent trustees, ensuring a supply of highly professional advice on how the Fund should be managed. By 1999, it had also been agreed that Prudential would eventually take over the scheme, and although it was another twelve years before this happened, the Fund was extremely well managed. In particular, because it was agreed that the Fund should continue to invest in the London Stock Exchange, buying low-risk assets that would eventually be converted into annuities secured by Prudential, it benefitted enormously from the boom in stock exchange fortunes from the 1990s up to 2007. By the time the Fund was formally wound up in February 2011 and transferred to Prudential, all pensioners and deferred pensioners received a 15% increase to their basic entitlement, while additional higher level guaranteed increases of 40% had been achieved. At the very least, Albert Dodd and his advisors had protected Ferranti pensioners' interests, providing some compensation in retirement for the traumas experienced in the early 1990s.

8.4 Epilogue

One can hardly express in words what the events of the period 1989–93 meant to the 26,000 or so people who worked for Ferranti International at the time the fraud was revealed. Up to a quarter had invested in the employee share option scheme, relying on the expected gains to help pay for either luxury purchases or a relaxing retirement. Instead, many were faced with either redundancy or being sold as a commodity in the asset disposal programme pursued relentlessly by both the Ferranti International board and receivers. In the meantime, their investments were practically worthless. Those who were transferred to other firms after the asset disposals also seemed to have an uncertain future, while the closure of plants at Moston and Wythenshawe symbolised the cloak of misery that descended on to the firm after 1989. More importantly, though, an engineering tradition died in the early 1990s, as parts of the Ferranti group were sold off, closed or slimmed down. Although it is possible to argue that, after the defence cuts and severe macro-economic downturn starting around 1989, the company would more than likely have been forced into a major rationalisation programme, leading to some significant changes, as a result of the decisions made up to that year the group was working from a highly disadvantageous position.

When assessing this scenario, it is worth noting that there was nobody who felt it harder than Gene Anderson, the chief executive who had been hired to salvage Ferranti International after the September 1989 revelations. When the group was placed in the hands of receivers this represented 'a devastating blow to Eugene Anderson, the chairman, who has staked his reputation on the GEC offer'.[94] Indeed, over the course of the previous month he had worked hard to persuade shareholders to accept the GEC penny, while during his tenure as chairman and chief executive he had 'done as much as any mere mortal could ... to try to save [the group]'.[95] Of course, it is important to stress that had the GEC deal been completed, he would have benefitted to the tune of £1 million, payable as a bonus for negotiating the sale.[96] Anderson's remuneration package had also been significantly boosted, reaching £464,000 by 1993, compared to his original salary of £300,000. Although this made him eligible for statutory redundancy of £615,000,[97] he was obviously never able to claim the £1 million bonus, while the £250,000 he had invested in Ferranti International stock represented a complete loss. Of course, few of his fellow-employees would have sympathised with Anderson, because those who retained their jobs had been obliged to suffer a pay freeze since September 1989, while over 20,000 people had either been made redundant or moved to other firms. Nevertheless, he felt devastated about the overall outcome, whatever the personal financial situation, reflecting his enormous commitment to salvaging something from the wreck he inherited.

Whether or not one can describe Anderson as a failure is an extremely moot point. *The Times* was willing to take a broad perspective when assessing 'the day of reckoning', arguing that:

> No laurels for Robin Broadley, a director of Barings and a non-executive director of Ferranti since 1981. No laurels for Ferranti's former accountants Peat Marwick. No laurels for Robert Fleming who originally brought ISC to the London market in 1983. What Anderson inherited at Ferranti was a company which was the victim of 'hands off' management. If blame for the Ferranti fiasco must be apportioned, let it be apportioned with history in mind.[98]

This was a point made by many other commentators, with frequent references not only to the ISC fraud, but also a history of questionable management that could be tracked back through a series of episodes: the 1903 crisis, when the founder, Sebastian de Ferranti, was replaced by A.W. Tait; liquidity pressures during the 1950s, when Sir Vincent de Ferranti was investing massively in radio and television production; the *Bloodhound* profits issue in 1964–65; and quasi-nationalisation in 1974–75, when the third generation lost control of the firm and Derek Alun-Jones took over as managing director. More immediately, though, Gene Anderson was aware in

February 1990 that Ferranti International was beset by a lethal combination of challenges – the ISC fraud, acute difficulties associated with severe defence cuts, a global recession and strategic decisions that needed to be severely questioned – causing misgivings about whether there was ever a realistic hope Ferranti International would again become a viable operation. Above all, though, he persevered with a forward-looking strategy that was intended to inspire all employees and customers, arguing that this was the only positive message worth conveying.

In assessing why Ferranti International lost its struggle to overcome its challenges, the *Independent* asked some very tough questions:

> As Ferranti finally slips off the City's screens to become just another part of the GEC empire, many people will look at its extraordinary history and wonder whether things might have been otherwise. How was it that the company that built the world's first modern power station, the world's first commercial computer and Europe's first integrated circuit was now on its knees? Was it bad management? Bad luck? Or is there something about Britain that will always strangle innovation?[99]

While the last question is far too broad to be comprehensively assessed on the basis of a single case-study, we have seen plenty of evidence in the three volumes of this history that demonstrate the acute difficulties associated with commercialising technological innovations, from the zig-zag alternator developed by Sebastian de Ferranti in 1882 through to the highly advanced computers produced in the 1950s and 1960s and on to the sophisticated avionic and command and control systems of the 1980s and 1990s. As the *Scotsman* stated, Ferranti had spent 'A century pushing back the frontiers'.[100] On the other hand, the British market environment had never proved sufficiently conducive to encourage mass production of these innovations, limiting the firm's ability to generate profit that could be reinvested in further R&D. Only when the state proved willing to sponsor technological innovation and buy the end-product, mostly for defence purposes, did Ferranti prosper, persuading successive generations of chief executives from Sir Vincent de Ferranti and his son, Sebastian, to build a firm that was heavily dependent on military contracts. This reliance was also sustained, even extended, by their successors, providing a major challenge when after the mid-1980s defence markets collapsed around the world.

Having stressed the role played by a restrictive British market, however, it is worth commenting on the *Independent*'s claim that: 'Had [Ferranti] been American, it would probably have become one of the most successful companies in the world.'[101] Of course, in view of the lack of success Ferranti achieved with its 'USA Strategy', a vision espoused and implemented under the direction of Derek Alun-Jones, one would need to question this claim. On the other hand, building a more substantial presence in the world's biggest market for both defence and electronic equipment was a highly credible strategy that could well have produced rich rewards. Similarly, whatever the flaws associated with the 'USA Strategy', not least in the way that it was operationalised, it is vital to stress that some of the UK-based divisions were also beginning to struggle by the late 1980s. We noted earlier that after Gene Anderson made his first assessments of Ferranti International, he was immediately struck by the difficulties being experienced by several activities. These struggles had been best manifested in Ferranti Electronics Ltd, the chip-making operation that was sold in 1987 to Plessey, despite having achieved market dominance in customised hybrid chips during the early 1980s. Crucially, though, the major UK problems were to be found in the defence-oriented divisions, especially naval systems and at Ferranti Instrumentation. In this respect, one must remember that in spite of rhetorical support for a strategy to reduce the dependence on defence markets, over the course of the 1980s Ferranti failed miserably to achieve this aim. When one considers the acute difficulties in defence, caused partly by the UK government's desire to cut military expenditure, combined with the end of the Cold War and a major international reassessment of defence priorities, it is consequently vital to question the board's desire to sustain the firm's reliance – 65% of turnover and 75% of its profits – on defence. As one contemporary commented, 'the harsh reality that Ferranti is on the wrong end of the peace dividend' would make a full recovery impossible.[102] Of course, GEC was willing to buy all of these defence business units, but converting them into commercially viable enterprises would only be possible by integrating them into much larger activities that were supported with enormous financial resources.

A third question one must pose concerning the credibility of strategic decision-making in the 1980s relates to the civil ventures into which Ferranti diversified, most notably telecommunications. In principle, of course, this move represented a bold expression of intent to develop a more serious civil image, while the link with GTE on telephony and business communications, as well as combining with Electra Investments on mobile telephony, were strategically sound. On the other hand, a traditional Ferranti problem beset these ventures, reflecting a drawback that had also undermined other civil activities, such as radio and television, namely, poor marketing.[103] Although some effort was invested in developing a more progressive image, as we saw with Ferranti Creditphone contemporaries were highly critical of this aspect of the business, significantly affecting its ability to build a viable enterprise. Ferranti Creditphone consequently became a victim of the fate that had beset a plethora of Ferranti civil sales, passing into the hands of rivals who went on to utilise the core engineering expertise in a much more effective way.

By 1989, it is consequently clear that Ferranti International was already struggling with a range of strategic decisions that would present considerable challenges when both defence and civil markets took a decisive turn for the worst after 1990. As we saw earlier in the chapter, return on capital employed and net profitability had failed to reach the levels of the mid-1980s, pressuring the share price acutely (see Figure 8.1) by the time trading had been suspended in September 1989. One might consequently conclude that the ISC fraud merely compounded a range of internal problems that would have forced the board to take drastic action in the 1990s, either in the form of disposals or a merger with another defence-oriented conglomerate. This is not to underestimate the impact of what was a £400 million 'hole' in the balance sheet, not to mention the enforced disposal of the most profitable division, FDSL, creating massive financial challenges at a time when both civil and defence markets were proving increasingly difficult. Nevertheless, it is doubtful whether the strategic direction of Ferranti International up to 1989 was ever going to ensure a profitable, independent existence, especially when the economic and political environments deteriorated and as we saw with GEC the global electronics industry embarked on an era of consolidation achieved through aggressive acquisitions and rationalisation of capacity. In these circumstances, only the strongest firms with the deepest pockets would survive, characteristics that were not much in evidence at Ferranti International even in 1988. Moreover, once the £400 million 'hole' had been revealed and FDSL sold, it would never be possible for the firm to achieve these characteristics, in spite of the best efforts of every employee, from Gene Anderson and the board down to the remaining shopfloor workers.

A combination of massive fraud, strategic misdirection, and ineffective planning for the late 1980s defence market changes consequently combined to bring down Ferranti, terminating what had been a story which for 111 years had been replete with exciting and highly innovative adventures. Indeed, three generations of the de Ferranti family – Dr Sebastian, Sir Vincent and Sebastian – had invested their wealth and reputation in building a firm that almost from its very beginnings was a name well known across the engineering world for its pioneering work in a wide range of fields. Pursuing an engineering-led strategy, combined with a highly devolved organisational ethos that encouraged entrepreneurial activity, lay at the heart of their success, providing the conducive internal environment that produced a constant stream of ideas and products for an expanding number of departments and divisions. Although the external environment never proved as accommodating, limiting the market for high technology equipment in the UK at least, the firm developed a highly diverse product range that over the decades spanned everything from power equipment through to domestic appliances and on to electronic equipment and components. With 26,000 employees at its peak, this was a serious player in many markets that required the most advanced knowledge and skills. Much to the chagrin of its founding family, however, the venture was brought to its knees by factors which were anathema to the innovation culture on which Dr Sebastian Ziani de Ferranti had built the enterprise. While the transition from a family run firm to a typical example of managerial capitalism had occurred as a result of the shortcomings of the de Ferranti regime, not least inappropriate decision-making and severe illiquidity, the way in which Ferranti plc came to be dominated by City of London mores and traditions resulted in the development of a very different type of business culture, especially after 1986. As these mores and traditions pressured Sir Derek Alun-Jones and his board to merge with ISC, not to mention the total dominance of the banking syndicate after September 1989, they clearly contributed significantly to the demise of Ferranti International in 1993. It was an ignominious end which to employees, to customers, to suppliers, to shareholders and to the British electronics industry represented nothing short of a tragedy that could never be reversed. Returning to an earlier theme, however, one also wonders whether a French, Japanese or American government would have allowed the tragedy to unravel in this devastating way; Ferranti International disappeared irrespective of extensive evidence that British manufacturing was losing out to its global rivals, with successive British governments showing much more interest in financial services as the backbone of the economy. History will judge the wisdom of this policy.

Notes

1 This league table was based on earning capacity. *Sunday Times*, 25 March 1990.
2 See, for example, the claims made in December 1991. *The Times*, 12 Dec 1991.
3 *Guardian*, 12 Dec 1990.
4 *Observer*, 18 Aug 1991.
5 *The Times*, 31 Oct 1991.
6 Brummer and Cowe, *Weinstock*, p.221.
7 FBM 1, 6 Feb 1992.
8 FBM 9, 6 Feb 1992.
9 FBM 11, 6 March 1992.
10 FBM 5, 3 Sept 1992.
11 FBM 5, 3 Sept 1992.
12 FBM 8, 3 Feb 1993.
13 See Felice, 'State ownership and international competitiveness', pp. 622–28.
14 FBM 1, 24 Sept 1992.
15 FBM 5, 1 Oct 1992.
16 FBM 3, 6 May 1993.
17 FBM 6, 4 March 1993.

18 See above, pp. 240–1; FBM 5, 5 Nov 1992.

19 FBM 11, 1 Oct 1992.

20 FBM 7, 4 March 1993.

21 FBM 11, 6 May 1993.

22 FBM 8, 27 July 1993.

23 *Daily Mail*, 16 Dec 1992.

24 FBM 6, 28 July 1992.

25 See Vol. 1, pp. 259–61.

26 FBM 8, 3 Dec 1992.

27 FBM 6, 5 Nov 1992.

28 *Independent*, 30 June 1993.

29 *Daily Mail*, 30 June 1993.

30 *Independent*, 14 Sept 1993.

31 *The Times*, 13 Sept 1993.

32 *The Times*, 27 Oct 1993.

33 *Daily Mail*, 27 Oct 1993.

34 See above, pp. 15–21, and Vol. 2, pp. 365–78.

35 *Financial Times*, 3 Jan 1992.

36 See earlier, pp. 214–16.

37 See earlier, pp. 15–19.

38 *Financial Times*, 5 March 1993.

39 See Vol. 2, pp. 171–4, for details of MESS and how it supported Ferranti Electronics Ltd in the 1970s. The DTI had originally asked for the return of £4.5 million, but Dr Shepherd was able to persuade them to accept the lower sum.

40 FBM 1, 23 March 1993.

41 FBM 2, 16 June 1993

42 FBM 9, 2 Sept 1993.

43 FBM 1, 1 Oct 1993.

44 FBM 1, 7 Oct 1993.

45 FBM 2, 7 Oct 1993.

46 FBM 1, 12 Oct 1993.

47 *Independent*, 14 Sept 1993; *Daily Mail*, 8 Oct 1993.

48 *The Times*, 13 Sept 1993.

49 FBM 1, 12 Oct 1993.

50 Quoted in S. Aris (1998), *Arnold Weinstock and the Making of GEC*, Aurum Press, p.204.

51 FBM 8, 20 Jan 1993.

52 Ibid.

53 FBM 7, 26 March 1993.

54 FBM 7, 6 May 1993.

55 Brummer and Cowe, *Weinstock*, p. 223

56 FBM 7, 27 July 1993.

57 FBM 8, 2 Sept 1993.

58 FBM 1, 7 Oct 1993.

59 FBM 1, 12 Oct 1993.

60 FBM 7, 4 Nov 1993.

61 *Sunday Times*, 14 Nov 1993.
62 FBM 2, 18 Oct 1993.
63 FBM 5, 28 Oct 1993.
64 FBM 3, 28 Oct 1993.
65 See, for example, *The Times*, 27 Oct 1993; *Daily Mail*, 27 Oct 1993.
66 *The Times*, 27 Oct 1993.
67 FBM 2, 10 Nov 1993.
68 FBM 3, 28 Oct 1993.
69 *The Times*, 27 Oct 1993.
70 Quoted in *Sunday Times*, 31 Oct 1993.
71 *The Times*, 26 Nov 1993.
72 *The Times*, 6 Dec 1993.
73 *Independent*, 30 Nov 1993.
74 *Herald*, 30 Nov 1993.
75 *Observer*, 31 Oct 1993.
76 *The Times*, 18 Nov 1993.
77 FBM 2, 17 Nov 1993.
78 FBM 1, 30 Nov 1993.
79 *The Guardian*, 4 Dec 1993.
80 FBM 1, 1 Dec 1993.
81 FBM 1, 1 Dec 1993.
82 *The Times*, 2 Dec 1993.
83 *Daily Mail*, 10 Dec 1993.
84 Letter to all employees, 10 Dec 1993.
85 *The Times*, 6 Dec 1993.
86 Ibid.
87 See Vol. 2, pp. 320–6.
88 *Daily Mail*, 23 Dec 1993. See also author's correspondence with Phil Burton.
89 *The Times*, 23 Dec 1993.
90 Correspondence with Phil Burton.
91 *Daily Mail*, 2 Dec 1993; *Guardian*, 4 Dec 1993.
92 Brummer and Cowe, *Weinstock*, pp. 222–3.
93 *Defence News*, 18 Jan 1993.
94 *The Times*, 3 Dec 1993.
95 *Sunday Times*, 14 Nov 1993.
96 *Independent*, 15 Nov 1993.
97 *The Times*, 4 Dec 1993.
98 Ibid.
99 *Independent*, 31 Oct 1993.
100 *Scotsman*, 29 Oct 1993.
101 *Independent*, 31 Oct 1993.
102 *The Times*, 27 Oct 1993.
103 See Vol. 1, pp. 309–16, for discussions of this weakness.

Appendix A: The financing of Ferranti, 1970–1993

	Issued capital	Net borrowings	General reserve
1970	4,500,000	9,038,000	13,392,000
1971	4,500,000	10,424,000	12,974,000
1972	4,500,000	4,373,000	13,534,000
1973	4,500,000	4,093,000	15,016,000
1974	4,500,000	9,645,000	18,083,000
1975	4,500,000	16,911,000	17,993,000
1976	7,833,000	8,193,000	20,527,000
1977	7,833.000	8,201,000	35,349,000
1978	7,833,000	23,693,000	40,363,000
1979	13,167,000	22,875,000	44,662,000
1980	13,167,000	17,576,000	41,501,000
1981	23,833,000	(1,040,000)	67,051,000
1982	23,833,000	(3,299,000)	82,816,000
1983	43,200,000	(1,200,000)	89,100,000
1984	45,200,000	(5,200,000)	93,100,000
1985	45,500,000	25,400,000	112,500,000
1986	45,600,000	65,100,000	137,800,000
1987	45,900,000	41,600,000	159,200,000
1988	77,100,000	145,600,000	130,200,000
1989	77,300,000	226,600,000	115,200,000
1990	78,300,000	275,500,000	152,200,000
1991	96,800,000	94,900,000	15,700,000
1992	96,800,000	66,500,000	(24,900,000)
1993	96,800,000	90,600,000	(42,300,000)

Appendix B: Profitability and return on capital employed at Ferranti, 1970–1993

	Gross profit (£)	Capital employed (£)	Return on capital employed (%)	Net profit or (loss) (£)
1970	1,591,498	33,258,710	4.7	935,000
1971	(826,590)	33,816,411	(2.4)	(348,000)
1972	1,188,483	32,626,098	3.6	915,000
1973	2,710,675	33,348,777	8.1	1,810,000
1974	53,880	42,871,749	0.1	373,000
1975	(488,006)	49,716,438	(1.0)	11,000
1976	4,101,353	46,700,000	8.8	3,600,000
1977	6,136,381	51,800,000	11.8	4,800,000
1978	9,123,000	72,300,000	12.6	5,800,000
1979	9,944,000	77,100,000	12.8	7,800,000
1980	11,186,000	78,850,000	14.2	4,700,000
1981	18,081,000	99,840,000	18.1	14,900,000
1982	23,800,000	107,770,000	22.1	19,400,000
1983	31,500,000	123,900,000	25.4	29,800,000
1984	38,800,000	141,900,000	27.3	22,300,000
1985	46,000,000	195,100,000	23.6	30,100,000
1986	41,100,000	217,000,000	18.9	28,000,000
1987	50,200,000	233,500,000	21.5	31,500,000
1988	54,500,000	354,100,000	13.8	15,500,000
1989	13,100,000	477,100,000	2.7	(800,000)
1990	(161,700,000)	342,200,000	(47.2)	43,200,000
1991	(98,100,000)	208,100,000	(47.1)	(165,200,000)
1992	(39,600,000)	141,200,000	(28.1)	(44,100,000)
1993	(12,600,000)	147,300,000	(8.5)	(22,700,000)

Appendix C: Turnover and employment at Ferranti, 1970–1993

	Turnover (£m)	Labour force (at 31 March)
1970	54.7	17,859
1971	57.2	16,559
1972	63.7	16,042
1973	65.1	16,453
1974	70.2	16,688
1975	86.3	16,079
1976	108.3	16,302
1977	125.4	16,786
1978	156.9	17,360
1979	192.1	16,464
1980	214.6	16,545
1981	271.5	18,254
1982	306.9	18,850
1983	372.2	18,966
1984	451.7	19,448
1985	567.9	20,981
1986	595.8	21,791
1987	628.7	21,683
1988	755.9	24,818
1989	927.5	24,549
1990	794.9	21,299
1991	458.0	10,325
1992	362.6	7,311
1993	230.9	4,690

Appendix D: Chairmen and directors of Ferranti, 1905–1993

Chairmen

A.W. Tait	(1905–28)	B.Z. de Ferranti	(1982–87)[b]
Dr S.Z. de Ferranti	(1928–30)	Sir Derek Alun-Jones	(1987–89)[a]
Sir Vincent de Ferranti	(1930–63)[a]	E.A. Anderson	(1989–93)[a]
S.Z. de Ferranti	(1963–82)[a]		

Directors

A.W. Tait	(1905–30)	T. Edmondson	(1963–76)
A. Whittaker	(1905–53)[b]	A.J. Gray	(1968–76)
J.M. Henderson	(1905–22)	R.H. Davies	(1968–76)
A.B. Anderson	(1908–14)[a]	Sir Donald M. McCallum	(1970–87)
R.W. Cooper	(1913–63)	J.R. Pickin	(1970–83)
O. Winder	(1916–17)	J.J. Ratcliffe	(1973–76)
P.D. Thomas	(1917–29)	P.F. Dorey	(1973–88)
Sir Vincent de Ferranti	(1924–63)[a]	G. Boyd	(1975–89)
H.W. Kolle	(1930–43)	H.W. Broad	(1975–86)
D.Z. de Ferranti	(1933–51)	Sir Derek Alun-Jones	(1975–89)[a]
R.H. Schofield	(1934–35)	W.L. Hetherington	(1976–79)
J.W. Davies	(1942–57)	M. Elderfield	(1976–77)
W. Tyldesley	(1942–43)	Dr A.A. Shepherd	(1981–93)
W.A.G. Bass	(1943–60)	C.F. Scott	(1981–93)
C.W. Bridgen	(1943–46)	R. Broadley	(1981–93)
W.C. Pycroft	(1943–58)	P.E. Atterton	(1986–92)
A.B. Cooper	(1947–54)	Sir John Hoskyns	(1986–93)
S.Z. de Ferranti	(1954–82)[a]	J.H. Guerin	(1987–89)[b]
B.Z. de Ferranti	(1957–87)[b]	N.C. Blackwell	(1987–92)
Sir Frank Rostron	(1958–68)	A.E. Dodd	(1987–93)
J.H. Thomson	(1958–71)	J.M. Fox	(1987–89)
Sir John Toothill	(1958–75)	J.A. Heywood	(1987–93)
E. Grundy	(1959–71)	R.C. Ivy	(1987–89)
O.M. Robson	(1959–68)	J.H. Zilligen	(1987–89)
J. Prince	(1959–68)	E.A. Anderson	(1989–93)[a]
R.M. Hobill	(1961–69)	I. Ball	(1990–93)
Dr N.H. Searby	(1962–75)	W. Broekhuizen	(1990–91)
F.W. Hardstone	(1963–73)	R. Davies	(1991–93)

Note: [a] Indicates that this person was also a managing director at some stage in their career with Ferranti.
[b] Indicates that at some stage this person was also deputy chairman of Ferranti.

Bibliography

Primary sources

Interviews and correspondence

Sir Derek Alun-Jones	Lester George
Eugene Anderson	Tom Grime
Ian Ball	Roy Handley
Bruce Calveley	David Knowles
Alan Cooper	Tom Lunt
Basil Z. de Ferranti	Sir Donald McCallum
Sebastian Z. de Ferranti	Charles Scott
Albert Dodd	Dr Alan Shepherd

Company documents

THE FERRANTI ARCHIVES

Since the 1990s, this rich set of family and corporate records has both expanded considerably and moved regularly. Today, it is housed in the archives section of the Manchester Museum of Science and Industry, Castlefield, Manchester, where the records are professionally indexed and secured. It was not always thus, because from the early 1960s they were cared for by a senior employee, Arthur Ridding, who was instructed by Sir Vincent de Ferranti to bring all the records together for the first time. Ridding performed an impressive job, indexing what must have been one of the largest set of company records in the country. He was succeeded by Charles Somers, who continued Ridding's work with a most able assistant, Edith Walsh. They, in turn, were succeeded by Cliff Wimpenny, undoubtedly the most able Ferranti Archivist. Cliff Wimpenny contributed enormously to the development of a truly company-wide archive, extending Ridding's interests from Hollinwood and Chadderton to Edinburgh, Bracknell and the increasing number of overseas subsidiaries. By the time the company's crisis in 1989 had brought an end to the archives department, the collection had expanded substantially in size and breadth. Indeed, new premises at Moston were acquired for the archive, after spending several unhappy years in the former transformer department drawing office. I am confident that at the Manchester Museum of Science and Industry the archive will become a major source of information for historians of every ilk.

The principal sets of records are:

Family papers
Correspondence, diaries and scrapbooks.

Technical notebooks
Including over thirty bound volumes of the work of Dr Ferranti.

Corporate records

Minute books	Annual Reports
Correspondence	Photographs
Patents	Films
Account books	Ferranti News.
Agreements	

Ian Ball (1990), 'Report to FBI on ISC'.
C. Scott, 'The 1987–90 three year plan and its message', 1987 Chief Executive's Conference, 1987.
Ferranti Annual Reports 1976–93.
Ferranti Board Minutes, 1974–93 (FBM).
Flemings Research, 'International Signal & Control Group plc', 1987.
Sir Donald McCallum, 'Ten year performance and our position in 1987', 1987 Chief Executive's Conference.
Nicholson Report to the NatWest Bank, 1974, in FBM, Nov 1974.
Charles Scott and Alan Bardsley (1986), 'A report on International Signal & Control Group plc'.
C. Scott (1987), 'Acquisitions strategy', Ferranti Chief Executive's Conference.

Newspapers and trade papers (covering the period 1980–2005)

Accountancy Age	*Investors Chronicle*
Business Age	*Jane's Defence Weekly*
Cellular Business	*Lancaster New Era*
Corporate Money	*Lancaster Sunday News*
Daily Mail	*Legal Intelligence*
Daily Mirror	*Observer*
Daily Record	*Oldham Evening Chronicle*
Daily Telegraph	*People*
Defence News	*Philadelphia Inquirer*
Electronic Times	*Scotsman*
Engineer	*Sunday Business*
Ferranti News	*Sunday Correspondent*
Financial Times	*Sunday Observer*
Financial Weekly	*Sunday Telegraph*
Guardian	*Sunday Times*
Herald	*The Times*
Independent	*Today*
Independent on Sunday	*Wall St Journal.*
Intelligencer Journal	

General sources

M.S. Chance (1996), 'The investigation of the audits of the International Signal and Control Group PLC', Joint Disciplinary Scheme, June, Institute of Chartered Accountants for England and Wales.

Scott Report (1996), *Report of the Inquiry into the Export of Defence and Dual-Use Goods to Iraq and Related Prosecutions*, House of Commons Papers 115, 1996.

US Department of Justice Bulletin.

Secondary sources

Alun-Jones, D. (1982), 'My business experience at Burmah Oil and Ferranti', paper presented to the Business History Unit, LSE.

Aris, S. (1998), *Arnold Weinstock and the Making of GEC*, Aurum Press.

Aylen, J. (2012), 'Bloodhound on my trail: building the Ferranti Argus Process Control Computer', *International Journal for the History of Engineering and Technology*, Vol. 82, No. 1, 1–36.

Brummer, A. and R. Cowe (1998), *Weinstock. The Life and Times of Britain's Premier Industrialist*, HarperCollins.

Cassis, Y. (2011), *Crises and Opportunities. The Shaping of Modern Finance*, Oxford University Press.

Chapman, P. (1994), 'Overview: the UK labour market', in T. Buxton, P. Chapman and P. Temple (eds), *Britain's Economic Performance*, Routledge.

Charkham, J. (1995), *Keeping Good Company. A Study of Corporate Governance in Five Countries*, Oxford University Press.

Clark, Alan (1993, 2002), Vol 1: *Diaries. In Power 1983–1992*; Vol 3: *Diaries. The Last Diaries 1993–1999*, Weidenfeld & Nicolson.

Cock, J. and L. Nathan (1989), *War and Society. The Militarisation of South Africa*, David Philip.

Epstein, E.J. (1989), 'Who killed Zia?', *Vanity Fair*, Sept, 27–9.

Felice, E. (2010), 'State ownership and international competitiveness: the Italian Finmeccanica from Alfa Romeo to aerospace and defense (1947–2007)', *Enterprise and Society*, Vol. 11, No. 3.

Friedman, A. (1993), *The Spider's Web. The Secret History of How the White House Illegally Armed Iraq*, Alan Friedman Books.

Goold, M. and A. Campbell (1987), *Strategies and Styles. The Role of the Centre in Managing Diversified Corporations*, Blackwell.

Greenwood, D. (1984), 'Managing the defence programme and budget', *The Three Banks Review*, No. 142, June, 34–50.

Howson, P. (2004), *Commercial Due Diligence*, Gower.

James, G.R. (1995), *In the Public Interest*, Little Brown.

Jones, G. (2005), *Multinationals and Global Capitalism*, Oxford University Press.

Lovering, J. (1995), 'Opportunity or crisis? The remaking of the British arms industry', in R. Turner (ed.), *The British Economy in Transition*, Routledge.

Matthews, D. (2006), *A History of Auditing. The Changing Audit Process in Britain from the Nineteenth Century to the Present Day*, Routledge.

Miller, D. (1996), *Export or Die. Britain's Defence Trade with Iran and Iraq*, Cassell.

Owen, G. (1999), *From Empire to Europe. The Decline and Revival of British Industry since the Second World War*, HarperCollins.

Polakow-Suransky, S. (2010), *The Unspoken Alliance*, Vintage.

Seagrim, M. (1992), 'The effect of defence spending upon the UK economy', *Royal Bank of Scotland Review*, No. 173, March, 27–38.

Whisler, T.R. (1999), *The British Motor Industry, 1945–94*, Oxford University Press.

Wilson, J.F. (1995), *British Business History, 1720–1994*, Manchester University Press.

Wilson, J.F. (2000), *Ferranti. A History*. Volume 1. *Building a Family Business, 1882–1975*, Carnegie Publishing.

Wilson, J.F. (2007), *Ferranti. A History*. Volume 2. *From Family Firm to Multinational, 1975–1987*, Crucible Books.

Wilson, J.F. and Andrew Thomson (2006), *The Making of Modern Management. British Management in Historical Perspective*, Oxford University Press.

Index

Note: page numbers in **bold** refer to figures, page numbers in *italics* refer to tables and 'n.' after a page reference indicates the number of a note on that page.